Touch the Future
TEACH!

Touch the Future
TEACH!

W. Robert Houston
Renee Tipton Clift
H. Jerome Freiberg
Allen R. Warner

University of Houston
Houston, Texas

West Publishing Company
St. Paul   New York   Los Angeles   San Francisco

Production Credits
Copyediting   *Miriam Frost*
Artwork   *Alice Thiede, Cartographics*
Cover   *John Och*
Cover Image   *The Image Bank*

COPYRIGHT © 1988   By WEST PUBLISHING COMPANY
50 W. Kellogg Boulevard
P.O. Box 64526
St. Paul, MN 55164-1003

Library of Congress Cataloging-in-Publication Data

Touch the future.

   Includes index.
   1. Teaching.   2. Teaching—Vocational guidance—
United States.   3. Education—United States.
I. Houston, W. Robert.
LB1025.2.T685   1988   371.1'02   87-25441
ISBN 0-314-62759-6

C O N T E N T S

Preface ix

SECTION ONE

Reflecting on Schools and Society 1

CHAPTER ONE
Beginnings 3

A New Experience 4
Teaching as Reflective Inquiry 7
Analyzing Schools 13
Deciding to Teach 14
Conclusion 16

CHAPTER TWO
Schools: A Reflection of Society 21

Historical Antecedents of Modern Schools 22
Trends in Education 33
1965: The Hinge 38
The Decade of Experimentation 39
Alternative Futures for Schools 40
Conclusion 45

CHAPTER THREE
Reflective Teachers Are Students of Teaching 49

Teaching as a Process of Inquiry 50
The Teaching Day 50
The Responsibilities of Teaching 54
Personal Philosophies of Teaching 62
Why Teachers Enjoy Teaching 68
Conclusion 69

CHAPTER FOUR
Students—The Future of Society 73

Looking Beneath the Surface 74
Learning as Function of Prior Learning 74
External Factors Affecting Success in School 81
Conclusion 92

CHAPTER FIVE
Communities and Schools 97

School and Community 98
The Community School 98
Types of Communities 99
Communities in Transition 100
Impact of Social Changes on Schools 105
Discovering a School's Community Constituency 109
Conclusion 111

CHAPTER SIX
Exploring School Quality 115

Research on Effective Schools 117
Other Conceptions of Quality Schools 122
Schools Cannot Provide Quality Education 126
Commission Reports and Recommendations of the 1980s 127
High School Reform 133
Conclusion 134

SECTION TWO

Inquiring Into the Processes of Teaching 141

CHAPTER SEVEN
The Concept of Curriculum 143

What is Curriculum? 144
The Participant-Observer and the Curriculum 146
The Language of Curriculum 147
Who Decides Curricular Issues? 148
The Contemporary Curriculum 149
Curricular Trends 154
Curriculum and Instruction 159
Goals and Objectives 160
Domains of Learning 161
Conclusion 164

CHAPTER EIGHT
Planning to Teach Students 167

What is Instructional Design? 168
Analyzing the Curriculum 169
Instructional Objectives 172
Planning for Instruction 178
Lesson Design 180
Planning for Evaluation 186
Unit Plans 187
Conclusion 188

CHAPTER NINE
Varying Instruction for Effective Teaching 191

Five Elements of Effective Teaching 194
Teacher Directed Strategies 196
Student Focused Strategies 205
Conclusion 211

CHAPTER TEN
Creating Effective Classroom Management 215

The Importance of Management 216
Perspective of Classroom Management 223
Communications 232
Setting the Stage 236
Conclusion 239

CHAPTER ELEVEN
Measurement and Evaluation 249

Using Measurement and Evaluation in Making Decisions 250
Assessing Instructional Objectives 255
Measuring Student Progress 260
Testing as a National Movement 273

SECTION THREE
Reflecting on the Contexts and Challenges of Teaching 283

CHAPTER TWELVE
Governmental Influence on Schools 285

Federal Role in Education 287
Judicial Influence on Schools 291
States' Responsibility for Public Education 302
Local School Districts 303
Decision-making in Schools 311
Conclusion 313

CHAPTER THIRTEEN
Issues Facing Educators Today 317

Exploring Educational Issues 318
The Purpose of Schools 319
Substance of the School's Curriculum 324
Achieving Its Purpose 329
Conclusion 337

CHAPTER FOURTEEN
Don't Trip on the Threshold 343

The Rest of Your Program 344
There IS Life After Certification! 349
Conclusion 358

APPENDICES

A. Exploring Elementary, Middle, and Senior High Schools 361

B. The Public's Responses to Gallup Polls in Chapters 2 and 13 371

C. Working in Schools 375

D. State Certification Offices 377

Touch the Future: Teach! blends current research on teaching, teachers, and school contexts with an historical, socio-cultural, and legal understanding of the profession of teaching. The text is written for people who are beginning to explore teaching as a career and for people who have made an initial commitment to teaching. With constant change in schools and with the continued expansion of the knowledge base of teaching, prospective teachers need skills for analyzing the students with whom they work, the situations in which they are involved, and the organizations and social contexts that fashion their working environment. Thus, this text provides more than a summary of the knowledge base of teaching.

Reflective Inquiry As a Life-long Approach to Teaching

We view the teaching process as one which is both reflective and analytical. The materials in this book are designed to facilitate your development as a reflective inquirer. This process of *reflective inquiry* is the heart of the text. To know only the *what* of a situation or problem is not enough. Of greater importance is to know also the *how* and *why* of problems or situations and to be able to formulate alternative solutions as a part of your professional repertoire. We hope this text will reduce the amount of time needed to become an expert teacher by creating situations that support a reflective and analytical approach from the beginning of your professional preparation. Rather than focus on static solutions to changing problems, this text incorporates the philosophy of an ancient saying:

If I give you a fish you will eat for a day.

If I teach you to fish you will eat for a lifetime.

Learning To Use Reflective Inquiry

The text is a thorough, detailed introduction to teaching. We have attempted to create a resource book that will be useful beyond an introductory course because our own students have expressed the need for such a text. *Touch the Future: Teach!* is a practical, as well as a conceptual, introduction to what it means to be a teacher.

In the first section, we cover many of the topics typically included in a general introduction-to-education text. The first chapter reintroduces you to the school and to schooling, then explores the concept of reflective inquiry. Using reflective inquiry as a tool for further study of teaching, Section I includes a brief historical sketch of educational developments to provide perspective on where we have been, then speculates on possible future movements in education. Three chapters explore the constituencies of education—teachers, their students, and the communities in which they live and work. The last chapter in this section explores the nature of school quality. Some people believe that schools are effective only when they increase student achievement; some when they bring about social change. Others relate school quality primarily to learning to learn more effectively. Which are more important?

The second section in the book considers topics central to the act of teaching. The first chapter examines the curriculum studied by students. Four interrelated chapters include ideas that beginning teachers need in order to survive and enjoy their first year of teaching. These chapters focus on teaching—planning for instruction, approaches used in actual teaching, processes useful for effective classroom management, and strategies for assessing teaching and learning effectiveness.

The final section introduces you to the complex societal forces that continue to affect the teaching profession. Public schools are *public*, and thus they are affected by governmental forces at the national, state, and local levels. They also are affected by social forces, technological advances, and economic conditions. Two chapters in this section explore the organization of education in this nation, the influence of the judicial system, and the issues arising from national and even international socio-cultural movements. Finally, the profession of teaching, its opportunities and challenges, its rewards and responsibilities are considered. Through study of this third section, we hope you will be able to extend your understanding of the various factors influencing the lives of teachers.

Each chapter is introduced with a set of objectives for the chapter and a listing of key words and concepts. As you study the research on teaching, you will find that people learn more effectively when they have before them clear objectives of what they intend to accomplish and an overview of new words and concepts. The expository section of each chapter introduces major concepts and illustrates them with actual episodes that have occurred in schools. Research, too, has shown that if abstract concepts are illustrated with actual events, they are more meaningful to learners. Our goal, however, is to facilitate your understanding of the basic concepts of teaching so that you can then apply them in many diverse situations. A series of quotations, found in the margins provide material for further discussion.

Each chapter has a part that introduces you to a new technique for becoming more sensitive to the nuances of teaching. Entitled "Building Reflective-Inquiry Skills," this part focuses on skills of interviewing, observing (using different types of instruments and for varying purposes), completing historical studies of a school, and conducting ethnographic and sociological studies. Finally, each chapter includes a set of "Explorations" that are designed to enhance your inquiry skills as well as to further extend your knowledge of professional education. Our ultimate goal is for you to apply professional knowledge as you teach children and youth, and these activities are designed to facilitate your skill development.

The concepts and skills developed in this book are drawn from our years of experience as teachers and as teachers working with teacher education students and beginning teachers. The content also is drawn from a review of research in the field and from studies of the needs of beginning professionals.

So many people have contributed to this book. Our students and teachers with whom we have worked over the past few years have challenged us to probe more deeply the nuances of professional practice. Particularly, we want to thank Pat Cothren, Scott Evers and Pam Menard, three teachers who shared their insights of teaching and permitted us to record their busy days. Bob Bartay, Assistant Superintendent of Galena Park (Texas) schools, made data available and stimulated our thinking about the realities of teaching. Deputy Superintendent for Instruction Ann O'Donnell and Assistant Superintendent for Elementary Schools Betty Bennett Best of the Alief (Texas) schools shared their time and wisdom with us as well. Gwen Hodgkins was our communicator and organizer.

Our families supported us even when writing took precedence over family activities, and we are grateful to them not only for their support but also for their ideas and wisdom. Our spouses—Elizabeth, Richard, Linda and Hildy, respectively—deserve our special, continuing gratitude.

The purpose of the text is not only to introduce you to teaching as a career, but also to expand your vision of the many factors that affect that career. In later portions of your preprofessional development, you will study many of these areas in greater depth, but this initial experience is designed to provide perspective for further exploration. While an introductory text, this book is designed to provide a solid base for profession-long learning.

For those who want to **touch the future**, teaching provides an effective way to make a difference.

W. Robert Houston

Renee Tipton Clift

H. Jerome Freiberg

Allen R. Warner

Touch the Future
TEACH!

Reflecting on Schools and Society

CHAPTER ONE

Beginnings

OBJECTIVES

By the end of this chapter, you will be able to:

1. Recognize that the massive societal changes reshaping America today are also changing education and schools.
2. Discuss the concept of reflective inquiry as it applies to preprofessional teachers.
3. Describe similarities and differences between elementary schools, middle or junior high schools, and high schools.
4. Consider the importance of making informed, reflective decisions about becoming a teacher.
5. Conduct interviews with students and teachers.

KEY WORDS AND CONCEPTS

Elementary schools
Functional school facilities
High schools
Magnet schools
Middle schools
Reflective inquiry
Societal changes and schools
Theory
Third Wave

A New Experience

Schools are continually beginning; beginning new ideas, new programs, new techniques, new content, new organizational patterns, admitting new students, hiring new personnel. Schools change as new and more effective ways of working with students are perceived. It is in this dynamic institution that you will teach.

The modern school is a complex institution. Yet you may feel that you understand the organization and the activities that constitute a good school. After all, you have spent more than a decade (and perhaps most of your life) there. Such a feeling is natural even though you were a student *in* rather than *of* the school, and thus your knowledge of what actually was happening is limited to your own personal experience. The situation is analogous to viewing an iceberg of which only ten percent is visible above water while the vast mass is hidden beneath the sea. There are at least three reasons why you probably are not fully informed.

First, as a child or teenager, you knew very little about how the school operated, or why; what its mission and goals were; or the basis for its instructional program. You experienced only the *result* of such important factors in the school as state curriculum requirements, school administrative policies, teacher/staff development programs, research on teacher and school effectiveness, and sources of community pressures. In the intervening years since you were a student in precollegiate schools, your own understandings have broadened and modified. Thus, sights and sounds in schools perceived today may take on quite different meanings than they did at that time. Not only the passage of time but also the change in your purposes for being in the school affects your perception.

Students never know the whole story of being an effective teacher.

Second, schools have changed considerably during the past few years. Studies about human learning and instruction in a wide range of fields have resulted in important gains in our knowledge of effective teaching and about effective school settings. Schools may be organized differently (for example, a community may have middle schools rather than junior high schools; it may have alternative high schools; a school's students may be drawn city-wide rather than from just the immediate neighborhood surrounding a school). Schools today generally have larger enrollments than in past years, and they are more complex in their organization and programming. The development of new instructional materials and equipment such as microcomputers, interactive and closed circuit televised courses, and self-contained teaching machines and instructional kits, as well as the wider availability of audiovisual aids such as overhead projectors, films, and VCR cassettes have changed schooling. Professional personnel with specialized skills and abilities (counselors, psychologists, social workers, nurses, special education resource teachers, diagnosticians) are being employed in greater numbers to support classroom teachers.

Since 1983, when the U.S. Department of Education published the special commission report, *A Nation at Risk*, more than 300 national, regional, and state task forces and commissions have analyzed every facet of education and made recommendations for reform. Legislatures and state boards of education in every state have made major changes in schools; many have strengthened high school graduation requirements, specified essential curriculum elements, required criterion-referenced tests, and systematized teacher evaluation. Federal programs and court decisions on desegregation, schooling of children with disabilities, student rights, and school responsibility have modified school practice. As you study and reflect on school practice and as you become a teacher, you will experience these changes.

Third, we live in a dynamic society. The impact of single-parent families, increased mobility, the large proportion of working parents without child care arrangements after school, the increased need for free lunch and breakfast programs in schools, almost universal school busing, violence and drama on television, and the ready availability of instant world-wide news (mostly sensational and negative) have all influenced students, teachers, and the school itself.

Many educational programs appropriate a few years ago are no longer applicable. Consequently, the educational program often has been modified to cope with these new demands and realities. Schools have assumed additional functions and responsibilities that differ from those of even the immediate past, and this trend is unlikely to change. For example, substance abuse and AIDS so concern some communities that information about them is being taught in schools. Bilingual education has become more prevalent with the influx of legal and illegal immigrants.

In half a century, our nation changed its values, its economics, and its culture as in no other period—changes so dramatic as to be revolutionary. During the 1930s, we were a depression-ridden nation. Hunger and unemployment were prevalent. The forties brought war and its aftermath. The fifties were characterized by extensive technical and industrial growth in America. The sixties were shrouded by an unwanted war, open rebellion by the youth against traditional values of society, and the first recognition that the United States could not institute democracy all over the world. The seventies became a transitional decade as the values and practices of the liberal sixties began to be questioned, and a conservative social movement was initiated that continued through the eighties.

In the process, more people in our nation now provide services than produce goods. Only 30 percent of workers are employed in industries manufacturing products, and this is decreasing. Only 3 percent of the work force is in agriculture, which was the major job classification just 50 years ago, and this proportion is still decreasing. Between 1950 and 1980, jobs in the United States grew from 59 million to 99 million, a 67 percent increase. The proportion of these jobs in the professional, technical, and managerial fields expanded from 17 percent of all jobs to 27 percent (Newman 1984, pp. 5–6).

The new period, called the Third Wave by Alvin Toffler and the post-industrial era by John Naisbitt, has resulted in educational needs that are quite different from those of only ten years ago. The organization, content, and extent of educational opportunities evolve as the needs of society and individuals change. Schools you attended differ from those of today, and those you will be teaching in a decade from now will likely have evolved even more.

Thus, the vantage point from which we view and evaluate our schools, social structure, and value system is a shifting and evolving one. Schools not only *transmit* the culture to a new generation, but are obligated to *translate* the meaning of that culture. This obligation is even more important, considering the extremely rapid growth of innovations that characterize the civilization of our times.

Because of the rapid changes transforming society, each new generation is partially forced out of touch even with the immediate past. It is important for teachers to help young people sense the greatness, growth, and vitality of America and the significance of a student's personal heritage. Likewise, teachers must understand and deeply sense their own personal heritages. Effective professionals understand the implications of the massive cultural changes occurring in America and are able to help the new generation establish relationships between the present and the past.

Teachers also need a broader and deeper view of the school, its culture, organization, and mission in society. Rapid societal changes will continue to occur. Students attending school today will live and work in the twenty-first century; in fact, those entering kindergarten in 1988 will graduate from high school in the twenty-first century.

This dynamic atmosphere makes all the more important a teacher's responsibility to draw on new concepts, new approaches, and to build upon past achievements rather than simply to mimic the teaching patterns and curriculum of the past. Analyzing what is appropriate, what is relevant, and what is needed based on future, not past, considerations is not only a skill that requires knowledge, but also an attitude that is important to tomorrow's teachers. We refer to this as *reflective inquiry*.

Teaching as Reflective Inquiry

Education: Noun or Verb?

As you begin to engage in professional study, your view of schools and schooling and of yourself as a professional will be shaped by your view of education. Do you regard education as something to be achieved or as something in which to be engaged? In other words, do you perceive the term *education* as having a *noun* quality, or as having a *verb* quality?

How you make this distinction will influence your study of education and your behavior as a teacher. The noun use of the word *education* indicates that something already has been attained. The verb use implies continuous inquiry. In our view as well as in that of many educators, seeing education as a verb results in more effective learning. We are firmly convinced that this view leads to the fullest development of professional teachers and of their students.

Three dimensions permeate education: the *answering of questions*, the *questioning of answers*, and the *questioning of questions*. Education, when used in the verb sense, insists upon the questioning of answers and the questioning of the questions themselves. While often trying and sometimes a bit frightening, these dimensions nonetheless form the essence of effective teaching. In professional education, they distinguish the student from the teacher, the craftsman from the professional, the novice from the master.

> *E*ducation makes a people easy to lead, but difficult to drive; easy to govern, but impossible to enslave.
>
> Lord Brougham, in a speech to the British House of Commons, 1828.

Reflective Inquiry

Teachers are deeply involved in such activities as explaining, defining, proving, inferring, and classifying. They not only transmit knowledge, attitudes and skills, they help students translate these into useful and personally meaningful behaviors. Teachers press for thoughtful speculation about phenomena, for formulation of hypotheses and hunches, and for evaluation of activities and results. The well-educated person is concerned with all three dimensions (the *answering of questions*, the *questioning of answers*, and the *questioning of questions*). Too often students who are unchallenged by the breadth and depth of educational thought in school seek other less productive outlets for their energies.

This process of synthesis and analysis we refer to as *reflective inquiry*. To *inquire* is to question, to probe, to extend one's understanding of a situation. *Reflection* implies speculation, assessment, and consideration of factors with respect to desired goals. Reflective inquiry combines both notions in the verb sense of education. It is an active, dynamic, living process engaged in by professional teachers. They examine social and physical phenomena and actions; they not only answer questions, but question both the answer and the question.

Teachers need to apply this process in four circumstances: (1) as individuals who continue to be vibrant, active learners (that is, as students), (2) as teachers who challenge their students to be reflective learners, (3) as professionals who continually reflect upon their effectiveness as teachers, and (4) as professionals who promote the worth of their profession.

Being a reflective inquirer requires the ability to listen to what others are *really* saying.

In each of these circumstances, reflective inquiry requires a set of well-understood educational goals or objectives, a set of strategies for achieving these goals or objectives, and a set of processes for assessing the effectiveness of strategies for achieving the goals, as well as a reexamination of the desirability of the goals themselves. Thus, while the target itself (goals) may be shifting because of changing conditions, the strategies also must be modified to most effectively achieve these goals. This "mid-course correction" is part of an active endeavor; it reflects educational practice in the verb, not the noun, sense.

In the coming weeks, as you study the content in this textbook, learn from your instructor and fellow students, and explore schools through actual experiences, you will be afforded an opportunity to explore and to reflect upon the goals of schools and of your teacher education program; you will learn strategies for achieving those goals based on societal/cultural/organizational conditions that affect both goals and strategies and techniques for determining the extent to which both are successful.

Practicing Theorists. Teachers are both theorists and practicing philosophers. They tend to deny this, for common opinion views theory as abstract, ethereal, vague, and impractical. Considerable confusion surrounds the term *theory*; however, sound theory is the most practical knowledge one can have—it has concrete, immediate applicability. A theory is like an hypothesis that describes (explains) how things occur. It is a hunch that considers cause and effect; it attempts to predict or explain the probable outcome of certain actions based on antecedent conditions.

*T*he spirit of inquiry can be got only through and with the attitude of inquiry.

John Dewey, *The School and Society*, 1899, p. 93.

The teacher exemplifies hypothesis-making when writing lesson plans. First, the teacher assumes that selected objectives are appropriate for students at a particular time. Then, the teacher assumes that certain instructional procedures will bring about increased achievement of those objectives. The hypothesis may be sound or not, but its soundness is confirmed through practice.

Professionals attempt to make basic concepts or theories *explicit* on the grounds that when they are conscious of theoretical constructs, they can test them to determine their validity. They can improve practice because they understand the undergirding basis for their actions and results. The tradesman or apprentice, on the other hand, tends to ignore theory or to keep them *implicit*. Hence, the basis for actions is largely unexplained, often even unrecognized. They may be able to improve their performance, but if so, it is often only by chance.

Implications for Preprofessionals.   As a person and as a preprofessional, what does reflective inquiry mean for you? First, it implies that you consider your own values—those activities and things that are rewarding to you—and that you are candid and honest with yourself about these. Second, it implies that you consider the personal and professional goals and accomplishments you hope to achieve in life. Third, it implies that you identify the current conditions and relevant factors related to these goals. Fourth, it implies that you reflect on your education and activities as they contribute to these goals. And finally, it implies that you periodically reconsider goals, actions, and assessments.

Making such a personal and professional assessment is an important dimension in your life; it is a private endeavor and a private commitment. Others can help to sharpen the relevant factors and can provide a context for a more public exploration, but the desire for personal examination of life and its factors is a private affair. We encourage you to consider it as you explore teaching as your chosen vocation.

Actions As the Tip of the Iceberg

Like the iceberg mentioned earlier, much of the professional substance of teaching is not visible to the casual observer. Your observations of actions and interactions in classrooms permit you to hypothesize about the professional decisions teachers make and later verify your hunches. Two brief vignettes, one from an elementary school and one from a high school, illustrate this process of reflective inquiry. An observer's notes of events is followed by the reasoning, or reflective inquiry, as described by the teacher.

EXHIBIT 1.1   **Elementary School Classroom**

Observer's Notes

9:03 A.M. As I entered the second grade classroom, students were sitting at their desks, writing a story. The teacher was walking around, stopping occasionally to say something to a child or to write something on his or her paper.

9:07 A.M. Three students finish, look up at the chalkboard, then go to learning centers (one to the listening center, one to the home center, one to the computer center). One child goes to the back of the room, picks up a restroom tag, and leaves the room; returns two minutes later.

9:15 A.M. The teacher asks all boys and girls at Table 1 to go to the class discussion center. They get up, push their chairs in (all but one boy), then proceed to a throw rug near the side of the classroom. The teacher says, "I like the way Table 1 pushed their chairs under their table," whereupon the boy went back and pushed his chair completely under the table. The teacher then called on students at other tables, one table at a time, to go to the class meeting.

9:18 A.M. All students are seated closely together on the floor surrounding a small chair for the teacher. "Can you think of different ways Christmas is celebrated in other countries?" (repeated in Spanish for those students who didn't speak English). This leads to a discussion of Christmas in Mexico (described by one girl in Spanish and translated by the teacher); of cutting trees in Michigan (described by a boy in English and translated by the teacher); and of celebrations in Germany (described by a boy in English and also translated by the teacher).

9:28 A.M. The teacher tells the class they now are going to see a filmstrip about Christmas around the world. The teacher calls out table numbers, and students return to their seats while she rolls out a cart with a filmstrip projector and audiotape machine on it, plugs in the AV equipment, turns on the projector and focuses it. After showing slides of the first country the teacher asks a question. . . .

Teacher's Discussion

When you entered the room, we were writing about our field trip to the woods yesterday afternoon. On that walk I asked my students to feel the bark of trees, find and keep a leaf (for splatter painting later), stand quietly and listen to the sound of the forest (even if we are in the middle of the city), and to smell the freshness of the air. I even asked them to put their noses to the bark of pine trees and guess what they smell like (caramel pudding). I want them to experience life, using as many of their senses as possible.

We talked afterward about our experiences, and today they are writing about them. I want them to learn to express feelings in writing without being constrained by spelling or grammar; that is why I wrote words down for several students.

Peter was getting restless, so I encouraged him; then stood nearby. I have found that I can be more supportive and can influence children more when I am closer to them.

Yesterday afternoon after school, I wrote on the chalkboard a list of activities for the children to do in different learning centers. As students finished their stories today, they could work on the activities in any of the learning centers. It is their responsibility to go directly to the next activity. I should not have to tell each what to do next, just as I should not have to give students permission to go to the restroom. They know that only one boy and one girl can be gone at any time and that if the restroom tag is missing, they must wait until someone returns it.

Children at this age need to change activities about every ten minutes, or they become restless and lose interest. I try to move them around the room or out to the playground to assure a varied setting and different activities. That is why I took them to the class meeting area: to let them walk, then sit on the floor. Learning centers provide opportunities for individual activities and a change of pace.

I ask students to do only one thing at a time; multiple instructions simply lead to chaos. I also try to tell them what to do, not what not to do.

Our class meeting area permits students to be close together. This seems to help us to be more unified, more of a team. It also makes talking together easier and helps me make eye contact with individuals I want to contribute to the discussion. I try to get everyone involved, if possible; especially new or quiet students. That is why I asked about Christmas in other lands. Maria is new, speaks almost no English, and is shy. The other students have not yet included her in their free play, and I wanted her to have an opportunity to tell something impressive to the class. That's the reason I looked at her and smiled when I asked the question.

Communication is so important—not only students learning to listen to each other and to me but being able to articulate ideas and concepts. I provide as many opportunities as possible for students to discuss, such as we did today after showing each country's celebrations on the audio-filmstrip.

EXHIBIT 1.2 **High School Classroom**

Observer's Notes

11:02 A.M. The corridors are crowded as students rush to their next class. Some exchange quick messages (I hear "lunch" and "this evening" mentioned in two such passing conversations). Each teacher stands by his or her door, greeting students as they enter the classroom. Mr. Henry teaches mathematics, and as the bell sounds at 11:05 A.M.

for the beginning of the period, he closes the door, walks to the front of the room, and asks students to get out their homework assignments. He calls out the correct answers to the six problems, accompanied by groans and "all right!" He then responds to student questions about why certain answers were correct or not and gives a detailed answer to one question.

11:15 A.M. "Last week, NASA launched a space exploration rocket that is supposed to provide information about our solar system. In designing that rocket what are some of the questions NASA would need to answer?" Responses ranged from the size and weight of instruments, the length of the mission, the need for backup systems in case of failure, the cost of the rocket, to the feasibility of the mission in terms of available technology and knowledge. These were recorded on the chalkboard.

"You may wonder what this has to do with mathematics;" the teacher continued, "but actually mathematics is critical to answering all of the questions you have posed. Some of the mathematics are very complex and advanced, requiring computers and Ph.D. mathematicians; others are fairly straightforward and relatively simple. Some simply require logical reasoning that is facilitated by knowledge of mathematics. Today, we are going to explore the answer to one question: How much fuel is needed? NASA has provided several charts, but we must assume . . ." (and so on, into the lesson).

"You will find this same process to be useful in your own life; now that we have used mathematics to solve NASA's problems, we will learn more about its uses and differing functions. Turn to page 149 for an introduction . . ."

Teacher's Discussion

We have only fifty-five minutes in a period, and every minute counts. The first few minutes are particularly important. If I am slow to begin class, if I spend time calling roll or listening to accounts of the basketball game played yesterday or of Tom's new car, if I talk with one student at the front of the room while the others wait, then I convey to them that I don't think this class is very important. I know about time-on-task research, but I think it goes far beyond the actual time one teaches; it includes the psychological climate of the classroom, the work ethic needed for successful learning. Sometimes I give my students an assignment to begin the instant they enter the room. I want all to be working when the bell rings, and in that case I write instructions on the board.

My students want to know how they are doing, so for any homework due that day, I give them the correct answers at the beginning of the period. They know how well they fared, and I don't have to grade all those papers. This also gives me a chance to answer their questions and to correct any misperceptions. I find immediate feedback to be the most effective. I also never criticize or laugh at a student who asks a question. There must be no stigma attached to doing something wrong; only in not trying at all.

We are going into a new area of study, so I want students to understand mathematics' potential usefulness to them personally and to NASA. I would not generally spend that much time exploring a topic, but motivating students, giving them a sense that they can be successful in the new process, and helping them to understand its usefulness seems to lead to better attitudes toward mathematics and greater success.

The teachers in these two vignettes were using professional reflective thinking. They were using their knowledge of learning theory, developmental psychology, and effective instruction as a basis for their actions. As you begin to explore the science and art of teaching, carefully observe what effective teachers do in classrooms and subsequently ask why they made certain decisions.

Many teachers are conscientious and concerned about their students' welfare. They may have a reasonably good grasp of the content they teach, an intuitive flair for working with children and youth, and greater awareness of the community's impact on the school than the schools' impact on the community. However, they may not be *professional teachers* for several reasons. They may lack depth in their knowledge of the subjects they teach or of professional theory; or have a limited range of instructional strategies; or be relatively unsuccessful in radically different types of teaching situations; or do not practice professional introspection or reflective inquiry.

Professional teachers exhibit the depth of knowledge, level of generalization, and range of applicability that allow them to function in a wide variety of conditions. They develop with experience, for in their reflection they learn to practice professional behavior more effectively.

In doing we learn.

George Herbert, *Jacula Prudentum*

Why Reflective Inquiry for Teachers?

Why is such an emphasis being placed on reflection in this initial phase of your professional program? Wouldn't reflection be better accomplished after you have had more teaching experience to analyze? Perhaps not.

Reflection on teaching begins as you make the transition from student to teacher—a transition you are making at this time. You have had at least fourteen years of school experiences, experiences that affect the ways you think about teaching and learning in school settings. But your experiences are not universal; no one has experienced school in exactly the same way you have, and many people have had experiences directly opposite to yours. Realizing this is an important first step in becoming a teacher.

Going beyond that realization leads you to thoughtful questioning of your own experience: Why am I interested in becoming a teacher? Do I expect all schools to be like the ones I attended? Do I expect all students to think about schooling and learning in the same ways that I did? What do I really know about how children learn? About how curriculum is developed and implemented? About designing and evaluating instruction? About managing large groups of children? These, and other questions will help you re-evaluate your past experience as a student. This text will deliberately encourage such re-evaluation to enable you to broaden your awareness of what teaching and learning are like in a variety of school settings.

But re-evaluation is only a beginning. You will be entering a profession in which you will exert a tremendous influence over the lives of students. You will influence them by the way you speak and act, through the curriculum you teach, through the activities you plan, and through the grades you assign. You will, in turn, be influenced by their responses to you.

As an inquiring prospective teacher, you will be able to examine these influences as an observer in some classrooms and as a participant in others. Once you have become aware of these influences, you can begin to think more deeply about what meaning this has for you and for your students. You can ask questions about equity in classroom participation, about differential treatment of students, about emotional responses to certain students, about learning, and about social interactions between students. And you can incorporate the answers to these questions into your new conception of what teaching and learning are all about.

You will begin to reflect on all of the information and advice you get from your coursework, your observations, and your colleagues. There is no prescription for good teaching. No one has yet developed an algorithm or a set of behaviors that will guarantee success in teaching. No day, no hour of your career will be exactly like any other. Patterns do begin to evolve in the teaching process, however. Certain situations will be similar to others, and we are beginning to develop a knowledge base for teachers that will enable you to reach informed conclusions and wise decisions about your teaching and your students' learning. Reflection will enable you to reach these conclusions and decisions after a period of information gathering followed by a period of thoughtful analysis of that information.

We have previously made the point that you are in a period of transition from student to teacher. Our goal, however, is to help you become a *student of teaching*. Professional teachers not only practice, they

Reflection means taking some time alone now and then.

speculate on that practice, consider the knowledge base that is rapidly developing in teaching, and make informed decisions. *Reflective inquiry* is the process by which one moves from student to teacher to student of teaching.

As you explore the implications of the teaching examples above, as you study the content and practice the skills of a teacher, and as you interact with practicing teachers, you will have opportunities to observe and to practice professional inquiry. It is a synergistic process; it feeds on itself, and it becomes more powerful with use. Ever greater depth of professional knowledge and skill results from such practice; so, too, does the usefulness of reflective inquiry.

Analyzing Schools

We want you to begin now to think about education and teaching as an active inquirer. We will start this process by asking you to think about the schools you attended as a student. A reflecting experience can be an opportunity to revisit events and places from your past. People known years ago can be recalled. To begin such an exploration into your educational past, get comfortable, relax, and let your mind drift back to your days as an elementary- or secondary-school student. You will want to make notes as your experiences unfold.

Think back to your years in school. You got out of bed in the morning, had something to eat, dressed, and headed for school. How did you get to school? Did you drive? Were you driven? Did you walk? Did you ride a bus?

However you got to school, think about what the school looked like as you approached it. What color was it? Which door did you enter?

As you entered the school, what colors greeted you? What odors? How did those odors change, for instance, from the chemistry lab to the cafeteria to the P.E. locker room?

What did the other students look like? Did they all seem to come from the same type of cultural environment and home, or did they represent a considerable amount of diversity?

Which teachers do you remember? What were they like and what did they do? What classroom activities do you remember? What was life like in corridors? Did you participate in extracurricular activities? What were they like? What events stand out in your mind as memorable? Why?

Now think about the community in which you lived. What did it look like? Was it an area of predominantly single-family homes, or apartment buildings? Densely populated, or not? Where did you shop? To what extent did your parents know others in the immediate neighborhood? What did you do after school and on weekends?

As you think about growing up, what are some events and people that influenced your life? What happened? What did they do, and how did you feel about it?

Carry this reflecting experience on into your growing-up years; then go back over your notes, analyze them, and list any principles of human interaction that you believe are important. What are some implications of events in your childhood for you as a teacher? Recalling the past is one thing; analyzing it, making hunches or hypotheses about human nature and learning, and reflecting on the implications of events in that past is another.

Three schools are described in Appendix A—an elementary school, a middle school, and a high school. These descriptions are designed not only to help you understand schools better, but to provide information you can use in reflective inquiry. Select one of these schools and read about it. In what ways is it similiar to the one you attended? How does it differ? Which do you think will better meet the needs of students in the future? The purpose of the activities in this section is to help you remember some of the things you already know about schools and to use this information later as a basis for further exploration.

Deciding to Teach

Combined with your reflecting experience, these vignettes of actual schools provide a background for a more in-depth study of education. During the coming weeks, you will have opportunities to speculate on your exploration of schools and teaching. You also will want to make an in-formed decision about teaching, and basing such a decision on evidence will be helpful.

Reasons To Teach

You may have chosen to prepare to teach for a variety of reasons.

▶ A relative whom you admire is a teacher.

▶ You have had some excellent teachers whom you would like to emulate.

▶ The working conditions seem attractive. After all, teachers only work from 8 A.M. until mid-afternoon and have summers off.

▶ You've worked with children through your church, synagogue, a daycare center, or coached soccer or swimming at the YMCA or YWCA, and those experiences have convinced you that you like to work with young people.

▶ You're thinking about picking up a teaching certificate as "something to fall back on" in case your *real* career plans take longer than expected to materialize or don't pan out.

None of these reasons to explore teaching as a career is a poor one—but neither are any of them sufficient to really make a commitment to teaching.

Choosing to teach because of family tradition is laudatory, but keep in mind that it is *your* career decision which must be made. The degree to which you can be happy and productive as a teacher is directly related to the strength of your decision to teach, how informed you are about the consequences of deciding to teach, and your careful and reflective examination of all aspects of teaching.

Similarly, if you are looking to teacher role models as your prime reason to teach, you are more likely to recall those teachers who liked you rather than those who were effective as teachers. When they took time to help you or praised a particular act of yours, you reacted positively. Of course these behaviors are important, and they are related to effective teaching, but they are not adequate, in and of themselves, to identify quality teachers.

Teaching is hard work and involves long hours. Recent studies from professional teacher organizations indicate that the average workweek of a teacher exceeds fifty hours, that many teachers have second jobs to supplement their income, and that summers are usually spent working at other jobs, teaching summer school classes, or completing graduate work toward advanced skills and degrees.

Working with children or young people in voluntary teaching settings may be far different from working with them in an elementary or secondary school each day. The children in voluntary settings are not required to be there until a certain age by state law; truant officers will not be looking for them if they are absent; your evaluations of their performance will probably not make a significant difference in their future opportunities (grades in school certainly do); and you are rarely evaluated on how well your charges succeed.

Finally, the decision to seek a teaching certificate as "something to fall back on" may not provide sufficient motivation to meet the increasingly rigorous requirements for teacher certification across the country. Supply and demand for teachers tends to be cyclical and regional. In some parts of the nation, the proportion of school-age children to the population is declining, while in other areas it is increasing. Within a given region, one school district may be declining in school population because housing prices in that district are escalating beyond what most parents with school-age children can afford to pay (or because layoffs in a major industry are causing parents to move elsewhere to seek employment).

None of this discussion is meant to discourage you from becoming a teacher. Quite to the contrary, the authors of this book sincerely hope you *will* decide to teach! We *are* teachers, we *like* teaching, we have dedicated our lives to improving the quality of schools and teaching, and we believe that this nation and world are in dire need of strong, well-qualified, and committed people who care about helping children and youth learn.

Career Choice as Reflective Inquiry

Because we *do* care, we are convinced that it is important for you to make an informed decision to teach and to have sound, realistic information upon which to base that decision. If you choose *not* to continue preparing to teach, preferring law, medicine, the liberal arts, or selling aluminum siding, we would rather that you make that decision before you commit so much of your time, energies, and resources in preparing to teach that it is too late to realistically change majors or courses. You will be better off, and so will the young people who might otherwise have to deal with someone who feels "trapped" in teaching and who really does not receive much enjoyment from what he or she does. You have probably experienced teachers like that from time to time yourself. Did you gain much from them?

Our primary focus here, then, is to engage you in explorations of the real world of the teacher—other teachers, students, schools, communities, parental expectations, paperwork, bus duty, cafeteria duty, and "potty patrol"—all of the elements that make teaching exhilarating and exhausting, fun and frustrating, pleasant and painful. In essence, this is the beginning of your use of the reflective inquiry process in education. You are using it to make one of the biggest decisions in your life—selecting a profession.

Conclusion

The purpose of this initial chapter was to provide a basis for further study of education by bringing your own personal experiences in schools into sharper focus. Through reading the first section of the chapter, we wanted you to recognize that a student's experience of school and of what teaching is all about is limited and often erroneous despite many years of school attendance. While this also applies to you, a later section in the chapter asked you to reflect on your own school experiences and then read a description of one of three schools. As you relived your own schooling and as you read this school description, you should have begun to recognize that you indeed do have the basic knowledge of schooling needed to begin serious study.

A second purpose of this chapter was to introduce the concept of reflective inquiry. Reflective inquiry provides the process by which your study of schooling can continue. Through studying and analyzing the con-

A teacher affects eternity; he can never tell where his influence stops.

Henry Adams, *The Education of Henry Adams.*

tent included in this book, through interactions with your classmates, and through the directed guidance and teaching of your instructor, you can gain a deeper understanding of the system called education, and through that understanding, become a better teacher. Education is an active process, and using reflection and inquiry strengthens your understanding of schooling.

In effect, then, Chapter 1 was designed to help you focus on schools as you now know them as a basis for further study and to initiate the use of reflective inquiry as a process by which such study can be enhanced. Chapter 2 traces the past and speculates on the future of education. With these foundations, we will explore the constituencies of schools—the lives and rewards of teachers in Chapter 3, their students in Chapter 4, and their communities in Chapter 5. Finally, in Chapter 6, we will consider the various definitions given to describe quality schools in our nation. Schools are greatly influenced by the needs, values, and goals of society.

Education is a fascinating study, one that will draw you deeper and deeper into its intricacies as you study it. Only you can control the depth of your exploration; we encourage you to expend the energy to do it well.

Building Reflective Inquiry Skills

In each chapter, you will have an opportunity to develop a skill that will facilitate reflective inquiry. In this first chapter, we will discuss interviews, since this is apt to be your first way to obtain information about schooling.

Conducting Effective Interviews

As you begin to learn about schools, teaching, students, and the factors that influence practice, you may discover some things from casual chats and overheard conversations; but to gain systematic information, a carefully planned interview is necessary. A successful interview requires careful preparation, a relaxed atmosphere, and a perceptive interviewer.

The importance of planning the content and strategy of the interview can hardly be overemphasized. The first step in the development of the protocol, or plan, for the interview is to determine why the interview is to be conducted. What is its purpose? What are the hoped-for outcomes? To explicitly state these purposes will aid immeasurably in the formulation of questions. For this reason, the purposes should be written and analyzed.

The stated purposes serve as a guide to the development of questions. Although an infinite number of questions might be asked, only a relatively

few may be required to elicit desired responses. Questions are written, then edited, eliminated, or rewritten after careful evaluation. Criteria such as the following may be employed in this process:

1. Are questions worded so as to elicit responses that will meet the purposes of the interview?

2. Is each question appropriately worded? Is it threatening as stated? How could it be less threatening (preceded by an anecdote or statement that indicates the interviewer's understanding, for example)? Is the wording and content appropriate for the age and background of the student or for the position and experience of the adult to be interviewed? Is the question open, or does it imply an expected answer or value judgment?

3. Are the questions ordered in the most appropriate sequence? Does the response to one question restrict the answers to subsequent questions? Are questions ordered so that they proceed from the general to the specific?

Determining a suitable place to hold the interview is another consideration. Facilities that are suitable and available for this purpose vary from school to school. Interviews with the principal are often held in the office, while interviews with teachers may be conducted in empty classrooms, the teachers' lounge, or during school in their classrooms for brief periods. Some interviews with students have occurred in the back of the classroom, in the hall, on a stage, or in the clinic. Scheduling interviews for certain times of the day or week may permit the use of facilities that are not in constant use.

When interviewing students, consult with the teacher before approaching students. You may need parental permission in some schools to conduct student interviews; check with your teacher.

As you begin the interview, explain the purpose of the interview and attempt to make the interviewee feel comfortable. If you don't first establish adequate rapport, many of your questions might easily be interpreted as threatening or as an unwarranted intrusion into the interviewee's personal life.

Focus attention on the interviewee, giving that person your undivided attention. Let the interviewee do most of the talking. You will learn little or nothing while you are talking.

Although you have a carefully prepared list of questions, pursuing unanticipated leads that occur during the interview may sometimes seem vital. You may need these digressions to clarify the response to a question or to explore important areas opened by responses. While feeling free to pursue these various trails, remember the basic purposes for the discussion, the time limitations, and don't let interesting ideas interfere with the basic purpose of the interview.

One's memory is tricky. Remembering fully the details of an interview is difficult, even a few minutes later. Note-taking is important, especially when recording the precise wording of the interviewee when this is needed for the flavor or accuracy of data. Notes generally are short, jotted phrases that are more fully developed immediately following the interview.

Some people use a tape recorder to reduce the need to take extensive notes during the interview. Place the tape recorder in an inconspicuous place (although it need not be hidden), so the moving tape won't be a distraction. Ask if you may record the interview before turning on the tape.

When possible, write thank you notes (no grammatical errors) to those persons who have been interviewed. Remember that they have not only given you their time but have also shared their expertise and talents.

You can learn many interesting facets of school life through interviews. With careful attention to the details of successful interviewing, you will develop both your skill in interviewing others and your understanding of the school.

Explorations

Exploration 1
Life in Schools
Several interesting accounts of life in schools have been written. Read from at least one of them and report your findings to the class.

▶ Jackson, P. W. (1968). Life in classrooms. New York: Holt, Rinehart and Winston. (While an older book, describes elementary school that is relevant for today).

▶ Lightfoot, S. L. (1983). The good high school. New York: Basic Books. (Descriptions of two urban, two suburban and two elite high schools that, while different, include a number of common elements).

▶ Perrone, V. (1985). Portraits of High Schools. Princeton, NJ: Carnegie Foundation for the Advancement of Teaching. (Descriptions of thirteen high schools which formed the basis for E. Boyer's High school: A report on secondary education in America).

Exploration 2
Developing Interviewing Skills
The beginning of a new course is a time when one meets new people. In your case, you probably will be in the same classes with many fellow students over the next year or two as you complete the same professional development program. Now is an appropriate time to become better acquainted with them. It also is an appropriate time to practice your interview skills before you use them in a school.

Select someone from your class whom you do not know or know only slightly but would like to know better. Interview that person about her or his background, skills, hobbies, reasons for pursuing teaching as a career, and other pertinent information.

Read the section on interviewing skills, then utilize them in this interview. Later, after that individual has interviewed you, exchange information with him or her on the interview, how you felt, some smooth and rough places, and how the interview could have been improved. You have a double reason for this exploration: learning about a colleague and learning to use interview skills more effectively.

Exploration 3
Exploring Educational Issues
Education has been central to the American culture for many generations. With the advent of the postindustrial era, education and communication are even more vital. Because of its centrality, education and the schools that provide it are often the targets of those who wish to shape public opinion or to control the development of American youth.

Some of the issues raised by these dynamic pressures include concerns over the curriculum students study, the quality of those teaching them, the processes used in that instruction, the cost of schooling, the effectiveness of schools, and the legitimate domains of church and home in the educational process.

During the coming weeks, the education of children and youth and the education of teachers will likely be the topic of research studies, public opinion, court decisions, and community concern. These will be reported in newspapers, journals, radio broadcasts, and other media.

Chapter 13 identifies a number of issues that traditionally are of concern. Others may be of particular interest during the coming weeks.

Begin now to prepare for dialogues and debates about relevant issues in education that will occur in conjunction with Chapter 13. Look for and collect accounts of educational perspectives reported during the coming weeks. At this time you may wish to review the issues raised in Chapter 13 as a way to familiarize yourself with the kinds of issues that might be considered; however, do not limit your search only to those issues.

References

Cruickshank, D. R. (1986). *Reflective teaching.* Bloomington, IN: Phi Delta Kappa.

Hullfish, H. G. (1978). *Reflective thinking: The method of education.* Westport, CN: Greenwood Press.

Naisbitt, J. (1984). *Megatrends.* New York: Warner.

National Commission on Excellence in Education. (1983). *A nation at risk: The imperative for educational reform.* Washington, DC: U.S. Government Printing Office.

Newman, F. (1984). *Higher education in an age of higher technology.* Presentation before the 1984 Indiana Governor's Conference for University Trustees, January 12, 1984, at Indianapolis. Mimeographed.

Schon, D. (1983). *The reflective practitioner: How professionals think in action.* New York: Basic Books.

Wittrock, M. C. (1986). Students' thought processes. Chapter 10 in Wittrock, M. C. (Ed.), *Handbook of research on teaching.* New York: Macmillan.

Schools: A Reflection of Society

OBJECTIVES

By the end of this chapter, you will be able to:

1. Sketch the historical development of schooling.
2. Describe the major contributions of some educational leaders.
3. Express your opinions on important educational issues and compare them with the opinions of respondents to Gallup polls.
4. Describe the cycles of change that have occurred in education during the past forty years.
5. Describe different scenarios of schools in the future.

KEY WORDS AND CONCEPTS

Decade of experimentation
Economic survival
Evolution of schools
Great Society
Outcome-based learning
Programmed instruction
Progressive education
Relevance and freedom of choice
Tabula rasa
Trends and futures in education

Historical Antecedents of Modern Schools

Becoming a professional requires more than facts, information, and the skills to teach in a classroom. Teaching requires a sense of what was, what is, and a vision that will allow you to project what might be. More than any other profession, teaching directly affects the future and is built on the past.

Society establishes institutions to reflect its values and beliefs in the hope that these cultural elements will transfer to the next generation. By studying the historical development of the school, you will begin to understand the development of society. In this section, you will be briefly introduced to the rich history of the school's development and how this development is, in fact, a mirror of our society.

Schools today have evolved from schools of the past, ideas and commitments of educational leaders, and societal movements and counter movements. To better understand the important characteristics of the schools described in Chapter 1 and the ones you attended, we need to explore briefly their historical context. This introduction is not meant to be comprehensive nor complete, but to be an overview that you may use for further study and exploration. It does, however, provide a basis for your initial study of teaching.

Education and Society

The development of education throughout history parallels the development of civilizations. Exhibit 2.1 outlines briefly the historical development of Western Civilization in relation to education. Development of both Western and Eastern civilizations, whether they be ancient Egyptian, Hebrew, Greek, Roman, Mayan or modern day European, North American, or Asian, have several common threads:

1. The concentration of people in large villages, cities, or city-states.
2. The development of a common language and forms of written communication.
3. The centralization of leadership/government.
4. Highly developed trade and commerce, with effective roads and waterway systems.
5. An effective system for educating the young.
6. The centralization of knowledge and information.
7. The diffusion of information and knowledge to a broad spectrum of the populace.
8. A common culture, common beliefs and a common value system.
9. A strong military (although not necessarily a dominate one).
10. Effective leadership.

Civilizations rise and fall on the ability of the society to transfer knowledge gained from past and present generations to future generations. Along with the ancient technological advances of fire, tools, bronze, steel, the wheel, and farming, came advances in teaching these "new" technologies to others. A breakdown in the educational system—no matter how crude—clearly indicated the demise of the civilization. Schools reflect the ills of society, and yet the school can be a place in which these ills can be corrected for future generations.

Education in Prehistoric Times

The evolution of the modern classroom and school has paralleled the development of society. Think of the time when humankind lived on the slopes of what is now the grasslands of southern Africa, the meeting points of the Tigris and Euphrates Rivers, the mouth of the Indus River, and the Yangtze Valley. The requirements of the hunter and gatherer of ancient civilizations were very basic.

According to anthropologists, the *Homo Erectus*, who lived nearly two million years ago, was a nomad who lived in a small group of family units that hunted the animals of the region and gathered nuts and berries. The males, females, and children all had specific tasks to perform in order for the group to survive. Without the benefit of a constant supply of nutrition, the nomads had to spend nearly 80 percent of their waking hours in the pursuit of food.

The teaching-learning process of the *Homo Erectus* was based on finding food, gathering food, and coping with a very hostile environment. Because they had a life expectancy of less than twenty years, the total living experience became teacher, classroom, and school. Survival for both the individual and for the family unit also depended on the ability of the group members to pass on to the younger members the experiences and knowl-

EXHIBIT 2.1   Education Parallels Civilization

PERIOD	TEACHING/LEARNING PROCESS	SOURCE(S) OF EDUCATION
Prehistoric (2,000,000–10,000 B.C.)	Watching/observing	Family/Tribal
Classical Greek & Roman (2,000 B.C.–A.D. 400)	One-to-one for a small elite group of the society	Tutor
Middle/Dark Ages (400–1500)	Religious education through the church	Priest
Renaissance (1500–1600)	One-to-one for nobility, apprenticeship, trades people, academy schools	Tutor, Mason, and Books
Colonial America (1600–1800)	One-to-one for elite; one-to-a few for the wealthy Start of schooling for religious education	Tutor, Teacher, Books, and School
Nineteenth Century America (1800–1899)	Start of universal schooling in urban areas	Teachers, Books, and School
Twentieth Century America (1900–1999)	Universal schooling is the norm; one-to-one tutoring with computers and laser disks could be common near the end of the century	Teachers, Books, Schools, Computers networks, Interactive-Television, and Media

edge gained by their elders. The children, through observations of adult activities and with specific assignments in gathering food and taking care of younger siblings, began to pattern adult behaviors in the transition from child to youth to adult.

This educational process remained remarkably unchanged for nearly two million years, changing only as civilization evolved away from hunting and gathering to the more complex social and economic organization required in farming and later in industrial and technological societies. The roots of modern schooling in the Western world may be traced back a mere three thousand years to the development of the Greek civilization.

Those who forget the past are doomed to repeat it.

George Santayana

The Roots of Modern Schooling

Let us begin by first defining a school. The term *school* is derived from the Greek word *schole*, meaning "leisure." "Of course, reasoned the Greek, given leisure a man will employ it in thinking and finding out about things" (Hamilton 1930, 28). The Western concept of school also evolved from the need of societies and civilizations to transmit the accumulated knowledge and culture to the young. Informal teaching, which occurred for thousands of years as humans evolved from hunters and gatherers to farmers and then city dwellers, faced a challenge as the ancient civilizations developed commerce, trade, and a written means of communicating with each other. The gaining of wealth (property, land, slaves, and other representations of ancient wealth) allowed a few members of the society to release their offspring and themselves from the labors of farming or industry. With the absence of work came the opportunity for leisure.

There came a time, in Greek society, when some men gained a greater knowledge than those around them. The younger members of the society gravitated to these thinkers and great teachers of wisdom. These teachers gave their students more than just the utilitarian skills of survival, opening a new world of learning and thought. Thus, the Greeks of ancient times were provided an *education*. Even today, the names of Plato, Aristotle, and Socrates are recognized as those of great teachers and educators.

The word *teaching* also has its roots in the Greek language. Teaching is derived from the word *deiknymi*, meaning "to point out." The Greek school was a place for those with time to learn, where teachers pointed out the path or paths to knowledge. It was still up to the students, however, to determine which path of knowledge they would take.

Socrates (469?–399 B.C.) was one of the greatest of the Greek philosopher-teachers. Although he did not write, his student Plato has described his teachings. Socrates taught by questioning people about their opinions and then asking further questions about their answers. Thus, he could show them how inadequate their opinions were. His goal was to stimulate them to go beyond opinion, to search out essential meanings. His guiding rule was "Know thyself."

Classical Greece. Edith Hamilton, in *The Greek Way*, cites a dialogue between Socrates and one of his students, which occurred in Athens nearly twenty-three hundred years ago and was reported by a Greek writer:

> . . . Socrates, just waked up in the early dawn by a persistent hammering at his door: "What's here?" he cries out, still half asleep. "O Socrates," and the voice is that of a lad he knows well, "Good news, good news!" "It ought to be at this unearthly hour. Well, out with it." The young fellow is in the house now. "O Socrates, Protagoras has come. I heard it yesterday evening. And I was going to you at once but it was so late—" "What's it all about—Protagoras? Has he stolen something of yours?" The boy bursts out laughing, "Yes, yes, that's just it. He's robbing me of wisdom. He has it—wisdom, and he can give it to me. Oh, come and go with me to him. Start now." (Hamilton 1930, 30)

The concept of *school* reflected the philosophy of the society. In Athens, the emphasis was the mind over the body, while in Sparta, the emphasis was the opposite. Much of schooling in ancient times was devoted to the development of religion. The ancient world was a place of fear of the unknown and of the commonplace. Regardless of the particular philosophy, the school represented a place (be it the house of Socrates, a Hindu Temple, Solomon's Temple, or an Athenian gymnasium) for people to be reflective and analytical.

Aristotle (384–322 B.C.) was a Greek philosopher whose writings and teachings extended into all areas of knowledge. He was more systematic in his philosophy than was his teacher, Plato. Aristotle developed a form of reasoning known as a syllogism and taught that it was the primary way to reach scientific conclusions. He lectured while walking about the corridors of the Lyceum.

Middle/Dark Ages

The opportunity for leisure—and thus learning—changed as the fortunes of the Greek states changed. When conquered by the Romans, much that was Greek was adopted by the new masters. The destruction of the Roman Empire at the end of the fourth century brought on the period known as the Middle or Dark Ages (A.D. 400–1400), so called because of the lack of enlightenment or new ideas. The last bastions of learning and scholarship remained in the monasteries, which were established throughout Europe during the second and third centuries, and continued through the sixteenth century.

Literacy was the key to life in the priesthood, while the laity had little need or time to be literate. Religion played a central role not only in the education of those preparing for priesthood but also in the lives of the everyday person. The Church, through its literate priests, became the translator of theology for the populace. The need for some members of medieval society to become literate outside of the monasteries paralleled the evolution of trade, commerce, and the development of cities.

The written records on the development of education and schooling from the classic Greek and Roman eras until the Renaissance are limited. The one exception was during the reign of Emperor Charlemagne (A.D. 768–814). He gathered scholars from the vast regions of his empire and created both a court library and an academy of education for the young.

Printing Press. The development of the printing press by Johan Gutenberg in the 1450s provided a new window of opportunity for education of the nobility and of upper class merchants. Learning to read became an important social and economic tool in achieving higher status in the society. The process of one person painstakingly copying one book for months or years was replaced by a movable printing press, which could produce several books a week. By today's standards, even this would seem slow, but the printing press radically altered how information and knowledge was disseminated.

Many of the writings of the Romans and Greeks preserved in the monasteries for nearly eleven hundred years were rediscovered in the fifteenth century and were printed, using the technology of the Gutenberg press. This rebirth of knowledge became known as the Renaissance period.

The Renaissance Period

The Renaissance era (A.D. 1500–1600) was a transitional period between the middle ages and the modern era of education which began in the late 1600s. C. H. Patterson (1973) provides a good overview of this period when he describes the following events:

Fifteenth century: Baldassare Castiglione's *Coutier*—a book which describes the universal man. (Woodhouse 1978)

1466–1536: Desiderius Erasmus *The Education of a Christian Prince.* (Erasmus 1548/1936)

1533–1592: Michel de Montaigne: *Cicero*—discussed the need for the teacher to also listen and learn from the student. (Noll & Kelly 1970)

1592–1670: John Amos Comenius: *The Great Didactic*—proposed a system of education without force or compulsion and one which progressed with the stages of development of the child. (Translation by Keating 1931)

Other scholars who influenced the development of schools included John Locke (1632–1704), among whose many works is *Some Thoughts on Education*. Locke emphasized the need to create a nonthreatening climate for learning. He coined the term *tabula rasa*, a concept of the child as a blank slate upon which life's experiences would be written. Current research on infant development would disagree with that notion, but for its time, the concept was revolutionary. Jean Jacques Rousseau, in *Emile* (1762), continued from Locke by describing four stages of child development, which he divided into infancy, boyhood, the approach of adolescence, and adolescence. He believed that education should reflect the child's stages of development (Patterson 1973).

John Locke (1632–1704), born in England, emphasized the importance of perception and experience in learning, through writings such as Essay Concerning Human Understanding (1691). He considered an infant at birth to be a tabula rasa, or blank slate, upon which life's experiences were written. He felt the structure provided by the teacher would enable the child to grow and develop. Locke stressed the need for discipline, mental toughness, and the integrity of character that would result in virtue, the ultimate aim of education.

In an era when whippings and other forms of corporal punishment were prevalent in schools, he believed in moderation and balance. His words, written over three hundred years ago, still have meaning for teachers.

> . . . and he that has found a way how to keep up a child's spirit easy, active, and free, and yet at the same time to restrain him from many things he has a mind to, and to draw him to things that are uneasy to him; he, I, say, that knows how to reconcile these seeming contradictions, has, in my opinion, got the true secret of education." (Locke 1693/1934, 37).

Locke stressed "the basics"—geography, mathematics, and history—in educational content and, to a lesser extent, formal language study and the arts. He encouraged vocational education for its value in the total development of the person.

The education of Emile was very different than the education of Sophie, his future wife. In a lesson on marriage in *Emile*, Rousseau discusses the role of Sophie and women in general. "But I still like a simple and coarsely raised girl a hundred times better than a learned and brilliant one who would come to establish in my house a tribunal of literature over which she would preside. A brilliant wife is a plague to her husband, her children, her friends, her valet, everyone." (Rousseau 1762/1979, 409) Even in the enlightened works of Locke and Rousseau, formal learning was for the male members of the society.

Jean Jacques Rousseau (1712–1788) was one of the leading philosophers of his time. He was a prolific writer who believed in the natural education of children, with a contract between the teacher and student; and in just governments, through a social contract between the government and the governed. Emile, the story of the education of a young boy, emphasized the need for a natural form of education rather than the harsh, ritualized forms common in Rousseau's day. Du Contract Social discussed the relationship between people and government. When his books were banned in Paris and burned, he went into exile.

Rousseau's philosophy of education differed from Locke's in two fundamental ways. First, he believed that children learned by observing concrete forms of life and later translating these into abstract thoughts. Locke, on the other hand, believed children should study abstractions before making natural observations. For Locke, the teacher was the primary source of information. For Rousseau, the tutor was more an interpreter of natural events than an instructor of those events.

Rousseau's philosophy, as described in Emile, has had a profound effect on education to this day. Four areas are important.

Individualization   A student and his tutor constitute an ideal learning situation, and one that Rousseau developed in the book Emile. The movement toward individualized instruction has its roots in Rousseau's philosophy.

Experiental learning   Rousseau favored the practical side of education as opposed to the theoretical side. He realized that education consisted less in precept than in practice and that the teacher needed to stimulate thinking in the pupil rather than to think for the pupil.

Student-centered education   He believed that teachers should permit students to follow their own instincts and desires rather than teaching them. He warned that our pedantic mania for instruction is always leading us to teach children things which they would learn better of their own accord. The student should be the focus, not the teacher.

Physical education   Rousseau advocated the development of the body as well as the mind—especially for the young. Their games were to teach them as well as their studies. (Rousseau 1762/1979)

The Colonial Period

Education in America may be divided into two eras: the colonial period (1607–1787), which began with the settlements in Jamestown, Virginia, in 1607 and concluded with the drafting of the Constitution in 1787; and the national period (1787–present), which began with the Constitution and continues to the present time (Cordasco 1976).

Key educational points in the colonial period in America are reflected in the chronology of events (Smith 1973 xxv–xxvii) in Exhibit 2.2. The chronology reflects the development of educational thought, institutions of higher education and public schools, and educational policy from 1635 until 1817.

Education in much of the early colonial period reflected new-found religious freedoms. Schools were instituted to provide for religious education in a country far removed from the interference of European monarchs and religious leaders. The educational requirements of the New England states (except for Rhode Island), starting in Massachusetts in 1647, mandated a tax levy and land to be set aside for the schools. This was a dramatic step toward a universal form of education.

Thomas Jefferson.   (1743–1826) The concept of universal education is reflected in early writings of Thomas Jefferson and in his Bill for the More General Diffusion of Knowledge, which was presented to the Virginia legislature in 1778. Jefferson was a firm believer in the separation of the Church from the state, and he saw this separation starting with the schools. Jefferson emphasized the need for a system of education that began with grammar schools, which were the equivalent of the elementary schools of today. Free elementary education for three years for all "free" (nonslave) male and female children was an innovation in its time. He saw a system wherein students would progress from the primary to the secondary, and later, to higher education.

The schools were to be secular, which was a radical departure from the religious-based schools of the late 1700s (Smith 1973). Jefferson believed that democracy would flourish if citizens were provided a free, secular education that included—at a minimum—reading, writing, and arithmetic. He also wanted the books for the children to include the history of the Greeks, Romans, English, and Americans. Although the bill was defeated, it created the framework for what is currently our system of education. As the chronology of educational events would indicate, education progressed more in two hundred years than it had in the previous ten thousand.

Education in the Nineteenth Century

Presenting a glimpse of the past provides the opportunity to develop a frame of reference for the present and future. As was the case in ancient China, India, Israel, Egypt, Greece, and Rome, the development of cities created the conditions for the development of people called teachers whose specialty was *knowledge*. Along with the other great artists and artisans of the time, the teacher was valued as an important member of society. In fact, few persons reached the upper levels of the society without walking with the great teachers.

As societies moved from hunters and gatherers to farmers and then to builders of machines, what is now the modern-day school began to evolve. The industrial revolution, which began in England in the early 1800s and in the United States by the mid-1870s, created a need for large concentrations of people to operate the factories. The schoolhouses of the farming communities were in stark contrast to the schools of the cities. The

EXHIBIT 2.2   Chronology of Colonial Educational Events from 1635–1817

1635   Founding of Boston Latin School.

1636   Founding of Harvard College.

1638   Printing press set up at Cambridge.

1642   Massachusetts law required selectmen of every town to make periodic inquiries concerning the training of children and apprentices, "especially of their ability to read and understand the principles of religion and the capital lawes of this country."

1647   Massachusetts law (the "ould deluder, Satan" law) required towns of fifty householders to hire a schoolmaster "to teach all such children as shall resort to him to write and read." Towns of one hundred householders were to establish Latin grammar schools where students could be prepared "as far as they may be fitted for the university." Similar acts by Connecticut, 1650; Plymouth, 1671; and New Hampshire, 1689.

1689   Founding of Friends Public School in Philadelphia (later the William Penn Charter School).

1690   John Locke, An Essay Concerning Humane Understanding.

1720   John Clarke, An Essay Upon the Education of Youth in Grammar-Schools (second edition in 1730).

1731   Founding of the first colonial circulating library by Benjamin Franklin at Philadelphia.

1732   First Poor Richard's Almanack.

1749   Benjamin Franklin, Proposals relating to the Education of Youth in Pensilvania.

1751   Benjamin Franklin, Idea of the English School.

1783   Noah Webster, A Grammatical Institute of the English Language.

1786   Benjamin Rush, Thoughts Upon the Mode of Education, Proper in a Republic.

1790   Founding of the Massachusetts Historical Society, the first American historical society. Enactment of law of copyright by Congress.

1802   Pauper School Act, Pennsylvania.

1817   Opening of law school at Harvard (Smith 1973, xxv–xxvii).

Source: Smith, 1973.

schoolhouses of the farming community were usually small, with one or two teachers and a large room with twenty to thirty students, from six to thirteen or fourteen years of age. Architecturally, the country schools looked like churches or farmhouses.

Horace Mann   (1796–1859) gave up his law practice in 1837 to become secretary of the newly established Massachusetts State Board of Education. He was instrumental in improving financial support and public control of schools. He founded the first state normal school in the United States in 1839 at Lexington, Massachusetts. Across the nation, normal schools subsequently became state teachers colleges, and many today are large comprehensive state universities in which teacher education is but one of several programs. His influence has been felt in every state, as others modeled programs on those he implemented. Because of his important contributions to public education, he has been called the Father of Common Schools. He also led the development of an elementary school system.

The industrialization of the cities attracted large concentrations of people to work in the factories. The workers who migrated to the cities from rural areas and other countries to seek employment brought their families. This large influx of adults and children created a need for larger schools. The city schools had anywhere from several hundred to several thousand students. Groups of forty to fifty students were placed in a grade level based on their age and assigned one teacher.

In many instances, the schools and factories were built at the same time, and many of the elementary and secondary schools even looked like factories. Similar materials were used to build both. With large numbers of students and teachers in the building, bells were used to identify periods of time for different activities, including changing classes, beginning and ending the day, and evacuating the building in the event of a fire. Many of the schools built at the turn of the century still exist today.

Inclusions and Exclusions.   The organization called "school" became more complex over the years as society's expectations grew. The schooling process of the past two thousand years had been one of exclusion. Only a small percentage of the total population was able or allowed to attend school. Schools of the sixteenth, seventeenth, and eighteenth centuries were for religious training of well-to-do males. Only in the late nineteenth century did the universal need for schooling begin to be recognized in the United States. A dramatic change toward the democratization of schooling began to take place. Woodrow Wilson (as cited by Perry 1908, 8), in a speech supporting common education that he delivered several years before he became President of the United States, addresses this point quite clearly.

> Popular education is necessary for the preservation of those conditions of freedom, political and social, which are indispensable to free individual development. . . .

Without popular education, moreover, no government which rests upon popular action can long endure: the people must be schooled in the knowledge, and if possible in the virtues, upon which the maintenance and success of free institutions depend.—Woodrow Wilson, "The State," Boston, 1904, p. 638.

Do you agree or disagree with the idea of popular education? How well have Wilson's ideas been implemented in today's schools? How did the schools reflect the society of the early 1900s? What are advantages and disadvantages of an inclusive versus an exclusive educational system?

Mark Hopkins (1802–1887) was a professor and president of Williams College. He illustrated his views on humankind and nature with diagrams, and he encouraged students to form their own opinions by questioning his. President James Garfield once said, "Give me a log hut, with only a simple bench, Mark Hopkins on one end and I on the other. . . ."

Into The Twentieth Century

The philosophy of Rousseau had a profound effect on education in America during the last few years of the nineteenth century and extending to this day. Rousseau believed that children should study things of importance to them rather than to adults. In 1895, the influential Committee of Fifteen, composed of leading educators, reported the findings of their study to the National Education Association. In their report, they stated: "Modern education emphasizes the opinion that the child, not the subject of study, is the guide to the teacher's efforts. To know the child is of paramount importance" (National Education Association 1895, 242). G. Stanley Hall, a prominent educator, wrote in 1901 that rather than the child being forced to fit the school, the school should fit the needs of the child. John Dewey, whose writings shaped much of education during the first half of this century and still guide many of our actions, wrote, "The child is the starting point, the center, and the end. It alone furnishes the standard. To the growth of the child all studies are subservient; they are instruments valued as they serve the needs of growth" (Dewey 1902, 14).

Charles W. Eliot (1834–1926) was president of Harvard University for forty years. He was a major developer of university programs and educational standards in the nation. He actively led in improving secondary schools, chairing the Committee on Secondary School Studies which recommended a more standardized and difficult course for high school students. The committee's report shaped secondary education during the early 1900s; its impact can still be felt in the core curriculum of high schools today.

The work of John Dewey has had an enduring impact on education.

John Dewey (1859–1952) was the most influential American educator of all time. His philosophy was practical—actions were judged according to whether or not they worked (called pragmatism). His philosophy has been called experimentalism, because he believed that ideas must always be tested by experiments. He believed that no knowledge is so certain that it is not subject to new evidence that might be provided by experimentation and experiences. His educational philosophy has been called "progressive education," which dominated educational thought from the turn of the century through the 1940s.

Among Dewey's most important books are The School and Society (1899), Essays in Experimental Logic (1916), Experience and Nature (1925), The Quest for Certainty (1929), Art as Experience (1934), and Logic, the Theory of Inquiry (1938).

Active Learning.   A second trend that shaped education in the first half of this century was the belief that students must be active learners and that instruction is more effective when it involves depth of learning in a small number of disciplines rather than superficially covering all subject areas. In a book published in 1962, a decade after his death, Dewey cautioned that quality rather than quantity in knowledge is the key.

> The frequent criticism of existing education on the ground that it gives a smattering and superficial impression of a large and miscellaneous number of subjects, is just. But the desired remedy will not be found in a return to mechanical and meager teaching of the three R's, but rather in a surrender of our feverish desire to lay out the whole field of knowledge into various studies, in order to "cover the ground." We must substitute for this futile and harmful aim the better ideal of dealing thoroughly with a small number of typical experiences in such a way as to master the tools of learning, and present situations that make pupils hungry to acquire additional knowledge (Dewey 1962, p. 12).

*W*hat you teach, teach thoroughly.

Alfred North Whitehead in *The Aims of Education* 1929, 14.

The philosophy underlying curriculum change was to teach only a few important ideas, but to teach them well so that students learned them and used them as part of their lives. Ralph Tyler, pioneer educational leader whose influence began with the Eight Year Study in the 1930s and extended into the 1980s, summarized this position in specifying the school curriculum.

> Thorndike's investigations of transfer of training had destroyed the earlier confidence in the educational value of school subjects as such. Formal discipline could no longer be invoked to justify the inclusion of such fields as Latin and geometry in high school programs. The relevance of the content of the curriculum to the problems and activities of contemporary life had to be considered. Furthermore, scientific studies of memorization showed that children forget material in a short time unless they have frequent occasions to recall what they have memorized. These findings suggested that curriculum content must be selected which children will have early and frequent occasions to use (Tyler 1971, 26).

By the 1920s, educators were expressing faith in the scientific method as important for students to apply and as important in teaching and in the content of subjects taught. Individual differences began to be demonstrated through test results during the 1920s. I.Q. scores, achievement tests, and aptitude tests became the norm and were used to measure educational accomplishments.

In summarizing the educational program during the first quarter of this century, Robert Schaefer identified several dichotomies that focused the educational debate: ". . . the academic versus the practical, the college preparatory versus the general student, education for life versus education for college, and education for an elite versus education for a 'democracy' " (Schaefer 1971, 11). Lawrence Cremin concluded that Dewey believed that:

> [T]he aim of education is to make not citizens or workers or soldiers or even scientists, but human beings who will live life to the fullest, who will never stop expanding their horizons, reformulating their purposes, and modifying their actions in light of those purposes. Given this conception of growth, a democracy can be defined simply as a society in which each individual is encouraged to continue his education throughout his lifetime. (Cremin 1966, 19)

Booker T. Washington (1856–1915) organized Tuskegee Institute, a school for blacks in Tuskegee, Alabama, and served as its president until his death. He believed that blacks could advance themselves by being efficient and educating themselves. The curriculum of Tuskegee consisted of preparation for a number of trades and professions as well as traditional academic subjects.

Trends in Education

Cycles of Change

Trends in education seem to flow like waves in the ocean. The first wave begins to form a swell far from the shoreline. It then reaches a crest and finally breaks on the shore. While the first wave is reaching its crest a

Booker T. Washington pioneered educational opportunities for black youth.

Maria Montessori's ideas continue to influence the education of young children.

second wave is beginning to form. The cycle then repeats itself. The progessive movement sparked by the work of John Dewey and others was reaching its peak in the early 1940s just as the United States was entering World War II.

Historical Motivations for Public Education

The United States was the first nation to make a major commitment to mass public education. Education is now considered an inherent right of citizenship, a right which cannot be denied without constitutional guarantees of "due process of law." As a result, the public education enterprise has become so massive that the number of people involved in delivering educational services cannot be precisely known. Certainly, every citizen has not only had the opportunity, but has been required by laws in the various states, to attend school.

Maria Montessori (1870–1952) was born in Italy. As a young child, Maria became very interested in the field of mathematics. She considered careers in engineering and biology but eventually decided to study medicine. Despite opposition, Maria Montessori was admitted into medical school and became the first woman in Italy to receive the degree of Doctor of Medicine.

Dr. Montessori's interest in education came while working with handicapped children at the Psychiatric Clinic in the University of Rome. Her work with these children led her to believe that learning disability was a problem to be solved by teachers rather than by doctors. Her teachings and methods are incorporated into what we know as Montessori's Method. This method is designed to encourage a child to move and act in a prepared environment that supports self-development. A child's physical and psychological development is seen as being comprised of distinct phases, or "sensitive periods," with the most crucial period being from birth to age six. Montessori also recognized the elements important to a young child's learning. These elements include programmed preparation, practice, imitation, and repetition (Standing 1962).

Parents have even brought sleeping bags to camp overnight to be in line to register their children for the Montessori Program. The typical Montessori classroom contains instructional materials worth fifteen to twenty thousand dollars that are designed to provide children with concrete learning experiences. Montessori's concepts continue to have a significant impact on the education of children nearly one hundred years after she expressed her revolutionary ideas about the teaching/learning process.

Education and National Defense

A Nation Mobilizes. World War II began with horse-drawn artillery and ended with the atomic bomb. In a period of four short years the United States moved into a new technological era, one which would demand more from its citizens than any other in the history of this country. Major political and social events have a direct effect on educational trends and patterns, and this period was no exception. World War II was a benchmark for the nation and its educational system.

The mobilization of men from each of the states brought a rude awakening to reality to those responsible for the war effort. Many of the recruits were either illiterate or semi-literate. A modern army with new technology required soldiers who could read and follow directions. The armed forces became the largest school in the world (Bishop & Regan 1962). Training programs were developed to provide a quick way for instructing the new recruits. The term "90-day wonders" referred to the amount of time provided to make a citizen into an officer. But the experiential learnings proposed by the progressive movement would not work in such a short period of time. Outcome-based learning and programmed instruction were developed to help in the effort of educating these millions.

Outcome-based Learning. In this approach, the emphasis is on the end product, or objective, of the learning activity, which must be demonstrated in observable terms. The outcome-based learning approach takes a large objective (for example, learning to shoot a rifle and hit a target in the center eight out of ten times) and breaks it down into smaller objectives. (For example: (1) "The soldier will be able to load and fire a rifle in ten seconds." (2) "The soldier will be able to load, fire a rifle in ten seconds, and hit a target fifty yards away." (3) "The soldier will be able to load, fire a rifle in ten seconds, and hit the solid red circle in the target in eight out of ten tries.")

The objectives allowed for a standard by which all learners (in this case, soldiers) could be measured. If the soldier could not master one of the steps, the instructor would then spend additional time on that part of the task with the learner. If a soldier could achieve the last objective of hitting the target eight out of ten times the first time, then he would move on to another task. Outcome-based learning was combined with programmed instruction to form a new basis for instruction that shaped the learners' responses.

Programmed Instruction. The use of outcome-based learning and programmed instruction is the application of the psychologist B. F. Skinner's work on operant conditioning. The principle of operant conditioning is based on the process of increasing the likelihood of a new behavior in the learner by reinforcing the desired behavior (Skinner 1957). Programmed instruction is used primarily when a systematic body of information must be known (Watson 1963); for example, the steps required for cleaning a rifle or the taxonomies used in any of the sciences. Programmed instruction gave the military instructor greater control over the learning process and enabled the military to train large numbers of recruits in a short period of time. Programmed instruction was also designed for transmission by machines so that the student could receive instruction without a teacher being present. The student would press a button in response to a picture or question, and the machine would indicate whether or not the response was correct, and if not, specify next steps in instruction.

The end of World War II in 1945 brought home over twelve million soldiers. The end of the war also began what the media today call the "baby boom" generation. Millions of new families began looking for inexpensive homes, outside of the more expensive cities, in places like Levittown, New York. This pattern created what was termed *suburbs—sub* ("near") and *urbs* ("city"). (Webster 1967).

Demographics. Following World War II, the nation first embarked on an expansion of its school system as the baby-boom crest entered first grade in 1952. The number of students increased by 33 percent, staff by 50 percent, and construction of schools by a staggering 600 percent. Schools in the fifties were under enormous pressure to expand to meet the needs of the influx of new students.

Technology Not Always The Answer. A wave of new technologies in teaching developed in response to the growing student populations. By the early 1960s, technologies tested in schools included educational objectives, teaching machines, computers, programmed textbooks, and instructional television. Norman Crowder, who worked for the military during World War II in developing training materials that employed programmed learning and outcome-based instruction, is quoted in the *Saturday Evening Post* as saying "By the mid-1960's most systematic teaching in U.S. schools and colleges will be done by teaching machines and programmed textbooks." (Foltz 1962). That trend may have happened in some schools, but it did not become the dominant force Crowder and others had expected.

America Challenged

In October 1957, the Russians launched a small sphere into earth orbit. The reverberations of Sputnik were heard around the globe, including the halls of America's schools and universities. One almost immediate response to this event was the National Defense Education Act of 1957, which for the first time identified education in national policy as a vital element of national defense. Scientists challenged the relevancy of the content of the curriculum in schools and the methods being used to deliver it. Under their direction, new programs were completely developed, resulting in the "new math," the "new biology," and the "new physics." Distribution of these materials was made possible through Title III of the National Defense Act (Spring 1976). Taking the most advanced thinking in a field such as mathematics, scientists refashioned concepts into intellectually correct but appropriately simplified ideas for children to learn.

The scientific method became more important than it had ever been before. In 1959, thirty-five prestigious scientists, scholars, and educators gathered for ten days at Woods Hole, Massachusetts to discuss how to improve education. As a result, Jerome Bruner, conference chair, wrote *The Process of Education*, which shaped educational thought for several years. He summarized the thinking in the conference with these words.

> Intellectual activity anywhere is the same whether at the frontier of knowledge or in the third grade classroom. . . . The schoolboy learning physics is a physicist, and it is easier for him to learn physics behaving like a physicist than doing something else . . . the curriculum of a subject should be determined by the most fundamental understanding that can be achieved of the underlying principles that give structure to that subject. Teaching specific topics or skills without making clear their context in the broader fundamental structure of a field of knowledge is uneconomical . . . such teaching makes it exceedingly difficult for the student to generalize from what he has learned to what he will encounter later. (Bruner 1963, 14, 31)

The 1960s brought another wave of change to schools—social and political currents of contemporary society, which divided and polarized American youth. An unpopular war in Vietnam, desegregation of schools in this nation, and disenchanted youth challenged every aspect of schools. School discipline and contemporary American heroes fell together.

The federal government expended billions of dollars for educational reform during the sixties and seventies. Between 1963 and 1968, Congress enacted twenty-four major educational laws, more than in its entire history. The new legislation touched every aspect of education from preschool to postdoctoral studies. As will be discussed in greater detail in Chapter 12, the federal government greatly accelerated its interest and its funding of education—and its power to influence schools, teachers, and the curriculum.

Teacher Shortage

In 1960, the National Education Association, the nation's largest teachers organization, reported a shortage of 135,000 teachers and identified another 100,000 teachers as having substandard credentials (Foltz 1962). The dramatic increase in the number of young students was placing a severe strain on the ability of states and local communities to respond to that increase with enough qualified teachers, schools, supplies, and support personnel. The resources to meet the growing educational needs were not

The foundations of any subject may be taught to anybody at any age in some form.

Jerome Bruner, *The Process of Education*, 1957.

always available locally. The states and local communities began to look to the federal government for assistance. That assistance came by way of sweeping federal legislation in 1965.

1965: The Hinge

Ira Shor (1986) uses the term "hinge" to describe the dramatic changes that occurred in schools and society between decades. We can apply that term here to describe changes resulting from federal legislation in 1964 and 1965, which altered the direction of education for the next fifteen years.

The Great Society

The assassination of President John F. Kennedy in 1963 ended what some would say was "the age of innocence." Social pressures for change, including racial and social equality, had been building since blacks fought side by side with whites during World War II and women took the places of men on the assembly line. A new social consciousness, which emphasized individual freedom, was beginning to crest. The schools (elementary, secondary, and college), considered by many reformers to be the great equalizers, were seen once again as the vehicle for social change.

> *T*oday ... our Nation can declare another essential human freedom ... freedom from ignorance.
>
> President Lyndon Johnson, Message to Congress February 5, 1968.

Lyndon B. Johnson, carrying a mandate from the people and Congress and continuing in practice what Kennedy had begun, forged social legislation that impacted the foundations of American society. Johnson and his advisors evisioned a Great Society wherein all people—regardless of race, gender, or ethnic origin—would have equal opportunity to learn, work, earn, and succeed; in other words, there would be an opportunity for equality in all aspects of life. The War on Poverty was but one part of this vision.

Legislation. The following is a summary of Lyndon Johnson's key education legislation, which was enacted during 1964 and 1965 (Burns 1968).

▶ Civil Rights Act of 1964
Title VI. The act focused on an end to segregated schools by prohibiting the use of federal funds to support racial bias.
▶ Elementary and Secondary Act of 1965
Title I. The goal was to improve the education of disadvantaged children. The act impacted over 17,500 school districts.
▶ Economic Opportunity Act of 1966
Head Start. This legislation provided health care and early preschool learning experiences to over two million children.
▶ Teacher Corps Legislation of 1965

This legislation was a local version of the Peace Corps but for American schools in large urban districts and in poor rural areas. Teacher Corps emphasized the need to bring minority teachers who were college graduates into urban schools to provide the same quality education that was available for the suburban schools.

The legislation forged during the Johnson administration sounded the bell of equality for all Americans. It initiated the first of four "Es" (Equity, Experimentation, Excellence, and Economics)—**equity**—to characterize educational reform during the past quarter of a century.

The Decade of Experimentation

The 1970s ushered in an era of **experimentation** (the second E) in life-styles, family patterns, education, and schooling. The movement toward a standardized "teacher-proof" curriculum in mathematics and the sciences that required little teacher input or thought reached its peak in the late fifties and early sixties. The materials were developed, in many cases, by scientists in response to the space race and to the generally low level of content expertise held by teachers in mathematics and science at the elementary school levels. During the same period, the seeds of a very different educational movement were taking hold. The key words to the new educational movement in the seventies were *relevance* and *freedom of choice*.

Relevance and Freedom of Choice

The critics of the educational system of the fifties and sixties attacked its rigidity and lack of creativity. Many educators questioned the wisdom of removing the teacher from control of the curriculum and instruction. Donald Barnes (1986) reported that critics like Edgar Friedenberg (*Coming of Age in America*) called for alternatives in education; Charles Silberman (*Crisis in the Classroom*) endorsed open education and a movement away from the "mindless" education of the fifties, and Jonathan Kozel (*Death at an Early Age*) pleaded for educational equality (Barnes 1986, 30). Also, John Holt (*How Children Fail*) talked about the need for greater success in the classroom.

The New Critics

The wave of educational experimentation combined with a ground swell of protest from students in colleges and high schools both about the relevance of education and American involvement in the Vietnam War. The decade of experimentation reached its peak in the late seventies. A new wave was beginning to break on the shores. Critics in the eighties called the late sixties and the seventies the era of permissive education, with "too little writing and reading, too many soft electives and too few required hard academic courses" (Shor 1986, 67). A dramatic drop in Scholastic Aptitude Test (SAT) scores, taken by millions of high school students, was a clear indication to some that the era of experimentation had failed. The trend for educational **excellence** (the third E) and the "back to basics" movement in the eighties were beginning to build in the seventies.

Shor, in his text *Culture Wars* (1986, 104) selected the quotes from John Goodlad and Peter Brimelow to highlight the concerns expressed by many educators about our system of education.

*I*t is possible that our entire public education system is nearing collapse.

John Goodlad, *A Place Called School*, 1984.

*F*rom the bottom to the top of the system, professional social reformers abound, they are more interested in equality than excellence . . . The war for the public schools will be fought at the local level, where parents and back-to-basics educators find themselves in alliance with a conservative White House.

Peter Brimelow, *Fortune*, 1983.

The 1980s

Economic Survival

This decade is witnessing a new challenge to the American system—that of economic survival—and with that challenge, the birth of the fourth E for educational reform: **economics.** From World War II to the early 1980s, America was a creditor nation; we loaned money to other nations and have always had a trade surplus with the world economic community. During the eighties, however, the United States became a debtor nation. In 1986, the United States imported nearly 180 billion dollars more than was exported. For the first time in the modern history of this country we imported more agricultural products than we exported. The major reason given in consumer surveys for buying foreign goods was the poorer quality of American products. The push toward excellence was a move toward making the United States competitive in the economic world market place through a greater emphasis on excellence in the public schools.

Alternative Futures for Schools

Trends in education have taken us to the late 1980s. The future of our schools will depend on the economic, social, and technological directions of our country. If history is a good teacher, then societal needs will shape the curriculum, instruction, and organization of schools in the future. Although the future is unknown, we can conclude that schools will continue to change and reflect the needs of society. The following scenarios are examples of possible directions of schooling in the future.

The Changing School

Society has given educators the task to transmit its culture, skills, values, and beliefs. Additionally, schools are expected to care for the youth while parents are on the job, to prepare students for the world of work, and to provide a place where the social fabric of the society is strenghtened and where democracy can be nurtured. This is no small task for the eighties and nineties, and in the future it will become an even greater challenge. The quality of education directly affects the quality of our lives and our nation's success in the world marketplace.

A four-nation study (Japan, West Germany, Sweden, and the United States) was conducted by the Economic Policy Institute to compare quality of life and economic performance, using data from 1960 to 1985. The research institute concluded that Sweden ranked first and the United States ranked last in seventeen overall indicators of quality of life. The quality-of-life indicators included such areas as: mortality rates for infants; life expectancy; unemployment levels; homicide rates; income levels; medical care; home ownership; and average working hours. The United States was also last in the overall scores on seventeen economic indicators, with Japan being first. Only in housing did the United States receive a top score. (Gorham 1986).

A country with the best performance was given four points on an indicator. Countries with lesser performances were given either one, two, or three points. Exhibit 2.3 shows the quality-of-life rankings and total points.

The same study examined economic indicators for the United States, Japan, Sweden, and West Germany. The economic indicators looked at these areas: productivity; inflation; growth in products; personal savings; trade balance; research and development; and investments. The same point system was used in determining the points for economic indicators. Exhibit 2.4 shows the economic rankings and points for each of the four countries.

EXHIBIT 2.3 Quality-of-Life Rankings		EXHIBIT 2.4 Economic Indicators	
1. Sweden	54 points	1. Japan	113 points
2. Japan	52 points	2. Germany	80 points
3. West Germany	44 points	3. Sweden	65 points
4. United States	32 points	4. United States	50 points

Source: Economic Policy Institute, 1986   Source: Economic Policy Institute, 1986

When students in the United States are compared to other western nations in computation skills and higher-level mathematics skills, we are scoring near or at the bottom of the list of nations. In 1957, our schools responded to the technological challenge of the launching of Sputnik. It began a new era for mathematics and science in our schools and a subsequent lead in the space race. However, if the United States hopes to retain its international leadership into the next century, our schools and educators must also respond to this latest challenge.

Schools of the Future

The schoolhouse of the future may be similar in structure to the schools of today, but what is learned there and how it is learned will be very different. The classrooms of the future will see greater changes than the schools themselves. We have moved from the one-room school to the town school to the comprehensive school. Our next step may be to national and global schools.

National Schools. The seeds for national schooling have already been planted. A student in a rural high school in South Dakota is taking a calculus course over interactive television. The course is being taught by an instructor two thousand miles away in San Antonio, Texas. The student can interact live with the teacher through a telephone link. The students in this calculus class are scattered among thirty school districts in fourteen states. The TI-IN Network, in cooperation with a state-sponsored and taxpayer-supported educational service center in Texas, has begun a series of classes from calculus to physics, which are beamed via satellite to high schools around the country that are too small to support the range of course offerings required for their students who wish to attend college. Similar arrangements have been established in Alaska and other states, where schools are small and scattered great distances from major population areas.

Elite Schools. The same technology that allows one instructor to teach calculus to students across the nation also allows a Nobel Prize professor in physics, for example, to teach the top two students in each of the fifty states. In this case classroom teachers would provide assistance to the students after each of the seminars. Classes would be formed in other key areas of mathematics, science, and the social sciences. Students would communicate with each other in the different states after class, using existing computer network links.

The students would be members of two schools: the one they are physically attending and the school within a school, which provides access to the top researchers and educators in the nation.

Global Schools. The same satellite technology that allows for national links could also be used for the development of global schools. Students from fifty countries could form a world school in which students would share a common curriculum and interact with each other and with the leading minds throughout the world. The number of schools would only be limited by available resources.

Career Schools. Other types of schools may also become more common in the mainstream of educating our youth in the future. Career schools, which have been developing through district-wide (magnet) school programs nationally during the past twenty years, will expand to provide parents and students greater opportunities to specialize in fields that require advanced training to become an expert. Schools will begin to mirror the organizational divisions at most universities. There will be schools for the education professions, law enforcement, arts and drama, music, mathematics and science, social welfare, business and management, architecture and engineering, and the liberal arts.

Year-Round Schools. The concept of the nine-month school year was appropriate when we were an agrarian society. Farmers planted seeds in late May and harvested in the late summer. Children were an important part of the economy of the farming community. Students needed time off during the planting, tending, and harvesting times of the year. With less than 2 percent of the nation's population directly involved in farming, the continued two-to-three-month summer vacation seems unnecessary.

Some school districts are moving to year-round schools to avoid the boom-or-bust enrollment cycles that have caused numerous districts in the northeast and midwest to close schools in the late 1970s and early 1980s. Having some students and teachers in the building all year allows for greater utilization of facilities and equipment. Most year-round schools have teachers and students attend one of four tracks. Each track provides for three months of school and one month of vacation time, three times during the twelve-month period for a total of nine months. Students in track A may attend school in July, August, and September and be on vacation in October. They would return to school again in November. While one track is on vacation other tracks will be in session. The Los Angeles and Houston public schools are implementing year-round programs.

According to Charles Ballinger of the National Council of Year-Round Education, 409 schools in 16 states have some type of year-round schedule. Scores earned on standardized tests by students in year-round schools may be as much as 20 percent higher than those of non-year-round students. (Ordovensky 1986). School boards are beginning to look for ways to spend less on buildings and more on the materials and people that benefit the students directly. The year-round school may be another future schooling trend.

Resident Academies. The cycle of poverty that extends from one generation to the next will continue into the future. The idea of resident, or boarding, schools is not new, but its application to poverty-stricken families may be one approach used to break the poverty cycle in America. The gap between middle- and upper-income groups and lower-income groups will continue to widen. It is difficult, if not impossible, for schools to furnish all the needs of poverty-stricken students during a normal six-hour day. The resident academy could supplement the students' social and academic environment and present greater opportunities for the future.

Super Schools. According to *NEA Today* (1987, 11) North Carolina, Illinois, and Louisiana have developed state-wide, high-technology boarding schools for academically gifted high school juniors and seniors. The schools, labeled "super schools" by the media, emphasize math and science curricula. Most of the teachers hold advance degrees, including doctorates, in their subject areas. Legislators and educators in other states, including Texas, Oklahoma, New York, Indiana, and Maryland, are observing the results of these high-tech schools for possible future development in their states.

Home Schools. The movement toward schooling students at home has been a growing trend since the 1970s. Parents were beginning to complain that schools were not reflecting their religious beliefs or the values they wished for their children. In response to values clashes with the educational system, parents began educating their children at home. They felt that teaching their children at home would provide them with a better future. In some states, groups of parents have joined together to form home schools for up to ten or twelve students. Although many states are beginning to restrict home education by requiring certified teachers, the trend toward home education may continue to grow as computer software and instructional materials become more available.

Computer-Intensive Schools

Electronic technology has become an important part of the teacher's world. While television, the overhead projector, and the filmstrip and 16-mm movie projectors have been tools for enhancing instruction for decades, the most significant contemporary shift is to the use of microcomputers in instruction. According to figures compiled by Quality Data of Denver, Colorado and reported by the National Educational Association, each computer in the nation's schools served an average of 125 students in 1983–84. In 1984–85, the figure dropped to 75, and in 1985–86, there was one microcomputer for every 50 students. The lower the number of students per microcomputer, the greater the opportunity for hands-on experiences. (NEA Today 1987, 7).

The microcomputers uses a variety of modalities: tactile, since a keyboard or "mouse" is normally used by students to communicate with the computer; visual, because the computer most often communicates with its user through images on a video display terminal (VDT), often called a television monitor; and auditory, in some cases, because voice synthesizers allow the computer to "talk" with its user.

In any case, a major value of the use of microcomputers as instructional tools is that the computer provides immediate feedback to the student, with minimal need for immediate supervision by the teacher. Software programs (programs which tell the computer how to interact with its user) are increasingly simple to use and have progressed far beyond the computer's usefulness as an "electronic flashcard" for drill purposes. Students can now use word-processing programs to produce class reports, for example. And the teacher can use a variety of programs to manage and monitor student progress and attendance, to compute numerical grades, and to perform a variety of other tasks that make his or her routine less laborious and provide more time for instructional—rather than managerial—purposes.

The Customized Teacher

The use of computers for instruction has expanded dramatically since 1980. The future, however, is not confined to floppy disks, the future resides with newer technologies. The compact disk (CD), similar to the disk you can buy in a record store, may revolutionize the teaching-learning process. When the compact disk is connected to a microcomputer, it can hold up to 250,000 single-spaced, typewritten pages. It can also store pictures, sound, and movies on the same disk. The computer is used to retrieve, in seconds, any order or sequence of information needed by the student. The new technology is called CD-I (Compact Disk-Interactive). Steven Frankel, from the Montgomery County Public Schools outside of Washington, D.C., in an article in the Outpost section of the *Washington Post*, presents the following scenario in Exhibit 2.5 about the impact of CDs in schools.

Frankel identified a software company that has placed the story of whales on CD-I. It mixes music with text and underwater photographs, narration, and detailed charts of whale migration patterns.

The possibility for fewer teachers with higher salaries or smaller classes, as Frankel suggests, is a provocative direction for our schools.

*S*ome men see things as they are and ask "Why?" I dream of things that never were, and ask "Why Not?"

Robert Kennedy.

EXHIBIT 2.5 **The Profit Potential**

Because they'll require fewer teachers for the same number of children, CD-I-based schools will be able to pay their teachers much more and/or offer much smaller classes. At the same time, by assaulting all of a student's senses and ensuring that instruction is neither too hard, nor too easy, they'll be a lot more appealing. If public schools are slow to react to these developments, they may cause an explosion in the growth of private schools that use CD-I technology.

CD-I-based elementary schools could easily be the next product that day-care corporations such as Kindercare will offer. If these corporations start successfully teaching kids reading and math on the disks while they're still preschoolers, the number of parents willing to move their kids into conventional public schools may be very low. Instead, an enormous market may open up for similar but more intensive experiences in the center's elementary programs—along with before- and after-school care.

Meanwhile, the pioneers in developing the satellite-based CD-I systems will probably be the fundamentalist Christian broadcasters. They are already years ahead of the public sector in satellite broadcasting. With their deep pockets, established audiences, and experience in running schools, they could build "universal school systems" which could make deep inroads on public schools.

The nation's brightest and most dedicated public school teachers, meanwhile, may be heading toward the growth area of developing the CD-I disks themselves. Many of the nation's most committed teachers gravitated to the Peace Corps or the Job Corps during the War on Poverty. Look for a similar exodus to publishing companies and small start-up firms as the rush to develop innovative education experiences for the CD-I players develops.

1986. Reprinted with permission. Steven Frankel

Conclusion

Many Entrances

The schoolhouse of the future will have many entrances. The above examples represent some possible directions for schooling in the twenty-first century. The effectiveness and quality of schools in the future may be determined by our ability to be on the cutting edge of a changing world.

Some of the directions, for example, home education and elite schools may fragment our society, while other directions, such as year-round, national, and career schools may have a unifying effect. The concept of global schools may be an important force for international understanding.

One Exit

It appears that a quality school will be defined in the future by how students succeed throughout school, in their personal lives, in the work world, and ultimately, how our country fares in the world marketplace. Paralleling the variety of quality schooling options will be a greater movement in the future for a national curriculum and standards for graduation for all students from elementary school through college. Uniform testing may act as the single door that will be a common exit for all students. The greatest danger of this trend is for those students who never make it through the door.

Whatever directions or combinations of possible schooling alternatives that evolve in the future, education and those of us who teach will be the key to our nation's success.

Building Reflective Inquiry Skills

How Would You Rate Our Schools?

For the past 12 years, Phi Delta Kappan, an educational journal with a circulation of 150,000, has commissioned the Gallup organization to survey the public's attitude toward schools. We have selected some key questions about schools from the 1976 and 1985 Gallup Polls.

Complete the poll, then compare your responses with those of the other students in your class. How do you, as a group, feel about each question? To what extent are your responses congruent with those of your classmates? Use this poll to understand their viewpoints and to broaden your own understanding. Finally, compare the responses of your class to those found in the general public. These are found in Appendix B.

School Survey

Circle one answer for each question.

1. Students are often given the grades A, B, C, D, and FAIL to denote the quality of their work. Suppose the public schools themselves, in this community, were graded in the same way. What grade would you give the public schools here? 1) A   2) B   3) C   4) D   5) FAIL   6) don't know

2. How about the public schools in the nation as a whole? What grade would you give the public schools nationally? 1) A   2) B   3) C   4) D   5) FAIL   6) don't know

3. Now, what grade would you give the teachers in the public schools in this community? 1) A   2) B   3) C   4) D   5) FAIL   6) don't know

4. Do you think salaries in this community for teachers are: 1) too high   2) too low   3) just about right or   4) no opinion?

5. How do you, yourself, feel about the idea of merit pay for teachers? In general, do you: 1) favor it   2) oppose it or   3) have no opinion?

6. Before they are hired by a school district, do you feel all teachers: 1) should or   2) should not be required to pass a basic competency test to measure such things as their general knowledge and ability to think? or   3) do you not know?

7. What do you think are the biggest problems with which the public schools in this community must deal?

_____

_____

8. Lack of discipline is often cited as a problem confronting the public schools. Please look over this list and rank in order from 1 to 10 which of these possible solutions you think would be most helpful in improving school discipline.

_____ Classes for teachers on how to deal with problem children

_____ Discussion groups with parents of problem children

_____ Required classes for parents of problem children

_____ Suspension of students with extreme behavior problems

_____ Formation of special classes for students who have behavior problems

_____ Creation of a system of work-study programs, with problem children doing useful work half-time and attending school half-time

_____ Classes for administrators to help them create more orderly behavior

_____ Tougher courts, probation systems, and work programs for delinquents

_____ Creation of a curriculum more relevant to the interests and concerns of students

_____ Alternative schools

9. How do you feel about the spending of public school funds for special instruction and homework programs for students with learning problems? Do you feel that more public school funds should be spent on students with learning problems than on average students, the same amount, or don't know?

_____

_____

_____

10. Should all high school students in the United States be required to pass a standard, nationwide examination in order to get a high school diploma? 1) yes, 2) no, 3) no opinion

11. Suppose you could choose your child's teachers. Assuming they all had about the same experience and training, what personal qualities would you look for?

_____

_____

_____

_____

Source: Reprinted with permission from Phi Delta Kappan 1976/1995.

Explorations

Exploration 1
Historical Antecedents of Modern Schooling

A number of today's school practices are rooted in the philosophies and teachings of educational leaders of previous generations. Re-read the sections about them in this chapter, listing their recommendations for effective education. Compare their concepts with practice today. What evidence do you find that their teachings are part of schools today?

Exploration 2
Needed Skills for Future Students

After reading the section on Alternative Futures for Schools, list some skills you feel students will need in order to succeed in schools of the twenty-first century. Compare your list with others in your class. What conclusions would you make about student skills for the future? What special skills will teachers need to be effective in the twenty-first century? From the descriptions of possible types of quality schools in the future, which ones do you think will be the most prevelant and why?

References

Barnes, D. L. (1986). Recent trends in education. *The Teacher Educator, 21*(4).

Bishop, C. K. & Regan, J. J. (1962). Programmed instruction in the armed forces—An overview. In S. Margulies & L. Eigen (Eds.) *Applied programmed instruction.* New York: John Wiley and Sons.

Bruner, J. (1963). *The process of education.* Cambridge, MA: Harvard University Press.

Burns, M. J. (1968). *To heal and to build.* New York: McGraw Hill.

Cordasco, F. (1976). *A brief history of education.* New Jersey: Littlefield Adams.

Cremin, L. A. (1966). *Genius of American education.* New York: Vintage Books.

Dewey, J. (1902). *The child and the curriculum.* Chicago: University of Chicago Press.

Dewey, J. & Dewey, E. (1962). *Schools of tomorrow.* New York: E. P. Dutton.

Elliot, C. (1910). *English philosophers of the seventeenth and eighteenth centuries.* New York: Collier.

Erasmus, D. (1936). *The education of a Christian prince* (L. K. Born, Trans.). New York: Columbia University Press. (Original work published in 1540.) (Erasmus, 1540/1936).

Foltz, C. I. (1962). Aids to teaching: A survey of the current status of teaching machines. In S. Margulies & L. Eigen (Eds.) *Applied programmed instruction.* New York: John Wiley and Sons.

Frankel, S. (1986). Finally, the revolution in teaching. *Washington Post*, November 23, 1986, D3.

Gallup, G. H. (1976). The 8th annual Gallup poll of the public's attitudes toward the public schools. *Phi Delta Kappan, 58*(2), 187–200.

Gallup, G. H. (1985). The 17th annual Gallup poll of the public's attitudes toward the public schools. *Phi Delta Kappan, 66*(1), 23–38.

Gorham, L. (1986). *No longer leading: A scorecard on U.S. economic performance and the role of the public sector compared with Japan, West Germany and Sweden.* Washington, D.C.: Economic Policy Institute.

Hamilton, E. (1930). *The Greek way.* New York: W. W. Norton.

Keating, M. W. (Ed.). (1931). *Comenius.* New York & London: McGraw-Hill.

Locke, J. (1934). *Some Thoughts Concerning Education* (Translated by R.H. Quick). London: Cambridge University Press, (Original work published in 1693.) (Locke, 1693/1934).

National Education Association. (1985). *Addresses and proceedings.* Washington, DC: National Education Association.

NEA Today (1987). Volume No. 6, March 1987.

Noll, J. W., & Kelly, S. P. (Trans.). (1970). *Foundations of Education in America: An anthology of major thoughts and significant actions.* New York: Harper & Row.

Ordovensky, P. (1986). Some USA schools never close. *USA today.* (D) 1.

Patterson, C. H. (1973). *Humanistic Education.* Englewood Cliffs, NJ: Prentice Hall.

Perry, A. C. (1908). *The Management of a City School.* New York: Macmillan.

Rousseau, J. J. (1979). *Emile.* Translated by Allan Bloom. New York: Basic Books (Original work published in 1762.) (Rousseau, 1762/1979).

Schaefer, R. J. (1971). Retrospect and prospect. Chapter 1 in *The Curriculum: Retrospect and Prospect.* Seventieth Yearbook, National Society for the Study of Education. Chicago: University of Chicago Press.

Shor, I. (1986). *Culture wars.* Boston: Routledge & Kegan Paul.

Skinner, B. F. (1957). *Verbal behavior.* New York: Appleton-Century-Crofts.

Smith, W. (1973). *Theories of education in early America 1655–1819.* New York: Bobbs-Merrill.

Spring, J. H. (1976). *The sorting machine, National educational policy since 1945.* New York: McKay.

Standing, E. M. (1962). *Maria Montessori, Her life and works.* New York: New American Library.

Tyler, R. W. (1971). Curriculum development in the twenties and thirties. Chapter 2 in *The Curriculum: Retrospect and Prospect.* Seventieth Yearbook, National Society for the Study of Education. Chicago: University of Chicago Press.

Watson, F. G. (1963). Research on teaching science. In N. L. Gage (Ed.) *Handbook of research on teaching.* Chicago: Rand McNally.

Webster, M. (1966). *Webster's seventh new collegiate dictionary.* Springfield: G & C. Merriam Company, 1966.

Woodhouse, J. R. (1978). *Baldesar Castiglione.* Edinburgh: Edinburgh University Press.

Reflective Teachers Are Students of Teaching

OBJECTIVES

By the end of this chapter, you will be able to:

1. Identify four major responsibilities shared by all teachers.
2. Discuss the concept of academic learning time and its relationship to students' potential for learning.
3. Discuss teaching philosophies and begin to form your own philosophy of teaching.
4. Conduct qualitative observations of teachers and combine them with interview data as you continue your study of what it means to be a teacher.

KEY WORDS AND CONCEPTS

Academic learning time
Essentialism
Existentialism
Intrinsic rewards
Mastery learning
Perennialism
Progressivism
Social reconstructionism

Teaching as a Process of Inquiry

All teachers teach students, but thoughtful teachers also *study* their students so that they may meet their individual needs and accommodate individual differences. Such teachers study the process of teaching and the outcomes that may be associated with these processes. They also study the intellectual and emotional processes of their students in both academic and social settings. Through such study teachers are able to reflect on the possible relationships between their teaching and the students' responses to that teaching.

As we discussed in the previous chapter, the teacher's role changes as the demands on schools change. When you were in school, you may have been unaware of the demands on teachers other than classroom instruction, or extracurricular responsibilities. Now that you are deciding to become a teacher, you need to investigate the time, effort, and knowledge that is a prerequisite for successful teaching. In this chapter, we will investigate teaching in elementary, middle, and high schools through the accounts of three teachers as they take you through a typical teaching day. From their perceptions of the demands on their time, patience, and professional expertise, we will begin an exploration of some of the research on teaching that investigates the relationships between teaching and learning in classroom settings.

While research provides us with the knowledge to guide our thoughts on teaching responsibilities, it does not prescribe any one way of teaching, nor does it present laws of teaching that automatically guarantee a specific student response. As you begin to conduct your own personal inquiries into the relationships between teaching and learning, research on teaching will provide you with a starting point, but you will be responsible for deciding what is most desirable for your students. As you know, debate continues about which educational goals are the most important goals for our students. These arguments usually represent different philosophies of education; therefore, at the end of this chapter we will look at different philosophies of teaching and at various teachers' stances concerning the practice of teaching. By that time, we hope that you will have begun to develop your own personal philosophy of teaching.

The Teaching Day

Although teachers share many activities and actions, there is no such thing as a "typical" teacher or a typical school day. A teacher's day is shaped by the school context, by the assigned duties in addition to teaching, and by the content he or she teaches. Elementary teachers usually work with fewer students each day than do secondary teachers and, therefore, are able to establish closer relationships with those students. Secondary-school teachers are often asked to monitor public areas and to control students whose names they don't know and probably never will. Teachers who sponsor clubs, who coach sports, or who work in the performing arts spend more time in school than do teachers whose responsibilities are in the classroom only (although those teachers are often grading papers and planning lessons at home) and often serve as explicit mentors and role models to their students. The school community also makes an impact on a teacher's assignment.

In the following exhibits we present three teachers who will discuss their daily routines. As you read these accounts, consider the experiences they all share and consider the differences between their work responsibilities both in and out of class. Our first teacher, Paula, teaches in a rural elementary school. She commutes about sixty miles round trip from her home in a nearby city to her small fourth-grade classroom.

EXHIBIT 3.1   **Paula, a Fourth-Grade Teacher in a Rural School District**

A typical day begins at 6:00 A.M. While getting ready and while traveling to school, I think about what we will learn that day. I think of ways to make long division seem easy, ways to motivate my students, and ways to make science and social studies concepts more applicable and exciting. Once I arrive at school at 7:45, I prepare the classroom for the day. Lessons are written on the board, dittoed work is organized, and notes are placed everywhere to remind me of things that need to be done. I read over my lesson plans and lessons and straighten my desk, only to see it unorganized again by mid-morning.

The children come in at 8:15. My students range in age from nine to thirteen, which often causes social problems. Many read below grade level and one-third of the class receives some remedial instruction with a resource teacher. Morning lessons include science, physical education, mathematics, and spelling. Afternoon lessons include reading, language, handwriting, social studies, art, and music.

The school day ends at 3:30, but usually my work is just beginning. Once I am home, there are papers to grade, lessons to plan, progress reports to write, and materials to create. Some nights I spend two or more hours preparing for the next day. Teaching does not end when the final bell rings or the school year is over. I spend much time in the summer months preparing for the year ahead.

With all its challenges, teaching is often fun.

Stan, urban high-school social studies teacher, is married, but has no children. He commutes each day though heavy city traffic to a high school that has been targeted for a special program emphasizing academic achievement. Many of his students are performing well below grade level and are tutored before and after school.

EXHIBIT 3.2   **Stan, a Teacher in an Urban High School**

BEEP! It is 5:45 A.M. and the feet respond to a request for automatic pilot. I "breeze" through a shower and breakfast, grab a cup of coffee and—after a minimum of twenty-five minutes on the freeway—I pull into the school parking lot. I sign in, check my information box, and head off to unpack my "teachers' tidbits" (homework, grade book, duplicating masters prepared the night before, and so on).

Since first period is my conference period, I write objectives and homework assignments on the board until the first-period bell rings. That way I can avoid the horde of last minute duplicators (teachers) who accumulate in the workroom prior to first period. After the halls begin to clear, I head to the workroom. The first duplicator refuses to feed the paper properly. It thinks it is a trash compactor! The next machine has no duplicator fluid. So, I go to the office, fill out a requisition (nothing in my school moves without a requistion), pick up the fluid, and go back to the workroom. Duplicating completed, I find that I have wasted thirty of my fifty minutes. I start back to my room.

As I enter the second floor hallway, I encounter a group of boys loitering near a locker. I kindly ask them to go to their classes, but they continue to stand around. Welcome to the hit gameshow—test that TEACHER! I move in closer and inform them in a slightly less civilized manner that my intention was for the movement to occur immediately. With facial expressions designed to intimidate me, they move toward the stairs. Occasionally I have to follow them all the way to class; occasionally they shout obscenities. This type of problem is typical when the loitering students are not my own. Several times I have encountered a group that includes one of my students and have listened to a smart remark followed by my student's remark, "He's cool. Let's go."

Back in my room, I stack the assignments on the table and glance over my notes. Soon the bell rings, and I greet my students and urge strays into class. By second period the students are awake and fairly spunky. This class proceeds without interruption.

The next period is deceptively labeled "tutorial." Approximately thirty students from three different classes seat themselves in my room. These are students who are failing and who need additional instruction. First, I have to find out where each different class of students is in the curriculum. Then I look at the work assigned for each one. These students seem to lack self-discipline and to need a lot of external motivation. I don't find them enjoyable to work with. Today I am able to adjust my instruction and to make routines flow smoothly. They also remain fairly alert and respond well.

Fourth period—lunch—arrives and so do my hungry students. This period is a split lunch, thirty minutes of instruction followed by thirty minutes of lunch and then thirty minutes more of instruction. After lunch, time is wasted as students rethink themselves into the classroom mode. This class always ends early (or so it seems).

Ahora es tiempo para mi estudiantes de Español. Even though I don't speak Spanish fluently, it is thought that if I speak slowly and use more gestures I can be an ESL (English as a second language) teacher. ESL is usually a learning experience for both the students and the teacher. I teach them the subject matter, and they help me improve my Spanish and my cultural awareness of Latin American nations.

By the time sixth period arrives, I need to recharge in order to motivate the tired, wandering minds awaiting freedom for the day.

After school I spend a few minutes talking to students and then gather my materials to take home. Once home I eat, and after those two or three hours I've spent away from the job, I go into my study for another two or three hours of grading papers and preparing new ideas for tomorrow.

Marsha, a middle-school math teacher, lives and teaches in the same suburban school district. She feels that living near her work is important to help her balance her responsibilities as a teacher and as a parent—both of which occupy a great deal of Marsha's time.

EXHIBIT 3.3   **Marsha, a Suburban Middle-School Teacher.**

What is that noise? It can't be time to get up—it's still dark outside. However, the clock says 5:15 A.M. and if I can just make it to the coffee pot, maybe I'll feel better.

It's amazing what a shower and coffee do for you. Now, wake up my daughter and then my husband—I hope everyone has clean clothes to wear. I had better make the bed and straighten the kitchen (thank goodness everyone gets their own breakfast). I'll eat a piece of toast while I make my lunch. Oh, I mustn't forget to sign Suzy's paper, give her lunch money, and ask when to pick her up from practice.

6:35 Head for the car after I check to see if I have everything—graded papers, purse, lunch and aspirin to take before my 6th period class. In the two minutes I drive to school I think about the forthcoming day: no morning duty this week; tutoring this week after school; parent conference at 7:00 A.M.; no lunch duty until tomorrow.

By 6:50 I'm at school, and I meet with other teachers for the parent conference. We would all like the same thing from the child—homework and supplies brought to class. Is that too much to ask?

First period, at 7:20, is a conference period. I record grades on the computer, make out a test, and call parents about progress and lack of progress. I would like to visit with my colleagues over coffee, but that would put me behind for the entire week.

Second period—announcements and the pledge of allegiance. Sometimes I worry that we get off to a slow start in this class.

Between classes I visit with another teacher as I supervise the halls—and then third period. I feel that I have a real rapport with this class. They really seem to enjoy math.

During fourth period I check roll, and then we go to lunch. I really want to hurry as much as they do—I want to beat the crowd to the teachers' restroom. The first rule of teaching: You must have a strong bladder. After lunch we return to class—my only seventh-grade class. They are so different from the sixth graders. Seventh graders are more interested in socializing and less interested in academics. I have to keep a tight lid on them, or they will get me off the topic. I often implore them to study if only because they want to be eligible for sports or band or because they need to know percentages in order to shop sales at the mall!

Fifth period and a return to sixth graders. I overhear a student remark that she really likes math and it makes my day. It doesn't take much to make a teacher happy.

Sixth period is where I really earn my salary. I wish I had these below-level math students earlier in the day. By sixth period I don't know if I'm teaching manners or mathematics because they are so tired of school. Still, even though it is a very stressful class, I know I'll reach at least one of them, and I'll be able to help them learn.

At 2:40 I'm running out of steam.

The next period is my tutoring period. I wish the ones who needed help the most would come in, but today there are only people wanting to make up a test.

Time to go home after I collect the papers I need to grade. I stop and pick up Suzy, go by the grocery, and then I go home and cook dinner, wash dishes, wash a few clothes and . . . grade papers. WHEW. By 9:00 I put my feet up and try to relax fast. Teaching and caring for a family is not for the weak, nor for the faint-hearted.

These teachers all teach in very different schools, but they all share at least four common elements.

1. Although the time teachers are *required* to be on campus is somewhat less than other occupations, most teachers' days start early and end late. While there may be a break to eat supper or to take care of family responsibilities, the end of school is often only a prelude to an evening of evaluating student papers and assignments.
2. Classroom teaching occupies the largest amount of a teacher's time, but teachers are also responsible for supervisory duties around the school building and for tutoring students who are not doing well in regular classroom work.
3. Teachers often compete for resources within the school building. Whether a movie projector, a computer, a duplicating machine, or overhead projectors, teachers have to plan their use of these resources carefully so that their materials are ready for each class.
4. Teachers are concerned primarily with student welfare, and positive relationships between themselves and their students are their major sources of satisfaction.

Simply put, teachers work long hours in and out of school, but they are not "super people." They must learn to plan ahead so that their personal time is not wasted and so that their classroom time will be used to teach rather than to do clerical work. This is especially important in classes where students experience academic problems, for these students are the challenges of teaching. Effective planning is also important for teachers whose responsibilities include sponsoring extracurricular activities or working at another job after school, the conditions experienced by over one-third of all teachers.

Philip Jackson conducted extensive investigations of teaching and of teachers that documented the intense, moment-to-moment demands on teachers' time. He concluded that

> The job of managing 25 or 30 children for 5 or 6 hours a day, 5 days a week, 40 weeks a year, is quite a bit different from what an abstract consideration of the learning process might lead us to believe . . . . There is evidence to show that the elementary school teacher typically engages in 200 or 300 interpersonal interchanges every hour of her working day. (Jackson 1968, 149)

Although secondary-school teachers may have fewer interchanges, they typically work with more students. Some 125 to 160 adolescents walk in and out of classes each day. Let us look carefully at the responsibilities of teaching—keeping in mind the numbers of student-teacher interactions that teachers must attend to and account for.

The Responsibilities of Teaching

Sociologist Willard Waller studied the work of teaching and described a teacher's primary responsibility as one of commanding students' attention and of prodding students toward learning.

> The teacher, following out his customary role, attempts to delimit the social interaction of the classroom. . . . Thus the teacher continually strives to evoke in students the attitudinal set which we call "attention" . . . The attention of the students tends to wander from the cut-and-dried subject matter. As attention wanders, the social interaction broadens. The teacher brings it back in a manner very similar to that of a dog driving a herd of sheep. (Walle 1932, 333)

Many teachers today would agree that their first responsibility is to command students' attention and to then find ways of securing that attention long enough for learning to occur. But many teachers would disagree

TABLE 3.1 Teaching Duties

PERCENTAGE OF TEACHERS PERFORMING DUTIES AT LEAST WEEKLY					
0	20	40	60	80	100

Keeping students on task	x x x x x x x x x x x x x x x x x x x x x x x
Recording attendance	x x x x x x x x x x x x x x x x x x x x x x x
Adjust plan in class	x x x x x x x x x x x x x x x x x x x x x x x
Monitor out of class	x x x x x x x x x x x x x x x x x x x
Plan class lessons	x x x x x x x x x x x x x x x x x x x x x x x x
Discuss work with colleagues	x x x x x x x x x x x x x x x x x x x x x x x x x
Counsel students	x x x x x x x x x x x x x x x x x x x x x
Respond to administrator's questions	x x x x x x x x x x x x x x x x x x x x
Meet with parents	x x x x x x x x x x x x x x
Attend faculty meetings	x x x x x x x x x x x x x x x x

Source: *NEA Today*, May, 1986, 4. Used with permission.

with Waller's contention that social interaction is not desirable in a classroom. These teachers would argue that helping students learn to work together and to share ideas is a very important part of the teaching/learning process. In our opinion, both are important. Teachers' responsibilities include the management of time, the planning and implementation of classroom learning environments, and the facilitation of positive social interactions between students. Most importantly, good teachers monitor the effects of their teaching to assess the relationships between what they intended and what the students actually experience.

Management of Time

Teachers are time managers. They must plan so that the classroom time promotes learning through careful implementation of appropriate learning environments that will help students accomplish educational goals. One such goal is educating students to work with other students in school settings, even though they may come from different social or cultural backgrounds. To accomplish this, teachers are responsible for helping to establish positive interpersonal relationships within the classroom. Teachers are also responsible for evaluating educational outcomes, whether these outcomes are academic or social. To some people, evaluation may imply a test, but evaluation in teaching is far more than test construction and scoring. The thoughtful teacher is one who continually assesses the classroom environment and its impact on the students. This reflection on the teaching/learning process is one of the most basic responsibilities of teaching.

Academic Learning Time. Many research efforts have been geared toward the use of time in classrooms. The earliest efforts were by John Carroll (1963), who believed that differences in student achievement were not so much related to differences in innate ability, but that different students need different amounts of time to master the same concepts. Benjamin Bloom (1968), another educational researcher, developed this idea into a concept called *mastery learning.* Teachers and schools that use a mastery approach to teaching work with students individually or in small groups and permit students to study, rework assignments, and retake tests until mastery is achieved. A mastery approach to teaching usually necessitates the cooperation of the entire school, because individual classes and yearly promotions will vary with the amount of time the individual student needs to complete the given curriculum; thus, individual teachers may have trouble implementing mastery learning in their own classrooms. There is a considerable body of research on time management that has made the biggest impact on teaching and on individual teachers—the concept of *academic learning time.*

Think about your most recent experiences in precollegiate studies. Did you ever experience situations in which the PA system interrupted a lesson? Did you ever have a teacher who was so busy with one student that he or she did not start class on time? How about a situation in which the substitute teacher had no lesson plans to help as he or she struggled through each hour of the day? All of these situations illustrate a potential waste of a portion of the fifteen thousand hours children spend in school. Classroom researchers (Fisher, Filby, Marliave, Cahen, Dishaw, Moore, and Berliner 1978) have observed numerous teachers in both elementary and secondary schools and have found that those teachers who spend less time on non-academic tasks and who have each class session organized for instruction are more likely to produce higher academic achievement in their students. This concept, although it sounds simplistic, is one of the most basic skills of teaching—and one that first-year year teachers find the hardest, because they have not yet developed the expertise to manage noninstructional tasks, such as roll taking, talking with individual students, and distributing supplies. Let us look at academic learning time more closely.

Think about the time available in one class period. Let's say fifty minutes, for math. This is the total amount of time that the teacher and the school allocate for instruction. Now suppose you decide to take the first five minutes of class to check for permission slips for a field trip. Subtract five minutes from the total time allocated for instruction.

Then the next ten minutes you lecture on a new mathematical operation. Four of the students are not listening—they are preparing their history assignment. They have no contact with the material. Although you have allocated time for teaching, they are not taking advantage of it—they are not *engaged* in learning math (although they may be learning history). Fifteen minutes have been subtracted from their potential learning time. The next fifteen minutes you allocate to seatwork, using the operation you have just presented. Those students sit, helplessly, because they are not able to complete the assignment.

Five other students are not sitting idle, but they are not learning because they did not understand your presentation, and they are being frustrated by their inability to complete their assignment. While they are engaged, they are not *actively learning*, because they are not successfully making the connections between instruction and independent application of instruction.

Maximizing academic learning requires three elements: learning time must be *allocated*, the students must be *engaged* in the learning process, and they must be *actively learning* through experiencing the appropriate degree of success. Determining that appropriate degree is the key to why teachers are professionals and are *not* skilled laborers. There is no algorithm or rule that determines the appropriate success level. Professional judgement is necessary to understand when a student is challenged—or frustrated. The

FIGURE 3.1
The concept of academic learning time

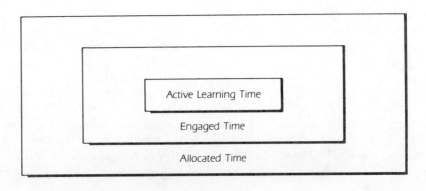

appropriate degree of success for each student is the attainment of his or her maximum potential as a student. Students who are not accustomed to frequent success on academic tasks need a structure that will permit them to succeed easily at *least* 80 percent of the time; students who are accustomed to academic success can tolerate more of a challenge (Rosenshine & Stevens, 1986).

Different Learning Environments for Different Goals

A large part of being a teaching professional is the ability to design learning tasks and establish settings that will enable your students to meet diverse educational goals. Many of your decisions concerning learning environments will be academically oriented, but "academic orientation" can imply at least three equally important goals. The first of these goals relates to acquisition of facts, skills, and concepts. According to many instructional designers, these might be classified as lower order processes, because they do not ask the student to generate additional information or to create essentially new ideas, hypotheses, or theories based on a set of given information. The second of these goals relates to moving beyond the "lower order processes," as we ask the student to analyze an unfamiliar problem or process or to synthesize discrete bits of information into a "new" solution or product. These are referred to as higher order processes. The third goal relates to the creation of expression and meaning through the interpretation of literature, music, or art, through the creation of a literary or visual work, or through a musical or dramatic performance.

There is a growing body of research on effective teaching that can help us design learning environments to accomplish the first goal. In a review of this research, Barak Rosenshine and Robert Stevens list nine components that research has identified as important for teaching the acquisition of basic facts and skills.

1. Begin a lesson with a short review of previous instruction that is important for the lesson.
2. Briefly inform students of the goals for the lesson.
3. Present new material in small steps with brief practice after each step.
4. Give clear, detailed instructions and explanations.
5. Provide a high level of practice.
6. Ask many questions and provide many opportunities for all students to demonstrate understanding.
7. Guide students' initial practice with a new skill or procedure.
8. Provide systematic feedback and correction.
9. Provide explicit instruction for seatwork and monitor student progress.
(Rosenshine & Stevens 1986, 377)

Rosenshine and Stevens emphasize that these elements are most effective for well-structured learning goals. When the knowledge base is well defined, or when the procedures for solving problems can be specified in advance, teachers are advised to directly instruct students about the knowledge base and the procedures. Such direct instruction does not promote problem solving when both the problem and the steps for solving the problem are unknown. Similarly, direct instruction does not encourage creativity. For those goals, teachers and students need to work in fundamentally different learning environments.

Inquiry-oriented instruction and discovery learning are only two of the strategies that will help students to move beyond knowledge acquisition to the more complex processes of analysis and synthesis. In the learning environment Rosenshine discusses, there is a high degree of certainty. The student knows exactly what is expected and how to set about accomplishing the academic task; in inquiry-oriented tasks, defining the problem may be as important as solving it.

Evaluations for well-structured assignments are closely related to the information provided by the teacher and by the texts. But as assignments become more complex, the student must deal with more ambiguity. The more complexity and ambiguity in the task, the harder it is for a teacher to evaluate the students' achievement or to be held accountable for it.

I t is in the formulation of the problem that individuality is expressed, that creativity is stimulated, and that nuances and subtleties are discovered.

Herbert Thelen, *Education and the Human Quest*. 1960, 26

Accountability

Accountability, or *proving* to others that you, the teacher, have helped students to learn, is a very big issue that all teachers face. In some school districts, standardized subject matter tests are administered to all students. Teachers are then evaluated on the results of the tests, and those teachers whose students do not score well receive poor evaluations of their teaching, while teachers whose students make acceptable scores will receive higher salary increases. In other school districts, teachers are evaluated by observation instruments that document observable indicators of recommended teaching practices. At the present time it is unclear whether such evaluations of teaching practice are contributing to increases in student performance on well-structured problems, on ill-structured problems, or on skill development. The effects of such evaluation on sustained changes in the ways teachers teach and on changes in teacher morale are also unclear.

Evaluations of teaching performance and knowledge assume that there *is* a knowledge base of teaching. One portion of this knowledge base is provided by content area knowledge—for example, knowledge of history, mathematics, or literature. A second portion of the knowledge base is knowledge of pedagogy—teaching strategies, classroom management, instructional design. The third area of the knowledge base is knowledge of learners and of learning—the reading process, individual differences in learning style and in motivation, individual differences in the capacity to process information, and the like. Within the past fifty years, the last two areas have been the foci of researchers who study teaching. Although much of this research is referenced in later chapters, the U.S. Department of Education (Bennett 1986), which sponsors much of the research on teaching, attempted to summarize this research in a monograph entitled *What Works: Research about Teaching and Learning*. While this document is not a *prescription* for teaching, it does offer an insight into some of the more effective parenting and teaching strategies that help children do well academically.

TABLE 3.2   Numbers of States and Mandates for Improving Teaching

	1982	1985	1986
Performance based incentives	not given	30	40
State financed in-service training	n/g	36	n/g
State mandated testing for new teachers	12	31	35

Sources: *Education Week*, February 26, 1986, 12–13; February 18, 1987, 20–21. Used with permission.

Interpersonal Relations

Teaching means that you will be working with other people daily. You will interact with students formally in classroom settings and, possibly, informally out of class. Excellent teachers are able to demonstrate that they care about their students' academic achievement *and* that they care about the person who is capable of achievment. A recent poll, conducted by *Phi Delta Kappa* (Clark 1987), suggests that most students perceive schools and teachers favorably. Seventy-two percent of the students would give their schools a grade of either A or B; 74 percent gave their teachers similar grades. In addition, 22 percent of the students stated that they would like to become teachers. As Table 3.3 indicates, students appreciate teachers who are understanding and who are both knowledgeable and fair. But Table 3.4 shows that some students who are having problems in school may feel alienated from teachers, thus underscoring the importance of establishing positive relationships with *all* students.

We cannot think about school settings solely as structures for thinking about academic concerns. Sociologist Steven Bossert, who has studied social relationships in schools, has documented the interaction between the *tasks* teachers assign students, the evaluations of those tasks, and the social relationships that are formed as a result. The following quote is an excerpt from an interview with Mr. Stone, a third-grade teacher, who has adopted a multi-task environment in which groups of students work cooperatively on projects.

EXHIBIT 3.4   **Key Points From** *What Works*

► Reading ability improves with the amount of reading children do.

► Reading assignments are more effective when the teacher precedes the lesson with background information and follows it with discussion.

► Science lessons are more effective when children are able to do experiments, so they can witness "science in action."

► Writing is best taught as a process of brainstorming, composing, revising, and editing.

► Mathematics instruction for young children is more effective when they use physical objects in their lessons.

► When students tutor other students, both can improve academically and often develop more positive attitudes toward coursework.

► When teachers regularly assign homework and students conscientiously do it, student achievement improves.

TABLE 3.3   **Highlights From *Kappan* Poll of High School Seniors**

	CHARACTERISTICS OF TEACHERS	
Characteristic	*Percentage of students saying this characteristic is important*	*Percentage of students noting the characteristic is demonstrated*
Understanding	82	66
Knowledgeable	81	87
Fair	78	71
Interesting	72	41
Organized	67	69
Competent	62	75
Friendly	60	80
Creative	44	33
Demanding	22	62
Strict	10	48

Source: *Clark* 1987, 504. Used with permission.

TABLE 3.4   **Teacher's Perceived Favoritism**

	STUDENTS AVERAGE GRADE			
	A/A−	*B+/B/B−*	*C+/C*	*C−/D*
Teachers seem to teach mainly for the benefit of top students.	7.4%	11.2%	13.7%	21.7%
Teachers do not appear to care whether all students learn the subject or not.	6.7%	10.7%	14.6%	21.7%

Source: *Clark* 1987, 505. Used with permission.

> I used to use a lot more structured things in my teaching. However, I felt I was being less responsive to each child. You know, when you're up there talking and trying to get the stuff across to the kids, it's really hard to handle each one's needs. That's why I like to be able to work with them [in small groups] . . . When I can immediately help them with their problems, things work out much better. (Bossert 1979, 54)

Mr. Stone's experience as a teacher has led him to work with his students in groups so that he can interact with them on an individual basis. The students in his class learned to work with each other and to share ideas and solutions to problems. Bossert found that the students in Mr. Stone's class were more likely to work with all class members, not just a few, and that they were not highly competitive. They were learning to work with children from different cultures and to help students of different academic abilities.

In contrast, when these students were promoted to a fourth-grade teacher's class that offered class rewards for completing assigned work quickly and accurately, they became more competitive and formed tightly-knit friendships with students who were their equals in the competitions. Although the students who had Mr. Stone the previous year had some difficulty in adjusting to this more competitive approach to teaching, they recognized that the classroom environment and the teacher's expectations were clearly different, and they adapted to the demands of the new setting.

Robert Dreeben (1968) argued that learning to compete is one of the most basic lessons learned in school. Researchers on cooperative learning in small groups (Cohen 1986; Bossert 1979; Johnson, Johnson, Holubec, Roy 1984) would agree that individual competition is dominant in most school settings, but they would disagree that it *must* be that way. Their research on cooperative learning has shown that students *can* learn from each other, *can* work together productively, and *do* improve academically. The teacher is the one who determines whether the climate of the class will be cooperative or competitive.

The relationships between academic settings and personal feelings of achievement and self-worth make the teacher an important personal, as well as an important academic, force. To many teachers, one of the most important aspects of a teacher's job is establishing personal contacts with students. This does not mean that one must become "best friends" with one's classes, but it does mean demonstrating a sincere caring for the students' welfare. Balancing professional conduct and personal concern is an important skill. Some teachers are able to learn it early. Kevin Ryan and colleagues (1980) conducted longitudinal case studies of first-year teachers. One of these teachers, Sandy, found that learning how to interact with students was one of her most important lessons in learning to teach effectively:

> Sandy liked students; she enjoyed being around them and playing sports with them. She reflected, "I guess I am like a good friend to these girls. I like that. But being a friend makes it hard to get tough with them." When the roles of teacher and friend became confused, the students, particularly the ninth graders, were difficult to control . . . As the year drew to a close, Sandy felt more sure in her interactions with the students . . . She found that a healthy relationship with students was the result of personal concern and involvement, not jokes and discussions on clothes. (Ryan et al. 1980, 142, 145)

Teachers are able to create positive classroom atmospheres through the learning tasks they assign and through their positive interpersonal interactions with students both in and out of class. As a novice teacher, it will be important for you to think about the classroom environment you want to establish. Then you will need to continually work toward achieving your ideal. In our opinion, careful planning for instruction and thoughtful evaluation of one's own instruction are the foundations of excellence in teaching.

Reflections on the Teaching/Learning Process

Donald Cruickshank (1987), a teacher educator from Ohio State University, began a program for experienced teachers that encouraged them to reflect on their daily experiences with other teachers and to improve their teaching based on this reflection. The teachers who participated in the program found that they were able to share problems with others in a nonthreatening, helpful environment, and that they were able to review their classrooms using different perspectives and thereby understanding those classrooms more completely.

This concept of being a reflective practitioner is important to medicine, to architecture, and to any other profession in which one person makes decisions and takes actions to affect the lives of others. Donald Schön (1983) has studied reflective practice in several occupations. He distinguishes between reflection *in* action and reflection *on* action. His analysis of tape recorded discussions between expert practitioners and novices led to the observation that experts in a given profession are capable of an automatic ability to "read" a situation and to modify their thoughts and actions based on their reading of that situation. This almost instantaneous analysis, reflection, and action has long been associated with improvisational actors and musicians, but has only recently become a major focus of research on teaching.

Reflection on action, or on teaching, occurs after the active teaching has ended as you think about the class day while driving home or while grading students' papers. This is a time to stand back from a situation and to examine that situation from many perspectives. This kind of reflection can lead to modification of plans, or it can lead a teacher to seek more information about a child so that the teaching and learning cycle can be improved.

Teaching without reflection becomes mechanical and routine. Some teachers often follow patterns established years ago without asking if the present situation is any different from the past. Such teachers tend to blame the child or the parent for academic difficulty without inquiring into the nature of the difficulty or into the many alternative instructional procedures that might help that child.

Teachers who hold fundamentally different assumptions about the nature and purpose of education may act in very different ways—all of them appropriate. But a philosophy of teaching implies thoughtfulness; there is never an excuse for thoughtlessness or teaching by an outdated recipe.

Personal Philosophies of Teaching

The phrase "philosophy of teaching" may sound abstract and rather foreign if you are not accustomed to thinking about teaching as the practical implementation of your own personal philosophy. The *Random House Dictionary* gives as its first definition of philosophy, "the rational investigation of truths and principles of being, knowledge or conduct." In our opinion, it is impossible to be a thoughtful teacher without a commitment to inquire into the truths and principles of what it means to be a student in your classroom, to inquire into the truths and principles of what constitutes valuable knowledge, and to inquire into the truths and principles related to the ethical, effective, and exciting conduct of teaching.

First let us consider what it may mean to be your student. Earlier, we discussed teachers' responsibilities for using time effectively, for creating positive learning environments, and for promoting desirable interpersonal relations between students. Let's turn that around for a minute and look at it from students' viewpoints. Is the time spent in the classroom focused on academic content? What is that content? Is it predetermined, or does it emerge throughout the course of the school year? Who has made that decision and on what grounds? Did the students have *any* input into the content? Is the learning environment focused on the teacher's knowledge and opinions? What room is there for the students' experiences or viewpoints? Are all classes held inside the classroom, or are some held in the community? How involved is the community with the class—and how involved is the class with the community? The answers to these questions, and questions of similar importance, begin to identify what philosophy is being transmitted to your students.

Your identification of what knowledge is—in your particular area(s) of instruction—and of the values that are placed on that knowledge are closely related to the nature of being a student in your classroom. Who determines what you will teach? Do you adapt the content when you feel that it would then be more relevant to your students? *How* does that adaptation take place? Do you ever ignore the mandated curriculum? Do you and your students ever create your own curriculum just because it is deemed mutually desirable to do so? As you think about your answers to the questions in this paragraph and the preceding paragraph, we will introduce five philosophical doctrines that explain how other people, many of them teachers, have categorized the diverse answers to these questions.

A knowledge of differing philosophies and a knowledge of one's own philosophy are both vital elements in becoming a reflective professional. In many cases, educators disagree with one another and may believe that they are arguing over "semantics"—when in fact the argument is really a manifestation of philosophical differences concerning why schools should exist in the first place.

In this section five basic educational philosophies will be emphasized: perennialism, essentialism, progressivism, social reconstructionism, and existentialism. Each of these is important in understanding the controversies that surround schools.

Differing Philosophies of Education

Perennialism. The perennialist teacher is concerned with opening students' minds to rational thought and to the truths that can be found in the "classics," works of Aristotle, Plato, Saint Thomas Aquinas, Shakespeare, and other "great" authors, which achieve immortality through survival over time and through the acclaim of leading intellectuals over generations. Students would learn through the examples set by these authors and through discussions with their teachers in which they argued over the ideas and assumptions found in the texts.

Mortimer Adler (1982) is a perennialist scholar who advocates a curriculum based on the study of the classics. His *Paideia Proposal*—for twelve years of education for all students—includes physical education and manual arts, but the core of the curriculum is for fundamental knowledge in history, literature, languages, sciences, fine arts, and mathematics, with an emphasis on the basic intellectual skills of reading, writing, and computation. Students who would go through his program would develop the

Perennialists rely on classical texts such as readings from Plato and Aristotle as the basis for the curriculum.

abilities to reason critically and to conduct scientific investigations in their search for knowledge. They would also develop aesthetic sensitivity as they study and criticize works of art. The goal of this curriculum is to develop students who can recognize "excellence" in thinking and who strive toward that excellence in their own thinking.

The search for excellence and mental discipline means that education also becomes a sorting process, identifying and fostering the brightest and best. The perennialist's classroom, then, would be replete with materials like the *Great Books of the Western World*. The teacher would be exploring ideas and engaging students in Socratic dialogue—forcing them to question their underlying assumptions. Teachers would be critical of students' thinking in an effort to sharpen students' abilities to articulate their own ideas and interpretations. Student participation that is combined with thoughtful teacher response is the core of the perennialist classroom.

Essentialism. An essentialist believes that schools should exist to see that certain, selected elements of the culture are passed on to succeeding generations. The primary emphasis for the essentialist is on the subject matter rather than the student. The student is viewed as a recipient (often passive) of those parts of human knowledge deemed of sufficient importance to be included in the curriculum. The essentialist teacher represents the mainstream of contemporary American educational belief that the basic skills of reading, writing, and mathematics should be mastered before one goes on to learn the specific disciplines of history, biology, Spanish, literature, and so on. The fine arts and the physical arts receive a very low priority, but they may be tolerated.

Standardized textbooks are the normal reference for the essentialist, and lecture/practice/recitation is the preferred instructional mode. The teacher is transmitter of important knowledge and skills, the students are recipients, and standardized tests measure whether or not everyone is meeting "minimum expectations." Essentialist teachers stress the importance of adopting the values and traditions of the society (defined as the dominant group in the society). Students are drilled and tested over their ability to perform the basic skills and over their ability to retain the essential knowledge within a given discipline. They are also evaluated on their knowledge of social traditions and on their social conduct.

Essentialist curricula can be found in almost every school district in every state. While the perennialist teacher emphasizes the rational thinking process and encourages discussion, argument, and debate, the essentialist teacher emphasizes the mastery of academic content and desirable social values.

Progressivism.   The progressivist believes that schools should focus on developing the unique talents, capabilities, and interests of each child. The emphasis is on the individual child rather than on society or the subject matter. John Dewey (1916) was the major educator who elaborated on progressivist thought. For Dewey, the responsibilities of living in a democratic society demand *social* as well as *academic* knowledge and skill. The progressive curriculum emerges from the needs and the interests of the students, much as a democratic government is (or should be) formed from the needs and the desires of the populace.

The progressivist teacher is very different from both the perennialist and the essentialist in attitude and in pedagogy. At the core of this difference is the progressivist view that to learn is to change and that neither learning nor change ever stop. Learning in a progressivist classroom is an end in itself. Students learn the social skills of working with one another. They apply their prior knowledge and develop problem-solving skills and inquiry skills as they work through individual projects or in small groups. The teacher serves as a student's guide, intervening when necessary, but always letting the student(s) set the agenda.

What would a progressive classroom be like? Would standardized textbooks be used for instruction? Not by the purist! If each student's expressed interests and needs are to form the basis for the curriculum, the role of the teacher changes from the traditional "sage on the stage" to "guide on the side." The teacher becomes a resource, helping students identify their interests and directing them to other resources and activities as those interests and needs become apparent. Students take major responsibility for deciding both what they will learn at any particular time and the means for learning that content.

Social Reconstructionism.   While the progressivist views the changes in the student as the central element of education, the social reconstructionist emphasizes that education changes society. The reconstructionist believes that schools should be active agents of social change, leading the way to a new and more ideal social order. Students are encouraged to question traditions and traditional values and even to question the value of academic content.

Society becomes the subject matter, and the function of the student is to effect social change through skills and attitudes learned in the school set-

Social Reconstructionists emphasize changing society.

ting. This deep-seated set of values held by a teacher would have definite, visible impact on the decisions that teacher makes about what to teach, choices of learning materials to use, decisions about learning activities in which students would be involved, and certainly the sorts of outcomes that teacher is working to foster in his or her students. The reconstructionist curriculum cannot be separated from the current events taking place within the community. A group of students might learn math by analyzing the possibilities of feeding a family of six given an income below the proverty level and a reduction in welfare benefits. They might practice writing by writing letters to the local newspaper or by forming a community newspaper of their own. Their teacher serves as a guide and a leader for these projects and often learns as much or more than the students.

What would a classroom look like if operated by a teacher who held to the basic values of reconstructionism? Likely, there would be very few textbooks. The emphasis would be on current society, with newspapers, news magazines, videotapes, on-line television, and other contemporary media scattered about the room.

Would students be memorizing facts and repeating them on paper-and-pencil tests? Likely not. Much more likely is a scenario in which students engage in study and debate about current issues and seek information on ways to affect social decisions. The focus of student attention is outside of the school setting rather than inside (although social action might be directed at school policies once in a while, too).

Existentialism. Of the five dominant educational philosophies, existentialism is the one most concerned with developing the individual student.

The existentialist believes that the most important human activity is the search for the meaning of one's own existence in an irrational world—a search that can take place in or out of school settings. Carried to the extreme, an emphasis on existentialism could lead to a society without formal schools.

The existentialist teacher is aware that although some people may hold rational thought as the ideal, the human animal is capable of many irrational and thoughtless acts. Teachers and students assume the wonderful and the terrible burden of individual freedom, and they accept the consequences of those actions. For the existentialist teacher, students are subjects, not objects. This means that the student is respected as a unique individual and her needs or his needs and wishes are considered as important as the teacher's own. Students are never to be used as objects to fulfill a teacher's need, a school's needs, or even a society's needs.

The existentialist curriculum could be anything negotiated between the teacher and the student, and the relationships between teacher and student are very important. The teacher serves as an expert guide when the student asks for guidance; as a listener who encourages the student to examine, to reflect, and to introspect; and as one who cares that each individual student reaches his or her own individual goals. Such relationships necessitate small teacher to student ratios and small schools, so that the students can work with many caring adults as they grow and develop.

Of course, very few teachers fit neatly into one or another of these categories. As you begin to think about your own vision of the purpose and structure of education, you may find that you will incorporate ideas from each of the philosophies, although one may be emphasized more than another. As you discuss your thoughts and ideas with friends, relatives, and colleagues, you will probably notice that there are people who disagree with your views. There are also school principals and school-district personnel who will want your philosophy to conform to the district philosophy (or to their own). Our point is not that one or more philosophies should dominate, but that you be aware of where you stand and aware of how the different philosophical positions lead to many arguments over educational policy and practice.

Teacher Stances

As you begin to meet and observe teachers you may notice differences in the way they view the practice of teaching. Just as educators have differing philosophies about the purposes of education, educators also hold different beliefs concerning professional responsibilities. In order to understand more of how teachers think and feel about professional conduct, one-hundred elementary-school teachers were interviewed about their beliefs, teaching actions, and future aspirations. In addition to the interviews, these teachers were observed, and their students and teaching colleagues were also interviewed, in order to obtain information that would validate the interviews with the teachers. From these data the researchers were able to identify seven teacher *stances* or views on teaching and on the professional conduct of teachers (Olmsted, Blackington and Houston 1974).

The first three stances, child-focusers, task-focusers, and pragmatists, describe what we might term *professional teachers*, or teachers who believe in the importance of schooling. They are all effective in their ability to work with students but in very different ways. Child-focusers are able to develop childrens' positive self-concepts and, through that, promote achievement. Task-focusers, who exhibit the behaviors described by Rosenshine and Stevens (1986), are primarily concerned with achievement. Pragmatists are the politicians in school; they understand the system, and they know how to use it to help students succeed. Although all three are concerned with self-concept and achievement, they vary in emphasis.

The next two stances, contented-conformists and time servers, describe teachers for whom school is a place to earn a living. Their real life is outside of school, and they prefer that school responsibilities not interfere with that life. Beginning teachers are often intimidated by teachers who are time servers because of their negative comments about everything from the administration to innovative instructional methods to the "naive" enthusiasm of novice teachers.

Ambivalent teachers feel that "things will get better," although they never do. They have no consistent concept of their role as teacher. Alienated teachers, the last stance, are clearly in the wrong occupation and, fortunately, they are a small minority of the teaching force. Many of them would be more successful working with objects or with mathematical concepts rather than with people, particularly children, who depend on teachers for emotional support. These two groups have little or no control over their classes, and they don't even seem to want to establish that control. The alienated teachers feel that there is no hope, that nothing will improve—ever. These teachers no longer enjoy teaching and may try to force their views on you.

Why Teachers Enjoy Teaching

At the beginning of this chapter, three teachers talked about their teaching day. Each of them discussed the challenges posed by a particularly difficult situation and their responses to those difficulties. Stan discussed his Spanish-speaking class, the one in which he improved his Spanish while the students improved their English. Marsha mentioned her sixth period math class, the one in which she really earned her pay. For Paula, each day was a challenge as she coped with a shortage of materials in her rural classroom. Meeting these challenges and having an impact on the lives of students are the major reasons that teachers enjoy their profession. Jackson's (1968) study of teachers (referred to earlier) also found that working with students and helping them to achieve personal and educational goals were the most rewarding aspects of teaching.

A group of researchers at Stanford University (McLaughlin, Pfeifer, Swanson-Owens and Yee, 1986) have been studying teachers throughout the San Francisco Bay area. Their data reveal that the demands made by the school setting and the demands made by society are interfering with teachers' abilities to teach and thus to reach students. McLaughlin and colleagues suggest that the structure and the administration of schools may debilitate teaching success in any one of five ways:

1. Class sizes that are overly large and classes composed of a number of students with special needs.
2. Working without adequate books and supplies, even when teachers have been able to supplement school funds out of their own pockets.
3. Administrators who interrupt instruction or who do not protect teachers from noninstructional duties.
4. Teachers who work in isolation from other teachers and who never have the opportunity to share ideas and to reflect on common experiences receive no feedback and no help when situations become problematic.
5. Teachers who work in schools where no one says "thank you" and where parents, administrators, and the media constantly criticize teaching and teachers.

Thus we may conclude that although working with children is a major source of satisfaction for teachers, the context of the workplace can either enhance or diminish this satisfaction. Prospective teachers must consider school settings carefully as they begin to look for jobs, for different schools offer different opportunities for collegial support and for professional growth.

Sociologist Dan Lortie (1975) studied teachers in Dade County, Florida in 1964. More recently, Kottkamp, Provenzo, and Cohn (1986) repeated Lortie's study. Together, these studies document that both the joys and the problems of teaching have not changed much in twenty years. For most teachers, the intrinsic rewards are the most compelling. Of the teachers surveyed in Dade Court, 76.3 percent in 1964 and 70.2 percent in 1984 identify the opportunities to study, to plan, to master classroom management, to "reach" students and to associate with colleagues and children as their most important category of reward.

Many researchers have documented that teachers enjoy their work when they have an opportunity to interact with colleagues (Little, 1984), to help a child understand something for the first time, and to give children a positive vision of their future (Jackson 1968). In other words, teaching is a service-oriented occupation, which means that teachers have a primary obligation to their clients (students) rather than an obligation to stockholders (as in a profit-oriented occupation) or to self-expression (as in the visual and performing arts). Service in teaching can be defined as a positive relationship between a teacher and a student that enables the student to achieve personally, socially, academically, or in any combination of the three. The rewards of successful service are usually *intrinsic*; that is, teachers have an internal desire to succeed in helping students and when they meet with success, they feel that they have done a good job. Remember Marsha's comment, "It doesn't take much to make a teacher happy."

Conclusion

In this chapter we have seen that all teachers share the responsibilities for managing time effectively, for designing and implementing productive learning environments, for demonstrating that their efforts are successful, and for maintaining positive interpersonal relationships among students. We have noted that while there are certain roles and responsibilities that concern all teachers, there is a great deal of variation in how teaching is accomplished. Although variation is often a matter of personal choice, it can usually be attributed to differences in educational philosophy or to different stances regarding the practice of teaching. Excellence in teaching does not imply that all teachers must think and act alike, but it does imply thoughtful consideration of the relationships between one's teaching and the responses of one's students. Thoughtful teachers will continue to learn about their content, pedagogy, and their students through study and through reflection.

Building Reflective Inquiry Skills

In this chapter, we have discussed a teacher's day through accounts of teaching and through research on teaching, but this is no substitute for investigating teaching on your own. While we could have you conduct a survey of several hundred teachers or interview two or three teachers about their lives as teachers, we believe that these are only substitutes for reality. One way to learn more about the details of teachers' work and how they feel about their work is a technique called "shadowing." This technique is exactly what the name implies, the subjects of the study agree to let someone (in this case, you, whom we will refer to as the student) follow them throughout their working day for one or more days and to discuss their perceptions of the day's events. This enables the student to understand the subject's actions and conversations from the subject's perspective rather than trying to infer what is happening only from an observation of the action.

Shadowing a Teacher

Before you begin your observations, you will need to discuss the conditions of the observation with a teacher who is willing to give her or his time to this assignment. The two of you should agree on how long (and how often) you may observe, and you should guarantee that your observations will be confidential. When you write up your observations, or when you refer to your teacher, you should use a code name. It is your responsibility to get the school's permission for you to observe on those days you and your teacher agree upon. It is also your responsibility to meet the dates once they are set and to accommodate your schedule to the teacher's.

In your prior discussions with the teacher and the school, you will know if you are allowed to audiotape your observations or your interviews. If you are using audiotape, make sure that you have a sufficient supply of batteries and clean tapes. You will also need a note pad and plenty of pencils for recording those things that will not be picked up on tape, such as classroom arrangements and decorations, nonverbal communications, and conversations that are inappropriate for audio recording.

Be as unobtrusive as possible while you are observing your teacher. You are a guest in the school, and you are there to watch and learn, not to interfere. Yet you must be a careful observer. You should follow your teacher throughout her or his day, making notes on each setting you visit, the people with whom your teacher talks, the time she or he spends in each of the many activities of the day. You should also keep a list of questions or topics that you would like to discuss with your teacher at the end of the observation.

Your list of questions and topics will frame the debriefing of the assignment observation. This is a time for you and your teacher to discuss her or his perceptions of the day's events and to reflect on their significance. Do not feel pressure to get through your entire list. A lot of information about a few incidents is more valuable than surface information about six or sixteen incidents. You should record the debriefing either on tape or by taking careful notes.

Once you have completed all observations and interviews, it is important to make sense of the data you have collected. That means that you should review thoroughly all of your notes and identify at least three themes that are the most informative about your teacher and your teacher's work. Then you are ready to write a report that explains these themes and presents evidence to support your conclusions. In the write-up, fictitious names of all people will preserve confidentiality.

The write-up can be shared with the teacher, if you both agree to this, but the most important function of the write-up is to provide you with a better understanding of what it means to teach.

Explorations

Exploration 1
Philosophy in Action
Arrange to visit a preschool that welcomes visitors. Make a diagram of the room and note whether or not the classroom has many learning centers with children spread out among centers. Learning centers would be indicative of which educational philosophy(ies)? If possible, talk with the preschool director about her or his thoughts on how children learn.

Exploration 2
The Use of Classroom Time
Read through the section in this chapter on academic learning time and distinguish between allocated time, engaged time, and active learning time. Use these distinctions to monitor yourself as you sit through a class. How much time is allocated for the class? How much time is spent on academic content? How much time are you involved with the class? How much time are you actively manipulating ideas related to the class?

Then reflect on the differences between teachers in a university setting and teachers in an elementary school or a secondary school. Are the responsibilities the same? Do university professors have the right to expect different responses from their students than do elementary or secondary teachers? How much should university students be expected to accomplish on their own? How much should be expected

of elementary students? of secondary students? What is academic learning time in a university setting?

Exploration 3
Students' Responses to Different Learning Environments
Become involved as a volunteer tutor in a local school and get to know one student fairly well. Observe that student in three or more different classes or class settings. Are there any differences in observable behavior among settings? Are there any differences in the student's attitudes? Are there any differences in the student's interactions with the teacher(s) among settings?

Exploration 4
Developing a Philosophy of Education
Begin by writing a short paper on what you feel is important in education. Try to identify what you believe about the nature of knowledge, the nature of learning, and the purpose of society. Then, follow up on that by reading any of the sources discussed in this chapter or read an introductory text on educational philosophy. In your readings, what arguments appeal to you? What arguments do not make sense to you personally? As you continue to read, revise your short paper to reflect your new insights.

References

Adler, M. J. (1982). *The paideia proposal: An educational manifesto.* New York: Macmillan.

Bennett, W. J. (1986). *What works: Research about teaching and learning.* Washington, DC: Department of Education.

Bloom, B. S. (1968). Learning for mastery. *Evaluation Comment, 1*(2). Los Angeles: University of California Center for the Study of Evaluation.

Bossert, S. (1979). *Tasks and social relationships in classrooms: A study of classroom organization and its sequences.* American Sociological Association, Arnold and Caroline Rose Monograph Series. New York: Cambridge University Press.

Carroll, J. B. (1963). A model of school learning. *Teachers College Record*, 64, 723–733.

Clark, D. L. (1987). High school seniors react to their teachers and their schools. *Phi Delta Kappan, 68*(7), 503–509.

Cohen, E. G. (1986). *Designing groupwork for instruction.* New York: Teacher's College Press.

Cruickshank, D. (1987). *Reflective Teaching.* Reston, VA: Association of Teacher Educators.

Dewey, J. (1916). *Democracy and education.* New York: Macmillan.

Dreeben, R. (1968). *On what is learned in school.* Reading, MA: Addison Wesley.

Education Week. (1986). State education statistics: Student performance, resource inputs, and population characteristics, 1982 and 1985, 12–13.

Education Week. (1987). State education statistics: Student performance, resource inputs, and population characteristics, 1982 and 1986, 20–21.

Feistritzer, E. (1986). What teaching crisis? Houston, TX: *Houston Chronicle*, Sunday, July 6: 1,4.

Fisher, C.; Filby, N.; Marliave, R.; Cahen, L.; Dishaw, M.; Moore, J.; & Berliner, D., (1978). *Teaching behaviors, academic learning time, and student achievement: Final report of Phase III–B, Beginning Teacher Evaluation Study.* San Francisco: Far West Laboratory.

Jackson, P. W. (1968). *Life in classrooms.* New York: Holt, Rinehart, and Winston.

Johnson, D. W.; Johnson, R. T.; Holubec, E. J.; & Roy, P. (1984). *Circles of learning: Cooperation in the classroom.* Alexandria, VA: Association for Supervision and Curriculum Development.

Kottkamp, R. B.; Provenzo, E. F.; & Cohn, M. M. (1986). Stability and change in a profession:

Two decades of teacher attitudes, 1964–1984. *Phi Delta Kappan, 67*(8), 559–567.

Little, J. W. (1982). Norms of collegiality and experimentation: Workplace conditions of school success. *American Educational Association Research Journal, 19*(3), 325–340.

Lortie, D. C. (1975). *Schoolteacher: A Sociological Study.* Chicago: University of Chicago Press.

McLaughlin, M. W.; Pfeifer, R. S.; Swanson-Owens, D.; & Yee, S. (1986). Why teachers won't teach. *Phi Delta Kappan, 67*(6), 420–426.

NEA Today. (1986). *Today's Education, 1986–1987.* Washington, D.C.: National Education Association.

NEA Today. (May, 1986). Washington, D. C.: National Education Association.

Olmested, A. C.; Blackington, F. H.; & Houston, W. R. (1974). Stances teachers take: A basis for selective admission. *Phi Delta Kappan, 55*(5), 330–334.

Rosenshine, B. & Stevens, R. (1986). Teaching Functions. In M. C. Wittrock (Ed.) *Handbook of Research on Teaching*, Third Edition. New York: Macmillan.

Ryan, K.; Newman, K. K.; Mager, G.; Applegate, J.; Lasley, T.; Flora, R.; & Johnston, J. (1980). *Biting the apple: Accounts of first year teachers.* New York: Longman.

Stallings, J. (1980). Allocated academic learning time revisited, or beyond time on task. *Educational Researcher, 8*(11), 11–16.

Thelen, H. (1960). *Education and the human quest.* New York: Harper.

Schon, D. A. (1983). *The reflective practitioner.* New York: Basic Books.

Waller, W. (1932). *The sociology of teaching.* New York: John Wiley and Sons.

Students: The Future of Society

OBJECTIVES

By the end of this chapter, you will be able to:

1. Define and discuss information processing theory and developmental learning theory.
2. Discuss the application of theories of learning to the way we think about teaching and learning in school settings.
3. Identify factors beyond the school's control that may affect students' performance in school.
4. Discuss the effect of individual student differences on the ways in which children experience life in schools.
5. Begin to develop a concept of teaching students that incorporates multicultural awareness and individual difference.

KEY WORDS AND CONCEPTS

Accommodation
Assimilation
Developmental learning theory
Information processing theory
Cultural pluralism
Latch-key child
Socioeconomic status

Looking Beneath the Surface

As you begin to study school settings—classrooms, playing fields, lunch-rooms, and even settings on your college campus—there are many ways to describe the students as they work on academic tasks or talk together about matters that are not related to school. The most obvious descriptors are the physical characteristics, such as height, weight, hair color, and skin color. Social characteristics, such as patterns of friendship, preferred language and dialect, body language, and style of dress are also readily observable if you listen to conversations and take some mental notes on who is talking with whom.

But listening and observing rarely provide sufficient information about psychological characteristics, such as intelligence, problem-solving ability, feelings of competence, and feelings of security. Casual observations of student groups reveal very little about the students' lives at home, their obligations and responsibilities after school, or their talents and abilities that are not a part of the normal academic routine. Knowing your students well includes this type of information.

While it may be easiest to form opinions about students based only on what one can observe in the classroom or on the playing field, this limited information may be dangerously incomplete. In Chapter 1, we mentioned that the observable actions of teaching represent only the tip of an ice-berg—that much of the substance of teaching is not readily accessible to the casual observer. The same thing can be said for the substance of each student. Most of what makes each child a unique and special individual cannot be seen by a casual observer, who only thinks about students as faces in a classroom. As you seek to learn more about the individual talents, abilities, and needs of each child, you may need to explore beyond the classroom, to make detailed observations of a student in different settings, or to interview the child about her or his perceptions of life at school and at home.

In this chapter we will examine those factors lying beneath the classroom surface that make a difference in the ways students think about themselves and the schools they attend. To begin this examination, we will first consider relevant theories that explain how people think and learn as we explore the rich diversity among students. Then, we will examine some factors that are external to the school, and possibly outside of the school's control, but which may make a tremendous impact on how your students think and feel about learning and about themselves.

Learning as Function of Prior Learning

Cognitive psychologists who study the way in which people think and learn have developed a theory that explains how we each build our own set of perspectives and how we acquire, retain and create information (Norman 1968; Wittrock 1974; Shuell 1986). This theory, called *information-processing theory*, is not the only explanation of how people learn, but it represents the current thought of most leading educators and psychologists. More importantly, it represents our view of the relationships between teaching and learning. As teachers learn more about educational settings, they can ask better questions about how to work most effectively within those settings.

A compatible theory, *cognitive-developmental theory*, presents the case that children develop increasingly sophisticated understandings of the world. Thinking (cognition) is shaped by our interaction with the environment *and* by our innate biological structures. Together, information-processing theory *and* cognitive-developmental theory offer powerful explanations of the ways students learn.

Although we have chosen to emphasize only two learning theories, we would be remiss if we implied that these are the only two theories that seek to explain how humans acquire and organize information. Two other learning theories, *behavioral-learning theory* (Skinner 1953) and *social-learning theory* (Bandura 1977), also offer explanations of how people learn.

Behavioral theorists believe that the environment is the main determinant of learning and behavior. As humans interact with the environment, they encounter certain stimulus situations. These stimuli can be either pleasurable or punishing, and people respond accordingly. Humans (and animals) come to associate these sensations with the stimuli. According to behaviorists, learning occurs as we build up a set of associations. We learn that certain events are associated with other events and, over time, we build sophisticated knowledge structures based on these associations.

Social-learning theorists argue that association alone is an insufficient explanation for all types of learning (Bandura 1977). Many situations are too dangerous or too novel to permit the gradual accumulation of associations. Therefore, they argue, another factor must be operating. Social learning occurs through observation and through the *modeling* of others' behavior.

Both the behaviorists and the social-learning theorists agree that we cannot study learning if we can not see it or measure it, thus cognitive developmentalists and cognitive information-processing theorists are investigating something that cannot be proven to exist—the quality of the mind. Exhibit 4.1 compares all four theories with regard to their assumptions about the acquisition of knowledge, the role of the environment, and the function of the teacher. For more detailed information on these theories, you may wish to complete Exploration 4 at the end of this chapter.

Information-Processing Theory

To help you understand the basic premise that undergirds information-processing theory, pause for a moment in your reading and take a survey of all of the sights, sounds, smells, flavors, and textures that surround you. What noises do you hear? What can you feel with your hands and your feet? What odors are present in the room? What can you see when you lift your eyes from the printed page? Can you taste anything in particular? Chances are that until you paused to take a sensory inventory of the world around you, you were only aware of the immediate connections between your eyes, this text, and your thoughts about this text. You have selected to pay attention to only a fraction of all of the information available to you through any combination of your five senses.

EXHIBIT 4.1   Theories of Learning

	BEHAVIORAL THEORY	SOCIAL-LEARNING THEORY	INFORMATION-PROCESSING THEORY	DEVELOPMENTAL THEORY
Knowledge	When two behaviors occur together many times, they are associated with one another. Later, when one occurs, the other is recalled.	We observe the actions and the reactions of others. One learns by imitating physical, cognitive, and social skills.	People actively select sensory information for attention. Some of the stimuli are encoded into long term memory. Others are not retained.	We are biologically programmed to learn through genetic structures. Through maturation and through interaction with the environment, we develop more complex knowledge structures.
Environment	Learning is a function of the environment. Stimuli that reinforce other events, or stimuli, facilitate learning. Events that are not reinforced are not learned.	Behaviors that are observed are models for subsequent behavior. The available models in the environment shape what is learned.	The individual imposes meaning on the environment. Given the same environment, two different people will have different perceptions.	Although the individual interacts with the environment, the interpretation of the interaction changes as the individual matures.
Teacher's Functions	Learning is controlled through manipulation of learning experiences. Teachers must reinforce desirable learning behaviors.	Teachers serve as role models for learning. Therefore they must consciously demonstrate desirable learning behavior.	Teachers must focus students' attention on meaningful environmental stimuli and then must monitor students' perceptions of those stimuli.	Teachers must design tasks that are appropriate for students' level of development and must guide students' progress.

Why is this? Why do humans attend to and respond to only a fraction of their environment? And why do they remember even less? We may all be exposed to the same set of stimuli, but we perceive (or process) those stimuli in different ways. According to information-processing theory, so much information is available that humans cannot possibly deal with all of it. Therefore, they simplify their world by selecting only a small portion of that environment to work with at any given time (Sternberg 1984).

Working Memory.   Information-processing theory (Rummelhart and Norman, 1978) suggests that people actively determine which environmental stimuli are important and which are not. Each person makes a slightly different decision about importance and about which of the five senses (or sensory channels) will most likely help him or her get the information needed. Information obtained through sensory channels is held for a brief period of time in working memory (otherwise known as "short-term memory"), or that part of the memory that is alert, conscious, and actively manipulating information. You are using working memory as you read this chapter, and you are also using working memory when your thoughts wander away from the chapter in a daydream. But just paying attention to something and allowing it to occupy some time in working memory does not guarantee that you have "learned" it.

Working memory is not very large and cannot hold more than a few (three to five) pieces of information at any one time. To help you think about this concept, try to remember the fifteenth word that your instructor said on the third class meeting. You probably heard it, you may have even written it down, but we doubt that many people will be able to recall that word—including your instructor! Once information leaves short-term memory, it is gone from memory unless it is somehow stored (although it may still exist in the environment, and you may be able to get it back through your sensory channels; that is, you may listen to an audiotape recording of the third day of class and make a special effort to pay attention to the fifteenth word).

Long-Term Memory.   Information-processing theorists refer to the place where information is stored as "long-term memory." Long-term memory is an all-important storage facility. New information that is related to previously stored information (prior knowledge and experience) is more easily incorporated into long-term memory. Information that has a special significance or meaning is more easily retained and recalled (Ausubel 1963). To help you understand this, think about what you did on your last birthday. Chances are that you can recall this information rather easily, although you were not thinking about that particular day as you read this passage. Chances are also good that you cannot recall what you were doing on any other given day in 1979 unless the day was highly significant, or unless you work very hard to reconstruct that information. Learning and remembering involve getting information into long-term memory (storage) and getting it back out of long-term memory (retrieval).

Learning in Classrooms

As your students work with the facts and the ideas in your class, they will be involved in several cognitive (mental) processes:

1. Attending to the appropriate environmental cues.
2. Selecting relevant information for manipulation in working memory.
3. Manipulating information in working memory.
4. Encoding (or organizing) the information for storage in long-term memory.
5. Retrieving the information from long-term memory so that it can be manipulated in short-term memory.
6. Producing that information to the external environment so that others can be aware of the information.

A student's task is to figure out what needs to be learned and to select and encode that knowledge so that it can be retrieved or revised at some later date when the student later needs to retrieve the information. He or she must employ retrieval strategies and then must externalize that knowledge through some medium such as writing, speaking, drawing, or filling in the appropriate circle on a standardized test.

A teacher's task is to facilitate that process. Learning experiences designed to help students acquire relevant information, plus instruction that will help them acquire strategies for learning, will enable the students to concentrate on content. Here are a few suggestions that you may want to consider when planning for your students.

1. Help students highlight those topics that merit special attention, and minimize distracting environmental stimuli that may compete for their attention.
2. Check to see that students have selected the relevant information for the task at hand and that they are actively working with that information.
3. Ask questions and give writing assignments, or other projects, that will encourage students to grapple with information, not just attend to the information.
4. Help students develop strategies for relating new information to previously-acquired knowledge and/or to prior experience with similar information, so that they can more easily store new ideas in long-term memory.
5. Help students develop strategies for retrieving the information from long-term memory, through reviews, through questions that provide a sufficient context for information retrieval, and through practice in working with both storage and retrieval.
6. Help students feel comfortable about expressing their own ideas, through non-graded speaking and writing activities and through other expressive forms, such as drama and art. Provide feedback that will help students develop communicative ability.

As you encourage students to become aware of their own cognitive processes and to develop their cognitive abilities, you will become even more aware of how people can start with the same pieces of information and yet perceive that information very differently from one another. Nowhere is this more apparent than when you work with young children who have not developed the capacity to understand that even though an object is hidden, it may still exist—much less the capacity to think abstractly using algebraic symbols.

Learning as a Function of Development

Infants and young children are just as active as are older children and adults in perceiving the environment. Studies by T. G. R. Bower (1974), a developmental psychologist who studies the visual abilities of infants, and others (for example, Ross 1980) have demonstrated that even young infants can use their senses to obtain information, that they can discriminate between objects, and that they can perceive irregularities in the environment. But while these processes are present, they are not the same as those of adults, and they do not represent the full array of cognitive processes that adults possess. In addition to the attentional processes, infants and young children are not very good at storing and retrieving information. In fact, they have fundamental misconceptions about how the physical world operates, as well as how society operates. Therefore, infants and children spend a lot of time trying to interpret their environment and attempting to understand how elements within that environment fit together.

Jean Piaget, a Swiss psychologist, was one of the first people to study the different perceptions children have of their world and how these perceptions change over time. He began his career as a biologist. His observations of the ways that animals both affect their environment and are also affected by their environment led him to conceptualize learning as a similarly interactive process. Consider, for example, a beaver who creates a home by building a dam in the middle of a small river or a stream, thus creating a lake or altering the course of the river or stream. The beaver has changed his environment. Darwin's theory of evolution (Darwin 1859) is based on his many observations of plants and animals that have biologically adapted to their environments over a period of time and over a number of generations.

Assimilation and Accommodation

Piaget reasoned that knowledge acquisition in humans was similar to biological change in plants and animals. His thesis was that the human mind perceives the environment in ways that make sense through one's own familiar ways of thinking about phenomena. But as one begins to acquire more and more information, some of the new knowledge is not understandable through old (or earlier) ways of explaining phenomena. One then begins to adapt earlier perceptions, as new information is integrated with older information. Piaget suggested that all people are continually balancing incoming knowledge with prior knowledge in the dual processes of *assimilation* and *accommodation*. John Flavell, one of the first people to introduce Piaget's work into this country, explains the processes this way: "Assimilation essentially means interpreting or construing external objects and events in terms of one's own presently available and favored ways of thinking about things. . . . Accommodation roughly means noticing and taking cognitive account of the various real properties and relationships among properties that external objects and events possess" (Flavell 1977, 7).

Assimilation occurs as we think about the world, only through the ideas and concepts with which we are already comfortable. Thus, if our only experiences with school have been positive, we tend to see all schools as positive environments. If we are only familiar with the customs and the values of our own family and close friends, we judge all new people by those values.

Accommodation occurs as we change the way we think about school as we learn that schools have properties that are negative for certain groups and individuals. In the opening chapter we invited you to become a student of, not in, schools. Essentially, our first chapter invited you to accommodate your previous knowledge and experiences of schools to some facts and ideas you may not have considered while you were an elementary-school student, or even a high-school student.

Piaget (1926), Jerome Bruner (1966), and many other developmental psychologists have documented that children perceive their environment in a fundamentally different way than do adults. For example, infants of about three months seem to believe that if you hide a toy by covering it with a cloth, the toy is really gone. What is not seen does not exist, or, all knowledge must be immediately perceived by one of the senses. Four-year-olds, given a choice between a row of five pennies placed close together and a row of five pennies spread apart, will choose the row spread apart and will defend their choice by saying that there are "more" in that row, because they do not understand that the number of objects remains the same, even though the space between objects may vary. Ten-year-olds can solve logical problems if those problems are based in reality, but they cannot work through abstract problems or identify and test probable hypotheses. To put this in other terms, children assimilate more and more information about their environment and about those who populate that environment. This leads to their accommodating earlier assumptions and older knowledge structures to account for the new information, thus forming new knowledge structures. The developmental stages are summarized in Exhibit 4.2.

Development and Learning in Classrooms. Our point is not to make you an expert in child development, for the text has provided a brief overview of a large and very important body of research on the ways learners develop increasingly sophisticated cognitive skills. We would like to emphasize, however, that students of different ages have different ways of dealing with information. And, because we are talking about ranges of ages instead of a particular grade, children within one grade level may exhibit wide variations in intellectual development. This is true for *all* grade levels, not just the elementary grades. As you reflect on the differences among your students and form your own hypotheses about why one is reading above grade level and one below, we hope you will consider differences in development as one highly plausible explanation—but not the only possible explanation.

Frequently, a student will tell us that studying child development is only for elementary teachers, that secondary teachers do not need to know about developmental issues. We would like to emphasize that this is a false and potentially dangerous assumption. Although Piaget documented that the ability to conduct formal operations occurs during adolescence, subse-

EXHIBIT 4.2   Stages of Development

	AGE RANGE	CHILDREN'S CHARACTERISTICS	RELATIONSHIP TO CLASSROOM LEARNING
Sensorimotor	0–2	Capable of imitation, recognizes that objects are permanent, even when they cannot be seen, begins to be goal oriented, begins some verbal activity.	Provide a rich context for language development; encourage short, goal oriented activities.
Preoperational	2–7	Language develops, capable of working through simple physical operations, tends to focus on one physical dimension at a time.	Provide opportunities to manipulate objects. Provide visual examples of concepts; encourage language use.
Concrete Operational	7–11	Focuses on more than one physical dimension at a time, understands that rearranging physical objects does not change their basic properties, begins to classify.	Provide opportunities to work with physical transformations; provide visual examples of abstract concepts.
Formal Operational	11–15	Capable of abstract thought, manipulates variables, deals with hypothetical situations.	Provide opportunities for hypothesis generation and testing; do not expect abstract thought in every area.

quent research (Flavell 1977) has shown that most people do not reach the formal operational stage in all areas and that prior knowledge and experience have a great deal to do with how well one can think abstractly about any given topic. Thus, as a college student, you may experience the failure to think abstractly when you are introduced to an unfamiliar topic, such as computer science or statistics. You may need concrete examples or practical exercises to help you understand unfamiliar concepts or processes. This does not mean that you are "stupid" or "unmotivated;" it does mean that you have to spend more time developing base-level knowledge before you can begin to manipulate abstraction with ease and comfort. Even university faculty members need to be reminded that their students have individual differences related to cognitive development and that those students may need special instruction.

We have reviewed two theories that help to explain how children learn and how that process of learning may differ from child to child. Now let us turn to a child's life outside of the school as we seek to understand the many factors that affect learning in schools.

External Factors Affecting Success in School

Teachers who live and work in small suburban or rural communities may get to know their students individually simply because they all share the same community experiences and they all are aware of the few distinct cultures of the small area. But teachers who live in urban environments need to make a special effort to understand their students' life experiences. Simply taking the time to ask students about their day may yield some surprising information about their responsibilities outside of school.

In planning for instruction, it's important to know your students as well as your subject-matter.

EXHIBIT 4.3   Elena, a Seventh-Grade Student

My mother goes to work at 5:00 a.m., and so I have to help my brother and sister get ready for school. This is difficult for me because my school starts one hour earlier than theirs, so I have to get all of my things together, wake them up, feed them breakfast, and make sure they will be ready to catch their bus before my bus leaves at 6:45. Sometimes I am really tired, and I oversleep because I helped close the restaurant the night before. When I oversleep, I miss my bus and I have to call my friend's mom to come and get me. That makes us both late, but my teacher doesn't make me get a tardy slip. She knows I work.

I have five classes in a row before lunch. On the days when I skip breakfast, it is pretty hard to concentrate in fifth period. That class is English. It is pretty boring to have to listen to all that stuff about parts of a sentence, but I like the days when she lets us read anything we want to. I don't read so good, but she has a lot of books, and she helps me find ones I like.

After lunch I always feel sleepy. I have a hard time staying awake in sixth period math. We do a lot of worksheets and stuff in there, and I have to concentrate real hard.

After school I go to work. I used to go home to take care of my brother and sister, but they are in fifth grade and second grade now, and they are old enough to take care of themselves until Mom comes home at six. My brother can even cook supper sometimes and that makes Mom happy.

When I get old enough to go to high school, I am going to get a better job. This one doesn't pay too good, but I was lucky that they would let me work at fourteen. I'm doing real good there. I got a raise after only two months, and they let me help with closing some nights. That means they trust me.

I don't know what I want to do after I get out of school, except that I don't want to go to more school. Maybe I'll get married or maybe I'll just get a job.

Elena and her brothers and sisters are typical of many students whose parents (or one parent) have no other alternative than to let the children take care of themselves while they work. Those children who come home to empty houses and apartments face a set of circumstances that force them to grow up fast as they cope with the fear of being attacked or insulted by older children, the danger of being robbed or raped, and the general loneliness of being a youngster who has no adult to talk to about the triumphs or the problems of the school day. And like Elena, many of these children are also responsible for bringing in additional income to aid the family. Two of the major problems facing children today are the problems of returning home to an empty house and of coping with financial pressure.

Children Without Adult Supervision: Latch-Key Children

The Children's Defense Fund (1986) estimates that twenty-two million children, age thirteen and under, live in one- and two-parent families in which all of the adults work full time outside the home. Only 54 percent of these children of employed parents have identifiable child-care arrangements. The remaining 46 percent have been given the label "latch-key children" because some of them wear house keys around their necks. A significant portion of these children (and no one knows exactly how many) don't even have keys. They must find some place to wait until someone comes home to let them in the house.

Adolescence and the Absence of Adult Guidance

This situation can breed alienation and hostility for adolescent children, according to Urie Bronfenbrenner, a psychologist who specializes in social

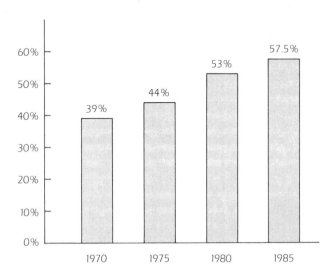

FIGURE 4.1
Children Whose Mothers Are Working Outside the Home

Source: Adapted from **NEA Today**, reporting U.S. Department of Labor statistics, 1986, 37. Used with permission.

development. Longitudinal studies of delinquency suggest that without adult love and guidance (a combination of direction and challenge), there is a strong possibility that young people will become alienated and will develop delinquent behavior patterns (Bronfenbrenner 1986). When adults are not present, or are too preoccupied with their own troubles to attend to their children, they cannot provide the challenge and the support their children need in order to become socially and psychologically healthy. Without adult guidance, Bronfenbrenner and his colleagues argue, adolescents begin to depend more heavily on their peers and often find their challenges in drugs, promiscuous sexual activity, and juvenile delinquency. Some of them turn to suicide, the third leading cause of death for persons between the ages of fourteen and twenty-four (see Figure 4.2). Supportive adults, working and non-working parents who make time for their children, teachers, and community leaders, can help adolescents to feel loved and valued.

The dilemma of after-school care is really a community problem and not a problem belonging to schools and to teachers—or is it? *What Works* (Bennett, 1986), summarized in the previous chapter, highlights the importance of parental involvement with their children's education, from reading in the preschool years, to making sure that homework gets done—and done correctly—as children progress through the grades. When there are no parents (or other knowledgeable adults) to provide guidance after school hours, the community problem becomes a problem for students and for schools.

In addition, school systems are the only institutions charged with caring for future citizens; no other social institution works with children eight or more hours every day. Many people argue that for schools to cope with the problems of before -and after-school care is both logical and functional. In light of this, some schools have begun experimental "extended day" programs for before- and after-school care, but most school districts cannot

The U.S. is the wealthiest nation in the world, but it is rapidly becoming a nation whose political will to provide its children with the necessities for physical, intellectual, emotional, and moral growth is weakening. Look at the national scene, and ask yourself who is the champion for children.

Former U.S. Commissioner of Education, Harold Howe II (1986, 192)

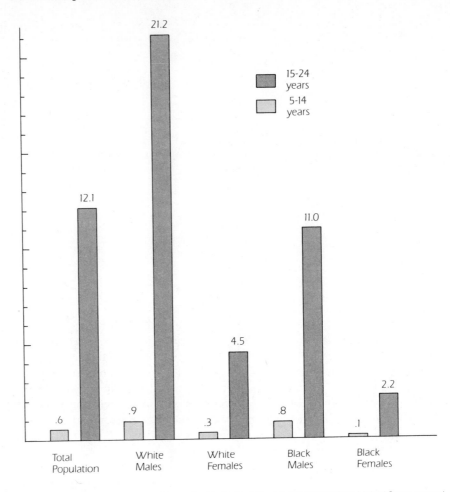

FIGURE 4.2
Suicide Rates for Every
100,000 Children
1970–1982

Source: Adapted from U.S. National Center for Health Statistics, Vital Statistics of the United States, annual by Statistical Abstracts of the United States 1986, 78.

afford such programs. Until communities find the resources to deal with this growing national problem, children will continue to struggle for themselves. As a teacher who looks beyond the classroom and who inquires into the circumstances that affect a child's poor grades or that lead to withdrawal from class activities, you may become a major source of support for children who need the guidance and the advice of a caring adult.

Financial Pressures

More than one-third of all high-school students between the ages of sixteen and nineteen are formally employed. Like Elena, economic necessity motivates many of these students, for approximately 20 percent (see Figure 4.3) of our youth live in families whose income falls below the poverty line. Other students work because of the readily available cash a job can provide. These children are pressured, by family circumstances and by their own desire to contribute to the family well-being, to take jobs that

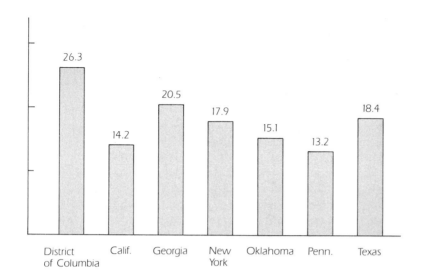

FIGURE 4.3
Percentage of Children
(5–17) Who Live in
Poverty

26.3

20.5

17.9

14.2

15.1

13.2

18.4

District
of Columbia Calif. Georgia New
York Oklahoma Penn. Texas

Source: Adapted with permission from **Education Week**, February, 1987, 20–21.

promise short-term income. For some students, the feelings of responsibility and self-worth that result from success at work are important psychological factors that enhance overall success—academic as well as personal. Although the knowledge one acquires while working may be a valuable asset when one graduates and enters the work force permanently, focusing only on short-term gains may prevent students from developing the skills that will enable them to move into higher-paying positions in the future.

I help them fill out their college applications, and I begin to find financial support for them. Then an uncle, a grandparent, or a parent talks them into taking a job at the supermarket, making a minimum wage. The family can't see the sense in sacrificing this potential income for something as far away as a college degree.

School Coordinator, who works with economically disadvantaged children.

High school students believe teachers should be understanding and fair with students, and knowledgeable about the subject being taught.

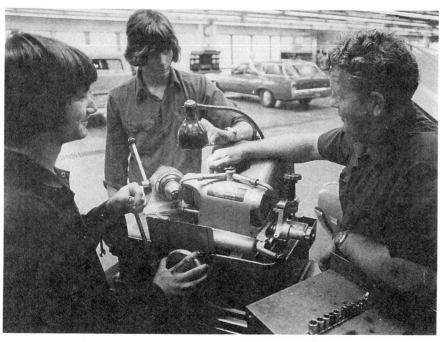

Students who try to maintain a rigorous academic program while working often suffer from fatigue in school, and they often have a difficult time working through homework assignments or completing projects assigned out of class. This difficulty may encourage some students to withdraw from the traditional academic program or to drop out of school entirely.

More and more students, whose families do not depend on their income for survival, take jobs so that they can save for college (estimated average cost by 1988 is thirteen thousand dollars per year), drive a car, buy trendy clothing, and enjoy nonessential luxuries. Many fast food restaurants and grocery stores depend on the relatively inexpensive labor of the part-timers who work for minimum wage or less and who receive no benefits (such as health insurance or pension). These students, like those who work from necessity, may suffer from fatigue during school and may be unable to complete out-of-class assignments. In addition, educational values may be undermined by the more immediate reward of a paycheck.

> *he students for whom the school fails most dramatically do not stay around long enough to become seniors.*
>
> David L. Clark (1987, 509)

Socioeconomic Status

The pressures of work and the dilemmas of what to do with children after school are, in part, related to the social and financial condition of the family. Sociologists frequently use the term *socioeconomic status* (SES) to categorize a person's social class or financial position relative to others. SES is determined by the income level of parents, the highest grade in school they have completed, their occupations, and by other indicators, such as the number of rooms in the home and the number of books owned. Although every child in the United States is guaranteed the right to an education (through the Fourteenth Amendment to the Constitution), regardless of social class or academic condition, children who come from higher SES homes often have material advantages that are not available to lower SES children.

EXHIBIT 4.4   **Greg, a First-Grade Student**

I get up at seven o'clock. School begins at 8:15. I dress myself and go downstairs and eat my breakfast. Usually I make myself cereal (I learned how to do that when I started first grade this year). Sometimes Dad makes pancakes or Mom makes muffins for a special treat. My little brother gets up later. When my Mom doesn't go to work early, she and my brother walk to school with me. Next year I can ride my bike by myself.

I go to homeroom and then to reading. I could read before first grade. I never wrote answers to questions about the stories before. We write a lot. I hate boardwork and I hate writing. Sometimes I go too slow, and then I have to work during recess. My teacher and my Mom had a conference. I am trying to work faster and to not daydream so much.

In first grade we have one teacher for homeroom and one for reading and math. Then we go to lunch. I take my lunch because I don't like all the things they give you at school. After lunch we have science with my homeroom teacher or social studies with a different teacher. We also have music, library, and P. E. I like them best—especially library.

I take piano lessons, and I can read music too. Sometimes my teacher lets me play for the class.

After school I go home. My grandmother takes care of me if my Mom isn't home. I do my homework and then I play outside. Sometimes I watch TV. When Mom or Dad gets home, I help set the table for supper.

Next year I am going to learn to cook. After supper I play until it is time to go to bed. My parents used to read me a bedtime story, but now we read to my brother. I have a lot of books that I share with him.

Next year I'll be in second grade. Mom says I will learn to write in script. I still don't even print very good. I wish I could use Mom's computer for school! I will like second grade, except for the writing.

Greg's parents are both college graduates; his mother is a professional who is informed about the latest technological innovations and shares these innovations with her children. Although there is probably no difference between Greg's intelligence and the intelligence of Elena's second grade sister, Greg has the advantage of a secure home environment and access to many educational resources. Greg's parents both have sufficiently flexible jobs that permit them to accompany Greg to school and to attend school activities. They chose their present home so that he could walk to school and so that his Dad would only be five minutes away should there be any emergency. Clearly, this family places a high value on education and is willing to arrange family life to accommodate schooling and extracurricular activities, such as Greg's piano lessons. For some students, however, advantages become liabilities as students are pressured to achieve academic and social success at early ages.

Pressure to Achieve

Children in the 1980s face pressures from almost every corner of society to grow up fast. "Back-to-school" advertisements feature designer clothing for teens, elementary students, and even preschool children. Parents who want their toddlers to "dress for success" shop in special boutiques for children that stock clothing with the same designer names that they themselves buy. Once a toddler is properly dressed, she or he can then prepare to attend the "right" preschool, preferably one that will assure admission to an Ivy League college.

In *The Hurried Child*, David Elkind (1981) documents the many ways that children are not allowed to be children. Parents who work may encourage their children to be independent so that the parents can get on with their work. Single parents sometimes confide details about courting and marriage that are beyond a young child's comprehension or emotional capacity. The media—video, radio, and recordings—present adult topics to six-year-olds and give the impression that adult behavior is the only acceptable norm. Rock music has moved from sexually-suggestive to sexually-explicit lyrics, and young children puzzle over their meaning.

But, Elkind points out, the schools are as much to blame as are parents and the media. The schools' reliance on standardized testing as a measure of student "success" has led many educators to sacrifice the developing child on an altar of achievement gains. This violates a basic principle of developmental psychology—that while all individuals grow and develop, the rates of growth differ from child to child. Competition for test scores, for grades, and for entry into elite academic programs can transform children's basic desires to do well and to please parents and teachers into a feeling that they will not be loved if they aren't "Number One."

Competition in school is often surpassed by competition in extracurricular activities. And competitions between schools heighten competition for positions on a team, for parts in the school play, or for chairs in band. The public nature of these competitions can tempt many students to focus their time and attention on competitive sports or arts as well as on academic studies, thus creating twice the pressure. This pressure can be very stressful for children who want to be "first" in everything.

Mommy, what does she mean when she says, "I've made up my mind, I'm keeping my baby"?

Seven-year-old child upon hearing "Poppa Don't Preach" by Madonna.

Extracurricular activities do not have to create a negative, debilitating pressure for children, however. Many times the sports, the arts, and the youth groups offer students their only public opportunity to display talents and to achieve recognition in nonacademic areas. Participation in extracurricular activities can teach social skills and life skills that will reach far beyond the classroom. In addition, achievement out of class can help children feel good about themselves, a feeling they might not get from a routine of academic mediocrity—or failure. In a recent survey of high school students, 67 percent reported that extracurricular activities made high school more enjoyable, and 53 percent said that they were an important part of their education (*NEA Today* 1986, 23).

Elkind is also careful to point out that some pressure is both healthy and desirable. Commitment to a job, to a sport, or to the arts is a sign that children can set individual goals and then work to achieve those goals. But whether we are speaking of academic achievement or nonacademic achievement, it is important to help children set their own goals and to work toward those goals (Elkind 1981).

Your reading thus far clearly indicates each child has a life outside of school that may affect the way he or she behaves in your classroom. In addition to individual life experiences are differences in ability, language, and culture that affect the way a student perceives the school experience.

Language and a Student's Perception of School

Although considerable controversy surrounds the issue of bilingual education, no one would argue that for many students, in virtually all school systems, English is not their first language and their parents do not speak English at home. Although this is not a new phenomenon, the problem of teaching the non-English-speaking child is receiving a great deal of attention from the media and from policy makers. United States Census data record that in all major cities, over thirty different languages are the first languages of large numbers of students.

Language Barriers and Education

Understandably, this causes great difficulty for those teachers who are fluent in only one language—English. Even those teachers who are multilingual are seldom fluent in more than three languages and certainly not fluent in thirty. But the teachers' difficulties are small compared to the problems faced by students who are not proficient in English. Understanding a lecture is difficult, discussion is virtually impossible, and a simple reading assignment is an arduous task.

The language barrier is also problematical for those students who live with relatives and friends who do not speak a Standard English dialect. Standard English is the language of textbooks, television announcers, and grammar workbooks. It is not street talk, nor is it the common dialect of many ethnic groups in urban or rural communities. For these students, papers are filled with corrective marks and discussions are punctuated by teachers' grammatical corrections. The child's verbal fluency, which may

*I*n a time of increasingly technical language, bureaucratic formulations, simulation games, and a lingua franca deriving from the media, it may become more and more necessary for teachers to create the kinds of speech situations in which and through which learners can open themselves to their lived worlds, to one another, and to themselves.

Maxine Greene, philosopher of education, (1986, 498)

be very evident outside of school or on the playground, may disappear completely inside the classroom (Labov 1972). Conversely, some children may learn the standard dialect well, only to be teased by their friends once off the school campus.

Language and Self-concept

The language we learn as very young children shapes the way we view our world and the way we construe new information. As we grow in years and in experience, we learn to use words as symbols to represent feelings and concepts, and we rely on words to help establish our status within a given society. Language—my speech, your speech, my writing, your writing—is a very personal expression of self. When that expression is consistently rejected by teachers, the child (or the adult) often feels rejected too. You may have had personal experience with such feelings of rejection on occasions when you have turned in a paper on which you labored for hours, even weeks, only to be told by a professor that it was "sloppy" or "illogical" or a "C" paper. Although the comments and the grade may have been justified, they have a personal, as well as an academic, impact.

Differences in language are intimately connected to students' abilities to perform academic tasks and to students' feelings about themselves and their relationships to schools and teachers. We can provide students with models for standard grammar and syntax; we can help non-English-proficient students become more proficient; and we can suggest that in certain situations, proficiency in Standard English is desirable and is often advantageous. As you reflect on why a child may choose not to participate in class or not to write a paper, one reason may be that the child has learned to avoid the humiliation and pain that accompany attempts at self-expression.

An implicit message that a student is "deficient" or unacceptable because of differences in preferred language or dialect may prevent the student from becoming fluent in English or from mastering the standard dialect, thus leading to a vicious succession of similar messages in later school years and beyond. As you look beyond the classroom to more fully understand students' abilities and needs, you may see that language differences and cultural differences can be a major liability in schools where such differences are penalized. Specialists in urban education and in multicultural education urge teachers to incorporate the concept of cultural pluralism into their conceptions of teaching.

Culture and a Student's Perception of School

James Banks, known for his work in multicultural education, defines culture as ". . . the behavior patterns, symbols, institutions, values, and other human-made components of society . . . the unique achievement of a human group that distinguishes it from other human groups" (Banks 1981, 181). While language is a significant aspect of culture, it is only one of the components that give human groups a singular identity (Brooks 1979). Thus, the issues related to cultural differences are related to those of language, but they are not identical.

Cultural Differences and Social Messages

Students come to schools having learned social behaviors from their interactions with their relatives and friends. These social behaviors may not be
acceptable in school settings, necessitating some teacher-led socialization
into the culture of the school and the classroom. The importance of this is
obvious. Less obvious, and potentially problematic, are the social messages
conveyed by some curricula and some texts.

For many years, United States history was comprised only of the
achievements of white males, predominantly from European cultures. Literature classes formerly emphasized the writings of white British and
American authors, most of whom were male. These conditions are changing in many communities that are sensitive to avoiding an environment that
promotes a single cultural heritage and that excludes, ignores, or deni-
grates other cultures.

Parallel to the community's growing awareness of the importance of
celebrating cultural diversity is the rapid growth of minority groups in
schools. By the year 2000, one-third of all students will be "minority"
(Alexander 1986), which means that teachers of these children must be
aware of their cultural backgrounds and must enable them to succeed in
schools. The number of school dropouts attests to the importance of this
awareness. While 63.3 percent of all eighteen- and nineteen-year-olds have
completed high school, and 84.7 percent of all twenty- to twenty-four-year-
olds have completed high school, these figures drop by 10 percent for
black students and by 20 percent for Hispanic students.

Cultural Differences and Schooling.   Banks (1981) and other scholars
who are interested in cultural phenomena advocate the adoption of a multicultural approach to curriculum that includes the art, the literature, the music, and the achievements of many cultural groups. Following are four
principles summarized from Banks that can guide the development of a
curriculum that includes all cultures, not just a few.

TABLE 4.1   Public High School Dropout Rates

CHARACTERISTIC	RACE/ETHNICITY			
	White	Black	Hispanic	Total
High-school program				
Academic	4.8	7.1	14.8	5.8
General	15.9	18.1	18.4	16.6
Vocational	18.0	23.5	21.1	19.7
Socioeconomic status				
Low	23.7	18.0	23.1	22.3
Low-middle	12.6	10.3	19.5	13.2
High-middle	10.2	15.6	11.3	10.7
High	6.3	13.8	10.6	7.0

Source: U.S. Department of Education, National Center for Educational Statistics,
September, 1984.

Teachers are often very important people in the lives of students.

1. Diversity should be recognized and respected at the individual, group, and societal levels.
2. Diversity provides a basis for societal cohesiveness and survival.
3. Equality of opportunity must be afforded to all cultural groups.
4. Cultural identification for individuals should be optional in a democracy.

From these principles it follows that students deserve a classroom environment in which they feel respected by their school, their teacher, and their peers. This environment should include activities and materials that celebrate diversity and that enable all students to understand the importance of diversity in a democratic society. The environment should also provide opportunities for all students to succeed in academic tasks and in social interactions without pressuring those students to adopt a particular cultural identity if they choose not to do so.

Strategies for Teaching in Multicultural Settings

One very successful program, led by Elizabeth Cohen and her students (Cohen 1986), sponsors summer workshops in which teachers design academic tasks that encourage interdependence among students as they work in groups. Each student makes a valuable contribution to the group, but no student is assigned a task that is outside of the range of her or his talent or ability. While Cohen's work is targeted specifically toward classrooms composed of different cultures and speakers of several languages, there are other forms of cooperative learning environments (Aaronson 1978; Johnson & Johnson 1984; Slavin 1980) that also promote positive social relationships without sacrificing intellectual achievement.

Working With Handicapped Children

Although multicultural education does not typically include the education of children with handicaps, special children must also be considered when thinking through curricular and instructional issues. Public Law 94–142, the Education for All Handicapped Children Act, has resulted in growing numbers of students with physical, mental, or emotional disabilities being placed in all classrooms. Special students are assigned an *Individualized Educational Plan* (IEP), which is a schedule of the times they attend class with non-handicapped children and the times they are in special classes. The intent of the law is to place children in the *Least Restrictive Environment* (LRE) that will enable them to accomplish academic work. Because of this law, children with visual or auditory problems may take a full academic program.

Some teachers have not been trained to meet the special needs of children with physical and mental handicaps. Coping with these special needs requires innovative instructional designs that include peer tutoring, small group cooperative work, and some degree of individualized instruction. Curricular materials that depict what children with handicaps can do, and do well, are important aids that facilitate children's understandings of one another's accomplishments.

Conclusion

We have titled this chapter "Students: The Future of Society," because you will be helping to shape the future through the students you teach—or fail to teach—today. Education in the United States is designed to prepare people who live and participate in a democracy to do so intelligently and productively. Teachers prepare the future voters, the future presidents, and the future inmates. They teach those who will become altruistic contributers to, as well as those who will become selfish consumers of, society's

TABLE 4.2 **Persons With Handicaps Who Are Served by Educational Programs**

	% of total enrollment	
	1978–79	*1983–84*
All conditions	9.14	10.98
Learning-disabled	2.66	4.62
Speech-impaired	2.85	2.88
Mentally handicapped	2.12	1.86
Seriously emotionally disturbed	.71	.92
Deaf, or hearing-impaired	.20	.18
Orthopedically handicapped	.16	.14
Other health impairments	.25	.13
Visually handicapped	.08	.07
Multihandicapped	.12	.17
Deaf-blind	.01	.01

Source: U.S. Department of Education, Office of Special Education and Rehabilitative Services, September, 1984.

goods and services. Many times teachers help students make choices that will affect their visions of what the future holds and that will affect their visions of themselves.

As you think about the responsibilities you have to your students, remember that the people you will be teaching do not leave their life experiences outside the door when they enter the school building. Their languages, their cultures, and their life situations have shaped the way they view themselves and the way they view school. Sometimes your students will be coping with pressures that distract them from your assignments; sometimes your students will form opinions about their work that will prevent them from further progress. These are the times when you will need to reflect on the situation and develop plans to gather the information you need to help the student.

There will also be times when your students will delight you with their original and innovative ways of synthesizing information, with their unique perspectives on course content, and with their creative projects. Teachers who take the time to probe beyond the mass of faces in a classroom learn that students are fascinating and capable individuals who will make contributions to the present world of the classroom as well as to the real world of the future.

Building Reflective Inquiry Skills

In this chapter we have discussed two complementary theoretical explanations of how individuals perceive their environment and process information from that environment: information-processing theory and developmental-learning theory. In this section we will introduce you to one way of learning more about how individual students may work through the same assignment very differently, a "think-aloud" protocol.

Think-Aloud Task

First ask four students of the same age if they will agree to work through a familiar school task while you observe them and ask them questions about what they are doing in order to complete that task. Then, in consultation with a teacher, identify a task or assignment with which the students are familiar, one that is assigned often—such as a word problem in math, a writing assignment in English, or a skill drill in physical education.

Once the students and the task are chosen, you must prepare for the assignment yourself. First prepare the materials that each student will need in order to complete the task. Include the following:

1. A set of instructions that you will give to each student.

2. The paper, texts, and equipment that each student will need to complete the assignment.

3. An audiotape recorder and one clean tape for each student, labeled with that student's name.

4. A set of debriefing questions that you will use to question the student once the task has been completed.

5. A place to work with the student that is free from interruptions and noise.

Notify each student when she or he is expected to work with you and be prepared when each one arrives. Be sure that you have not scheduled students too closely together. Spend some time at the beginning of each session talking to the student before you begin giving instructions.

When you begin the session, read the instructions to the student. These should explain the task and that the student is to talk about what he or she is doing while working through the task. You may want to give an example of "thinking aloud," using a different task.

Let the student begin. If he or she has not begun to talk to you early in the task (after about fifteen seconds), you may need to prompt a response by asking, "What is going through your mind now?" Allow students to work completely through the task, prompting only when, they do not verbalize their thoughts.

Once the task is completed, ask the students to explain how they set about working through the task and the strategies they used to get the task done. Also ask which times they knew they were working well and which times they experienced frustration with the task. Make certain that you record their responses.

After all students have been through the task, compare their responses. What were some of the different strategies they used to work through the task? Which strategies were the most successful? Did the students differ in their feelings about the task?

Write a short paper reflecting on the students' responses to the task. What did this assignment teach you about individual differences? What did it teach you about how students process information in order to complete an academic task?

Explorations

Exploration 1
Students' Feelings about School
Interview four students, who attend the same school and are in the same grade, about their school experiences. Include questions like these:

1. What do you like most about the school day?
2. Which subjects are most interesting to you?
3. Which subjects are least interesting?
4. What makes a subject interesting? uninteresting?
5. What do you do when you have a problem with schoolwork?
6. When do you get a chance to see your friends at school? after school?
7. What do you and your friends do at school? after school?
8. What thing about you are you most proud of?
9. What thing about you are your teachers most proud of? your parents? your friends?

Exploration 2
Children Outside of School Settings
Work with a community service agency to find a program that will let you volunteer to work with children for a few hours each week. Here are some suggestions:

1. A local "latch-key" program.
2. The YMCA.
3. A youth sports organization.
4. A day-care center.
5. A church youth group.
6. A choir or choral group.

Exploration 3
Examining Textbooks
Obtain a copy of a textbook used to teach literature (or history). Examine the Table of Contents, noting the gender of the authors and, where possible, the ethnic background. Read through the first story (or chapter) and take notes on the people who figured prominently and their actions. Do the same for a story (or chapter) in the middle of the text. Then skim through the entire text to see if the two chapters you have chosen are representative of the book.

What patterns did you notice? Are some groups represented more than others? Are some groups ignored? Is there any sexual or cultural stereotyping? If you had to use this text in your classroom, would you be satisfied with it? What other materials would you consider using to supplement the text?

Exploration 4
Theories of Learning
Beginning with the references listed in this chapter, collect at least five documents (books, journal articles, other textbooks) that discuss any one of the four learning theories mentioned in this chapter. Summarize the major facets of the theory. What phenomena are explained by the theory? What empirical research documents these theories? How might the application of this theory appear in a classroom you might teach?

References

Aaronson, E., Blaney, N., Sikes, J., Stephan, G., & Snapp, M. (1978). *The jigsaw classroom.* Beverly Hills, CA: Sage Publications.

Alexander, L. (1986). Time for results: An overview. *Phi Delta Kappan, 68*(4), 202–204.

Ausubel, D. P. (1963). *The psychology of meaningful verbal learning.* New York: Grune and Stratton.

Bandura, A. (1977). *Social learning theory.* Englewood Cliffs, NJ: Prentice-Hall.

Banks, J. A. (1981). *Multiethnic education: Theory and practice.* Boston: Allyn and Bacon.

Bennett, W. J. (1986). *What works: Research about teaching and learning.* Washington, D.C.: U.S. Department of Education.

Bossert, S. S. (1979). *Tasks and social relationships in classrooms.* New York: Cambridge University Press.

Bower, T. G. R. (1974). *Development in infancy.* San Francisco: Freeman.

Brooks, N. (1979). Parameters of culture. In H. Baptiste (Ed.), *Developing the multicultural process in classroom instruction.* Lanham: University Press of America.

Bronfenbrenner, U. (1986). Alienation and the four worlds of childhood. *Phi Delta Kappan, 67*(6), 430–436.

Bruner, J. S. (1966). *Toward a theory of instruction.* Cambridge, MA: Harvard University Press.

Children's Defense Fund. (1986). *Employed parents and their children: A date book.* Washington, D.C.: Children's Defense Fund.

Clark, D. L. (1987). High school seniors react to their teachers and their schools. *Phi Delta Kappan, 68*(7), 503–509.

Cohen, E. G. (1986). *Designing groupwork for the classroom.* New York: Teacher's College Press.

Darwin, C. (1859). *The origin of the species.* New York: Modern Library.

Education Week. (1987). State education statistics: Student performance, resource inputs, and population characterisitics, 1982 and 1986, 20–21.

Elkind, D. (1981). *The hurried child: Growing up too fast too soon.* Reading, MA: Addison-Wesley.

Flavell J. H. (1977). *Cognitive development.* Englewood Cliffs, NJ: Prentice-Hall.

Greene, M. (1986). Philosophy and teaching. In M. C. Wittrock (Ed.), *The handbook of research on teaching, 3rd edition.* New York: Macmillan.

Howe, H. (1987). The prospect for children in the United States. *Phi Delta Kappan, 68*(4), 191–196.

Johnson, D. W., Johnson, R. T., Holubec, E. J., & Roy, P. (1984). *Circles of learning: Cooperation in the classroom.* Alexandria, VA: Association for Supervision and Curriculum Development.

Labov, W. (1972). *Sociolinguistic Patterns.* Philadelphia: University of Pennsylvania.

NEA Today. (1986–87). *Today's Education, 5*(1), 23.

Norman, D. A. (1968). Towards a theory of memory and attention. *Psychological Review, 75*, 522–526.

Piaget, J. (1926). *The language and thought of the child.* New York: Harcourt Brace.

Ross, G. S. (1980). Categorization in 1- to 2-year-olds. *Developmental Psychology 16*(5), 391–396.

Rummelhart, D. E. & Norman, D. A. (1978). Accretion, tuning and restructuring: Three modes of learning. In J. W. Cotton & R. L. Klatzky (Eds.), *Semantic factors in cognition.* Hillsdale, NJ: Lawrence Erlbaum Associates.

Shuell, T. S. (1986). Cognitive conceptions of learning. *Review of Educational Research, 56*(4), 411–436.

Skinner, B. F. (1953) *Science and human behavior.* New York: Macmillan.

Slavin, R. E. (1980). Cooperative learning. *Review of Educational Research, 50*, 317–343.

Sternberg, R. J. (1984) Mechanisms of cognitive development: A componential approach. In R. J.

Sternberg (Ed.) *Mechanisms of cognitive development*. New York: W. H. Freeman.

Wittrock, M. C. (1974). Learning as a generative process. *Educational Psychologist, 11*(2), 87–93.

CHAPTER FIVE

Communities and Schools

OBJECTIVES

By the end of this chapter, you will be able to:

1. Discuss the complex relationships between schools and the communities they serve.
2. Examine the impact of social changes and trends on communities and schools.
3. Demonstrate skills in describing a school's community-service area.
4. Demonstrate skills in analyzing the impact of a school's community-service area on the operation of that school.

KEY WORDS AND CONCEPTS

Community school
Cultural diversity
Nuclear family
Participant observer
Physical mobility
Social mobility
Societal migration
Urbanization

School and Community

The relationship between schools and their communities should be one of symbiosis—a relationship in which each feeds and draws nourishment from the other, to the benefit of both. It is from the community that the school draws its clients, its students. And since across much of the nation public schools are heavily dependent on local property taxes for operating revenues, the community is—in the most real sense—the constituency of the school.

In this chapter we will examine the diverse nature of contemporary American communities, the relationships between communities and the schools which serve them, and trends affecting communities. We will also provide you with the skills needed to analyze communities and the variations in expectations which communities have of their schools.

The interaction between schools and their communities is a subject of much discussion and debate. In his book *The Real World of the Public Schools*, Harry S. Broudy poses the following question:

> How far is the rhetoric about teachers from reality? If we take the rhetoric seriously, the teacher is expected to act in loco parentis, in loco communitatis, in loco humanitatis, that is, in place of the parent, the community, and the culture—and to do so as an expert in pedagogy. (Broudy 1972, 44)

Under the "reserved powers" clause of the Constitution, education is one of those powers reserved to the states—a point to be expanded in Chapter 12. Unlike France, Great Britain, West Germany, Japan, Brazil, and Indonesia, we do not have a national educational system. Instead, education is a responsibility of each of the states; and the federal government becomes involved, usually, only to the extent that state or local policies and practices violate the rights of United States citizens guaranteed by the Constitution, or when programs are supported by federal funding.

Most states, in turn, leave considerable discretion for the direction of schools to local boards of education. Of the fifty states, only Hawaii has a single, centralized, statewide educational system. Thus the United States has at least fifty different systems of education—and in reality and practice, many more than that—due to the broad discretion of local boards. The issue of local control of schools is a continuous source of debate.

The Community School

Politicians and other opinion leaders (as well as Americans in general) are fond of talking of the values of the "community school" as an idealized setting in which the wishes of all parents are realized for their children, in which "outside interference" is minimized and dominant community values transmitted to the young, and in which every child is treated as a winner—with the exception of the "discipline problems" (always someone else's offspring), who are dealt with firmly and fairly.

The vast majority of students in America, however, attend public elementary and secondary schools that serve not a single, cohesive commu-

Teacher: Today we are studying the letter M.
Child: It's my mother's birthday.
Teacher: This is not the time for that; we're talking about M.

Exchange in a primary classroom

nity but a diverse mix of small communities, which often hold differing value systems and expectations for their children. The notion of a community school (one in which a single, cohesive community is served) is more rare than common in contemporary American education.

Nonetheless, at a very general level there seems to be considerable agreement about major goals, or expectations, for schools. John Goodlad and his colleagues found the following:

> At the beginning of A Study of Schooling, several colleagues and I examined a vast array of documents reporting the ongoing effort to define, over a period of more than three hundred years, the goals of education and schooling in this country. . . . We concluded that four broad areas of goals for the schools have emerged. They are the following: (1) academic, embracing all intellectual skills and domains of knowledge; (2) vocational, geared to developing readiness for productive work and economic responsibility; (3) social and civic, related to preparing for socialization into a complex society; and (4) personal, emphasizing the development of individual responsibility, talent, and free expression (Goodlad 1984, 36–37).

Goodlad and colleagues also asked parents, teachers, and students to rate these four goal categories in order of importance. They found a high degree of agreement between parents and teachers. The results were:

Top priority:	Intellectual goals
Second:	Personal goals
Third:	Social goals
Fourth:	Vocational goals

General agreement among teachers and parents concerning the broad goals of schools seems supported by these data. The actual implementation of those goals in a specific school and community setting, though, is often more complex.

Types of Communities

The professional teacher may be employed to perform the variety of Broudy's expectations in greatly differing settings. Among them, (1) *Inner-city* settings in which the dominant community ethos is one of despair over unemployment, underemployment, lack of economic opportunities, and often a jaundiced view toward the potential of schooling to make a difference in that cycle of despair. (2) *Rural or small-town* settings in which the school is the center of community life, in which the Future Farmers of America provide a direct linkage between what is learned in school and the realities of everyday life, in which the teacher is among the most learned members of the community, and in which nearly everyone supports the school sports teams and the marching band. (3) *Bedroom suburbs* populated by professionals who often hold higher academic credentials than do the teachers to whom they entrust their children, who hold high expectations for education, but who may be so consumed by the competitive press of corporate advancement that their progeny rarely see them and even more rarely have the opportunity to interact with, and learn from, them.

Obviously, each of these settings (and this certainly is not an exhaustive list) places differing expectations on the teacher and on the school. And each is really a simplistic scenario, because, as mentioned earlier, schools rarely serve a cohesive, single community that has a unified set of values and expectations.

Some political scientists claim that the United States is not a single political and social system but rather a polity of special-interest groups. Schools respond to this diversity with bilingual education, English as a second language, programs for the gifted and for the handicapped, vocational education, and other efforts to make the school and its programs relevant to the needs of the local populace.

Because you, as a professional teacher, may work in a variety of school and community settings, it is important that you understand types of communities, recognize trends affecting the relationships between communities and schools, demonstrate skills in analyzing communities, and understand the implications of the local community for schools.

Communities in Transition

Changes in American society have direct impact on the communities that comprise that society and direct implications for schools as a major social agency within the culture.

In his book *Megatrends: Ten New Directions Transforming Our Lives*, John Naisbitt posits that American society is currently in the process of moving in the following directions.

EXHIBIT 5.1   Societal Trends (Naisbitt 1982)

From	To
Industrial Society	Information Society
Forced Technology	High Tech/High Touch
National Economy	World Economy
Short Term	Long Term
Centralization	Decentralization
Institutional Help	Self-Help
Representative Democracy	Participatory Democracy
Hierarchies	Networking
North	South
Either/Or	Multiple Option

© 1982 John Naisbett, Warner Books, N.Y., N.Y. Used with permission.

The implications of these trends for the curriculum in schools will be explored more fully in Chapter 7. The point here, however, is that our culture is constantly undergoing change from a variety of forces which constantly interact with one another. Schools must respond to those changes—while almost always lagging behind the rest of the culture. Some major forces which currently impact the ability of schools to respond to their constituencies are discussed in the following sections.

Physical Mobility

In our culture we take physical mobility for granted. The Interstate Highway System, initiated in the 1950s under President Eisenhower, allows one to engage the cruise control on the family vehicle and proceed for many hundreds of miles in the course of a single day, crossing unimpeded from state to state. A trip on that system is frequently a source of culture shock for sojourners from other nations for whom vehicular movement over great distances is hardly as cavalier. We also fly from coast to coast in a few hours by commercial airlines, which compete with one another for our patronage, with relatively low fares and frequent flights. We are accustomed, in short, to moving great distances in little time without a need for the prior approval of anyone.

As a result of our mobility, we are less and less likely to have lived in the same locale all our lives. We move from place to place, seeking work, or a promotion, or a more temperate climate, or a more congenial lifestyle. The tendency toward physical mobility can also result in a sense of rootlessness, of separation from family and friends, of drifting—a feeling that the sociologist Emile Durkheim years ago termed "anomie," or valuelessness.

As teachers, we may find a student in our class one Monday morning who left a school hundreds—or thousands—of miles away the Friday before, because of the transfer of a parent. We may have to find ways of helping a child who has been moved so frequently that her or his skills—those needed to read and to comprehend; to compute simple mathematical operations—have never been properly developed. And we often deal with young people who suffer a feeling of dislocation, a lack of friends, and likely a sense of rootlessness, of not really belonging. To focus the attention and effort of a dislocated adolescent on academic tasks is a major challenge. Table 5.1 gives some indication of the mobility of members of American society during just one year, from 1983 to 1984.

Urbanization

At the time of the American Revolution, only 3 percent of the population lived in cities or towns. The other 97 percent lived on farms. Today, the

TABLE 5.1 Mobility Status of the Population 1983–84

	Percent, By Region			
	Northeast	*Midwest*	*South*	*West*
Movers (Different house in 1983 than 1984)	11.6	15.4	18.5	21.3
Non-movers (Same house in 1983 as in 1984)	88.0	84.4	81.0	77.9

Source: Bureau of the Census (1986), *Statistical Abstract of the United States,* Abridged from pp. 14–15.

percentages are reversed. Due to immense technological advances in food production, a very small proportion of the population is able to produce more than enough food to supply the remainder of us—to the point of overweight becoming a cultural mania. Agricultural policies have even been set to prevent that small proportion of the population from producing foodstuffs beyond the point at which prices fall below profitable levels.

We have become an increasingly urbanized society. According to the U.S. Census Bureau, between 1980 and 1982 population in metropolitan areas grew by about four million people, while population in nonmetropolitan areas increased by only about one million people.

Those who move from rural areas to towns and cities are having to learn new habits and social patterns more appropriate to living in close quarters. Psychologists and social scientists conduct animal experiments on overcrowding, warning us that close quarters result in increasing aggression and physical violence. Yet dreams of opportunities for economic advancement and a more exciting lifestyle draw hundreds of thousands from country to city each year.

In addition to the movement of people from country to city, there is a corresponding movement, as Naisbitt puts it, from "North to South." The sun-belt southern and western states have experienced significant growth in population over the past two decades while northern states and cities have experienced a population decline. Between 1980 and 1984 the population grew by 8.3 percent in the West, by 6.9 percent in the South, by 0.4 percent in the Midwest, and by 1.2 percent in the Northeast. Texas is a prototypical example, gaining some two million in population from 1980 to 1985 and becoming the third most populous state (behind California and New York). Census Bureau estimates published in 1986 indicate that the three most populous states by the year 2000 will be California, Texas, and Florida.

In some cases this migration from North to South is due to individuals and families who are seeking a more temperate climate. In other cases, businesses (and the jobs which accompany them) have moved to southern states to find more favorable business and tax conditions.

The migration southward and westward has taken its toll on northern cities—some of which have been unjustly typified as "the Rust Belt." The decline of some major northern cities over the past decade, however, has been turned around through creative programs and incentives to attract and/or keep business interests active. The most recent migratory trends, in fact, are reported to be toward the East and West coasts of the United States, and away from the center of the nation (Church 1986).

Technology and Changing Work Skills

Over our national history we have moved from an agricultural economy to an industrial economy and now to an information-based economy. As Naisbitt wrote in *Megatrends*, "We now mass-produce information the way we used to mass-produce cars" (p. 16).

Information technology is exploding. Microprocessors have become both more powerful and more affordable. Home use of microcomputers has increased immensely in the past few years. In addition to providing word-processing capability and telecommunications, computer chips now control even the air-fuel mixture in automobiles, monitoring outside atmospheric conditions many times a second and adjusting for changes in those conditions. The growing use of robotics to do the repetitive, mechanical tasks once allocated to human labor has already displaced many workers and will no doubt displace more.

This shift from an industrial, manufacturing economy to an information economy results in dislocations of people and disruption of communities. Such disruption is especially common in areas which have, in the past, been dependent on manufacturing industries for economic stability.

In schools where typing was taught a few years ago, the skill taught now is "keyboarding." Many schools—and some states—require computer literacy for graduation even though the meaning of the term is still being debated. Does computer literacy mean having a knowledge of the historical development of computers? Or has computer use reached a developmental stage (analogous to learning about automobiles) in which one does not study the history of the computer but rather how to "drive" it?

Ethnic and Racial Identity, and the New Immigrants

Small towns in Iowa have significant populations of Southeast Asian immigrants, refugees from the war in Vietnam. The population of Miami, Florida is two-thirds Hispanic, predominantly from the influx of Cuban refugees. Fishermen from Southeast Asia ply their trade along the Texas Gulf Coast and come into conflict with more established residents of the area, because the Asian fishermen do not understand the cultural "rules" that have evolved over decades, which allocate certain fishing areas to individuals and companies, to alleviate earlier conflicts among natives of the region. School systems in New York, Los Angeles, and Houston report that more than ninety different languages or dialects are spoken in the homes of their students. Businessmen in the construction trades express concern over the hiring of undocumented aliens (predominantly from Mexico) at wages much lower than the going rate. This practice results in an unfair undercutting of competition, and also removes jobs that would otherwise be available to U.S. citizens.

It is a truism that the United States is a nation of immigrants. Over the course of our history, various factors of famine, unrest, and political and social upheaval have resulted in the immigration of millions from other nations, especially European, to our shores. Among the early motives for mass public education in this country was that of "Americanizing" these immigrants to the language and values of the dominant culture of the particular place and moment.

One major group, of course, did not immigrate willingly. Many Black Americans are the descendants of slaves, brought in chains to this land to do the labor others did not wish to do—predominantly backbreaking agricultural work. Once freed from slavery, they spent decades denied full and proper participation in political decision making and in educational opportunities. Many are still suffering from inadequate opportunities to be educated.

The United States continues to be an amalgamation of the cultures of the world.

The process of urbanization described earlier brought many ethnic and racial minorities to cities and towns, and the effects of their increasing participation in the political process is becoming more and more evident. Los Angeles, Chicago, Philadelphia, and Atlanta have elected Black mayors. Numerous smaller communities in the Southeast have elected Black officials to public office. Miami and San Antonio are two major cities in which Hispanic mayors have been voted to office—a reflection of the increased immigration of Hispanics from Central America, South America, and the Caribbean islands.

Southeast Asian refugees are making their mark in many American communities. For example, in those areas where they settle, Vietnamese students are often listed as the valedictorian or salutatorian of their high-school graduating class even though they may have come to school just a few years before, with little or no English-speaking capability.

Years ago historians gloriously described the United States as a "melting pot" for the cultures of the world. The melting pot analogy brings to mind a picture of various metals with differing qualities and properties being added and mixed until an alloy is achieved, an alloy which borrows from each of the ingredients to create a strong final product.

That would be well and good if it were not for the fact that in the "melting" process each of the properties loses its individual character. Rather than viewing society as an amalgamation in which cultural differences are extinguished as being somehow un-American, we need to celebrate the richness of diversity that each different culture adds to our society in the sense that Gold, Grant, and Rivlin (1977) suggest in *In Praise of Diversity*, or Garcia's (1982) emphasis on a *pluralistic* society.

How about beef stew as an alternative analogy? It does convey some important differences from the melting pot. In beef stew each of the ingredients retains its individual identity but complements other ingredients—to the point that the whole stew becomes more than the sum of the parts. We encourage you to think of better analogies to communicate the idea of maintaining the character of individual cultural elements while building a sense of community.

The Changing Nature of the Family

The American family is changing. Mom, Dad, Dick, Jane, Spot, and Puff (as well as Beaver Cleaver, brother Wally, and *their* parents)—idealized portraits of the middle-class, majority American family—have given way to a wide range of family configurations.

Today's family *may* be a standard, nuclear family, but it may also be:

► a nuclear family in which the marriage is by common law.
► a nuclear family in which the man and woman are not married to each other, by common law or otherwise.
► a single-parent family (most often headed by a female), the result of widowhood, divorce, or separation.
► an extended family, in which grandparents, uncles, aunts, cousins, or others are included.
► a mixed family, in which the two partners each bring with them children from earlier unions.

Regardless of the nature of a specific family, two trends are clear. First, more individuals will have more than one spouse during their lifetime, as a result of death or divorce (a tendency sometimes referred to as "serial polygamy"). And second, in an increasing number of families, both parents (or *the* parent, in single-parent families) work outside the home, and children are therefore left increasingly to their own or sibling care. Of all working wives, 55 percent have at least one child under eighteen. The most visible result of this phenomenon is the "latch-key child" (discussed in Chapter 4), so named because he or she carries or wears a key to the house or apartment, because no one will be home when the child returns from school.

Whatever the nature of the family, a child's home environment is a major determinant of, and a major contributor to, her or his potential success in school. The degree to which the student was read to at home as a small child will have an impact on reading in school. The degree to which the student was helped to develop a sound self-concept will impact a variety of areas of school achievement. And the value placed on academic success in the home environment is a major influence on the student's attitude toward school and school tasks.

*The child who is not plain and neat
With lots of toys and things to eat,
He is a naughty child, I'm sure—
Or else his dear papa is poor.*

R. L. Stevenson: *System.*

Impact of Social Changes on Schools

The School as Surrogate Parent

Schools are increasingly expected to perform functions that were once the responsibility of the family. To name just a few, schools have instituted programs to teach students to drive, to cook, to sew, to make moral and ethical decisions and programs to teach students about sex, about the prevention of sexually-transmitted disease, about child-care, and about the use and abuse of chemicals.

Individual teachers have historically been viewed by *some* students as surrogate parents, especially in the primary grades. A teacher's approval, or disapproval, can be extremely important to a five-, six-, or seven-year-old child. Soon thereafter, however, the peer group begins to determine appropriate behavior, dress, speech patterns, and other elements of socialization.

The School as Child-Care Agency

Single-parent families are increasing, and since the single parent often works, very special implications arise for the school as child-care agency. The same sort of child-care implications result from the increase in families in which both parents work outside the home, a phenomenon with a variety of causes, including economic conditions and increasing career opportunities for women. Both single parents and working parents depend on the school to perform major functions in the supervision of children when parents are not available for such supervision. If any doubt exists about the importance of the child-care function of schools, note the scrambling that occurs among working parents when a school is closed for some reason, such as a nearby fire, severe weather, or a water-main break. These parents must, on short notice, find some other means of providing supervision and child-care while they work.

Single parents and families in which both parents work, of course, are not the only segments of the community that depend on the school as a child-care agency. Our culture is replete with humorous cartoons in which the parent who does not work outside the home rues the onset of summer vacation and celebrates the beginning of the school year because of the relief it brings from constant child-care responsibilities and the freedom to do other things for significant periods of the day.

Exhibits 5.2 and 5.3 show data reported by the U.S. Census Bureau and the U.S. Labor Department's Bureau of Labor Statistics. These data underscore the pronounced trends toward single-parent families and working mothers. Are there other potential implications for elementary and secondary schools as you review these data?

The School as Transmitter of Changing Social Values

A major, ongoing debate concerns the school's role in the teaching of values. The teaching of values has been a focal point of schooling from the inception of public education. Many early educational materials explicitly addressed important social values of the time. *The New England Primer* of the eighteenth century taught the alphabet by using biblical homilies, while *McGuffey's Reader* and other readers of the nineteenth century addressed the values of nationalism, honesty, hard work, self-reliance, and thrift.

Significant controversy continues in many communities over the teaching of values in public schools. Courts are continually faced with suits over

EXHIBIT 5.2   Percent of Families Headed by a Single Parent, by Race,
1970 and 1980

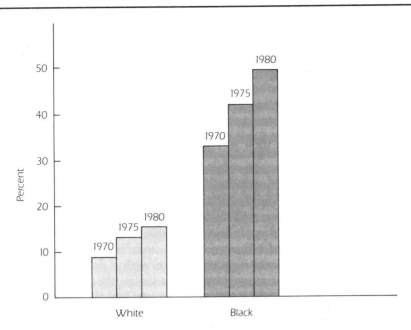

EXHIBIT 5.3   Labor-force Participation Rates of Mothers
in Two-parent Families, 1960–81

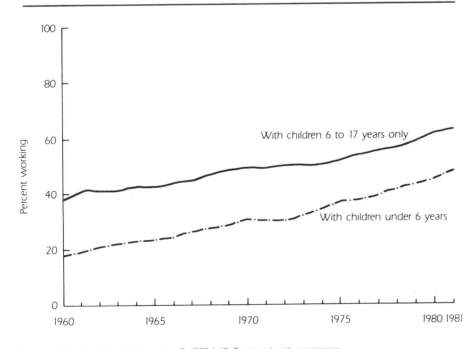

Source: Education Week—November 2, 1983 1, 18. Reprinted with permission.

allowing prayer in public schools, providing public assistance for religiously-oriented private schools, the teaching of creationism *or* evolution, and over other values which are claimed to be explicit or implicit in educational materials.

Societal values in contemporary America are hardly as clear, nor as universally agreed upon, as those reflected in the *Primer* or *McGuffey's*. We are in a time of confusion of values, in which choices must be made from among a variety of options, many of which are not clearly right or wrong by the criteria of contemporary social values. This phenomenon is called "over-choice," and the cumulative effect of having to make many such decisions from among unclear alternatives is often confusion and alienation.

Individuals may learn to live with the effects of over-choice and unclear social values, but the dilemma becomes especially complex when one make a career decision to teach. Teachers are directly charged with instilling social values in children and youth at a time when those very values are in flux and the subject of social controversy.

The School as Communal Acculturation Agency

Because so much discretionary control of American public education has been delegated to local boards of education and to local communities (which usually elect the members of those boards), the impact of community values is an important factor in understanding schools. The ethos of a school that serves a predominantly middle-class, upwardly-mobile community of professionals will be far different from that of a school that draws its clientele from a farming community.

A basic tenet of the American faith in education is the belief that education is important to social mobility. In addition to the physically mobile nature of American culture discussed earlier, we have taken historic pride as a nation in the degree to which individuals can change their status in life. Unlike the Indian caste system or even the British system of social class, the faith of Americans rests in the notion that every child has the opportunity to become president, or at least to better the station in life into which he or she is born. Education is viewed as a major avenue to upward social mobility, or the "American Dream."

The ways in which this faith is actualized in a given school setting vary by the expectations of the adults who are constituents of that school's community and by the capabilities that students, who are its clients, bring to the school. In their book *Schooling in Capitalist America* (1976), Bowles and Gintis argue that the net effect of local community expectations is often to hinder social mobility and reinforce social-class differences, rather than to equip students for changing their social class if they choose to do so. They argue that schools serving lower-class communities tend to emphasize rote learning, abiding by rules, and punctuality—all of which are desired behaviors for workers. Schools serving more professionally and managerially-oriented constituencies, however, tend to place greater emphasis on self-direction and student choice—both of which are desired qualities for managers and professionals. In either type of community, the school is directly responding to what its leaders perceive (likely accurately) to be the expectations of that local community.

The School as Center of Community Life

Schools have traditionally been a center of community activity. That quality has been enhanced with the increased social emphasis on what has come to be called "life-long learning," or continuing education. Adult education classes are often sponsored during the evening hours and on weekends in areas as diverse as automobile maintenance, arts and crafts, computer programming, English as a second language, defensive driving, and aerobic exercise. In many regions the school facilities, and often its staff, are extended to the community far beyond the teaching of academic skills to elementary- and secondary-age students.

Additionally, cocurricular activities, such as sports and music programs, often serve as a major force of community identity and pride. A winning school sports team or an outstanding marching band, orchestra, or glee club is an important element in marshalling adults as audiences and as supporters of other elements of the school program. Although many teachers would prefer that as much excitement was generated by students' academic achievements as by their teams, academic awards celebrations are not commonly attended by hundreds and thousands of community members.

Discovering a School's Community Constituency

Analyzing Community Structures

An astute educator does more than simply function within the confines of a school building. To best serve the students who are a school's clients, the teacher must seek to understand the community setting in which those students live and function outside of school time.

Likewise, the astute educator becomes a participant-observer in the local community—a methodology for sociological and anthropological re-

Parents have a vested interest in the quality of schools.

search pioneered by Margaret Mead in *Coming of Age in Samoa*, R. S. Lynd and H. M. Lynd's *Middletown*, W. Lloyd Warner's studies of Yankee City, and William F. Whyte's *Street Corner Society*.

The participant-observer methodology, as one work notes, requires "... a keen eye and an ear for life in the concrete and, most important, a capacity for detaching (oneself) from the beliefs and values of the local residents" (Vidich, Bensman & Stein 1964, viii).

It involves the ability to be a member of a culture while at the same time maintaining the objectivity to step back from time to time and reflect on the direction and values of that culture with as little unconscious interference as possible from one's own internalized value system.

You can observe a lot just by watchin'.

(Yogi Berra, quoted in Eric Hodgins's *Episode*.)

Probably the most difficult, and useful, set of skills to learn initially are the skills of observation and description, with as little as possible normative interpretation of those observations. We tend to unconsciously mix judgments of an event or interaction with our observations and thereby distort those observations.

The following passage is from the personal experience of one of the authors.

> Some years ago, I was working for a state university in Illinois. My primary job was to supervise student teachers in the Chicago area, and since the university was some distance from Chicago, I was provided a state-owned automobile for the travel involved.
>
> One morning I began my work at a large high school in a wealthy suburb on the Near North Side of the city. I arrived early, this being my first visit to the school, and waited outside for people to arrive. Some students walked to school, all well-dressed in the fashionable mode of the day. What really impressed me was the line of limousines, which began forming at the front entrance to the school. As each had its turn, the chauffeur would drive up, stop, get out, and open the right rear door. Out would step one or two students—often wearing faded (at the factory) jeans, with decorative patches of various colors.
>
> That afternoon I visited an elementary school in the midst of the public-housing projects on the South Side of the city. I pulled up in front of the school and walked toward the door. A small child, likely a five-year-old just completing half-day kindergarten, walked out of the school, looked at me (in my suit and tie), looked at the automobile with the State of Illinois symbol on the side, and asked me quietly if I was a "cop." I assured him I wasn't. He didn't seem fully convinced, though, until I showed him that the bulge under the left side of my suitcoat was not a pistol in a shoulder-holster, but rather a collection of papers and a pocket calendar.
>
> As I walked into the school, I noted fading and peeling paint, odors distinctly different from those I had experienced in a different school that morning, and a small display case mounted on the hallway wall that was covered with chicken-wire glass—the sort of glass that has wire embedded in it for security, so that smashing the glass still does not ensure a "quick snatch" of whatever is behind the glass.
>
> The only thing inside the display case was a branch from an apple tree, with a few leaves and blooms still on it. In talking with the principal and teachers later, I was told that there were very few trees within blocks of the school (a fact I later confirmed by my own observations) and that many of the children who attended there had never been outside the local neighborhood.

Note that the language in the preceding passage is descriptive rather than judgmental. The writer tells what happened, what was seen, with a minimum of value-laden language. Yet the passage has an emotional tone by the very choice of the events of that particular day that the writer chooses to share. No doubt many other things happened. Driving in the traffic of a major city is a constant adventure, but the writer does not choose to deal with the pressures of the drive from the north to the south side of Chicago.

Our perception is selective. We view only some elements of the reality that surrounds us at any given moment, and we recall only a portion of what we perceive. What we perceive and what we recall are, to a considerable degree, influenced by our unconscious value systems. We are all creatures of our own culture. To be an effective, reflective participant-observer requires constant examination of the accuracy we *think* we are applying in our observations.

Conclusion

Strong, effective schools are symbiotic with the communities in which they function. Leaders in such schools seek to identify local needs and respond to them, when at all possible, within the resource limitations of the school and their best professional judgment. Most American students attend schools that serve a multiplicity of communities rather than a single, easily identified, and homogeneous community. The degree to which teachers and schools succeed in meeting local needs, while concomitantly meeting broader societal expectations, is a major measure of the future of the second great American experiment: universal mass public education.

Building Reflective Inquiry Skills

As Conway, Jennings and Milstein (1974) and Oliva (1982) have pointed out in the context of program evaluation, the most important analytic skills are:

... asking questions
... asking the right questions
... asking the right questions of the right people.

When analyzing a community served by a school, the first step is to obtain a map of the area, mark off the boundaries of the area served by that particular school, and drive or walk through the service area. Some of the questions you should be seeking to answer, then, are these:

1. What is the economic base of the community? What do people do for a living? Do they tend to work in the community or live there and work elsewhere? Is unemployment high or low?

2. What do parents expect of the schools? Do they expect only that schools perform a child-care function? What proportion of high-school graduates go on to college? What proportion drop out before completing high school?

3. Does the school serve a single, readily identifiable community, with a unified set of expectations for the education of its offspring? Or is the constituency of the school characterized by diversity of ethnicity, race, culture, and/or income level? Does the school participate in free lunch (and sometimes breakfast) programs, which would indicate that a number of its students come from homes that fall below the poverty level?

4. How active and effective are other institutions in the community? Does religion play a large part in the life of the families of the community? Are children expected to learn moral and spiritual values at church rather than at school?

5. To what degree is the school the center of community life? How many other agencies compete for the attention of students and parents outside of school hours and meet needs that the school, then, is not expected to meet?

Answers to questions such as these (and you are encouraged to add to the list) can be obtained from a variety of sources:

1. Careful observation of people in the community. Become familiar with the sights, sounds, smells—in essence, the texture—of the area. Does it seem to represent one community, or several? Political boundaries are not always the same as community boundaries.

2. Interviews with parents—at school if necessary, but preferably in homes so that you can get a fuller sense of the conditions from which children come to school.

3. Examination of local media (newspapers, especially) for the sorts of information they publish about schools and the amount of space devoted to school items. Are the only things published concerning the lunch menu, interschool sports results, and an occasional scandal concerning a miscreant school official? Or is attention given to the achievements of students in academic and other pursuits?

Explorations

Exploration 1
Multicultural Education
Read the following excerpt from Nathan Glazer's Ethnic Dilemmas, 1964–82 from the perspective of a teacher working in a culturally diverse school. What is your reaction to this passage? Do you agree or disagree with Glazer? What is the impact on you as a teacher? Write your reactions down in your log.

The large question that multicultural education has not dealt with as yet is how very different are the desires and requirements of different groups in the area of bicultural and bilingual education. It is not possible for the state to legislate for each group separately, according to its needs and desires. That would run afoul of the state's need for general legislation, legislation that provides the "equal protection of the laws." Yet blacks, Mexican Americans, Puerto Ricans, American Indians, Cubans, Portugese from the islands and the mainland, French-speaking Canadians and Louisiana Cajuns, Jews, Chinese, Japanese, Poles, Italians, and so on need and want very different things. Some of these groups are concerned primarily with poor educational achievement: they want anything that will work, and if that means multicultural education and black English, so be it, but if it means the exact reverse, they will choose that. Some of these groups have only a transitional language problem and have no desire to maintain in a public school setting education in ancestral languages. Some want only to be recognized: if anything is to be done for any other groups, they want education in their own group's heritage, "equal time," but they may not even be sure they want their children to spend time taking it. And I have simplified the complexity, for in each group there are people with very different demands and needs. (Glazer 1983, 141)

Exploration 2
Observing in a Ghetto
Read the following expert from A Handbook for Teaching in the Ghetto School. The author here is talking of a Black ghetto, but you should keep in mind that ghetto is a Jewish word, which was initially used to describe the portion of any given city in which Jews were required to live, separated from the rest of the population. The term is now often used to describe any area that is inhabited predominantly or exclusively by a single racial or ethnic group. By this latter definition, do you know of any other ghettos? How about an exclusive residential country club?

Walk slowly up and down a street in the ghetto. Allow the life there to seep into your being. Fight past the rigid perception that comes of the fear of strangeness and see the forces that whirl around the children who will sit in your class the day you become a teacher in the elementary school in the area. On certain days you may see a policeman place a shabby man with his hands against the wall and frisk him. Children may walk by only mildly interested. You may see a sanitation worker hurl a garbage can cover at a rat that scurries past. You will likely see groups of men aimlessly drinking beer from cans hidden by brown paper bags. Children will probably be playing with tin cans or sticks in a rubble-filled lot, apart from the dull meanderings of nearby adults.

Go through the outdoor markets in the neighborhood. Feel the vitality of the people swirling around stores and stalls. Watch the children as they run to greet a teacher from their school. Breathe in the odors of the weekly Saturday pork chop fry held in front of a storefront church, and absorb the gaiety. Dwell on the pride-filled faces of adults as a class of children takes a neighborhood walk. Note the watchful care of a ten-year-old child as he leads a younger brother or sister to school. View the uncomplicated joy of the child whose teacher has taken a moment to joke with him.

Follow a child into his home. Walk into halls lit by one weak bulb. See his home with double-decked beds, with a television set blaring day and night, with half-dressed children hanging weakly to a skirt as you, the stranger, enter.

Look at the scrubbed faces, the starched dresses, the suit jackets of kindergarten children as they ven-

ture forth for their first day at school. Watch as sixth-graders enter the building for their last day of elementary school, the girls wearing dresses white from careful laundering, the boys clad in suits neat from pressing.

References

Bowles, S. & Gintis, H. (1976). *Schooling in capitalist America.* New York: Basic Books.

Broudy, H. S. (1972). *The real world of the public schools.* New York: Harcourt Brace Jovanovich, Inc.

Bureau of the Census, U.S. Department of Commerce (1986). *Statistical Abstract of the United States,* 106th Edition. Washington, D.C.

Church, G. J. (1986, September 1). A tale of two countries? A study finds America's coasts booming and its center sagging. *Time,* 16–17.

Conway, J. A., Jennings, R. E. & Milstein, M. M. (1974). *Understanding communities.* New York: Prentice-Hall.

Garcia, R. L. (1982). *Teaching in a pluralistic society: Concepts, models, strategies.* New York: Harper & Row.

Glazer, N. (1983). *Ethnic dilemmas 1964–82.* Cambridge, MA: Harvard University Press.

Gold, M. J., Grant, C. A. & Rivlin, H. N. (1977). *In praise of diversity: A resource book for multicultural education.* Washington, D.C.: Teacher Corps and Association of Teacher Educators.

Goodlad, J. I. (1984). *A place called school.* New York: McGraw-Hill.

Lynd, R. S. & Lynd, H. M. (1929). *Middletown.* New York: Harcourt, Brace & World.

Mead, M. (1961). *Coming of age in Samoa.* New York: Morrow.

Naisbitt, J. (1982). *Megatrends: Ten new directions transforming our lives.* New York: Warner Books.

Oliva, P. F. (1982). *Developing the curriculum.* Boston: Little, Brown.

Trubowitz, S. (1968). *A handbook for teaching in the ghetto school.* Chicago: Quadrangle Books.

Vidich, A. J., Bensman, J. & Stein, M. R. (1964). *Reflections on community studies.* New York: John Wiley and Sons, Inc.

Warner, W. L. (1941). *The social life of a modern community.* New Haven: Yale University Press.

Whyte, W. F. (1955). *Street corner society.* Chicago: University of Chicago Press.

Exploring School Quality

OBJECTIVES

By the end of this chapter, you will be able to:

1. Compare different definitions of school quality.
2. Articulate basic elements of research on effective schools and apply them as criteria in examining a school.
3. Discuss the recommendations of commissions and task forces proposing changes during the mid-1980s.
4. Speculate on school quality as it might be considered in the future.

KEY WORDS AND CONCEPTS

Commission reports
Deschooling society
Effective schools research
Goal-directed actions
Quality schools
School accreditation
Stimulating environment
Team building and cohesion

Basis for Quality

Schools have reputations, some deserved, others not. The bases for their reputations are many; some valid and others based on hearsay. Schools may have poor reputations because of the neighborhood in which they are located (ghettos), the condition of the building (old or dirty), or a particular issue that was resolved differently from that which a segment of the community wanted (school boundaries changed in their area).

Other schools have reputations as being "good"—students like them; they are in higher socioeconomic neighborhoods; the school has a special focus or special resources (for example, school for exceptional children, high school for the health professions, comprehensive microcomputer labs); a high proportion of graduates attend college; or they have winning athletic teams. The reasons for strong reputations of schools vary widely.

Often, the reasons for strong reputations of schools are valid, but a number capitalize on external circumstances for which schools take undue credit (for example, a higher proportion of high-school graduates whose parents graduated from college are more likely to attend college themselves than the general population; schools in more affluent neighborhoods tend to have greater resources; the achievement scores of students from low-income, minority families and from inner-city schools tend to be lower).

Several of the factors that make a school strong or not-so-strong are cultural, economic, or situation-specific; professionals in those schools have little control over them. Other factors (a winning football team, for example) may be irrelevant to the concept of quality schools when the basic mission of the school in society is considered.

Varying Indicators of Quality

*A*n effective school is a work of art. It orchestrates . . . its students and parents and community in concerted efforts toward educational excellence. It enlists the creative abilities of all. . . . Above all, it is unique, responsive to personalities and values and needs and abilities that are never fully duplicated in any other school.

Doxey Wilkerson, *Educating All Our Children*

How can you determine whether a school has quality or not? What are indicators of quality? The bases for answering these questions are numerous. In this chapter we explore several notions about quality schools. Each grows out of a conception of the contribution schools make to society.

Beginning in the late 1970s, quality schools were defined as those that brought about changes in student achievement. An extensive series of research studies, funded primarily by the federal government, examined practices in schools with both high and low achievement to determine which practices were related to increased achievement by students. The movement, called *effective schools research*, was closely aligned with studies of effective teachers, (teachers whose students score higher on achievement tests) or process-product research (teaching procedures that result in greater production of student achievement) discussed in Chapter 3. The U.S. Department of Education heavily funded the research on effective schools and later supported the dissemination of its findings. This major movement in improving school practice is described in the second section of this chapter.

Other definitions of school quality have developed out of the conceptualizations of educators, needs of special interest groups, school accrediting agencies, and societal trends. In the third section of this chapter, several of these criteria are considered, including the extent to which schools (1) teach eternal truths, beauty, and goodness; (2) teach skills for democratic living; (3) include student exploratory activities; (4) teach how to learn; (5) have adequate staff and resources; (6) meet national needs; (7) improve the education of disadvantaged groups; (8) are similar in student body values; and (9) provide multiple choices for students. These alternative positions for assessing the quality of schools, along with effective schools research, provide a context for better understanding of events in schools. These varied notions of quality are reported in the third section of this chapter.

Some persons have advocated doing away with schools altogether. They believe that society would be better served if students did not attend school at all. Their position is considered in the fourth part of the chapter.

Beginning about 1983, in response to mounting public criticism of the quality of schools, a number of national and state commissions and task forces made recommendations to improve schooling. The first and most-often quoted was *A Nation At Risk*, a publication initiated by the U.S. Department of Education. The high school was particularly criticized during this period, with several important studies of it made by educators. The fifth section of this chapter includes summaries of several commission reports and analyses of high schools.

The purpose of this chapter is not to make you a specialist in determining school quality, but to suggest different conceptualizations so that you can better understand the schools in which you visit or work. Quality can be defined in many ways; controversy occurs over what is considered quality.

Research on Effective Schools

About fifteen years ago, several teams of researchers began exploring the basic characteristics of effective schools. They wanted to eliminate from consideration extraneous factors such as socioeconomic status of students, location of school, or winning athletic teams. Most began their studies by asking educators to identify the best and weakest schools in a school district, then studying those schools to determine differences in their curricula, instructional processes, organization, administration, and attitudes of students and teachers.

One of the leading researchers who explored effective schools was Ron Edmonds. Edmonds (1979) based his research on the assumption that the basic purpose of schools is academic achievement. He secured achievement scores, socioeconomic indices, and information on other factors that might affect students' achievement. He analyzed achievement test scores and used a statistical procedure to eliminate the effects of factors (such as socioeconomic conditions) over which schools had no control. The results were revised achievement scores that reflected school practices rather than community settings. Then he studied the differences in practices between two sets of schools: those in which students scored much higher than would be expected and those in which students scored lower than expected. He sought practices found in the higher achieving schools that were not evident in schools with lower student achievement. These practices, he concluded, distinguished effective schools.

Rutter (1979) observed secondary schools in England to determine practices that made a difference in student achievement. Lortie (1975) and Brookover and Lezotte (1979) were others who studied the bases for effective versus ineffective schools.

Their findings are amazingly similar. Schools that are effective tend to have similiar characteristics and practices. As you become a more sensitive observer, knowing this research may be helpful. Because classrooms are organizationally similiar to, and subsets of, schools, many of these same principles apply to classrooms as well as to schools. In the next few paragraphs we will explore some of the factors that define effective schools, whose students achieve higher scores than students of similar backgrounds but in other schools.

Strong Principal

In effective schools, the principal is a strong, consistent leader who clearly emphasizes instructional excellence (Austin 1979; Brookover & Lezotte 1979; Edmonds 1979). When budgeting scarce resources, the principal gives priority to factors that contribute to improved instruction. The principal is not closeted in the office but is around the school, a visible presence in its life. Effective principals make frequent informal classroom observations, press for greater commitment by teachers (Rutter, Maughan, Mortimore, Ouston & Smith 1979), and maintain open communications with parents and the community.

The quality of a learning environment is often reflected in students.

Goal Orientation

In schools identified as effective, the principal has a clear vision of the school's mission and communicates this vision to teachers, parents, and students. The mission is clearly defined in terms of student achievement; administrators and teachers agree this mission is important (Glenn & McLean 1981; Goodlad 1984); and a means is available to consistently implement it (Morris et al. 1981). The administrator conveys the importance as well as the essence of school goals (Brookover & Lezotte 1979; Glenn & McLean 1981). Havelock's studies indicated that goals should be realistically obtainable (Havelock & Huberman 1977).

Thirty years of research as well as common sense have signaled the importance of goals in life. Humans seek goals and are more likely to achieve them when the goals are explicit and recognized in advance. In an area of study in psychology referred to as incidental-intentional learning, researchers have found that individuals are more likely to attain an objective if they know it in advance of instruction (Duchastel & Merrill 1973).

Three educators, Benjamin Bloom, John Carroll, and J. H. Block, pioneered in the development of a method of instruction, evaluation, and advancement based on this principle in the book *Mastery Learning* (Block 1971). They demonstrated that when time is not a variable, almost all students can learn. Other goal-oriented instructional systems have been called competency-based education, education by behavioral objectives, and the Madeline Hunter method of teaching. In administration of schools or businesses, management by objectives (MBO) is an effective system based on this same premise.

Effective schools always are in the process of regular, focused, and goal-directed change, of which feedback is a vital part. Change is *directed by goals*, but *driven by feedback*. Feedback is important to effective principals. Lortie (1975) found that three-fourths of 113 principals believed that their major satisfaction was derived from evidence that their students were achieving. Teachers, parents, and students need to know how well they are achieving the goals and mission of the school. When they see progress, they tend to make even greater efforts and strides toward these goals.

When principals and teachers positively support actions that lead to school goals, the results are staggering—outcomes become even more powerful, complex, and dynamic. Principals of effective schools emphasize reward and positive ethos—*not punishment*—in the school.

High Expectations

Effective schools are characterized by high expectations (Brookover & Lezotte 1979; Resnick & Resnick 1985; Rutter et al. 1979). Teachers expect their students to do well, and they act on this assumption (Good 1981). They refuse to set aside basic skill acquisition, even for the lowest achievers (Wynne 1980). Principals expect their teachers to do well, and teachers, too, act on this expectation. An old saying reads, "Whatever you expect of others, you are not likely to be disappointed." Expect low achievement or poor performance and that is what you will get. Several years ago, a teacher was told that her new students were all extremely brilliant, even though they were just average students. A few months later, not only was the teacher praising the class, but achievement actually had increased.

Brookover and Lezotte (1979) found that teachers in schools with improving student achievement are less satisfied than staffs of declining schools. The latter reflect a pattern of complacency and satisfaction with current levels of educational achievement.

Team Building

Cooperation and collegial spirit permeate the faculty of effective schools, a spirit that says, "together we can improve." Teachers in effective schools are far less likely to be isolated. Effective schools are usually places of intellectual sharing, collaborative planning, and collegial work. Faculty activities are characterized by task-focused, cooperative, and frequent interaction (Little 1982).

In most cultures, ceremonies and initiation rites have been used in building esprit de corps. Clubs and fraternities often have such initiations. Whether through hazing or a spiritually moving rite, these initiations are designed to build a spirit of oneness in the group. Cohesion studies conducted in World War II demonstrated that performance in military platoons increased 25 percent through cohesion processes that bonded the men together. Effective schools have similar ways of building group identification—pep rallies, ceremonies, small work groups and clubs, contests with other schools, stickers, banners, and symbols painted on neighboring streets. Some elementary teachers name their rooms (Bailey's Beatles) and have "class hugs." The purpose is cohesion.

In developing team spirit and motivating students, schools could learn much from the business community. Corporations and agencies spend considerable resources in building cohesion (Houston 1986); it begins with the employment interview. After completing tests and initial screening, U.S. Border Patrol applicants, for example, are interviewed by current agents, who tell them that only one in five will be selected and recommended for employment. The Harris-Lanier employment process includes a two-hour test, initial interview, day-long series of sales calls with an experienced salesperson, and a final intensive two-hour interview by the staff. Applicants know that the selection process is serious and rigorous, and that the results are important to the organization and its members. When selected, applicants are pleased to be part of the team.

Specific efforts are made to communicate to the new employee the culture and mission of the organization. Walt Disney World's mission is to provide clean, wholesome fun appropriate for family entertainment in a safe, enjoyable, and different environment. Employees are expected to reflect a friendly, courteous, and clean-cut image. Even the language used conveys this message: employees are called "hosts" and customers "guests." In the spirit of Walt Disney, hosts treat guests quite differently than employees treat customers.

Traditions I is the first experience for all new Walt Disney World employees. Even the room environment, with its Walt Disney memorabilia on walls and in display cases, is designed to convey the mission and traditions of the corporation. Orientation includes a professional, motivating film and short, succinct, and stimulating talks by executives.

Teaching often lacks a sense of ownership, a sense among the teachers working together that the school is theirs, and that its future and their reputation are indistinguishable. Hired hands own nothing, are told what to do, and have little stake in their enterprises. . . . Not surprisingly . . . [teachers] . . . often act like hired hands.

Theodore Sizer, *Horace's Compromise*, 1984.

Mary Kay Cosmetics relies on human interaction for enculturation. New employees are identified by cute fur animals (called "warm fuzzies") stuck on their lapels. A regular, every-Monday-night meeting brings new employees together, as a group, with all the experienced salespersons in the office. These meetings are combination training sessions and pep rallies.

Some corporate practices have implications for school effectiveness; others do not. Attention to marketing the positive features of the company, both to the public and to its employees, and to enculturating new employees into the system are practices schools do, but not so effectively as if they employed some of these corporate strategies.

Time on Task

A strong relationship has been established between the amount of time a student spends studying a subject and that student's achievement. In effective schools, every effort is made to increase instructional time. Interruptions, such as loudspeaker announcements (Stallings 1980), school assemblies (Rutter et al. 1979), and other low-priority events (Glenn & McLean 1981), are minimized. Class changes are even organized to provide rapid movement of students.

Clean, Orderly, Stimulating School

Effective schools are clean and orderly without being rigid. They are quiet without being oppressive. Their atmospheres are conducive to a business-like approach to learning. The environment is stimulating. There are clear expectations for students in the form of rules, directives, and specifications of penalties (Rutter et al. 1979; Wynne 1980) that are enforced consistently (Morris et al. 1981). Evident in the room are colorful bulletin boards, displays, interesting programs, and supplies and equipment that stimulate students to explore. Edmonds (1979) found that students responded to unstimulating learning experiences predictably: they were apathetic, disruptive, or absent.

Caveat

In law, a caveat is a warning, an indication that the reader should beware of oversimplification and should refrain from an action until the caveat is considered. So it is with research findings on effective schools. The strengths of the research reported herein are considerable. The studies were carefully conducted and independent of one another, yet researchers found similar conditions that were consistent with the best of conventional wisdom and educational experience.

Three limitations should be noted, however. First, the current school effectiveness literature is primarily derived from studies on urban elementary schools in the northern part of the United States (Purkey & Smith 1983). The primary criterion of effectiveness in these studies was knowledge of basic skills in reading and arithmetic (Rowan, Bossert & Dwyer 1983). Standardized achievement-test scores were compared across schools with students of similar socioeconomic backgrounds. Only limited research has been conducted on effective junior or senior high schools.

Second, most studies examined the *relation* or *association* between practices in school and student learning, but not *causality*. This is an important distinction. For example, increased height may be *related* to increased weight, but it does not *cause* increased weight; neither does increased weight cause increased height. An old adage states that "correlation does not prove causation." Blue eyes and blond hair tend to occur together, but they do not cause one another.

When experimental studies have been conducted (which could show cause and effect), researchers relied on volunteer teachers rather than on a sample that represented all teachers. Thus, research conclusions could be flawed because the teachers involved were not representative of teachers in general.

Third, findings and conclusions do not provide a simple checklist of practices of effective schools. Classrooms and schools are complex, interactive social institutions wherein practices that work in one setting or situation may be less effective in another.

As a prospective teacher, you need to know the research on effective schools and effective teaching. It can form a basis for practice. It is difficult to improve your teaching if you don't understand the basic premises of instruction and the research in your field. Conclusions from research, however, cannot be blindly followed. Situations change and varying environments, people, and events modify conditions for effective practice. In reflective thinking, the teacher continually compares (sometimes subconsciously) what is known about effective practice with decisions to be made or probable actions to be taken in a particular event.

Other Conceptions of Quality Schools

The basic criterion for determining quality in the effective-school literature is *knowledge of basic disciplines as indicated by student achievement*. Schools whose students score higher on achievement tests are judged more effective. This perception of quality schools is held by persons referred to in Chapter 3 as essentialists.

As is true for most aspects of human endeavor, there are other definitions of quality in schools. In this section, we will briefly explore several of them. The purpose is to provide a broader perspective as you consider what is quality in education, not to provide a comprehensive or complete set of quality indicators.

As a reflective inquirer, you will find it interesting to study the premises upon which each conceptualization of quality rests. What do the holders of each belief assume when defining quality? What do they seek from schools? To what extent do such conceptions lead to a more effective nation?

Eternal Truths

Both perennialists and essentialists value knowledge, but for perennialists, *knowledge of unchanging principles* is most important—knowledge of what in all times and places constitutes truth, beauty, and goodness. They believe

*W*hen public schools are successful, they become a national treasure. They can instruct and inspire our young people. They can give life to local communities, contributing to their economic growth and social well-being. They can pave the road to employment, greater opportunity, and more productive lives. In our pluralistic democracy, the schools can forge a common culture while respecting diversity.

Committee for Economic Development, *Investing in our Children: Business and the Public Schools*, 1985, p. 1.

students should be well versed in the classics, languages, and other fields of traditional knowledge. Robert Hutchins, former President of the University of Chicago, for example, advocated study of the one hundred Great Books. Therefore, the quality of the school would be determined by the extent to which students studied these great historical writings. For example, while essentialists would administer achievement tests to document knowledge of eternal truths, perennialists would want students to learn about those truths, speculate on them, and continue searching for them.

Skills for Democratic Living

Progressive education, based on the theories of John Dewey, provides an interesting contrast to the essentialists and perennialists when defining quality schools. For progressive educators, the purpose of schools is to educate students to think, solve problems, and make intelligent adjustments in a changing world and for a democratic ideal. Traditional subject matter is not important, nor should the curriculum be organized around the basic elements of conventional disciplines.

Skills needed for collective inquiry and cooperative action are important; however, the key word is *sharing*. The aim of schools, and therefore the primary indicator of quality, is to educate *socially sensitive problem-solvers who can cooperatively cope with their environment*. Instruction is based on activities, broad units that synthesize content, and problem-solving experiences.

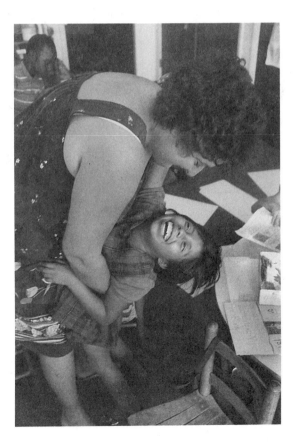

Can school quality always be judged by test scores?

Quality As Exploration

Some educators believe that quality in schools is to be judged by the *kinds of activities* in which students engage rather than by the *specific knowledge or skills they develop*. Maria Montessori, whom you read about in Chapter 2, was a leading advocate of this position. Montessori believed that the teacher should create a structured environment to provide sensory experiences with specially designed toys, manipulatives, physical activities, and an interactive curriculum. Once the teacher structures the environment, the intent is then to allow students to function freely within the environment. Each student learns differently according to needs, developmental level, and interests; there are no set outcomes for instruction.

Learning to Learn

Some educators believe that *learning how to learn* and *enjoying learning* is more important than learning a specific knowledge base. Their curriculum includes problem-solving activities that place the student in the position of inquirer, explorer, and discoverer of new information. They would want students to ask "why" and to seek underlying principles. Their school would be composed of science and social science laboratories in which to conduct experiments. Their students would learn how to use libraries and other resources for obtaining information. Their primary criterion of quality would be the extent to which schools provide explorations so that students would learn how to learn about the world.

National Needs

The commission reports of the mid-1980s, introduced in Chapter 2 and discussed in greater depth in a later section of this chapter, relate school quality to economic development. The reports call for shifts in curriculum so that this nation can compete more effectively in the international marketplace.

When the first Russian satellite was launched in 1957, the cry was for improved scientific prowess and technological advancement for national defense—and the National Defense Education Act was passed. The criterion for school quality is determined by immediate *national needs*; or at least such needs become the rallying cry for school reform.

Improving Disadvantaged Groups

One definition of quality schools involves the ability to bring about social change. More than fifty years ago, in the depths of the Great Depression, George Counts and other Reconstructionists proposed that schools should bring the benefits of a humane community—such as found in rural America—to city dwellers. His book, *Dare the School Build a New Social Order?*, described schools as part of a new democracy in which the populace arrived at more open and intelligent decisions.

Thirty years later, in the 1960s, activist social reconstructionists focused on the rights of the disadvantaged—poor, black and Hispanic, women, and persons with mental and physical disabilities. Civil rights legislation in

1964 marked a watershed in schooling. The fundamental criterion of quality was the *extent to which schools attended to the needs of disadvantaged groups.* Court actions led to busing and other means to achieve racial balance. Federal programs and grants required actions by schools to meet the needs of disadvantaged groups. School programs, organizational structures, and financial support would be modified as a result of the standard set by social reconstructionists. Their goal is to make schools more responsive to the needs of minorities by making student bodies more heterogeneous.

Homogeneity

Interestingly, the opposite viewpoint is also held in identifying quality schools. Some parents seek schools that are relatively homogeneous; students would be similar in their values, religion, income level, and race and ethnicity.

This view of quality schools holds that students do affect the values, attitudes, development, and achievement of other students. They believe that when children from poverty homes or other races are commingled with middle-class children, the achievement level of the middle-class students deteriorates, while discipline problems increase.

Based on this belief, parents have fought desegregation through the courts, moved from one community to another community which had a higher concentration of similiar homes and lifestyles, and sent their children to private schools. They believe that *homogeneity of student population* is a hallmark of quality schools.

Multiple Options

The quality of schools, for some, is judged by the *number of alternatives available to parents and students.* Elementary-school parents in Minneapolis have a choice of five kinds of schools for their children, including traditional and Montessori schools. Special schools for gifted and talented students are found in Louisiana and North Carolina. In Houston, high-school students may choose to attend either a neighborhood comprehensive high school or one of the magnet schools in the district that provides specialized opportunities for students (for example, hospitality careers, health professions, vocational careers, engineering professions, teaching professions, international baccalaureate, and performing and visual arts).

"Choice of schools" has been extended during the past few years to include the choice between public schools and tax-supported private schools. Because of the constitutional separation of church and state, state funds are not used to support church activities (as they are in Great Britain, West Germany, Iran, and most countries in South America); funding parochial schools directly is unconstitutional. Several means have been proposed, including the "voucher" system in which state funds would be paid to whatever schools students attended, whether public or private. This particular choice is a major issue, not yet resolved, facing educators and the general public today. In Chapter 13, where several issues in education are considered, it is discussed more fully.

The assumption behind each of these and dozens of other multiple approaches is that students will learn more effectively if they and/or their parents have a choice about the emphasis in their program, the school they will attend, or whether the school is public or private. *Quality schools, in this conception, involve choice.*

School Accreditation

Schools and universities usually are accredited by one of the following six regional associations that establish criteria for quality and judge whether or not their members meet those criteria.

▶ Association of Colleges and Preparatory Schools in the Middle States and Maryland
▶ Association of Colleges and Preparatory Schools of the Southern States
▶ New England Association of Colleges and Secondary Schools
▶ North Central Association of Schools and Colleges
▶ Northwest Association of Secondary and Higher Schools
▶ Western College Association

They base their criteria for quality primarily on the *availability of educational resources*. The assumption is that schools cannot provide quality education unless they meet certain minimum standards in their budgets, buildings, equipment, and faculty. Some of the criteria used in this assessment include the number of books in the library, student-teacher ratio, availability of properly furnished classrooms and laboratories, extensiveness of facilities and equipment, adequateness of the school's budget, educational levels of faculty preparation, and breadth and availability of curricular offerings.

Periodically, each school completes a self-study using the association's set of criteria. A team of educators then visits the school to determine if the report is accurate and if the school meets all criteria for reaccreditation.

Schools Cannot Provide Quality Education

In 1970, Ivan Illich challenged the educational establishment in *Deschooling Society* by proclaiming that schools limit rather than facilitate learning. He wrote, ". . . learning is the human activity which least needs manipulation by others. Most learning is not the result of instruction. It is rather the result of unhampered participation in a meaningful setting. Most people learn best by being 'with it,' yet school makes them identify their personal, cognitive growth with elaborate planning and manipulation" (Illich 1970, 39). To which eighteenth century educator discussed in Chapter 2 would you relate Illich's concept of education?

Students are schooled "to confuse teaching with learning, grade advancement with education, a diploma with competence, and fluency with the ability to say something new" (Illich 1970, 1). School programs do not educate, because they do not liberate the mind. While a major function of schools is supposed to be the forming of critical judgment, instruction uses static procedures, agreed-upon content, and previously approved measures of social control. The authority of the teacher causes multiple values in the classroom to "collapse into one. The distinctions between morality, legality, and personal worth are blurred and eventually eliminated" (Illich 1970, 32).

Schooling is a major first step in institutionalizing morals and values. Once the need for schools is accepted, people are easy prey to the dictates of other institutions. "This transfer of responsibility from self to institution guarantees social regression" (Illich 1970, 39).

Quality education, according to Illich, would include three elements: "provide all who want to learn with access to available resources at any time in their lives; empower all who want to share what they know to find those who want to learn it from them; and, finally furnish all who want to present an issue to the public with the opportunity to make their challenge known" (Illich 1970, 75).

He would reverse the responsibility for learning by shifting it from the school to the person. In Illich's system, students would be able to gain access to readily available resources as they define and achieve their own goals. Illustrative of these resources would be references available in libraries and other locations, skill exchanges so that persons could list their skills and availability to potential students, a peer-matching network so that a person might find a partner for a particular inquiry, and reference services for educators-at-large who could provide broader professional services, such as organizing networks, guiding parent and student choices, and guiding difficult intellectual explorations.

Commission Reports and Recommendations of the 1980s

Beginning in 1983, a wave of reports from government-, foundation-, and educational association-sponsored commissions defined what quality schooling was for them. In the following five years, more than three hundred such reports were issued. Some considered education in the nation; others made recommendations for particular aspects of teacher education; some related to specific subject areas (mathematics and science), and some to particular states (Washington, Florida, and New York) or regions of the country (Southern Regional Education Board). For the most part, the memberships of these commissions and task forces included business executives, politicians, and distinguished university administrators and liberal arts faculty. Very few members of the education profession were included. The perspectives and recommendations vary from report to report, but, when synthesized, provide another view of quality in schools.

These reports were precipitated by increasing evidence that America's schools had lost the luster of quality. Some of these indicators of poor quality were specified by the National Commission on Excellence in Education.

▶ International comparisons of student achievement, completed a decade ago, reveal that on 19 academic tests American students were never first or

*O*ur Nation is at risk. Our once unchallenged preeminence in commerce, industry, science, and technological innovation is being overtaken by competitors throughout the world. . . . If an unfriendly foreign power had attempted to impose on America the mediocre educational performance that exists today, we might well have viewed it as an act of war. As it stands, we have allowed this to happen to ourselves.

National Commission on Excellence in Education, *A Nation At Risk*, 1983, p. 5.

second and, in comparison with other industrialized nations, were last seven times.

► Some 23 million American adults are functionally illiterate by the simplest tests of everyday reading, writing, and comprehension.

► About 13 percent of all 17-year-olds in the United States can be considered functionally illiterate. Functional illiteracy among minority youth may run as high as 40 percent.

► Average achievement of high school students on most standardized tests is now lower than 26 years ago when Sputnik was launched.

► Over half the population of gifted students do not match their tested ability with comparable achievement in school.

► The College Board's Scholastic Aptitude Tests (SAT) demonstrated virtually unbroken decline from 1963 to 1980. Average verbal scores fell over 50 points and average mathematics scores dropped nearly 40 points.

► Many 17-year-olds do not possess the "higher order" intellectual skills we should expect of them. Nearly 40 percent cannot draw inferences from written material; only one-fifth can write a persuasive essay; and only one-third can solve a mathematics problem requiring several steps.

► There was a steady decline in science achievement scores of U.S. 17-year-olds as measured by national assessments of science in 1969, 1973, and 1977.

► Between 1975 and 1980, remedial mathematics courses in public 4-year colleges increased by 72 percent and now constitute one-quarter of all mathematics courses taught in those institutions.

► Average tested achievement of students graduating from college is also lower. (*A Nation at Risk* 1983, 8–9)

Recommendations from several of these commission reports are summarized below. Only their recommendations about curriculum and teachers are included even though several made important recommendations on school organization, school finance, and the relative responsibilities of federal, state, and local governments. If you wish to explore them in greater detail, a listing of major reports on educational reform in the 1980s is included in the References section of this chapter.

Between 1982 and 1987, more than thirty books were written on school quality. Several reflect major studies of schooling while others were based on the perspectives of leading educators. Several of these are also summarized in this section.

A Nation At Risk

The first and most widely publicized of the commission reports was initiated by Secretary of Education Terrel Bell in 1981. Concerned about the place of education on the national agenda, Bell appointed the prestigious National Commission on Excellence in Education, composed of eighteen educators and executives. Their report, *A Nation At Risk: The Imperative for Educational Reform*, followed eighteen months of study and numerous hearings across the country. Its major recommendations, summarized in the following paragraphs, were designed to correct the educational ills identified above.

Curriculum. Graduation requirements should be strengthened in five New Basics: four years of English, three years of mathematics, three years of science, three years of social studies, and one-half year of computer science. College-bound students should study foreign languages. Rigorous courses in the arts and vocational education should be provided. College admissions standards should be raised.

More time should be devoted to the New Basics. Consider seven-hour school days, 200- to 220-day school years. Reduce the administrative burden on teachers so they have more time to teach.

Grades should be indicators of academic achievement. Standardized tests should be administered at major transition points in a student's school experience.

Teachers. Employ qualified recent graduates in mathematics and science to overcome shortages. Provide grants and loans to attract outstanding students to teaching. Prospective teachers should meet high academic standards and demonstrate an aptitude for teaching. Develop career ladders and include peers in decisions about tenure and promotion. Make salaries professionally competitive, market-sensitive, and performance-based. Adopt an eleven-month contract.

Action for Excellence

The Task Force on Education for Economic Growth was appointed by the Education Commission of the States, an organization of forty-eight states and several territories whose purpose is to assist governors, state legislators, and state education officials develop educational policies. The Task Force was chaired by Governor James B. Hunt, Jr. of North Carolina and composed of forty-one legislators, educators, and business executives.

Curriculum. States and school systems should strengthen the public-school curriculum, enrich and increase the duration and intensity of academic learning, and develop a state plan for education and economic growth. States and communities should identify the skills they expect the schools to impart. Tests of general achievement as well as tests for specific skills should be periodically administered. Firm, specific, and rigorous standards for discipline, attendance, homework, and grades should be established.

Business leaders should become more active in schools through partnership programs.

Teachers. Improve the certification process. Make it possible for qualified persons without teacher education to serve in schools. Improve the recruiting, training, recognizing, and salary processes for teachers. Teacher effectiveness should be measured and rewarded. Principals should be explicitly in charge of educational quality.

> *W*e need to prepare the necessary human talent to keep the people in the nation responsive to the very competitive world of international commerce and trade.
>
> Task Force on Education for Economic Growth, Education Commission of the States, *Action for Excellence*, 1983, p. 28.

America's Competitive Challenge

The Business-Higher Education Forum, composed of top corporate executives and university presidents, published *America's Competitive Challenge:*

The Need for A National Response at the request of President Reagan. This forum stated that, "Our society must develop a consensus that industrial competitiveness on a global scale is crucial to our social and economic well-being." Its recommendations related to improving America's economic position in the world.

Curriculum. Prepare each student with a basic foundation in mathematics, science, and technology so the nation can better compete with foreign industries. Expand foreign-language studies.

Teachers. Upgrade skills of teachers in secondary science and mathematics.

Educating Americans for the Twenty-first Century

The National Science Board selected twenty educators, executives, and school board members to draft the report, *Educating Americans for the 21st Century.* Their goal: "By 1995, the nation must provide for all its youth a level of math, science and technology education that is the finest in the world, without sacrificing the American birthright of personal choice, equity and opportunity."

Curriculum. They proposed to require sixty minutes of mathematics and thirty minutes of science per day in Kindergarten through sixth grade, a full year of science in grades seven and eight, and more time devoted to mathematics, science, and technology in the secondary school. They would raise college entrance requirements to include four years of mathematics, four years of science, and one year of computer science. The school day, week, and year would need to be extended because of increased instruction in mathematics, science, and technology.

Local school districts should develop partnerships with governmental agencies and businesses. Business executives should develop plans for schools to use their new technology. States should establish rigorous standards for high-school graduation, and school districts for promotion; social promotion should be curtailed. The federal government should sponsor and finance national achievement tests, support excellent programs in math, science, and technology, and promote curriculum evaluation.

Making the Grade

The Twentieth Century Fund's Task Force on Federal Elementary and Secondary Education Policy was chaired by Robert Wood, University of Massachusetts. The twelve-person task force focused its report on the development of a coordinated federal policy that would support state and local efforts. Their recommendations dealt primarily with the federal role in education. The federal government should emphasize programs to develop basic science literacy for everyone and to promote advanced training in high schools. It should support special programs for the poor, handicapped, and in school districts with substantial numbers of immigrant children. It should maintain data banks of information on education and research on the learning process.

Curriculum. Although decentralized schools should be maintained, all should provide the same minimum core components. These include the basic skills of reading, writing, and calculating; technical capability in computers; training in science and foreign languages; and knowledge of civics. Every student should have an opportunity to learn a second language, but literacy in English is the schools' most important objective. Bilingual programs should be replaced with programs to teach non-English-speaking children to speak, read, and write English.

Teachers. Establish a master-teacher program funded by the federal government. (Master teachers would be experts identified through tests, recommendations, and observations who would be assigned as supervisors or curriculum-development specialists as well as teachers.)

> *T*omorrow I'll reform,
>   the fool does say;
> Today itself's too late;
>   the wise did yesterday.
>
> Benjamin Franklin, *Poor Richard's Almanack*, 1732

A Place Called School

After nearly a decade of research on thirty-eight public schools in seven states, John I. Goodlad published a report of his comprehensive study in *A Place Called School* and made recommendations for quality schools.

Curriculum. Too much emphasis is being placed on facts and low-level skills, with insufficient attention to writing, problem solving, analysis, and other higher-order processes. Facts must be tied to concepts. While teachers say they are teaching higher-order skills, they are not. The core curriculum should not be a common set of topics, but a common set of concepts, principles, skills, and ways of knowing. The curriculum should be organized with 18 percent of a student's time on literature and language, 18 percent on mathematics and science, 15 percent on social studies and society, 15 percent on the arts, 15 percent on career preparation or vocational education, and 10 percent on individual choice.

Vocational education should be a hands-on experience. Students should be able to change back and forth between vocational and academic programs. The best preparation for work is general education.

Teachers. Teachers should be better able to: teach in different ways for different purposes; vary the medium of instruction and student groupings; diagnose student problems; give clear instructions; give positive, helpful feedback; use time efficiently; provide personal attention to students; get and keep students engaged; and teach higher-order skills.

The Paideia Proposal

Twenty-two educators and scholars, under the direction of Mortimer Adler, recommended in *The Paideia Proposal* (1982) that schools should be more academically oriented.

Curriculum. Public schools should include no electives; the curriculum for all students should include three parts: (1) acquisition of organized knowledge by means of didactic instruction, lectures and responses, textbooks, and other aids—in three areas of subject matter: language, literature, and the fine arts; mathematics and natural science; and history, geography, and other social studies; (2) development of intellectual skills and skills of learning by coaching, exercises, and supervised practice in reading, writing, speaking, listening, calculating, problem solving, observing, measuring, estimating, and exercising critical judgment; and (3) enlarged understanding of ideas and values by means of Socratic questioning and active participation in discussing books (not textbooks) and other works of art and involvement in artistic activities (for example, music, drama, and visual arts).

Teachers. A liberal education is the best preparation for teachers. Teachers must know how to teach in the three ways outlined in the core curriculum and engage students more actively in their learning.

The Good School
Curriculum. In *The Schools We Deserve: Reflections on the Educational Crisis of Our Time*, Diane Ravitch presents her view of quality school programs.

> Now, in the interest of candor, I confess that I instinctively hew to John Dewey's admonition: "What the best and wisest parent wants for his own child, that must the community want for all of its children. Any other ideal for our schools is narrow and unlovely." The best and wisest parents, I expect, want their child to read and write fluently; to speak articulately; to listen carefully; to learn to participate in the give-and-take of group discussion; to learn self-discipline and to develop the capacity for deferred gratification; to read and appreciate good literature; to have a strong knowledge of history, both of our own nation and of others; to appreciate the values of a free, democratic society; to understand science, mathematics, technology, and the natural world; to become engaged in the arts, both as a participant and as one capable of appreciating aesthetic excellence. I expect such parents would also want a good program of physical education and perhaps even competence in a foreign language (Ravitch 1985, 277).

Teachers. Sara Lawrence Lightfoot provides portraits of two excellent urban high schools, two suburban high schools, and two elite private high schools in *The Good High School.* Each of the schools Lightfoot describes is very different, yet teachers displayed similiar qualities.

> One of the most striking qualities of these good schools is their consistent, unswerving attitude towards students. The first impression is that teachers are not afraid of their students. Ordinary adults often seem frightened by adolescents, fearing both their power and their vulnerability. . . . It is not that some teachers do not feel threatened by eruptions of violence, or do not wisely protect themselves from physical assaults, but rather that most good high school teachers seem to be unafraid of these young people who tend to baffle and offend the rest of us. (Lightfoot 1983, 342–343)

High-School Reform

Three other reports focused on reform in the American high school. The authors of the first two reports, Theodore R. Sizer and Ernest L. Boyer, described the elements of quality drawn from extensive exploration. The third report was drawn from discussions by more than two-hundred high-school and college teachers serving on committees of the College Board, and focused only on the college-bound student.

A Celebration of Teaching

Sizer's study was sponsored by the National Association of Secondary School Principals and the Commission on Educational Issues of the National Association of Independent Schools. His concepts were delineated in the provocative book, *Horace's Compromise*. In it, he shows teaching to be a subtle craft that is burdened by school bureaucracy, which stifles teachers' effectiveness. The report calls for secondary education to be reshaped into what he calls "Essential Schools." The elements of an essential school are as follows.

1. The ultimate ends of schooling are established by central authorities, but the detailed design for teaching and learning must be firmly in the hands of teachers and principals.
2. Strong incentives must be established to encourage students to learn and teachers to teach, and these will vary school by school.
3. Emphasis must be on quality of thought, with the traditional subject disciplines clustered into a few areas.
4. Students will assume considerable responsibility for their own education, as well as for some routine clerical and custodial jobs to keep the school operating.
5. Diplomas are awarded only upon the mastery of defined skills and knowledge.
6. Ethical values, such as fairness and tolerance, will be consciously a part of the school.
7. Per-pupil expenditure will not exceed that of conventional schools.

Traditional subject fields should be combined into a few broad, integrated areas of learning. Priority should be given to developing intellectual processes, such as reasoning power, expression, and interpreting data. Instructional focus is on quality of work rather than on sweeping coverage. Advancement would be by demonstrated understanding of the substance of a schools's educational program.

High School

In 1983, Ernest L. Boyer published *High School: A Report on Secondary Education in America*, which was sponsored by the Carnegie Foundation for the Advancement of Teaching. The report was based on field studies in fifteen high schools and research on secondary education. Boyer, former U.S. Commissioner of Education, framed the report to emphasize his own values about quality education.

Curriculum. Goals of secondary schools must be clarified. Mastery of the English language is the schools' most important priority. Writing skills are critical, and classes that teach writing skills should be limited to twenty students. Language proficiency should be assessed prior to entry into high school, with summer remedial courses for those needing special assistance. The interdisciplinary approach should be employed. The core curriculum includes literature, arts, foreign language, history, civics, science, mathematics, and technology. Seniors should complete an independent project. The three-track system—academic, vocational, and general—should be abolished.

Teachers. High-school teachers' loads should be limited to four courses, with a separate period to help individual students. An "excellence fund" should be established in each school to enable teachers to carry out special projects. Effective teachers should be recognized and rewarded; the average salary increased one-fourth over the next three years; a travel fund established; and a two-week Teacher Professional Development Term provided.

Academic Preparation for College

The College Entrance Examination Board established its Educational EQuality Project as a ten-year effort to strengthen the academic quality of secondary education and to ensure equality of opportunity for college entrance by all students. The focus of the report was college-bound secondary students.

Curriculum. The basic academic competencies are reading, writing, speaking and listening, mathematics, reasoning, and study skills. These competencies are the broad intellectual skills essential to effective work in all fields of college study. The basic academic subjects for effective college work are English, science, mathematics, social science, foreign languages, and the arts. Students should also have a basic knowledge of the computer.

Conclusion

Quality in schools—as in life—is defined in many ways. Some definitions are more valid than others; they are based on research or strong general perceptions that are important to a healthy society. In this chapter, we have explored several very different perceptions of quality in schools.

Some persons have defined quality as the impact schools have on academic achievement (effective schools), while others limit this definition to knowledge of basic skills or to knowledge of historic truths. Some consider schools' impact on society as the major criterion of quality, while others would judge quality by the schools' ability to respond to evolving national needs. Yet others consider processes used in school when specifying quality. In one conception, quality schools are judged by the kinds of activities in which students engage, while another perspective would consider the extent to which learning-activities help students learn how to learn. Some parents want their children to attend schools in which the population is homogeneous. Some educators have taken the position that quality schools include multiple options, and some parent groups have pressed for choice in schools as a major criterion of quality. Finally, some have despaired of schools as educational agencies, calling for deschooling America as the needed approach to improving learning.

These varying positions on quality schools reflect the diversity of values in America today. As we have seen, schools are a reflection of society, and America today is an amalgam of cultures. Schools in central cities, suburbs, and rural areas often convey different values and different conceptions of quality. Sometimes these differences are regional, with schools in the southeastern states differing from those in New England, the Midwest, or the Pacific coast. Indicators of quality shift with new pressures, new data on implications of schooling, and increased visibility of certain movements or factions in the nation.

These differing conceptions may be of value as you analyze schooling in America, in your area, and in specific schools that are of interest. How do your own values match with those of schools you observe or would consider for possible employment as a teacher? While we have defined central thrusts in quality indicators, no school is based on a single conception. Each reflects greater or lesser emphasis on each position. Which of the indicators of quality seem more relevant to you? How would you define school quality? In what ways does quality change over time? How is it affected by community mores and national needs? How does the definition of quality affect the school curriculum?

Building Reflective Inquiry Skills

Making A School Profile

By the time you completed high school, you had spent many days in school. This first-hand experience has given you an opportunity to reflect on the workings of schools and classrooms and perhaps has led you to consider teaching as your profession.

Seeing is not the same as observing. The process of seeing is mechanical, while observing requires analytical tools. In observing a school, be sure to collect data that reflect a broad-stroke picture of a school. As a student, much of your time was spent seeing rather than observing. Now that you are preparing to teach, a more analytical approach is needed to provide a clearer picture of the school. The research discussed in this and previous chapters has provided some basis for understanding the elements of quality schooling.

The twenty questions posed below provide structure for developing a school profile of an elementary, middle, or senior-high school. Responding to them may require contacts with a wide range of people and examination of school records. Work with other prospective teachers in collecting data and formulating your report. Some processes and sources for securing information include examining accreditation reports and curriculum guides; interviewing administrators, teachers, and students; driving around the school community; observing the school during breaks and lunch periods; and becoming acquainted with the layout and resources in the building.

School Profile

1. What is the history of the school?

2. How would you describe the facilities and the grounds of the school?

3. What type and size of school are you observing (for example, elementary, middle, junior high, senior high, magnet, or year-round)?

4. Does the school have any unique programs that might distinguish it from other schools in the area?

5. What is the ethnic composition of the students and teachers in the school?

6. Are the students ability-grouped for academic achievement? If so, how?

7. Does the school have specific rules and procedures for student conduct?

8. How would you describe the ambience of the school (for example, open, closed, warm, cold)?

9. Does the school emphasize one particular instructional format (for example, Madeline Hunter or Effective Use of Time)?

10. Do the students need to pass state, district, or school-based examinations to move to the next grade level?

11. Does the school have a PTA or PTO? How active is either organization in the school?

12. Has the school won any awards? If so, in what areas?

13. Do the teachers have a lounge area in which to meet and relax?

14. What is a typical day for a teacher at the observation-site school? (Give an hour-by-hour description for the day.)

15. How do most of the students arrive at the school?

16. What is the range of teaching experience of teachers in the school?

17. What percent of teachers have at least a master's degree?

18. How easy or difficult was it to obtain information about the school?

19. What would you do differently in collecting data the next time?

20. Once the above information has been collected, what one question would you ask that we did not include in this list?

Explorations

Exploration 1
Characteristics of Effective Schools
Read through the section of this chapter on effective-schools research and list characteristics of effective schools. Select one criterion and use it in observing in a school. To what extent does the school meet this standard? What incidents did you observe that indicated effective practice?

Exploration 2
Comparing Criteria on Quality Schools
Several definitions of "quality" in schools have been proposed in this chapter. Identify the salient characteristics of quality in each; then discuss with classmates the attributes of each. Are there any you would not subscribe to at all? Have you noted any of these characteristics of quality in the school in which you are observing? Any in the descriptions of the two schools in the Appendix?

How would you react to the statement: "There is no single set of quality criteria; there are only greater or lesser emphases of each in American schools."

Exploration 3
Understanding a School
Conduct a survey of a school. Describe and analyze the school plant and its equipment. Use diagrams, pictures, or drawings as illustrations if you wish. Some questions to guide your survey follow. You may also use the twenty questions in the Reflective Inquiry of this chapter.

General Features. How large is the school? How many and what kinds of classrooms? How are levels of instruction or departments grouped? When was the school built? What is the condition of the plant? Are the corridors and stairways wide and safe? Are there hall display cases and bulletin boards for students' work? How are they used? Are there any facilities planned for community use? What provisions are made to beautify the school and grounds?

Special Facilities. What special classrooms or other facilities are provided? If available, how is the auditorium utilized? Is there a health clinic? Physical education facilities? Conference rooms for parent-teacher conferences, student testing, meetings?

Classroom. What is the overall size of the room? What furniture is found in the room? What equipment and materials? How is the furniture arranged? How are bulletin boards and chalkboards used? What specific use does the teacher make of the physical setting?

Grounds. How large are the grounds of the school? What special playing fields or equipment are available? Is parking adequate?

Identify ways the building and other physical facilities enhance or limit the school program. What examples are there of flexible use of the physical plant and furniture?

Write a description of the school. How many students? What grades and how organized? What special personnel and how many classrooms?

References

Adler, M. (1982). *The Paideia proposal: An educational manifesto.* New York: Macmillan.

Austin, G. R. (1979). Exemplary schools: Search for effectiveness. *Educational Leadership, 37,* 10–14.

Boyer, E. L. (1983). *High school: A report on secondary education in America.* New York: Harper & Row.

Boyer, E. L. (1987). *The early years.* New York: Harper & Row.

Block, J. H. (Ed.) (1971). *Mastery learning: Theory and practice.* New York: Holt, Rinehart and Winston.

Brookover, W. B. & Lezotte, L. W. (1979). *Changes in school characteristics coincident with changes in student achievement* (ED 181 005). East Lansing, MI: Michigan State University, College of Education, Institute for Research on Teaching.

Counts, G. S. (1932). *Dare the school build a new social order?* New York: John Day.

Duchastel, P. C. & Merrill, P. F. (1973). The effects of behavioral objectives on learning: A review of empirical studies. *Review of Educational Research. 43,* 53–69.

Edmonds, R. R. (1979). Effective schools for the urban poor. *Educational Leadership, 37,* 15–23.

Feistritzer, E. C. (1986). *Profile of teachers in the U.S.* Washington, D.C.: National Center for Education Information.

Glenn, B. C. & McLean, T. (1981). *What works? An examination of effective schools for poor black children.* Cambridge, MA: Harvard University, Center for Law and Education.

Good, T. L. (1981). Teacher expectations and student perceptions: A decade of research. *Educational Leadership, 38*(5), 415–21.

Goodlad, J. I. (1984). *A place called school: Prospects for the future.* New York: McGraw-Hill.

Havelock, R. G. & Huberman, A. M. (1977). *Solving educational problems: The theory and reality of innovation in developing countries.* Paris, France: UNESCO.

Houston, W. R. (Ed.). (1986). *Mirrors of excellence: Reflections for teacher education from training programs in ten corporations and agencies.* Reston, VA: Association of Teacher Educators.

Illich, I. (1970). *Deschooling society.* New York: Harper & Row.

Lightfoot, S. L. (1983). *The good high school: Portraits of character and culture.* New York: Basic Books.

Little, J. W. (1982). Norms of collegiality and experimentation: Workplace conditions of school success. *American Educational Research Journal. 19*(30), 325–40.

Lortie, D. C. (1975). *Schoolteacher: A sociological study.* Chicago: University of Chicago Press.

Morris, V. C.; Crowson, R. L.; Hurwitz, E. & Porter-Gehrie, C. (1981). *The urban principal: Discretionary decision-making in a large educational organization.* Chicago: University of Illinois at Chicago Circle.

Naisbitt, J. (1984). *Megatrends.* New York: Warner.

Powell, A. G.; Farrar, E. & Cohen, D. K. (1985). *The shopping mall high school: Winners and losers in the educational marketplace.* Boston: Houghton Mifflin.

Purkey, S. C. & Smith, M. S. (1983). Effective schools: A review. *The Elementary School Journal, 83*(4), 427–452.

Ravitch, D. (1985). *The schools we deserve: Reflections on the educational crisis of our time.* New York: Basic Books.

Resnick, D. P. & Resnick, L. B. (1985). Standards, curriculum, and performance: A historical and comparative perspective. *Educational Researcher, 14*(4), 5–20.

Rowan, B., Bossert, S. T. & Dwyer, D. C. (1983). Research on effective schools: A cautionary note. *Educational Researcher, 12*(4), 24–30.

Rutter, M.; Maughan, B.; Mortimore, P.; Ouston, J. & Smith, A. (1979). *Fifteen thousand hours: Sec-ondary schools and their effects on children.* Cambridge, MA: Harvard University Press.

Sizer, T. (1984). *Horace's compromise: The dilemma of the American high school.* Boston: Houghton Mifflin.

Stallings, J. A. (1980). Allocated academic learning time revisited, or beyond time on task. *Educational Researcher,* December, 11–16.

Wynne, E. (1980). *Looking at schools: Good, bad, and indifferent.* Lexington, MA: Lexington Books, D.C. Heath.

Selected National Commission Reports

American Federation of Teachers. (1986). *The revolution that is overdue: Looking toward the future of teaching and learning.* Washington, DC: ERIC Clearinghouse on Teacher Education.

Business-Higher Education Forum. (1983). *America's competitive challenge: The need for a national response.* Washington, DC: Business-Higher Education Forum.

Carnegie Forum on Education and the Economy, Task Force on Teaching as a Profession. (1986). *A nation prepared: Teachers for the 21st century.* New York: Carnegie Forum on Education and the Economy.

College Board EQuality Project. (1983). *Academic preparation for college: What students need to know and be able to do.* New York: College Entrance Examination Board.

Committee for Economic Development. (1985). *Investing in our children: Business and the public schools.* New York: Committee for Economic Development.

Council of Chief State School Officers. (1984). *Staffing the nation's schools: A national emergency.* Washington, DC: Council of Chief State School Officers.

Council of Chief State School Officers Study Commission. (1986). *Education and the economy.* Washington, DC: Council of Chief State School Officers.

Education Commission of the States. (1985). *New directions for state teacher policies.* Denver: Education Commission of the States.

Education Commission of the States. (1986). *What next? More leverage for teachers.* Denver: Education Commission of the States.

Educational Development Center, Inc. (1985). *Improving our schools: Thirty-three studies that inform local action.* Newton, MA: Educational Development Center, Inc.

Holmes Group. (1986). *Tomorrow's teachers: A report of the Holmes Group.* East Lansing, MI: The Holmes Group.

Metropolitan Life. (1984–86). *The Metropolitan Life Surveys of American teachers.* Series of four documents: *The American teacher* (1984), *The American teacher 1985, The American teacher 1986: Restructuring the teaching profession*, and *Former teachers in America* (1986). New York: Metropolitan Life.

National Association of Secondary School Principals/National Education Association. (1986). *Ventures in good schooling: A cooperative model for a successful secondary school.* Reston, VA: National Association of Secondary School Principals/National Education Association.

National Commission for Excellence in Teacher Education. (1985). *A call for change in teacher education.* Washington, DC: American Association of Colleges for Teacher Education.

National Commission on Excellence in Education. (1983). *A nation at risk: The imperative for educational reform.* Washington, DC: Government Printing Office.

National Education Association. (1982). *Excellence in our schools: Teacher education, an action plan.* Washington, DC: National Education Association.

National Education Association. (1986). *The learning workplace: The conditions and resources of teaching.* Washington, DC: National Education Association.

National Governors' Association. (1986). *Time for results: The governors' 1991 report on education.* Washington, DC: National Governors' Association.

National Science Board, Commission on Precollege Education in Mathematics, Science and Technology. (1983). *Educating Americans for the 21st century.* Washington, DC: National Science Foundation.

Task Force on Education for Economic Growth. (1983). *Action for excellence: A comprehensive plan to improve our nation's schools.* Denver: Education Commission of the States.

Twentieth Century Fund, Task Force on Federal Elementary and Secondary Education Policy. (1983). *Making the grade.* New York: Twentieth Century Fund.

U.S. Department of Education. (1984). *The nation responds: Recent efforts to improve education.* Washington, DC: U.S. Government Printing Office.

U.S. Department of Education. (1986). *What works: Research about teaching and learning.* Washington, DC: U.S. Department of Education.

U.S. Department of Education. (1986). *First lessons: A report on elementary education in America.* Washington, DC: U.S. Government Printing Office.

Inquiring Into the Processes of Teaching

CHAPTER SEVEN

The Concept of Curriculum

OBJECTIVES

By the end of this chapter, you will be able to:

1. Differentiate between curriculum and instruction.
2. Distinguish between the formal, written curriculum of schools and the informal, or "hidden," curriculum.
3. Comprehend contemporary curriculum patterns and school organization.
4. Use basic curriculum planning terminology.
5. Distinguish between goals and objectives.
6. Write goals, and objectives derived from those goals.
7. Know the three major domains of learning (cognitive, affective, and psychomotor).
8. Know trends impacting elementary and secondary curricula.

KEY WORDS AND CONCEPTS

Affective domain
Articulation
Carnegie unit
Continuity
Curricular integration
Curriculum
Cognitive domain
Goals
Hidden curriculum
Instruction
Objectives
Psychomotor domain
Scope
Sequence

What is Curriculum?

In his book *Developing Attitude Toward Learning* (1984), Robert Mager begins with the following poem:

> There once was a teacher
> whose principal feature
> was hidden in quite an odd way.
> Students by millions
> and possibly zillions
> surrounded him all of the day.
> When finally seen by his scholarly dean
> and asked how he managed the deed,
> he lifted three fingers and said,
> "All you swingers
> need only to follow my lead.
> To rise from a zero to big campus hero
> to answer these questions you'll strive:
> > Where am I going?
> > How shall I get there?
> > And how will I know I've arrived?

"Where am I going?" is the question we attempt to answer in curriculum development. *Curriculum*, in this sense, is comprised of the statements of outcomes we are attempting to achieve with students as well as the subject matter (history, mathematics, science, music, art, and so on) to be offered in a school setting. "How shall I get there?" deals with the instructional delivery system. That is, given certain outcomes we want to achieve, and given the nature of the students with whom we are working, what strategies will be used to be most effective in achieving those outcomes with those students? "How will I know I've arrived?" deals with evaluation—not just evaluating how well students have done on a particular test or during a given grading period, but how effective the entire process of schooling has been.

The purpose of this chapter is to deal with questions of curriculum, of *ends* rather than *means* (the means of achieving the ends, again, are instruction). As an introductory note to this chapter it is useful to remember that the social motivations that have governed the curriculum in our schools evolved from religious motivations in the days of the seventeenth-century Massachusetts Bay Colony, to political motivations following the American Revolution (the need for an informed electorate in a representative democracy). The "Americanization" of masses of immigrants to an industrialized society was a driving force in the late nineteenth and early twentieth centuries, as was national defense in the 1950s. Today, schools seem to be struggling to keep up with a rapidly changing, dynamic society. All of these various motivations continue to affect curricular issues in a number of ways today, for their effects are cumulative over time.

When dealing with curricular issues the real question is, "What are we attempting to achieve in schools?" Obviously, schools have many functions, and there is seemingly no end to debate over adding more to the curriculum. Most schools at present are viewed as convenient means to address what is important to society, what used to be done by other social agencies (such as the family or church), and functions that are viewed as suffering from neglect. Many schools now offer classes designed to help students learn how to cook, sew, drive an automobile, raise livestock, build a bookshelf, repair an automobile, dance, choose a marriage partner. In addition, other classes deal with personal values, sexual relationships, and the dangers of chemical abuse.

How did all of these—in addition to the vaunted traditional mission of reading, writing, and arithmetic—come to be part of the school's curriculum? And more controversially, should they continue to be dealt with as part of the formal curriculum of schools?

Half a century ago, a prominent educator of the time, Harold Benjamin, wrote a satire entitled *The Saber-Tooth Curriculum* under the pen name of J. Abner Peddiwell. The book is an ostensible interview with Peddiwell, a professor of paleolithic (stone-age) education, held in a Tiajuana, Mexico bar over libations known as Tequila Daisies. Professor Peddiwell, when asked how formal education began, tells of a time when children learned all that they needed to survive and function in their culture from their parents. Boys learned to hunt and fish from their fathers, and girls learned about cooking, sewing, and gathering berries and other foods from their mothers.

One day, however, someone got the idea that perhaps the best hunter in the clan knew a little more than most of the other members and could be persuaded to pass that knowledge on to the younger generation if he received a larger portion of the communal meat supply. The idea took hold, and soon someone else had the notion that maybe the woman who had the best skills at food-gathering could do the same for the girls of the clan. Before long, classes for the younger generation were in full swing on topics like "fish-catching-with-hands" and "saber-toothed-tiger-scaring-with-fire." Everything seemed to be going very well with the new "school" system.

After some time, however, conditions changed. The fishhook was invented and proved to be much more effective than hands for catching fish. Saber-toothed tigers, alas, became extinct. Much discussion ensued about the worth of those classes, which still continued. Eventually, though, an attitude prevailed among the clan members that the traditional classes should continue because they were "good mental discipline" for children, even though knowledge of the subject matter had long since ceased to be of functional use to the survival of the individuals and the culture.

A constant challenge faced by educators today is the degree to which the ideas, knowledge, skills, and attitudes addressed in school curricula are current and useful. Consideration of that question, though, cannot be predicated solely on the basis of the moment at hand. As many writers have pointed out, change is accelerating to such an extent in our world that virtually by the time we implement an idea or approach in school settings, technological and social conditions have changed and the information may be outdated. Some estimates indicate that knowledge is doubling every four to five years, that the *amount* of information available about our world (and other worlds) is accelerating so quickly that it is almost impossible to make definitive decisions about what children should be taught in order for them to function as adults.

The Participant-Observer and the Curriculum

In Chapter 5 you learned about the participant-observer method of social research—a methodology involving being part of a group while still maintaining the objectivity necessary to scrutinize and analyze the culture and practices of the group. The participant-observer methodology is extremely important, as well, in seeking to understand the curriculum.

Many writers have distinguished between the *formal* curriculum of schools (the philosophy, goals, and objectives with which school people work to help students achieve) and the *informal, implicit,* or *hidden* curriculum. The hidden curriculum consists of those things that individuals learn in school settings that are rarely, if ever, written down and officially sanctioned as curriculum outcomes. In some cases, the hidden curriculum can be at least as powerful as the formal curriculum. For example, below are some outcomes that can be argued to be part of the hidden curriculum of many schools. While written in the form of instructional objectives, they are unlikely to be found as part of the formal, written curriculum of any school. But they are, nonetheless, things that are often learned in school.

▶ Students will learn to compete with their peers while conforming to authority figures.

▶ Students will learn to value a symbol of someone's perception of their achievement (A, B, C, D or F) more than what they may have actually learned.

▶ Students will develop the attitude that learning is like a vaccination. Once you've "taken" something you shouldn't have to "take" it again.

▶ Students will learn that mathematics is for boys, and literature and writing are for girls.

▶ Students will learn that schools, especially primary grades and preschools, reward traditionally feminine behavior more than traditionally masculine behavior. Children draw flowers and rainbows. Many preschool and kindergarten classrooms have a "traditional housekeeping" area with little counters, a miniature sink and stove. How many have an area for woodworking or taking apart a bicycle?

▶ Students will learn that being a superior student means being quicker than your peers at figuring out what teachers *really* want and being willing and able to give it to them.

▶ Students will learn whether they are "high-achieving" students or "low-achieving" students by the ways their teachers respond to them, and will tend to act in ways consistent with what they perceive to be their teachers' expectations.

The hidden curriculum is powerful. It is extremely important that educators understand its power and do the utmost to attempt to consciously shape its effects on students, rather than just leaving those effects to chance.

The Language of Curriculum

Every area of human endeavor has a specialized language. Curriculum specialists, including teachers, also have their own when talking of curricular matters. You will need to communicate in the "tongue" of curriculum. The purpose of this section is to provide you with a brief vocabulary lesson, which you will likely use over and over again.

Scope is a term which refers to decisions about the **breadth of the subject matter** to be studied. For example, mathematics is an important subject at literally every level of schooling. What should be the scope of mathematics taught in first grade? What mathematical concepts and information should be presented in first grade? Fifth grade? In high-school algebra? These questions are issues of the *scope* of the mathematics portion of the curriculum. Scope decisions occur at a number of levels. The curriculum guide for a one-year high-school course on United States History, for example, is the result of a number of scope decisions. Which elements of the nation's history are really worth studying? The individual teacher, in the same manner, makes decisions on scope while developing a one-week unit on the impact of the ideas of Thomas Jefferson on the country's founding. And the teacher must make even more limited scope decisions regarding which concepts from that unit to attempt to teach in a single lesson.

Sequence, as the term implies, deals with decisions about the **ordering of concepts, information, or ideas** for the most effective instruction. Returning to our mathematics analogy for a moment, is it important for students to show that they know how to multiply one digit by two digits before we confront them with learning tasks involving the multiplication of two digits by two digits? In the same vein, should students learn how to

Classrooms aren't the only places in which the curriculum is implemented.

compose words into sentences, and sentences into paragraphs, before we ask them to address the writing of an original essay?

Continuity refers to the **planned repetition** of concepts and ideas across various levels of the curriculum. In social studies, for instance, the basic concept of human groups begins with the family, in kindergarten, and proceeds throughout the elementary and secondary curriculum to encompass the neighborhood, city, state, nation, and world. In all cases the student is studying increasingly complex interactions among humans in group settings. In mathematics the basic concepts of number and numerals (the symbolic representations of numbers) are repeated in a planned manner from the young child's first learning to count, to the advanced high-school student's studying of linear programming.

Articulation is a term used to describe the **setting of boundaries** or parameters between courses of study. It is important, for instance, for the sake of efficiency and the elimination of unplanned and unnecessary duplication, that eighth-grade teachers of English language arts be able to assume that their students have learned some basic, prerequisite ideas in seventh grade, so that they can expand on those ideas rather than reteaching them. At the seventh-grade level, for example, students can learn the basic notions of following plot and character development and learn to recognize figurative language. The teacher can then challenge eighth-grade students to follow more complex plot and character development in stories and to recognize the ways in which figurative language and sound devices contribute to literary meaning. Because of careful articulation between English teachers at these two grade levels, eighth-grade teachers can assume that their students have been introduced to these ideas the previous year and need not begin "from scratch." Students will, of course, need some refreshing of the concepts before more expansive instructional activities begin.

Integration is the term used to describe efforts to **blend curriculum across subject matter lines.** A high-school course entitled "The Politics of Ecology," for instance, might be planned by American government teachers and by chemistry teachers. In such a course, students could learn to take soil and water samples, test them for contaminants, attempt to trace those contaminants to their source(s), determine which governmental agencies regulate the source or sources, and work to bring about more effective enforcement of environmental regulations. The higher the grade level, the more likely that "hardening of the categories" sets in, which artificially divides subject-matter specialists and their separate efforts, and the greater the need for conscious, systematic effort to integrate the curriculum across subject-matter boundaries.

Who Decides Curricular Issues?

States have authority over their educational systems and the curriculum—what is taught—in their schools, so long as curricular policies and practices do not deny rights assured under the Constitution. Most states delegate a considerable degree of their authority over schools to local boards of education or boards of trustees. A few states (such as New York) have established minimum statewide curricula, which their schools are expected to provide to students. These may range from a simple list of subjects to be taught (United States history, English, algebra, and so on) to rather highly-detailed specifications of objectives for each grade level and in each subject. Following, for example, are the minimum "essential elements" for third grade mathematics in Texas public schools.

EXHIBIT 7.1   **From Texas Education Agency, 1984**

d. Mathematics, grade three. Mathematics, grade three, shall include the following essential elements:

1. Concepts and skills associated with the understanding of numbers (whole, integer, and non-negative rational) and the place-value system. The student shall be provided opportunities to:

    A. compare and order;

    B. use odds, evens, and skip counting;

    C. use place value;

    D. identify decimal place value using money (tenths and hundredths);

    E. use fractions (models);

    F. recognize equivalent fractions (using models); and

    G. read and write whole numbers.

2. The basic operations on numbers (addition, subtraction, multiplication, division), their properties, and their uses. The student shall be provided opportunities to:

    A. add and subtract whole numbers;

    B. add and subtract decimals using money;

    C. multiply whole numbers;

    D. divide whole numbers (using concrete materials); and

    E. recognize inverse operations.

3. Experience in solving problems by selecting and matching strategies to given situations. The student shall be provided opportunities to:

    A. estimate with whole numbers;

    B. use basic operations with whole numbers and with decimals using money;

    C. use geometry; and

    D. use charts and graphs.

4. Measurement concepts and skills using metric and customary units. The student shall be provided opportunities to:

    A. measure (using measuring instruments);

    B. solve problems using metric and customary unit measures (no conversion); and

    C. find perimeter.

5. Properties and relationships of geometric shapes and their applications. The student shall be provided opportunities to identify characteristics of two- and three-dimensional shapes.

6. The representation of numbers on a line and pairs of numbers on a coordinate plane. The student shall be provided opportunities to:

    A. locate points on a number line; and

    B. work with addition and multiplication tables.

7. The use of probability and statistics to collect and interpret data. The student shall be provided opportunities to:

    A. collect and organize information; and

    B. interpret and construct picture and bar graphs.

The Contemporary Curriculum

The curriculum of elementary and secondary schools in the United States today is a product of all the previously-mentioned forces and is dynamic rather than static. A few states have general statewide curriculum patterns mandated from the state level, but most tend to leave many curricular decisions to local elected boards of education. Generalizing about the curriculum of elementary and secondary schools, therefore, is a risky enterprise and can only be done in very broad terms.

Nonetheless, you need to have some grasp of current emphases and curricular patterns, and that is what this section is intended to provide. The central notion is that deciding what to include in the curriculum of elementary and secondary education is an *economic* process. The basic principle of economics is that people have unlimited wants, but limited resources. In schools we have a limited amount of *time* (temporal resources), of *money* (fiscal resources), of *people* (human resources), and of *instructional aids* such as texts, workbooks, computers, and computer programs (material resources). How should those limited resources be organized and used? What must be *left out* of the curriculum because of limited resources?

Schools are commonly organized into the primary grades; the upper-elementary, or intermediate, grades; junior high school or middle school; and high school.

The Primary Grades

Primary grades is a term usually used to describe kindergarten through third grade. The clear, contemporary emphasis in the early grades of school is in the areas of reading, English language arts, and mathematics. Research over the past several decades, as well as practical experience, has shown that these skills are vital to success in later school grades and that if those skills are not assured in the early years of school, the child is disadvantaged for many years to come. The effects of *not* providing these "basic skills" early can be devastating for both the individual child and for the school.

"Reading, writing and arithmetic," though, do not constitute the entirety of the curriculum of the primary grades. The curriculum also includes the following:

► basic science concepts, such as skills in observing and classifying the elements of the world around us.
► health concepts, such as cleanliness and the importance of rest, sleep, exercise (and increasingly, information about the negative effects of the misuse of drugs).
► physical education concepts and skills, such as gross and fine motor skills, rhythmic body movement, and participation in games and sports.
► fine arts concepts and skills, such as expression through visual arts, listening to and participating in musical activities, and body and voice expression in theater arts.
► social studies concepts and skills, such as knowledge of social roles and being able to function in social groups, such as the family, class, and neighborhood; basic notions of economics (if you spend your money on candy you don't have it to buy other things); how rules are made and the importance of rules; basic geographic concepts, such as the use of maps and globes; and history of the state and nation.

The Upper-Elementary or Intermediate Grades

Upper-elementary or intermediate grades is a term often used to refer to grades four through five or four through 6, depending on how a local school system organizes its higher grade levels. Building on the basic ideas gained in the primary grades, the upper-elementary grades expand the basic concepts of reading, language arts, mathematics, science, social studies, fine arts, and physical education into increasingly complex and broad applications. In social studies, for example, the basic notions of human groups and social roles introduced at the level of the family in the primary grades are expanded into the notions of the neighborhood, city, state, nation, and world. Language arts and theater arts may be combined so that the student not only acts out a play or skit written by someone else but actually tries his or her hand in developing scripts that are then performed. In the same manner, games in physical education may be created by students; science information and concepts are used in original and creative ways to observe and classify phenomena and in the design of experiments; and mathematical reasoning is expanded to concepts as complex as exponential notation and factoring.

Allocating Time in Elementary Grades

One of the major decisions that must be made about allocating resources in the school curriculum is time allocation. How much time should be spent on various subjects? Should the same time be spent on everything, or are some subjects more important than others and therefore deserving of more time at the expense of other subjects?

Below is an actual school schedule that compares the amounts of time spent in certain subjects at the second-grade level (a primary grade) and at the fifth-grade level (an upper or intermediate grade). What does this display tell you about the relative importance that has been placed on certain subjects in these grades? Why do you think those decisions were made in this way?

	Second Grade	Fifth Grade
English/Language Arts	120 min.day	90 min./day
Mathematics	60 min./day	60 min./day
Science	100 min./week	225 min./week
Social Studies	100 min./week	225 min./week
Physical Education	100 min./week	120 min./week
Health	60 min./week	60 min./week
Fine Arts (Art, Music)	125 min./week	150 min./week

Middle Schools and/or Junior High Schools

A local school system may decide to organize middle schools (grades six, seven and eight) or junior high schools (grades seven and eight, or seven through nine). The contemporary trend is clearly toward the middle-school concept, a trend that will be discussed in greater depth later in this chapter.

Whatever the choice of the local school system, it is in these grades that a notion known as the "Carnegie unit" comes into play in allocating time for various subjects. Whereas in the early elementary grades decisions are usually made on what proportion of the school day and week will be devoted to certain subjects, in the middle school/junior high school the requirements are more commonly stated in terms of how many "units" are required for graduation and progression to high school. One Carnegie unit equates to one fifty-minute class period per day for the school year. Thus, a one-semester course carries one-half unit, while a course of study that is scheduled for the equivalent of fifty minutes per day for the entire year carries one unit of credit.

At the junior-high/middle-school level, the subjects studied each year are normally English language arts, mathematics, science (with greater specificity in terms of life and earth science in grades seven and eight), social studies (including both history and geography), fine arts (with, again, increasing options for specialization in music, visual arts, or theater arts), and health. Electives are made available on a limited basis.

Exhibit 7.2 is a reproduction of an actual seventh-grade course-selection sheet from a middle school for the 1986–87 academic year. Notice that the student, in this case, has a maximum of three, one-semester electives and that the majority of the courses are required. Why do you suppose that the asterisked (*) courses have the notation that the student can carry no more than two of these electives? What does this tell you about the values of the school and its leaders?

EXHIBIT 7.2   Course Selection Sheet—Grade Seven 1986–87

Name _____ Sex _____ Birthdate _____

Home Telephone No. _____ Parent's Work No. - Mom - _____

Dad - _____

REQUIRED COURSES

Language Arts or ESL	Life Science	Physical Education
Social Studies	Math	Computer Literacy (1 sem.)

ELECTIVES - Choose a total of 3 semesters. Number choices in order of preference.

_____ 712 French I-A (1 sem.)

_____ 710 Spanish 1-a (1 sem.)

_____ 711 German 1-a (1 sem.)

_____ 791 Art 7 (1 sem.)

_____ 781 Concert Choir (1 sem.)

_____ 103 Theater Arts 1 (1 sem.)

_____ 370 Intro to Industrial Arts 1-a (1 sem.)

_____ 271 Exploratory Homemaking 1-a, Foods (1 sem.)

_____ 272 Exploratory Homemaking 1-a, Foods (1 sem.)

_____ 100 Speech I (1 sem.)

*_____ 270 Crafts (1 sem.)

* Select no more than 2 of these classes.

*_____ 660 Piano Keyboard (1 sem.)

*_____ 273 Homemaking Special Projects (1 sem.)

*_____ 980 Enriched Reading (1 sem.)

APPROVAL NEEDED

*_____ 102 Performing Arts (1 sem.) _____

*_____ 475 Number Sense (1 sem.) _____

*_____ 762 Cadet Band (2 sem.) _____

*_____ 760 Concert Band (2 sem.) _____

*_____ 860 Symphonic Band (2 sem.) _____

*_____ 659 Concert Orchestra (2 sem.) _____

*_____ 665 Symphonic Orchestra (2 sem.) _____

*_____ 782 Chorale (2 sem.) _____

ALTERNATE ELECTIVES

Please write in the names of two other choices in case of schedule conflicts.

1. _____ 2. _____

Student Signature _____ Parent Signature _____

The High School

Contemporary high schools tend to be comprehensive high schools: that is, they offer not only academic coursework that provides a general liberal education and preparation for college, but usually offer vocational tracks as well, which equip graduates who choose those tracks with marketable skills.

Academic requirements for high-school graduation tend to be distributed in the following manner with, as discussed previously, each Carnegie unit equivalent to a year of study:

English language arts:	3–4 units, with the 4-unit requirement becoming increasingly common.
Mathematics:	2–3 units, with 3 units increasingly common.
Social Studies:	2–3 units, usually consisting of a year of United States history, a year of world history or world geography, a semester of American government, and increasingly a semester of economics.
Physical education:	1–2 units, but often allowing substitutions for other forms of physical activity such as marching band, Reserve Officers Training Corps (ROTC), drill team, and so on.
Health:	normally one-half unit (1 semester) of study.
Electives:	sufficient electives to complete minimum requirements of 21–22 units for graduation. These electives, of course, provide the opportunity for students to specialize in academic or vocational tracks.

The following chart gives a graphic display of the variation in requirements for high-school graduation among the various states.

TABLE 7.1 **Number of Course Units Required for High School Graduation in 1980 and 1984, Year Effective, and Increase in Number of Units Required, by State: 1984**

State	Number of Units Required, 1980	Number of Units Required, 1984	Year Effective [1]	Increase in Number of Units Required, 1980 to 1984
Alabama	20	20	1984	0
Alaska	19	21	1985	2
Arizona	16	20	1987	4
Arkansas	16	20	1988	4
California	([2])	13	1987	—
Colorado		Local boards determine		—
Connecticut	([2])	20	1988	—
Delaware	18	19	1987	1
District of Columbia	17½	20½ or 23	1985	3 or 5½
Florida	([2])	24	1987	—
Georgia	20	21	1988	1
Hawaii	18	20	1983	2
Idaho	18	20	1988	2
Illinois	[2]16	16	1988	0
Indiana	16	19½	1989	3½
Iowa[3]		Local boards determine all but 2½ units		—
Kansas	17	20	1988	3
Kentucky	18	20	1987	2
Louisiana	20	23	1990	3
Maine	16	16	1984	0
Maryland	20	20	1984	0
Massachusetts[4]		Local boards determine all but 5 units		—

TABLE 7.1   Number of Course Units Required for High School Graduation in 1980 and 1984, Year Effective, and Increase in Number of Units Required, by State: 1984

State	Number of Units Required, 1980	Number of Units Required, 1984	Year Effective [1]	Increase in Number of Units Required, 1980 to 1984
Michigan[5]	Local boards determine all but ½ unit			—
Minnesota	15	20	1982	5
Mississippi	16	16	1984	0
Missouri	20	22 or 24	1988	2 or 4
Montana	16	20	1986	4
Nebraska[6]	160 semester hours	200 credit hours	1991	—
Nevada	19	20	1986	1
New Hampshire	16	19¾	1989	3¾
New Jersey	18½	18½	1984	0
New Mexico	20	21	1987	1
New York	16 or 18	16 or 18	1984	0
North Carolina	16	20	1987	4
North Dakota	17	17	1984	0
Ohio	17	18	1988	1
Oklahoma	18	20	1987	2
Oregon	21	22	1988	1
Pennsylvania	13	21	1989	8
Rhode Island	16	16 or 18	1988	0 or 2
South Carolina	18	20	1987	2
South Dakota	16	20	1989	4
Tennessee	18	20	1987	2
Texas	18	21 or 22	1988	3 or 4
Utah	15	24	1988	9
Vermont	16	15½	1989	-½
Virginia	18	20 or 22	1988	2 or 4
Washington	15	18	1989	3
West Virginia	17	20	1985	3
Wisconsin	(²)	[7]13½	1989	—
Wyoming	18	18	1984	0

—Not applicable.

1. Effective for the graduating class of this year.

2. Local boards determine requirements.

3. Legislative requirements have been in effect for many years for 1½ years of social studies and 1 year of physical education/health. Local boards determine the remaining requirements.

4. Massachusetts has had legislative requirements in effect for many years. One year of American history is required along with 4 years of physical education/health. The local boards determine additional requirements.

5. Michigan's legislative requirements have been in effect for many years for a half a year of social studies. The local boards determine the remaining requirements in January 1984, the State board published graduation requirement guidelines which local boards are urged to incorporate.

6. In 1980, 160 semester hours were required for grades 9–12 with specific subject area requirements determined by local boards. Legislation enacted in April 1984 required 200 credit hours for graduation with at least 80 percent in core curriculum courses. The State board is conducting hearings to define core courses.

7. Electives are the option of local boards. The State recommends that local boards require a total of 22 units.

NOTE: If there are two numbers for units required, there are two different graduating programs available.

Source: Education Commission of the States, Department of Research and Information, *Clearinghouse Notes.* "Minimum High School Graduation Course Requirements in the States," August 1984. Reprinted with permission.

Curricular Trends

The curricula of elementary and secondary schools continue to be an issue of debate and change. What should be taught? At what levels should ideas be taught?

Trend: More and More, Earlier and Earlier

One major trend is that more and more complex information is being introduced earlier in schools. It is not uncommon for a concept that was taught in the fifth grade five years ago to be taught in the fourth grade today. With the increasing impact and use of preschools and televised instruction (such as found on "Sesame Street") prior to the formal beginnings of school, primary-grade teachers often find distinct challenges in meeting the differential needs, knowledge, skill levels, and experiences of their charges—who may (or may *not*) have been reared with day-care, preschool, and televised instruction.

Exhibit 7.3 is an extreme example of this phenomenon. It is an actual *first grade* mathematics quiz and worksheet, emphasizing geometric concepts, assigned to a child of one of the authors in 1987. Does this resemble any mathematics you learned in first grade?

EXHIBIT 7.3   First Grade Mathematics Worksheet, 1987

Name _____

Geometry Quiz - Fill in the blanks.

1. A circle has _____ degrees.

2. A triangle has _____ degrees.

3. This is called a _____ triangle when all the sides and the angles are equal.

4. These are called _____ lines.

5. These are called _____ lines.

6. A right angle has _____ degrees.

7. If an angle has <u>more</u> than 90° then it is called an _____ angle.

8. If an angle has <u>less</u> than 90° then it is called an _____ angle.

9. These are called _____ lines.

10. What is the missing angle?

$\angle A = 33°$
$\angle B = 50°$
$\angle C = \underline{\hspace{1cm}}°$

Answer box

90°	acute	perpendicular	square
360°	polygon	intersecting	rectangle
480°	equilateral	straight	triangle
180°	scalene	parallel	circle
97°	obtuse	lost	polygon
107°			

EXHIBIT 7.3 First Grade Mathematics Worksheet, 1987

Name _____

Triangles — Tell whether the triangle is <u>equilateral,</u> <u>isosceles,</u> or <u>scalene</u>.

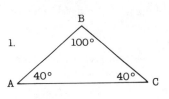

1.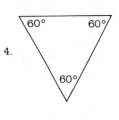

2.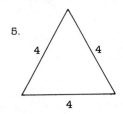

3.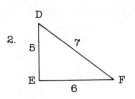

_____   _____   _____

4.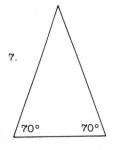

5.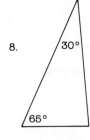

6.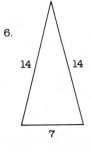

_____   _____   _____

In each triangle, write the measure of the third angle.

7. 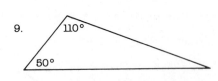   8.   9.

_____   _____   _____
_____

Trend: Increasing Elementary Subject Specialization

As a corollary to the preceding trend, the tendency for elementary teachers to be subject-matter specialists in addition to being generalists is growing. Most states require elementary teachers to be prepared to teach reading, English language arts, mathematics, science, social studies, music, visual arts, and physical education. The majority of elementary teachers are therefore prepared as generalists. Increasingly, however, elementary schools are "departmentalizing" along subject-matter lines to provide students with greater opportunities to study the various subjects in depth with teachers who are more highly prepared in a given subject.

Trend: From Junior High School to Middle School

The growth of middle schools has been one of the most significant phenomena in schooling in recent times. Junior high schools are what the name implies: preparation for high school. The emphasis in junior high schools is on subject matter and on providing students with the necessary prerequisites to enter high school with a sufficiently firm foundation of subject matter.

While middle schools do not ignore the importance of subject matter, they place emphasis as well on the importance of the student and the variety of transitions that students of this age undergo. In the early adolescent years, biological changes occur in their bodies and their brains. Hormonal secretion and the nature of social interactions change. New body hair appears, new urges compete for attention with academic pursuits, the peer discussion of girls centers on boys rather than dolls and boys' discussion centers on girls rather than sports. Girls often mature physically more quickly than their male counterparts, sometimes finding to their chagrin that they are the tallest persons in the class. Complexion problems and physical appearance become major concerns.

The middle-school concept differs from the junior high concept not only in grade levels addressed and in subject matter emphasis, but also in philosophy, which places considerably more attention on helping students cope with the multitude of personal and academic transitions common to the early adolescent years. From 1965 to 1978, the number of middle schools in the United States increased from 63 to 4,060, one of the most dramatic shifts in the history of American public education (Oliva 1982, 333).

Trend: From Basic Skills to Attitudes and Decision-Making

The "back-to-basics" movement of the early 1980s is giving way to an increased emphasis on student attitudes, critical thinking, and the ability to make moral decisions. Research over the past several decades on what actually occurs in elementary and secondary classrooms has resulted in criticisms that too much time is spent in rote memorization of information and too little time on the complex attitudes and skills needed to use information to make decisions in an increasingly complex society.

While basic skills certainly cannot be ignored and are vital to an individual's success in school and to the prosperity of a nation, the contemporary trend is toward teaching how to use information to make decisions. The emphasis on indoctrination of culturally acceptable "right" and "wrong" answers in the moral domain, prevalent in the earlier years of American schools, has given way to curricular materials that engage students in the process of making moral decisions (Costa 1985; Hensel 1986). Increasingly, emphasis is placed on the process of decision making.

Trend: Changing Graduation Requirements and Differentiated Diplomas

Just as schools are tending to provide more information in earlier grades, so too are they tending to demand more rigorous requirements for grade-level promotion and graduation and to recognize differential achievement through differentiated diplomas or transcripts.

Requirements for high school graduation have changed in the past several years (see Table 7.1) to include more required study of English and mathematics, and often the addition of economics. Several states have also enacted legislation or regulations providing for differentiated diplomas or transcripts for high-school graduation. In some cases, the distinction is literally between a certificate of attendance (documenting that a student attended school for the minimum amount of time), a diploma attesting to the successful completion of the minimum requirements, and an advanced "honors" recognition attesting to a high level of achievement in more difficult coursework, which may take the form of a differentiated diploma or transcript.

Trend: The Use of Standardized Tests

Spurred by research on effective schools, which shows that increased student achievement is closely linked with the attention paid by school officials to the results of standardized achievement tests, states have dramatically increased their reliance on standardized achievement tests to monitor student progress at the state level, and in some cases, to require minimum scores on standardized achievement tests for grade-level promotion and high-school graduation.

New York has, for decades, required high-school students to pass its Board of Regents examination in order to graduate; but in more recent times, Florida and twenty-two other states (see Table 11.6) have enacted test requirements for grade-level promotion, and still others have implemented broad-range testing programs to provide data on student progress from year to year so that curricular or instructional changes could be implemented to address any defiencies identified through those testing programs.

Trend: Preparing Students for an Unknown Future

Despite what futurists and other savants might say, the future is not readily predictable. Yet teachers deal in the future as much as in the present. Our profession's purpose is to empower young people, by providing the appropriate knowledge and tools, to function and persevere in a very uncertain future. Clearly, as futurists and economists tell us, we have moved beyond an economy based on manufacturing goods for the rest of the world. The future of our cultural well-being will be based more on the productivity of the mind than on the productivity of factory labor.

Electronic technology is a reality for today's students.

Curriculum and Instruction

In previous sections of this chapter, we have examined the essence of curriculum, patterns of curriculum in schools, and trends. As we pointed up earlier, curriculum and instruction are different—but interdependent—concepts. *Curriculum* refers to the outcomes we are attempting to help students achieve in a learning setting: the knowledge, skills, and attitudes we work to foster in students. *Instruction*, on the other hand, refers to the *means* we use to attempt to bring about those outcomes: lectures, simulations, laboratory exercises, discussions, inquiry sessions, and numerous other teaching techniques.

The approach we present to you is an *outcome-driven* conceptualization of the relationship between curriculum and instruction. That is, the outcomes we are attempting to achieve should be a major determining factor in the means chosen to bring them about.

Here is an example. Inquiry teaching (that is, teaching students to discover ideas on their own) is a very popular approach to teaching. On the other hand, despite its popularity, there are types of outcomes for which the inquiry approach is simply not appropriate: learning the alphabet, multiplication tables, or periodic tables, for example. Using drill and recitation until students have mastered some basic terms and have achieved some level of comfort with the new material is much more productive for the success of those outcomes. The ability to inquire assumes basic knowledge with which to begin the inquiry.

Goals and Objectives

Goals and objectives are the stuff of curriculum development and provide the basis for success suggested by Robert Mager's poem, quoted at the beginning of this chapter.

Teaching is intentional behavior change. As teachers, we are in the business of helping students who cannot spell or add to learn how to spell or add, who are captives of their own immediate experience to experience vicariously through reading, for example, of the hero's struggle to conquer fear in Stephen Crane's *The Red Badge of Courage* and Homer's *Iliad*. We are helping students to learn how decisions are made so that they can have a greater measure of personal power over their own destiny. We are, in short, in the profession of empowering others.

Goals and objectives provide direction. They are, in a very real sense, a map to the destinations we seek. Like the practice of medicine, teaching has elements of both art and science—perhaps best typified in Gage's book, *The Scientific Basis of the Art of Teaching* (1978). Effective teaching is systematic, aimed toward helping students achieve pre-defined knowledge, skills, and attitudes. For teaching to be systematic, goals and objectives must be clearly delineated. This section is designed to help you learn how to state goals and objectives.

Goals

"A curriculum goal is a purpose or end stated in general terms without criteria of achievement." (Oliva 1982)

Goals are broad, general statements of what schools seek to accomplish. They provide broad direction for educational programs. They are relatively timeless and do not provide measures of determining when they have been accomplished.

An example of a goal might be this statement: *"The students of this school will achieve mastery of basic skills and fundamental processes."* The preceding is a valuable goal, which provides direction for the conduct of educational programs. By itself, however, this goal also holds some difficulty for the teacher, since it does not clearly spell out how it is to be accomplished and since it can be interpreted in a number of ways. Transforming curriculum goals into more specific, observable elements that can help focus instruction involves the development of objectives.

Objectives

Objectives are derived from goals. In essence, objectives give substance to goal statements by identifying the evidence we may be willing to accept that a goal is being achieved. Mager (1975) points out that most types of well-stated objectives identify the following components:

1. **The behavior expected of the student.** What is it that we can observe that we are willing to accept as evidence that an objective is being achieved? The key to this component is the use of an action *verb*. *Write, describe, compare and contrast*, and *list,* for example, are all explicit action

words. They tell what we expect students to be able to do. Here, words like "understand" or "appreciate," by themselves, are not very helpful. How do we know if someone "understands the causes of the Great Depression?" What will we see that will lead us to believe that a student "appreciates classical music?" Understand and appreciate are marvelous words to use in goals. When writing objectives, however, they do not provide the necessary specificity.

2. Conditions under which the behavior is to be demonstrated. Do we want students to write their responses, to give them orally, to perform them, as in a play? Are we satisfied to receive responses via a multiple-choice test or do we want written essay responses?

3. The degree of mastery required. How good is good enough? If not otherwise stated, the degree of mastery is assumed to be 100 percent. The degree of mastery must be stated if anything less than 100 percent is acceptable. There is, by the way, no magic formula for deciding the proper degree of mastery. That is a professional decision which comes, at least in part, from the importance of the concept or idea being learned. If you are preparing someone to pick the winners of horse races, for instance, 51 percent is a pretty good success rate. Your student will make money at that rate. If, on the other hand, you are teaching someone how to pack parachutes—one mistake in a thousand is too much. Is learning twenty of the twenty-six letters of the alphabet good enough? No, because *all* of the letters are needed to communicate. How about solving problems in analytic geometry? Is anything short of 100 percent *un*acceptable?

Domains of Learning

A critical element in writing objectives is knowing that educational outcomes are generally divided into three areas, which educators call *domains*: cognition (intellectual operations); affect (attitudes, feelings, values); and psychomotor (body movement). The development of these domains was initiated by psychometricians (specialists in testing human performance) in the mid-1950s to provide structures for their work. Only later did these categories become incorporated into designing more efficient and effective ways to help people learn to perform those acts.

It is also important to understand that although these domains are categories for dividing up educational outcomes for purposes of analyzing them and systematically addressing them, all of them exist together in reality and in students. Take reading and writing, for instance. In reading and writing one must know what letters, words, and sentences mean and also the correct order for letter symbols (called spelling). In addition, though, one's attitude about reading and writing is important. And the psychomotor domain comes significantly into play in reading and writing. Reading involves rapid eye movement, and writing requires very close coordination between hand and eye.

While almost every element of learning involves more than one of these domains of learning, knowing the *taxonomies* for classifying educational objectives in each of these domains is crucial. Taxonomies are arrangements of order and complexity. The taxonomy in each of these domains is *hierarchical* and *cumulative*. That is, each level in each domain is more complex than the preceding level, and each successively advanced level assumes the ability to perform all of the levels which precede it.

The Cognitive Domain

The pioneering work of Benjamin S. Bloom and his colleagues in the mid-1950s paved the way for more systematic thinking in education. The cognitive domain deals with intellectual processes. Bloom and his colleagues (1956) delineated six levels of intellectual processes: knowledge (or recall), comprehension, application, analysis, synthesis, and evaluation.

Knowledge (or recall): This is the lowest level of the cognitive domain. It involves repeating back to the instructor (orally or in writing) exactly what was taught: the letters of the alphabet, or spelling, or pronunciation drill, or the multiplication tables.

Comprehension: Here students are asked to translate knowledge into their own words. "Summarize," "explain," and "tell in your own words" are operant action verbs at this level.

Application: At this level, the student can not only restate something in the same terms it was taught and translate it into his or her own words, but can also actually *do* something with the knowledge.

Analysis: Analysis in this sense means to break something into its constituent elements: for example, "The student will analyze and compare two bonding chemical reactions."

Synthesis: Synthesis here means to put elements together in a combination that is *unique for that individual*, as in, "The student will write an essay in which she or he takes a position on the use of the atomic bomb at Hiroshima and Nagasaki."

Evaluation: The term "evaluation" here means an assessment or judgment—but at the highest level of intellectual operation—requiring the ability to know, comprehend, apply, analyze, and synthesize in order to be properly and fully done.

The Affective Domain

In the affective domain of learning (Krathwohl, Bloom & Masia 1964) we deal with feelings, attitudes, and values rather than intellectual operations (keeping in mind that feelings, values, and attitudes all have a cognitive base). To best understand the levels within the affective domain (again, hierarchical and cumulative), it is helpful to preface the level descriptors with the words "willingness to." In the affective domain we deal less with the **ability** to perform certain operations and more with the student's **willingness** to do them.

Receiving (or attending): At the most basic level, we are interested here in the student's willingness to pay attention, (a prerequisite for additional learning in *any* domain).

Responding: Again, the willingness to respond—which assumes that some attention has been paid to what is going on. It is entirely possible (and often happens, of course) that students do know what is going on in class and are still unwilling to respond, for a variety of reasons.

Valuing: The student is willing to indicate that he or she places a value on something, considers it important and of a higher priority than something else.

Organization: At this level the student's discrete value judgments become organized in relationship to one another and affect overt choices: for example, the student makes a choice not to consume illegal drugs offered by a friend.

Characterization by a value or value complex: At the highest level in the affective domain, values become organized to the point of being internalized and a habitual part of the student's life; for example, the student follows classroom rules even when the teacher is not present.

The affective domain is a subject of serious controversy in education. Historically, schools have been accorded the responsibility more for the development of the intellect than for the development of student attitudes. Without meeting the most basic levels of the affective domain (receiving and responding), though, it is difficult to see how much in the way of intellectual development can take place. Increasingly, schools are also being called on to help students make value judgments concerning realms beyond the school setting. Controversy regarding the need or desire for affective education in public schools will continue. But the real debate centers more on *whose* values should be taught than on *whether* values should be taught.

At the very least, we agree with Robert Mager's (1984) minimal affective objective: When students leave your class they should like your subject matter *no less* than when they came to that class.

The Psychomotor Domain

The psychomotor domain deals with the use of the body in learning, whereas the cognitive and affective domains both involve the use of the mind. As Oliva (1982, 362–363) has pointed out, development of a taxonomy for the psychomotor domain has lagged far behind those in the cognitive and affective domains. Quoting Simpson (1972), Oliva lists the following categories:

Perception: The student will identify a woolen fabric by its feel.

Set: The student will demonstrate how to hold the reins of a horse when cantering.

Guided response: The student will imitate a right-about-face movement.

Mechanism: The student will mix a batch of mortar and water.

Complex overt response: The student will operate a 16-mm projector.

Adaptation: The student will arrange an attractive bulletin board display.

Origination: The student will create an original game requiring physical movements.

The lack of thorough development of a taxonomy of the psychomotor domain is problematic, especially when considered in the light of the importance of psychomotor skills in many basic learning outcomes. Reading and writing, for example, require a high degree of hand-eye coordination and fine motor skills, and they are unquestionably essential to much of what we do in schools. A fair amount of research indicates that students with communication-skill deficiencies improve markedly *if they learn to type*. The reasons are obvious but often overlooked. In many cases, students have not learned the necessary hand-eye coordination to be able to write something in a form in which *they* can read what they have just written! In learning to type, they must concentrate on each individual letter, and once typed on paper the letters are much more clearly readable than their own writing. Our experience, incidentally, is that this holds for high-school students as well as for young children.

Conclusion

Although many prospective teachers view the opportunity to lead and interact with students in a classroom setting to be the heart of teaching, increasing evidence demonstrates that the true core of teaching occurs in planning for that direct instructional contact. Curriculum development, the systematic planning of goals and objectives to be attained in working with students, gives direction and meaning to the interaction between student and teacher. Without that planning, the interaction can degenerate into meaningless dialogue day after day. With systematic planning and solid instruction, the learning setting can become a synergistic environment—one in which the needs of all are met together by their interaction.

Building Reflective Inquiry Skills

This is an exercise designed to help you become more skilled at writing objectives in at least two domains. Here is a curriculum goal from earlier in this chapter:

This school will help its students develop the abilities necessary for citizenship in a participatory democracy.

Your assignment is to write objectives in both the cognitive domain and the affective domain that would be consistent with this goal. Consider what an individual needs to know and to be able to do intellectually to be a citizen in a participatory democracy. What does she or he need to believe, to value, to feel?

Write at least four objectives in the cognitive domain, two of those above the level of knowledge, or recall.

Write at least three objectives in the affective domain.

Remember to state your objectives as learner outcomes, not teacher actions. Remember, too, that the objectives must be observable (something you can see), clearly stated, and—unless otherwise qualified by you—met with 100 percent mastery.

To get you started, here is an example of an objective that would address one part of the goal written above:

The student will demonstrate respect for the opinions of others by listening to differing points of view expressed by other students.

This objective addresses an attitude more than a skill, and therefore is primarily affective. How about the next example?

The student will know the procedures for registering to vote in local, state, and national elections.

Here the emphasis is on what the person knows rather than on an attitude or value, and is therefore primarily cognitive in emphasis. Now try writing your own objectives drawn from the goal above.

Explorations

Exploration 1
Finding Curriculum Guides
School systems usually have published curriculum guides to provide guidance and structure for different subjects at different grade levels. Find a curriculum guide and examine it. The following are some sources for curriculum guides:

1. The library of your college or university. Many libraries maintain collections of elementary- and secondary-school curriculum guides from school systems in their geographic area.

2. The Kraus Curriculum Development Library. This is a microfiche collection of literally thousands of curriculum guides, in every subject commonly taught in elementary and secondary schools, from across the country. Your library may be a subscriber to this microfiche collection.

3. School systems in your immediate area. Many school systems maintain professional libraries for their faculty and may allow you access to those professional libraries.

4. Teachers you know who may be willing to share a curriculum guide with you.

In examining curriculum guides, look for statements of goals and objectives. Are the objectives written in terms of student outcomes? Are most of them observable? Do they provide structure to the teacher in planning for instruction?

Exploration 2
Examining Local School Organization
This chapter provided you with a broad, general description of how various schools are organized. It is important for you to develop skills in inquiring into how elementary and secondary schools are organized in your locale. The questions you need to investigate, then, are these:

1. How are elementary schools organized in your area? Do they include K–5, K–6, K–8, or is kindergarten even included in most elementary schools? Do they operate on a "self-contained classroom" model, in which almost all subjects are taught to a group of students in one teacher's charge, or are the schools "departmentalized," that is, do students move from teacher to teacher for specific subjects? If so, is this true for all subjects and all grades? If not, which subjects and which grades?

2. Which seems to be prevalent, junior high schools or middle schools? Or, as alluded to in the previous question, are grades seven and eight included within an elementary context? If middle schools or junior high schools are evident, what are the requirements for graduation and entrance to high school? How do they vary from the patterns presented in this chapter?

3. Are high schools organized to include grades 9–12, or to include 10–12? What are the requirements for graduation? Do they issue differentiated diplomas or transcripts that depend on the student's program and achievement?

References

Association for Supervision and Curriculum Development (1985 Yearbook). *Current thought on curriculum.* Alexandria, VA.

Bloom, B. S., Ed. (1956). *Taxonomy of educational objectives: Handbook I: Cognitive domain.* New York: Longman.

Costa, A. L., Ed. (1985). *Developing minds: A resource book for teaching thinking.* Alexandria, VA: Association for Supervision and Curriculum Development.

Education Commission of the States (August 1984). Minimum high school graduation course requirements in the states. *Clearinghouse Notes.*

Denver: Department of Research and Information.

Gage, N. L. (1978). *The scientific basis of the art of teaching.* New York: Teachers College Press.

Giroux, H. A., Penna, A. N. & Pinar, W. F., Eds. (1981). *Curriculum & instruction: Alternatives in education.* Berkeley, CA: McCutchan.

Goodlad, J. I. (1984). *A place called school.* New York: McGraw-Hill.

Hensel, B. Jr. (1986, September 29). It's hip to be square: Teaching morals new trend in public schools. *Houston Post*, 1A, 10A.

Krathwohl, D. R., Bloom, B. S. & Masia, B. B. (1964). *Taxonomy of educational objectives: Handbook II: Affective domain.* New York: David McKay Company.

Mager, R. F. (1975). *Preparing instructional objectives.* 2d edition. Belmont, CA: Fearon Publishers.

Mager, R. F. (1984). *Developing attitude toward learning.* 2d edition. Belmont CA: David S. Lake Publishers.

Oliva, P. F. (1982). *Developing the curriculum.* Boston: Little, Brown.

Peddiwell, J. A. (1939). *The saber-tooth curriculum.* New York: McGraw-Hill.

Schubert, W. H. (1986). *Curriculum: Perspective, paradigm, possibility.* New York: Macmillan.

Simpson, E. J. (1972). The classification of educational objectives in the psychomotor domain. *The Psychomotor Domain, 3,* 43–56. Washington, DC: Gryphon House.

Texas Education Agency (1984). *State board of education rules for curriculum.* Austin, TX: Texas Education Agency.

Planning to Teach Students

OBJECTIVES

By the end of this chapter, you will be able to:

1. Differentiate between the forms and the purposes of behavioral, problem-solving, expressive, and affective objectives.
2. Design a lesson that incorporates one or more of these objectives.
3. Differentiate between an objective and an activity.
4. Incorporate a series of related lessons into a unit using all of these objectives.
5. Discuss the relationships between forms of instruction, students' activities, and instructional objectives.

KEY WORDS AND CONCEPTS

Activities
Affective objective
Behavioral objective
Expressive objective
Lesson plan
Prerequisite knowledge and skills
Problem-solving objective
Unit plan

What Is Instructional Design?

Some of you have had an opportunity to play a team sport; others of you have had the opportunity to watch football, basketball, baseball, or other team sports on television. You have probably heard coaches and sportscasters discuss the strengths and the weaknesses of each team and the contributions individual players will bring to the contest. Each coach has an idea of how his (or her) team can best meet the challenge and has communicated this to the entire team through discussions and practices of the strategy for that individual game. Designing instruction is closely analogous to preparing a game plan for a team.

Good classroom instructional designers know the strengths and the weaknesses of their students, and they know the challenges posed by the curriculum. They have a variety of instructional strategies that may be used to capitalize on the students' strengths, as well as strategies that will help reduce the areas of weakness. And, because most teaching is accomplished in large groups, the designers have an overall strategy that helps an entire class coordinate their efforts. Teachers spend up to twenty-four hours a week planning and evaluating instruction (Imig 1987), almost as much time as they spend teaching. As you begin your teaching career, we advise you not only to read about instructional design, but also to observe other teachers and to ask them about their planning strategies.

Notice that in the previous paragraph we used the term *classroom instructional designer*. This term was used deliberately to differentiate the instruction you will be designing for your students from the work that curriculum developers engage in as they write projects for industry, the military, commercial publishers, and entire school districts. This type of instructional design is often considered a specialization within itself (Gagne & Briggs 1979) and is beyond the scope of this textbook. In your first years of teaching you are unlikely to be charged with designing the instruction for the entire district or even for the school. You will be responsible for designing your own instruction to meet the special needs of your own students so that they can reach the goals established by your curriculum. Your curriculum may be set, but choice to implement that curriculum creatively and effectively is up to you.

EXHIBIT 8.1   **Thinking Through Instructional Design**

There are many ways to teach mathematical computation—worksheets, drill and practice sessions in small groups, computer drills, and the like. One first grade teacher we work with turns her class into a pizza parlor. She brings in red checked table cloths, flowers, and lots of construction paper. Then, the children order "supplies" for the restaurant, pay for the supplies, and "make" the pizzas. Other students, customers, come in and place their orders for construction paper pizzas. They are served pizza and drinks by a student who also figures the bill. The customers pay for the pizza with play money.

In this chapter we will discuss how one plans for classroom instruction, both the short term plan known as a lesson plan and the longer unit of instruction known as a unit plan. These plans will include:

1. An analysis of the curriculum;
2. The preparation of instructional objectives;
3. The activities one will use to accomplish the objectives;
4. The formative evaluations of success;
5. The summative evaluations of success.

Analyzing the Curriculum

Most schools or school districts will have prepared a curriculum guide for the grade level and the subject area that you will be teaching. Such guides provide an indication of what topics are covered at your particular grade level and for your particular subject area. This is the district's way of assuring that all important topics are covered without needless repetition. Although there may be no guide for all of the content areas you will be expected to cover, there are probably guides for similar content areas that you may use as resources. The curriculum guides for your grade level and content areas—and the guides for those grades and content areas immediately prior to, and subsequent to, yours—will be important resources as you think about your own class and your own students.

Another important set of resources are the texts that you will be using. In some states, texts are adopted at the state level, and teachers must choose their materials only from the state-approved texts; in some states school districts have an opportunity to choose the texts directly from the publisher. Although you may design instruction *without* using textbooks, you still need to examine carefully those texts that you will be issuing to the students. You should become familiar with the language demands of the texts, the content covered, and the organization of material so that you can evaluate when to use the textbook and when to supplement the text.

Once you have the texts and the curriculum guide, you are prepared to analyze the curriculum in order to teach. As you begin this analysis, it will be helpful to keep three points in mind:

1. The total amount of time you have available to cover the major topics you will be expected to cover;
2. The assumptions you have about your students' prior knowledge and skills as they begin each section;
3. The general learning goals you have set for your students.

Let us look at each of these points in detail.

Time

The total time you have available for the course, or for each content area, includes your expectations for students working outside of class. The content includes all topics you will be expected to cover, plus any additional information that you have elected to include. As we discussed in Chapters 3 and 6, time is an important consideration in any instructional decision. You never have enough time to do *everything* you want to do in a course. Therefore, you must consciously be aware of the total amount of time that you do have. A colleague of ours, who is a professor of social studies, is fond of telling about a number of his student teachers who have found themselves having to teach all of U.S. history from the Civil War to the present day in one month. Even experienced teachers sometimes find that the end of the year is approaching faster than the end of the syllabus.

Time may be defined as the total hours you have contact with the students, minus the administrative classroom duties and outside interruptions, plus the time you expect students to work outside of class. As we discussed in Chapter 4, that time outside of class may vary due to students' work responsibilities, their out-of-school activities, their home environment, and their individual commitment to completing homework. We do not recommend that you eliminate homework. Indeed, homework can be a very important learning aid if it is appropriately designed (Bennett 1986). We do recommend that in your preliminary analysis of your curriculum you refrain from *assuming* that students will do their homework because you assign it.

Once you have a sense of the content you will cover and the time available for that content, it is important to examine the curriculum to ascertain what is assumed about students' previous learning.

Prior Knowledge and Skills

Any textbook or curriculum guide contains unwritten assumptions about the knowledge and the skills that students bring with them to class. In your preliminary examinations of the curriculum, make as many of these unwritten assumptions as explicit as possible. For example, students in a computer programming class may be expected to have a basic level of knowledge about how to operate a computer. They may be expected to have used the computer as a tool in other classes, and now they will learn more advanced applications. For teachers whose students have never seen a computer before, the curriculum guide for this course would be far too advanced. The teacher may need to design *two* sets of instruction, one for the students who have the necessary prerequisites and one for students who do not have the necessary prerequisites.

Benjamin Bloom (1976) developed a theory that explains why student performance differs on any given learning task. According to this theory,

1. Up to 50 percent of the differences in achievement among students are due to the possession, or lack of possession, of the *cognitive entry skills* needed to begin the task. If, for instance, the learning task involves reading, are the reading materials at an appropriate level for these students? If the task is to teach individuals how to multiply two digits by two digits, can the individuals multiply two digits by one digit?
2. Up to 25 percent of the variance is due to what Bloom and his colleagues call *affective entry characteristics*. Most simply stated, does the learner *believe* she or he can succeed in the task—at least enough to give it a try? If a learner has the necessary cognitive skills but is not willing to try, the task is not likely to be completed. By the same token, learners with certain skill deficiencies may be able to overcome them if they are *willing* to make a major effort.

3. Up to 25 percent of the variance is due to *timely and effective feedback* from the teacher and/or the instructional materials. We may have the skills; we may believe we can do it; but without timely feedback, we may make a mistake that remains uncorrected and confounds the whole effort.

Keep in mind a number of cautions about this theory, however. The first is that it applies to *groups* of students and not to individuals. Other factors may enter into the effort of a single individual. That brings us to the second caution. Human behavior has multiple causes, and it is dangerous to be overly simplistic in attempting to explain any given behavior on any given day. Learners, for example, may have the necessary cognitive skills, may believe they can do the task, and may be provided sound, effective feedback and still do poorly, because they are ill that day; or their parents fought all night in the next room; or a relative, or a beloved pet, recently died; or any number of other variables that can distract them from academic work.

If this theory has any validity, up to 75 percent of the variance in achievement by a group of students on a given learning task is due to what they bring with them to the task. Skillful instructional designers must analyze the learning task to understand which prerequisite knowledge and skills are required. Then, through diagnostic tests, writing assignments,

Today's teachers rarely plan in quiet seclusion.

and discussion, they must determine if learners have the required background for the learning task. If not, the instruction should first provide that background.

To anticipate the prior knowledge your students will have *before* you meet them for the first time, discuss your curriculum with an experienced teacher who has taught the same content areas and ask which topics within the curriculum seemed to need more time and which topics needed less time. Talking with the teachers who have taught the classes and grades immediately prior to yours will also be helpful. This will tell you what content has been covered and what has not been covered. From your discussions and from your own knowledge of the subject matter, you can then begin to consider your own time frame for each topic.

As you set these time frames, it is helpful to know how your content relates to earlier coursework and to subsequent coursework. You may wish to spend more time on southwestern American literature in your seventh-grade survey course if you know that the sixth grade concentrated on early American literature. You may want to consider simple physical operations in your elementary science lesson if you know that last year's teachers concentrated on physical senses. Most schools have a school-wide plan that describes the scope and the sequence of the curriculum, but talking to the individual teachers who have just taught the students you will be teaching or who teach a course similar to yours will explain the difference between what was intended by the curriculum guide and how those intentions were carried out in practice.

Once you are familiar with the content you will be expected to teach and you have a sense of the time you will have to implement your curriculum, examine that curriculum to determine what you and the school consider to be the major goals for the students who will be in your class.

Instructional Objectives

In this section we will consider four types of objectives. **Behavioral objectives** define student learning in terms of observable, measurable outcomes that are considered proof that a student has accomplished a specific educational goal. **Problem-solving objectives** define student learning in terms of the processes they use to think through issues that have no specific solution. Although the problem is clear, the outcome cannot be specified in advance, and multiple acceptable outcomes are possible. **Expressive objectives** define student learning as the highly individual experience of sense making, whether or not the outcome was anticipated in advance. **Affective objectives** are similar to expressive objectives in that they deal with individual experience, but they acknowledge the importance of emotional responses to curriculum and instruction. Of the four, behavioral objectives are most often advocated by schools and school districts, and thus we will discuss these objectives in great detail. We caution you, however, that many educators emphasize behavioral objectives even to the exclusion of the other three. As you begin your teaching career, you may want to carefully consider the relationships between all four types of educational objectives and their impact on students.

Behavioral Objectives

The intellectual roots of this tradition can be found in behavioral psychology. According to the behaviorists, one cannot know anything if one cannot directly document it with one of the senses. If a teacher cannot specify what she or he means by *learning*, how can he or she possibly demonstrate that this learning has occurred? Furthermore, this learning must be measurable so that one can determine whether or not the learner has progressed from relative ignorance to relative enlightenment.

Robert Mager (1962) has written extensively on the process of formulating educational objectives. According to Mager, the objective is a statement of intent by the teacher to produce some *change* in the learner through instruction. This statement of intent is a three-part sentence that sets the criteria for monitoring the learning outcomes. The first part specifies the conditions for demonstrating the learning. The second part specifies the exact behavior the student will be expected to demonstrate. The third part specifies the evaluative criteria for success. An example of these parts is, "Given ten, three-column addition problems (the condition), the learner will add each of those problems (the behavior) demonstrating 90% mastery (the evaluative criteria)."

EXHIBIT 8.2   **Focus on Behavioral Objectives**

Writing good behavioral objectives is not difficult if you keep three questions in mind:

1. What is the learning context?
2. How will the student behave?
3. What is the student product that is acceptable?

Examine the following statements to see if they form an appropriate behavioral objective:

1. The student will listen.
2. We will fingerpaint.
3. At ten o'clock the lab session will begin.

None of them answer the three questions. Now let us rewrite them into proper form.

1. While the teacher reads a poem, the student will demonstrate the ability to identify descriptive language by writing four descriptive phrases used by the poet.
2. In a fingerpainting activity, the students will demonstrate knowledge of basic shapes by correctly drawing a circle, a square, and a triangle.
3. During the ten o'clock laboratory exercise, the students will demonstrate the ability to measure, using the displacement method, by correctly determining the volume of four solids, using only liquid measures.

As a teacher, you may be expected to write behavioral objectives for each lesson you plan. As you think about writing these objectives, keep in mind the purposes for teaching that particular lesson. Is there an overall target goal—a major objective that will take several lessons to achieve? Are there prerequisite objectives that must be mastered before the target objective is even attempted? What information within each lesson is most important and should be given the most time? Of this information, what should be committed to memory? What information should be available to use as the students work through an assignment without necessarily committing it to memory? How can students best demonstrate their ability to accomplish the objectives? The answers to these questions will help you to design the lesson—or the series of lessons—and to gather the materials you will need for the lesson.

The power of behavioral objectives is that they clarify for both the student and the teacher exactly what is expected and that they set definite criteria for success. This knowledge can be shared with other people—colleagues, parents, school boards, and legislators. The limitation of behavioral objectives is that many intellectual, scientific, and social problems cannot be defined so exactly, especially when the criteria for success are not known in advance.

Problem-Solving Objectives

One of the leading critics of relying solely on behavioral objectives is Elliot Eisner, an art educator and a curriculum specialist. Teachers should also establish problem-solving objectives (Eisner, 1985) for their students. Learning experiences would include a problematic situation and a fairly specific set of criteria for the solution of the problem. For example, students might be given a school-related problem, such as excessive littering on campus, and then be asked to pose solutions for that problem that do not depend on money, punishment, or adult enforcement. From there, the students are left to pose as many solutions as they can think of.

Social problems are not the only problems that students can attack. In a science class, the students could be given match boxes and paper from which they must design a structure that can support two or more bricks. Problems of this sort are posed in a national competition, called Odyssey of the Mind, in which students from many high schools compete to see which teams can create the most workable solutions to problems posed by a national committee. Some high schools even have special classes, or clubs, that work on the team. But problem-solving activity is not solely the province of the secondary school. It is important to begin problem solving exercises in the elementary grades—and even in preschool.

EXHIBIT 8.3   **Problem-Solving Objectives in the Primary Classroom**

Problem-solving objectives specify the conditions of the problem, but they are open-ended and may end in a question. Following are five problem-solving objectives for lower elementary school students.

1. Given five dollars in play money, the students will decide how to buy food for one day.
2. Two students will work together to create a block structure that will support another student.

3. A group of four students will act out a different ending to the story of The Gingerbread Man.
4. The students will discuss what life would be like if there were no cars.
5. The students will decide how to spend fifteen minutes of free time.

The problem-solving objectives differ from behavioral objectives in at least five ways. First, the solution to the problem cannot be defined in advance and is often a surprise to the students and to the teacher. Second, the process of thinking through the problem is as important as the solution. As Mortimer Adler points out (Adler 1986), thinking is not a product that can be specifically *taught*; one learns to think through the repeated process of being placed in situations where one must think.

Third, the teacher's role changes from one of explicit guide to that of an encouraging, friendly critic. When the outcome is specified, the teacher faces the challenge of helping a student master that outcome, but when the outcome cannot be specified, the teacher faces the challenges of helping students to deal with uncertainty, to critique their successes as well as their failures, and to design and implement novel strategies.

Fourth, as the teacher's role changes, so do the students' roles. In problem-solving situations, the students are not working toward a predetermined outcome. Very often, their expertise is equal (or superior) to the teacher's. The students face the challenge of relying on their own judgments, of learning from failure, and of tolerating the ambiguity of working toward a solution that may not exist. Therefore, the fifth difference between behavioral objectives and problem-solving objectives lies in the evaluation.

A teacher cannot evaluate a problem-solving exercise in the same way that she or he analyzes a behaviorally-oriented exercise. In behavioral objectives, the evaluative criteria are stated in the objective. In problem-solving objectives, the criteria for reaching a solution are specified, but the solution is not. Therefore, evaluative criteria can be organized around the following guidelines:

1. Did the student arrive at a solution that met all of the specified conditions?
2. Did the student work through the problem without deviating from the specified conditions, even though no solution was reached?
3. How would you describe the quality of the work? Did the student attempt to find an original solution? to adapt another's solution? to copy another's solution?

4. How would you describe the quality of the process the student used while working through the problem? Was the student on task? Was the student using a trial-and-error approach? a process-of-elimination approach? a theoretical approach?
5. What did the student learn from the experience? What factual knowledge? What procedural knowledge? What personal knowledge?

From these five guidelines you can begin to develop a set of evaluative criteria for a problem-solving project that focuses on process as well as product. The evaluation may also include information about students' personal growth as they work toward a solution.

Problem-solving objectives and behavioral objectives still do not describe the entire range of goals we may have for our students. They have not left space for those educational activities that are simply good experiences for the child (and the adult).

Expressive Objectives

Those of us who are parents are very familiar with expressive objectives. When our children are very young, we take them for walks and to the park. When they are a bit older, we go to the circus, to the fair, and to the beach. We also go to zoos and to museums and to holiday spots such as the Grand Canyon and Washington, DC. All of the outings can be considered educational, although we seldom specify what outcomes we expect our children to demonstrate after having been on an outing! Neither do we observe our children's working processes as we all try to figure out maps or subway lines. Elliot Eisner (1985; 1969) argues that a formal education must include experiences that have no *specific* goal, but that encourage children to interpret those experiences through language, music, art, dance, or drama or simply through the importance of having had the experience.

EXHIBIT 8.4 **Expressive Objectives**

In many schools you will be required to submit lesson plans and to write all of your objectives, even though you may prefer to let them emerge as the activity progresses. For those of you who will be in such schools, here are some examples of expressive objectives for reading, social studies, and science. But, remember, the power of expression is seldom, if ever, determined in advance.

Reading
1. The children will discuss how the main character feels when her brother gets married.
2. The students will illustrate how they feel about a poem read aloud in class.

Social Studies
1. The students will write about how it feels to be a slave.
2. The students will act out how it feels to be left alone.

Science
1. The students will act out arguments between people who disagree over how a piece of land should be used.
2. The students will identify music that reminds them of orbiting planets.

Unfortunately, the pressure for accountability by some legislatures and school boards has sharply curtailed a teacher's freedom to design a curriculum that includes the liberal use of expressive objectives. In Texas, for example, some school boards prohibit field trips. In these situations, teachers must learn to design lessons that accomplish several purposes and to work through the established curriculum, while providing instruction that is varied and that encourages children to respond to the excitement of learning in many verbal and nonverbal ways. In such cases it may be necessary to "operationalize" expressive objectives into affective objectives. To "operationalize a term" means to define that term into something that can be observed and measured in some way. "Enthusiasm," for example, is an internal state that cannot be readily measured. But if we define enthusiasm as the presence of a smile, we have begun to operationalize enthusiasm because smiles can be observed, their frequencies and their durations can be charted, and they can be correlated with other behaviors such as gestures.

Affective Objectives

In the previous chapter the affective domain of learning, the domain which deals with feelings, values, and attitudes was addressed. Unlike expressive objectives, which emphasize experiences that we want students to have and that do not have definable outcomes, affective objectives are *directional* and are stated in terms of observable student behaviors.

In review, the lowest levels in the affective domain are *attending* and *responding*. To help with understanding these ideas, it is useful to add the qualifying term "willingness to." Therefore, the teacher who uses affective objectives would write something like, "Students will demonstrate their willingness to pay attention by . . ." and then would describe the types of observable behavior he or she would expect to see if students are in fact paying attention to instruction. These behaviors might include maintaining eye contact with the teacher during a presentation, completing assignments once instructions are given without further procedural questions (evidence that attention was paid to those instructions), and so forth.

EXHIBIT 8.5   Sample Affective Objectives

Students will demonstrate a positive attitude toward the subject matter of U.S. history by—

1. voluntarily bringing newspaper or magazine items to class pertaining to a historical issue that has been studied.
2. voluntarily choosing reading materials on U.S. history.

3. voluntarily discussing issues in U.S. history outside of class time.
4. volunteering comments that link present events in the United States with historical precedents.

The key word here is *voluntarily*. The teacher can certainly assign or require students to do some of the above actions as learning activities, but only when students begin to do them voluntarily can the teacher have any confidence at all that a positive attitude toward the subject matter of U.S.

history is forming. Meeting an assignment probably indicates a positive attitude toward good grades more than a positive attitude toward the subject itself.

While affective objectives are stated in terms of observable behavior (from which we infer internal attitudes), we do not advocate attempting to use measurable, quantifiable means in the statement of affective objectives. At this stage in the development of the knowledge base of teaching, we simply do not know enough about the affective domain to say whether 60 percent of the class maintaining eye contact with the teacher during a teacher presentation indicates effective teaching, or not. Attempting to be too quantifiable when dealing with student attitudes often causes frustration, which can then lead to ignoring the affective domain entirely.

We encourage you to go back to the various levels of the affective domain in Chapter 7 as you become more adept at designing instruction, for the points made earlier concerning the interconnectedness of information and attitudes about learning are vital to designing effective instruction.

To summarize this section, we have discussed four forms of objectives, one of which is mandated by many school districts because the specified outcomes are both observable and measurable. We have argued that problem-solving outcomes, expressive outcomes, and affective outcomes are also desirable educational experiences for students. But objectives are only words and phrases that have no meaning—unless they are translated into meaningful educational activities.

Planning for Instruction

Figure 8.1 presents a normative planning model for designing instruction. We use the term normative because we suggest that you use such a model as you begin to design your own lessons. As you become more experienced, you can develop a personal model that works best for you. Studies of the ways experienced teachers plan instruction suggest that they have developed alternative planning strategies that are not as detailed as this one (Clark & Peterson 1986). Such teachers have developed instructional routines through their experience that have become automatic, and they no longer specify many of their instructional activities (Leinhardt & Greeno 1986). Until you have worked through the process for yourself (which usually takes several years of teaching experience), we advocate that you pay careful attention to lesson plans.

Beginning With Objectives

From this model you can see that instructional objectives include two categories of objectives, academic objectives (behavioral, problem-solving, expressive, or affective) and managerial objectives, the physical behaviors that you expect from your students as they work through an activity. The purposes of the lesson are communicated to the children either explicitly, through verbal interaction or through writing them on the board; or implicitly, through familiar instructional assignments for which the children have learned the appropriate managerial routines.

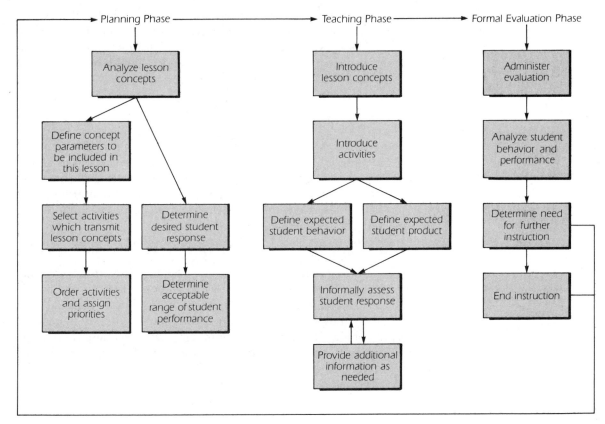

FIGURE 8.1
A model to guide early
attempts to design
instruction

Implementing the Activities

Once the purposes are communicated, the teacher can then provide clear and detailed instructions on the first activity. These instructions (oral and possibly written) should include information on how to work through the activity, information on any helpful cognitive strategies that will facilitate working through the activity, and information on what the teacher expects in terms of student behavior and student products that result from the activity. Exhibit 8.7 illustrates such instructions. Once the students begin the activity, the teacher can then monitor students' work to see if it follows the instructional guidelines, if any deviations are acceptable, or if students are off task.

Monitoring the Implementation

This monitoring procedure is also a part of the model in Figure 8.1. How many times have you been in a class where the teacher asks, "Are there any questions?" and although you had many questions, you did not ask them (1) because you were hesitant to admit ignorance; (2) because you did not want to hold the rest of the class back; (3) because you felt that the teacher really didn't want any questions; or (4) because there wasn't enough time in the period to answer questions anyway? Monitoring is far more than pausing for questions, and monitoring strategies should be planned in advance.

Evaluating the Lesson

The last part of the model presented in Figure 8.1 is a self check for the teacher. Evaluation is a continual process that begins *during* the instructional phases of a lesson. The teacher continually monitors progress to ascertain if the students are working appropriately, if they are encountering insurmountable difficulties, and if they are achieving the purposes of the lesson. If all goes well, the teacher can proceed to the next lesson, and if not, the teacher may need to go back to the instructional phase *or* to the planning phase.

Another important component of lesson planning is to make sure that all of the necessary resources will be available to the teacher and to the students. For example, in some large high schools, all dittoed material must be turned in to the clerical staff forty-eight hours before it is needed. Teachers are not allowed to operate equipment. Or, as we discussed in the chapter on teachers, you may find a log jam at the ditto machine on the morning you need to use it. In the case of demonstrations, have all of the equipment ready ahead of class so that you can begin the demonstration when the class begins. In your first lesson plans, check yourself and specify and obtain all of the necessary papers, texts, and materials before the day of the lesson. With this general planning model in mind, let us examine instructional design in more detail.

Lesson Design

For the purposes of this book we will define a lesson as the amount of time it takes to instruct students in a simple topic, whether a concept, a skill, or a process, or to discuss a brief piece of literature such as a poem, a short story, or a section of a novel. By "simple" we mean that each lesson is only one in a series of lessons that work together to help the students to understand a complex mathematic, scientific, social, or artistic phenomenon or to execute a complex mathematic, scientific, social, or artistic process.

For example, before one can understand the concept and the events of the Civil War, many social concepts and processes must be understood, as well as many historical and geographical concepts. Some of these are simple social lessons learned at home; some are historical and geographical lessons learned in elementary grades. In a given secondary-school unit on the Civil War, a helpful beginning might be to conduct several lessons on slavery in the United States in order to provide the students with a common understanding of the economics of slavery, the conditions under which slaves lived, the diversity of viewpoints regarding abolition, and the political tension caused by discussions of abolition. Then students can begin to study the war itself and to relate the process of war to the process of social change.

Each lesson can be divided into three parts: an introduction, an instructional section, and a summary. Although educators might fill each one of these three sections differently, they would all agree that each of these sections is important to the construct of a successful lesson. Let us look at each section more closely.

The Introduction

When you first introduce your students to a new topic, it is important to help them understand how that topic fits into the course in general. The lesson introduction can facilitate this understanding in at least four ways.

1. The introduction can help students connect what they have already learned to the new material. In our earlier discussion of learning theory, we noted that organizing new information and storing that information is easier if we can relate it to something familiar. A lesson introduction that recalls prior knowledge and relates the new information to that prior knowledge can be a valuable aid to students' new learning.

2. The introduction can provide a preview of what is to come so that students will be able to focus on the new information that will be most important and so that they can organize their new information around these important points. As we mentioned earlier, so much information is available to us every millisecond that we cannot possibly attend to everything. *Advance organizers* are statements that let students know what information will be important before instruction begins (Ausubel, 1963). They help us to deal with that new information more efficiently and effectively.

3. The introduction can arouse students' curiosity or excitement and can stimulate their attention and their continuing desire to learn. Just as the advertisement for a movie provides us with a teasing hint of what is to come, the introduction to a lesson can play with students' imaginations and can arouse their curiosity. Such introductions often have students begging for more information or activity.

4. The introduction can provide students with a sense of what you, the teacher, will expect from them as they work through the next few hours or days. Very often we assume that because we are involved in a classroom activity, students automatically know what to do and how to behave. This is not necessarily true, particularly when we plan something that is a little different from standard classroom routines. The introduction can help students understand what behaviors are appropriate and how they will be expected to respond both cognitively and affectively.

The first exhibit provides an example that combines the first two purposes; the second provides an example that combines the second two purposes.

EXHIBIT 8.6 **Sample Lesson Introduction Reviews Prior Instruction and Provides Advance Organizers for the Instruction**

Teacher: Last week we discussed the literary device known as foreshadowing. On your notepaper, write a definition of foreshadowing. (Teacher walks around the desks to quickly check for responses.) Anna, what is foreshadowing?

Anna: Foreshadowing is the author's way of providing a clue to future events in the story.

Teacher: Mario, can you give us an example of foreshadowing?

Mario: In the movie of Romeo and Juliet, the messenger and the priest pass each other on the road. The audience knows that the priest will not know about Juliet's faking a suicide attempt.

Teacher: Ah, so foreshadowing is also a useful device in film as well as in novels or short stories! Today we are going to begin our analysis of suspense literature. In suspense literature, foreshadowing is often used to establish the mood and to set the audience up for future events. Let us begin by listening to this recording of a story by Edgar Allen Poe.

EXHIBIT 8.7 **Sample Lesson Plan That Arouses Students' Curiosity and Communicates the Teacher's Expectations During Instruction**

The students arrive at the classroom and find that it is dark and that the door is locked. One student notices that the door has a message stuck in the casing. He reads the charred note that says, "In silence there is virtue. Those who hear my voice will be those who keep their own tongues still." The students crowd around the reader, wondering what is going on. The reader (who has been primed before class) asks the students what the note means. After some discussion, the students decide that they must be very quiet. They quiet down and urge new arrivals to do the same. When all is quiet, the door slowly opens and two figures (another student and the teacher) motion the class into the darkened room. The student confederates gently motion that all should be quiet.

Once all are in place, the teacher lights a candle while a tape recorded message invites students into the world of mystery and suspense and a story by Agatha Christie is begun. The teacher monitors the listening process.

The Instruction

Hunter (1984) discusses a "lesson cycle" that organizes teaching into a series of teacher-directed segments. Rosenshine and Stevens (1986), discussed in Chapter 3, present nine components that comprise an optimal lesson for well-structured information or procedures. Gagne and Briggs (1979) offer an analysis of instruction that includes nine steps that lead to the goals of retaining information and the transfer of information to new learning tasks. Our point here is that various educators, using different terminology and employing different numbers of instructional "steps," have attempted to separate instruction into discrete segments that can be used systematically to order a student's progress through an instructional sequence. Other educators (for example, Joyce & Weil 1986) argue that there are different models of instruction, many of which do not follow the systematic segmentation discussed above.

As you begin to think about your own instruction, it is important to understand that different designs are employed to accomplish diverse educational purposes. With that thought in mind let us look across the different educators' arguments to see what the purposes of the instructional portion of the lesson may serve.

1. Instruction may introduce a student to new information or to a new skill.
2. Instruction may encourage a student to review or to reinterpret information or skills that have been learned previously.
3. Instruction may enable a student to spot gaps in prior learning and to fill those gaps.
4. Instruction may encourage a student to develop or to strengthen new physical, cognitive, social, or affective processes.
5. Instruction may encourage a student to produce new information, to reorganize that information, or to express information in a creative manner.
6. Instruction may encourage a student to speculate, to wonder and to puzzle over ideas that are, as yet, undeveloped and to think about problems that are, as yet, unsolved.

These purposes may be very different, and they may even conflict at times. Your choices among these purposes will be determined in part by the curriculum and the discipline you are teaching and by your goals and the school district's goals for the students. They will also be influenced by your educational philosophy, by the time and materials that are available to you, and by your objectives for individual lessons and for related units of lessons. Knowing that these will differ, let us look at three sample lesson structures and see what elements, if any, they all have in common.

EXHIBIT 8.8   A Lesson Format From Madeline Hunter

The **anticipatory set** cues students toward the topics to be covered in the lesson. The **objective** and **purpose** explain why the topics are being covered and what the student is expected to accomplish during the lesson. The **instructional input** is the new information (or the information that is being retaught). **Modeling** is showing the students how to perform a task during the instructional input while **monitoring** students' responses and **adjusting** instruction accordingly. In **guided practice**, the students have the opportunity to work while being directed by the teacher until they are capable of **independent practice** on their own.

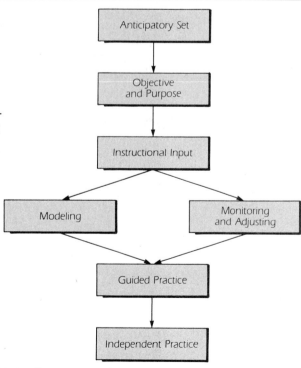

EXHIBIT 8.9 A Lesson Format From Gagne and Briggs

The Planning Stage

1. State the objective.
2. List the instructional events to be employed.
3. List the media, materials, and activities for each instructional event.
4. Make notes on the teacher's roles and activities, and the directions to students.

The Instructional Stage

1. State the objective of the lesson.

2. Further inform the student by providing a performance model.
3. Guide learning through questions.
4. Guide learning through verbal definitions.
5. Guide learning through a variety of examples.
6. Provide a stimulus that will elicit the desired performance response from students.
7. Provide feedback on their performance.
8. Assess whether or not the objective has been achieved.

EXHIBIT 8.10 An Instructional Activities Format From Joyce and Weil

Syntax for creating something new through synectics.

1. Students describe something that presently exists.
2. Students suggest direct analogies to the present condition.
3. Students then choose one for further elaboration.
4. Students "become" the analogy and describe how they feel.

5. Students take all descriptive phrases and juxtapose each pair of phrases that contradict each other (called compressed conflicts).
6. Students generate another direct analogy based on the compressed conflicts.
7. Teacher moves students back to the original condition or task, and then students write about the original condition using the metaphors created during the synectics exercise.

Notice that all of these lesson formats have some time for the teacher to make information available to the students. In the first two plans, the teacher presented all of the information; in the last plan, the teacher drew the information from the students. All of the lessons provide some time for the students to work with that information (and, in one case, to actively seek new information). All of the lessons include time for guidance and feedback from the teacher and possibly from the other students. We can infer, then, that there are three basic components of the instructional portion of the lesson: introduction of relevant information and materials; opportunities to manipulate that information; and feedback on one's performance. Whether you borrow a Hunter model or whether you opt for a different model, these three components should be an important part of your lesson design.

Planning for Instructional Activities

Instructional objectives are guidelines that enable you to think through the purposes of instruction, to decide which outcomes are the most important, and to relate your instructional goals to the curricular goals. Instructional *activities* are the academic tasks that students perform as they work toward the desired instructional outcomes. We emphasize that activities are what the *students* do, not what the teacher does, because learning depends on what takes place in the minds of students. A teacher may give a brilliant lecture, a faultless explanation, or a stimulating demonstration, but unless the meaning of that teacher's activity is perceived by students, no learning has occurred. For example, if you decide to explain a particular scientific concept such as "rotation" to your students, you may decide to have them listen to your explanation, to read a definition of rotation, to physically enact rotation, or to observe rotating objects. In all of these cases, the students' activities are emphasized, although you still have the responsibility for talking, for providing the passage, for setting up the enactment, or for arranging for the observation. Focusing on what the students will be doing makes it easier for them to understand what your expectations are and for you to monitor their response to your instruction.

Monitoring Activities

One of the most obvious monitoring techniques is to ask the students questions about the content of the instructional activity. This can be done rapidly, using a recitation format in which the teacher calls out a question and then asks the students for an answer. When using this recitation approach, call on students (rather than asking for volunteers) so that you can quickly see who may need further instruction (Groisser 1964). It is also helpful to pause for a few seconds between asking the question and calling on a student for the answer, for this will give students time to formulate an answer before one student provides the answer (Rowe 1974). This approach can also serve as a self-check for other students who were not sure if their answer was correct.

Another monitoring strategy is to ask the entire class a question and, through a given signal system, the entire class can nonverbally communicate the answer. An example of this is the "number cube" that has slots for six numbers. The teacher can call out the math problem and all of the students can flash the correct answer at her at one time. This system can also work for oral multiple-choice answers.

As students work alone or together, another monitoring strategy is the observation of student work. Recall that earlier we recommended that you specify the products that were expected from the student during the activity. In a lab class, that product may be lab notes that are written during the laboratory exercise. In a dramatic enactment, that product may be the physical activity that students demonstrate or the script or props they create for a planned enactment of a scene from history or a piece of literature. Both observation and question asking allow the teacher to guide the students back on task when necessary, to answer questions while moving around the room, to identify students who may be having trouble, and to provide those students with help, either by referring them to another student or by helping them yourself. Wise teachers do not make the mistake of assuming that just because they have told students how to work through something, the students will automatically be able to do so.

The Summary

A summary has many alternative names. It can be called a conclusion, a debriefing, a summative review, or attaining closure. A summary can serve three different purposes.

1. A summary can review the important details of the instruction.
2. A summary can permit students to reflect on instruction and to draw conclusions from the instructional experience.
3. A summary can foreshadow future instruction. Exhibit 9.6 illustrates all three purposes in one lesson summary.

EXHIBIT 8.11   A Sample Lesson Summary

Teacher: Raul, can you recall the three parts of an insect's body that we discussed today?

Raul: Head, thorax, and abdomen.

Teacher: As you think about the insects we examined today, can you think of one big difference between the insects and people?

Julia: People are bigger.

Antoine: People don't have wings.

Sharon: People have arms and legs.

Teacher: If insects don't have arms or legs, how do they build houses for themselves?

Andy: Do insects have houses?

Teacher: Tomorrow's lesson will focus on where insects live and on how some insects build their own places to live. Tonight I want you to go home and ask your family if they can show you any insect homes that might be in your yard or in a park.

Planning for Evaluation

Note that an important component of all planning is the plan for finding out whether your students are making progress toward the objectives you have specified as important and whether you are pleased with their progress. It is also important to note when students have accomplished an objective and are ready to move on to another, possibly more complex, objective. Earlier in this chapter we said that behavioral objectives contained an evaluative statement within the objective itself, that problem-solving objectives were evaluated on whether the criteria were followed and on the progress that a student made toward resolving the problem, and that expressive objectives often had no specified outcome and that evaluating such objectives must take an individual student's experience into account. These kinds of evaluations are often referred to as *summative evaluations*, or evaluations that summarize a student's learning at a given point in time.

In the last section we discussed monitoring strategies as an important component of all instructional activities. Questioning and observing students, responding to draft copies of papers, and responding to a physical or an artistic exercise are all examples of evaluation that occurs while a student is learning and provides feedback to the student on how he or she is growing and improving. This kind of evaluation is often labeled *formative evaluation* and is crucial to a student's intellectual progress.

Students, particularly older students, will focus on those aspects of the curriculum that will be graded (Becker, Geer, & Hughes 1968; Doyle 1983). Design your evaluations to be consistent with your objectives so that your students do not get mixed messages. For example, assume you have designed a creative writing unit around a nature theme and you are predominantly concerned with expressive objectives. You take your students outside on a windy day, and while they are outside you have them write phrases that describe wind. At home that night, you read over the phrases. If you decide to write comments back to the students that encourage them to elaborate on the phrases, to use more descriptive words, or to tell them when you find a particular phrase that is very well done, you are being consistent with your objective. But, if you choose to correct their spelling and their grammar and to give them a grade based on the number of correct phrases they have written, what do you think your students will focus on the next time you encourage them to express feeling and sensation in writing?

An inappropriate evaluation, whether formative or summative, can send an unintended message to the student that says you may signal one thing with your words, but your judgments signal something very different. Students are very practical people; they realize that once they have left your class, the grades will go with them as information to other teachers, parents, peers, and college admission offices. Students will focus on what is evaluated, particularly those evaluations that carry a letter or a number equivalent. Therefore, when designing your lessons, be sure that objectives, activities, *and evaluations* all carry the same message.

Up until this point, we have been discussing evaluations as though they were only the province of the teacher. Two other forms of evaluations should be considered as you think through instructional design. Because behavioral objectives are so specific, they lend themselves readily to self-evaluation. Many teachers design lessons that allow students to check their own work and to rework sections that caused them problems. For both behavioral objectives and for problem-solving objectives, having students check each other is helpful. In Chapter 3 we discussed cooperative learning groups, which rely on students to monitor and to help other students. Teachers often overlook the possibility that within their classrooms are many potential "teachers." Identifying those peer teachers and designing instructional activities and forms of evaluation that will take advantage of these peer teachers can multiply an individual teacher's effectiveness.

Unit Plans

Assume that you are a seventh-grade literature teacher, who will be teaching a unit organized around the theme of romance (a theme that will be relevant to many of your students' current interests). You have many topics you want to cover and many skills you want your students to develop, including the abilities to identify specifc authors within romantic literature, match authors with literary work, identify plot structure, think through the resolution of family conflicts, think about successful and unsuccessful communication between genders, interpret classical literature in modern terms, and write some poetry.

The students cannot accomplish all of these goals in one day. Unless you arrange your individual lessons carefully, this unit could become a meaningless hodgepodge of reading, writing, and floundering. As you think about designing instruction you will need to differentiate between *unit* objectives and individual *lesson* objectives. Unit objectives may take several weeks and many lessons before they can be accomplished. Lessons will build upon one another as they are ordered into cohesive units. For example, suppose you are a second-grade teacher and that you are studying careers in social studies. "Career" can be a rather meaningless term for second graders; so, in the unit you may want to include one or more lessons that explain what the term means and then to have guest speakers talk about different careers. You may also want to help students understand that careers are appropriate for both genders and for many different cultural groups. This implies that you will need to think through all of your objectives and to order the lessons in some way that will make sense for the students.

After the lessons are ordered, it is important to, once again, check for consistency between lesson objectives, activities, and evaluations. It is also important to check for consistency across lessons to determine that the lessons are enabling students to reach unit objectives.

Conclusion

Instructional design itself is a complex process. The sections at the end of this chapter will help you to begin thinking about how you will design your instruction; but you should not expect to become an expert in this area overnight. In this chapter we have discussed the importance of identifying realistic objectives for your students, of planning for lessons that include introductions, instructional activities, and summaries. We have also discussed the importance of evaluating instruction during the instruction as well as after a lesson or a unit has ended. The sections at the end of this chapter will help you begin your role as a classroom instructional designer.

Building Reflective Inquiry Skills

Studying Teacher Planning

Planning for instruction will vary between teachers and will vary within teachers, because new lessons require more extensive plans than do familiar lessons. Prospective teachers seldom, if ever, have an opportunity to learn about the decisions that go into planning, because most of the plans have been made long before a student teacher arrives on the scene, or because planning has become automatic for experienced teachers. In this skill-building session, we will ask you to study how planning is accomplished and to pay close attention to the decisions that need to be made regarding time, individual ability, content, and pedagogy.

Finding Cooperative Teachers

If you have been assigned to a school for your preservice fieldwork, you will be able to ask two or more teachers to work with you on this project. Otherwise, you will need to contact a nearby school and ask the principal if you might write a letter to all of the teachers, asking them to allow you to interview them about how lessons are planned.

Once your teachers have agreed to an interview, be sure to discuss the amount of time they will be willing to give you. The following questions may help you make those decisions.

1. How often do you write lesson plans?

2. When do you usually write them?

3. Does your lesson planning consist only of written plans, or are their other types of planning that you do? (If yes, ask the teacher to describe the plans.)

4. I am very interested in how planning gets done. Is there some time (or some place) that I could sit with you as you make your plans? I would like to hear you think out loud as you plan, and I would like to ask you questions after you have finished the planning session.

Then, arrange a time, date, and place to meet. Be sure that you follow through on the agreement; teachers are very unlikely to give you a part of their busy schedule if you have not been conscientious the first time.

The Planning Interview

You will need a tape recorder and a note pad. When you arrive at the interview, ask the teacher to please go ahead with the planning, but to think out loud while the session is in progress. Then try to be as un-obtrusive as possible while the planning session is in progress.

Once the teacher is finished, debrief the session using your adaptations of the following questions:

1. What materials do you plan to use? Have you used them before? How are these particular materials advantageous?

2. Is it necessary to modify the materials in any way? For example, are you presenting ideas in the same order as the textbook, or are you following a curriculum guide exactly as written? Did you create any of the materials yourself?

3. What do you expect the students to do during this lesson?

4. What do you expect the students to get out of this lesson? How will you know if this is happening?

5. What will be the biggest challenge of this lesson? How have you prepared to meet that challenge?

6. Have you taught this lesson before? Have you changed anything since the last time you taught it? Could you explain why you made those changes?

7. How do you feel about this lesson? How do you expect the students to feel?

Don't forget to thank the teachers for their time at the end of the interview

Reflecting on the Interviews

Go back through your tapes and your notes. Write a summary of each teacher's planning session that describes what happened. Then compare the sessions. Write your interpretations of the planning styles used by each individual teacher. How did they compare? How did they differ? Did they specify objectives? What orientation to the curriculum did their plans imply? How did they use course materials? How will you use this information to begin thinking about your own lesson plans?

Explorations

Exploration 1
Variation in Lesson Plans
Collect a variety of lesson plan formats, preferably ones that have been completed by teachers. What elements do they have in common? How do they differ? Practice writing your own lesson plans using the format that you find most useful.

Exploration 2
Observing the Results of Planning
If there is time, and if the teachers agree, observe the teachers whom you interviewed as they actually teach the lessons they planned. Take notes on any changes they make "in flight" and interview them about the classroom events that prompted those changes.

Exploration 3
Evaluating Student Performance in Nonacademic Settings
Interview teachers who work in the performance fields (such as art, music, drama, dance, and physical education) about how they evaluate students when they do not use written tests.

Exploration 4
Evaluation Outside of School Settings
Interview museum directors, musicians, artists, art critics, theatrical directors, or drama critics about how they evaluate performances.

References

Adler, M. J. (1982). *The paideia proposal: An educational manifesto.* New York: Macmillan.

Ausubel, D. (1963). *The psychology of meaningful verbal learning: An introduction to school learning.* New York: Grune and Stratton.

Becker, H. S., Geer, B. & Hughes, E. (1968). *Making the grade: The academic side of college life.* New York: John Wiley.

Bennett, W. J. (1986). *What works: Research about teaching & learning.* Washington, D.C.: Department of Education.

Bloom, B. S. (1976). *Human characteristics and school learning.* New York: McGraw-Hill.

Clark, C. M. & Peterson, P. L. (1986). Teachers' thought processes. In Wittrock, M. C. (Ed.) *Handbook of research on teaching, 3rd edition.* New York: MacMillan

Doyle, W. (1983). Academic work. *Review of Educational Research, 53*(2), 159–199.

Eisner, E. W. (1985). *The educational imagination, 2nd edition.* New York: Macmillan.

Eisner, E. W. (1969). Instructional and expressive objectives: Their formulation and use in curriculum. In Popham, W. J. (Ed.), *AERA monograph on curriculum and evaluation: Instructional objectives.* Chicago: Rand McNally.

Gagne, R. M. & Briggs, L. J. (1979). *Principles of instructional design, 2nd Ed.* New York: Holt, Rinehart, and Winston.

Hunter, M. (1984). Knowing, teaching, and supervising. In Hosford, P. L. (Ed.), *Using what we know about teaching.* Alexandria, VA: Association for Supervision and Curriculum Development.

Imig, D. G. (1987). Briefing: On competition and today's teachers. *AACTE Briefs, 8*(2), 2, 8.

Joyce, B. R. & Weil, M. (1986). *Models of Teaching.* Englewood Cliffs, NJ: Prentice Hall, Inc.

Leinhardt, G. & Greeno, J. G. (1986). The cognitive skill of teaching. *Journal of Educational Psychology, 78*(2), 75–95.

Mager, R. (1962). *Preparing instructional objectives.* Palo Alto, CA: Fearon Publishers.

_____ (1982). *Developing attitude toward learning.* 2d edition. Palo Alto, CA: Fearon Publishers.

Rosenshine, B. & Stevens, R. (1986). Teaching functions. In Wittrock, M. C. (Ed.), *Handbook of research on teaching, 3rd edition.* New York: Macmillan.

Rowe, M. B. (1974). The relation of wait time and rewards to the development of language, logic, and fate control: Part 1—Wait Time. *Journal of Research in Science Teaching, 11*(4), 291–308.

Varying Instruction for Effective Teaching

OBJECTIVES

By the end of this chapter, you will be able to:

1. Describe some of the roots of teaching methods we use today.
2. Identify at least five different teaching methods.
3. List the advantages and limitations of five teaching methods.
4. Explain the relationship between instructional variability and student learning.
5. Identify at least five elements of effective teaching.
6. Design a practice lesson with at least three teaching methods.
7. Explore the use of additional teaching strategies from a list of methods texts.

KEY WORDS AND CONCEPTS

Content
Discovery/Inquiry
Drill and practice
Grouping
Heterogeneous grouping
Homogeneous grouping
Instructional variability
Methods
Questioning
Student-focused methods
Teacher-focused methods

Teaching Roots

In Chapter 2 we discussed the early historical development of education and schooling. We saw how the teaching-learning process evolved very slowly from the time of hunters and gatherers to the present. Teachers of children during this time of prehistory were members of the tribe or family unit. The children would observe older children and adults complete a task and then try to imitate their actions. When special procedures or skills needed to be followed (for example, to make an arrowhead or pottery jar for water), the adult would describe, and then demonstrate, the steps to the young learner. The learner would then practice, sometimes for months or years, the steps until he or she had mastered the task. The "teacher" would work one-to-one with the learner to provide guidance and feedback.

This process developed experts in their trade who instructed other newcomers to the craft. During the middle ages, apprentices worked under the direction of a master craftsman to learn their trade. The educational process became an integral part of the economy of the local community and spread to other neighboring communities.

Telling and demonstrating by the "teacher" were combined with watching, listening, and practicing by the "learner" to produce a teaching-learning cycle. This cycle continued as the learner (apprentice) became the teacher (master craftsman) to a new generation of youth.

In the time of the Greeks the student had a tutor. During the middle ages the master craftsman had an apprentice. As society became more complex, public schools and institutions of higher learning evolved. Large numbers of students entering the educational system caused us to move away from the one-to-one learning experience to the group learning experience.

Group Learning

Major events from the past were conveyed by elder members of the tribe, as stories were told and retold to children and adults who gathered into a group during the evenings. Without a written language or books to preserve the collective history of the tribe, the story teller became the link between the tribe's past and present. The use of dance, with members of the tribe playing specific roles, was also used to share the collective history as a group. A great hunt would be depicted, with members of the tribe recreating the hunters and the animals. Prehistoric drawings in the caves of Europe depict the same type of scenes. The group became a social, as well as an economic, tool for learning. One person could teach many youth, freeing other adults to complete different tasks. The teacher, or storyteller, used a variety of methods to communicate information to the listeners.

Expert Teacher

Many of the teaching methods we use today have their roots in the need of people to share ideas, knowledge, skills, beliefs, and attitudes with the next generation. This chapter will explore teaching methods that link the knowledge of the teacher with the transfer of that knowledge to the learner. According to local newspaper accounts and critics, the best teaching occurs at a blackboard, with the teacher lecturing to students. However, just as teachers no longer stoke the potbelly stove, carry in the coal each morning, and sweep out the room each evening, they no longer simply stand at a blackboard and lecture. That old-time vision of teaching is not the reality. Successful teachers vary the instructional methods they use in the classroom.

Effective teachers use at least three instructional strategies per lesson (Stallings & Mohlman 1981). If you are familiar with only one or two strategies, exploring the range of strategies presented in this chapter will be worthwhile. During the various stages of your field experiences, look for the ways veteran teachers vary instructional methods in their classrooms.

The effective teacher has a strong command of the content and has mastered the instructional design of the subject matter to determine the steps needed to present the material to the students in a clear and logical manner. In a study Gaea Leinhardt conducted, of expert elementary math teachers in the Pittsburgh Public School District, some clear patterns begin to emerge. The lessons of expert teachers are described as "clear, accurate, and rich in examples and demonstrations for the students" (1986, 29). The same information is presented in a variety of ways. See Exhibit 9.1 for a description of how Dorothy Conway (one of the expert second-grade teachers in the study) teaches a math lesson on subtraction and regrouping.

EXHIBIT 9.1   Conway in Action

We observed Dorothy Conway teach a sequence of eight lessons on subtraction with regrouping. On the first day of the sequence, she quickly reviewed sums with ten (10 + 4, 10 + 8, 10 + 3, etc.) in order to (1) activate students' old knowledge and make it available, and (2) accentuate the base-ten aspects of the task or the additive composition of two (or more) digit numbers. Conway then switched to a series of two-digit subtraction problems done at the board with students giving choral support. Finally, she gave them two problems that required regrouping. By rehearsing the simple, two-digit column response for subtraction, Conway prevented students from counting up a clumsy way of getting the answer that does not require regrouping. Specifically, given the problem, 34 minus 17, the students could "count on" from 17, which would focus on the answer, but not on the need for adjusting the algorithm (you cannot take 7 from 4). Conway had students label these last two problems as "foolers." Then she went on to banded sticks, felt strips, and renaming two-digit numbers, each time pausing just before the solution to see if the children could come up with a way of doing it. This clarified and focused on the goal for the series of lessons that would follow.

By the end of the presentation, the children had used sticks to solve regrouping problems and had become skilled at re-expressing two-digit numbers as tens and ones. They learned this through demonstration and rehearsal. Essentially, Conway's first lesson set up the problem and built at least three separate ways for the children mentally to represent it before teaching the solution. Some of the more skilled students whom we interviewed after the first lesson, had already seen that "foolers" could be solved by some type of trading or transferring between the two columns. Special skill was involved in using the banded sticks. With

considerable showmanship, Conway had each child select some tens and some ones and then asked a student to give back some (always a number that did not require regrouping—if the child had 4 tens and 6 ones, Conway would ask for 5 ones, etc.). When she finally sprang a problem, 26 minus 8, on one child, the class was gleeful at the contradiction. Clearly, 26 was more than 8, but the student only had 6 ones. This elaborate focusing would pay off in subsequent lessons—when the numerical procedures were explained, rehearsed, and learned. Conway used "concrete" and "manipulative" materials in her example but, more importantly, she used them for a powerful illustrative purpose, one that would remain accessible to the students for the remaining days of the lesson sequence. This served to construct the first of three representations that Conway used. Expert teachers use good, tight demonstrations that clearly relate to the content being taught.

Still within the first lesson, Conway moved rapidly to a second more abstract example, one that was closer to the eventual algorithm to be taught. The second example involved felt strips. In using felt strips as a demonstration, Conway emphasized two points: (1) trading a ten strip for 10 ones, and (2) retaining the same value of the minuend. She proved the legitimacy of the trade move to her class of seven-year-olds by showing that the value remained constant. Obviously, not all of the children caught the subtlety of the point; however, many did. The trade operation more closely parallels the numerical regrouping than does the unbinding of sticks, but neither are precisely the same. By the end of the first lesson the students were familiar with three representations (sticks, felt, expanded numbers) but not their connections.

The second and third lessons of the sequence presented the numerical formalisms. By the end of the first day and a half, Conway had showed the following: (1) subtraction is both a type of problem and an operation; (2) subtraction problems consist of two types, those that do not require regrouping and those that do; (3) a subtraction operation can be represented as an unbinding of sticks, a trading of felt strips, or a regrouping of numbers; and (4) there are specific procedures for each type of operation. This structure was not suggested by the book or teacher's manual; Conway "invented" it.

Over the next few lessons, Conway's students explored subtraction in increasingly complex and ambiguous contexts: word problems, money, with addition and "regular" subtraction, and by correcting other students' work. Note that this practice reembedded subtraction into the matrix of arithmetic the students already knew, blocking the overuse of the regrouping procedure and, thus, recasting the new skill as a now familiar, and friendly, old one. (Leinhardt, "Expertise in Mathematics Teaching". *Educational Leadership* 43, (1986): 28–33.

What do you think students gain from such an expertly-tuned lesson? What relationship did you see between content and method? What teaching methods did Dorothy Conway use in teaching the math lesson? What are the implications for secondary teachers who are looking for greater variability in teaching?

Secondary teachers have been concerned about the lack of higher-level thinking and problem-solving skills of students. Pilot projects have been developed in several different content areas from social studies to writing to mathematics, to move students from memorizing facts to an emphasis on understanding concepts and problem solving. In mathematics, teachers are changing their instructional strategies from lecture and drill, which are fine for basic skills, to discover/inquiry and small problem-solving groups of three to four students (Simon 1986). Teacher-training programs are being redesigned to respond to the need for new approaches toward teaching.

For example, Martin Simon leads a summer mathematics program for teachers in Massachusetts. Teachers, who attend the sessions at Mount Holyoke College, must relearn teaching methods by giving up the role of "imparter of information and to become the architect and facilitator of active learning" (p. 42). Both teachers and students are responding with more enthusiasm, interest, and greater understanding of mathematics concepts.

Five Elements of Effective Teaching

As we noted in Chapter 7, the curriculum may be partly determined by the textbook, curriculum guide, or other instructional materials supplied and required by the school district or state. How effectively and efficiently the teacher is able to teach this content is determined by the following:

1. the teacher's expectations about the ability of students to learn;
2. classroom management skills;
3. the amount of time students spend engaged in academic tasks;
4. teacher decision making; and
5. the variability of teaching methods.

The first three elements are included in Chapters 3 and 10. The fourth element, teacher decision making, is a theme which runs throughout this text. Being reflective, examining the information presented, and making choices about your future and the future of students with whom you teach is at the heart of effective teaching. Finally, providing variability in teaching by using different methods is another key to becoming an effective teacher and will be considered in this chapter.

Content: The What of Teaching

The what of teaching is the specific content you will be teaching. Examples include adding single-digit numbers, spelling words from the reading book, learning the geometric formula for determining the area of a room, studying the elements on the periodic table, analyzing the causes of the American Civil War, and becoming aware of the risks Christopher Columbus took in coming to the new world and the "Challenger" crew took in exploring space. The *what*, or content of teaching, can range from simple facts, such as adding one plus one, to an analysis of complex issues, such as the genetic manipulation of DNA molecules to produce new organisms.

Methods: The How of Teaching

You will use two types of methods in teaching: content-specific methods and general teaching methods. For the elementary teacher, content-specific methods relate to how you would teach spelling or addition or to how you would select the appropriate approach for teaching reading or language arts. In the secondary classroom, the methods or strategies would relate to the specific content area.

This chapter addresses the second type of method: the general teaching strategies that are applicable to any grade level or content area. We will examine five teaching strategies: 1) lecture, 2) questioning, 3) drill and practice, 4) grouping, and 5) discovery/inquiry. The first three strategies are teacher-focused strategies, while the latter two are student-focused strategies.

Your Experiences With Strategies

Think back to your elementary and junior and senior high-school classroom years. What type of teaching strategies did most of your elementary teachers use? Did they present information, ask questions, give you assignments to work on at your seat, place you in small groups, or give you projects to complete? How did these strategies begin to change as you moved through the grade levels from first to third to sixth to ninth to twelfth grade? What instructional strategy was used most in your senior high school? What strategy is used most often in college? Which of the three levels—elementary school, middle (or junior high) school, and high school—tended to have the most teacher-focused instruction? Which were the most student-focused?

From Teacher-Focused to Student-Focused Instruction

Teaching methods change with the movement of students from elementary school through middle or junior high to high school and college. Some of the reasons for these changes relate to the previous experiences of the teachers, their training, and their philosophy of teaching. The elementary teacher uses more concrete, hands-on activities (as was the case in Dorothy Conway's second-grade classroom). Conway did more demonstrating than telling and had the students practice using concrete sticks to solve the problems. Many of the students were able to discover new applications for the rules of substraction presented in the class. Dorothy Conway used a balance of teacher-directed and student-directed strategies to achieve her goal of high student involvement along with mastery of the material.

Larry Cuban (1986) wrote that the history of education is one of a swing in philosophy from a teacher-centered curriculum to a student-focused curriculum. The type of instructional strategies used in the classroom may determine the type and levels of interaction in the classroom. The following strategies reflect the range of methods that are possible in classrooms from elementary school through college.

Teacher-Directed Strategies

Lecture

One of the most dominant strategies used in the classroom is that of the teacher telling or presenting information to students. This method dates back thousands of years and is a documented part of the teaching processes of the Greek civilization. The lecture method is the one with which we have had the greatest degree of experience. From the fourth grade through college, the predominant mode of instruction has been the lecture.

From our years as students, we may have experienced lecturers who have inspired, bored, threatened or cajoled us, provided humor or ridicule, were lively or exceedingly dull. In fact you can probably think of specific teachers who fit many of those descriptions. The point is that a strategy can be used in a variety of ways, and lecture is an important element to consider when designing and delivering the lesson.

Lecture Defined.   In the lecture method, the teacher is in control of the subject matter and orally presents information to a large group of students, generally without interruptions.

Types of Lecture.   In observations of teaching, several forms of the lecture method are used in the classroom, including the following:

1. *Pure lectures* are those in which the teacher orally presents information to the students, who passively listen or take notes. The lecturer (teacher) usually talks for the entire instructional period, leaving little or no time for questions. Pure lectures are usually found in high-school and college classrooms.

2. *Mini-lectures* include those in which the teacher presents information for short periods of time (five to fifteen minutes). Other strategies—including discussion, questioning and seatwork—may be interspersed with the mini-lectures during a fifty-minute period. Mini-lectures may be found in elementary classrooms as well as in middle-school and senior-high classrooms.

3. *Chalk-talk lectures* find the lecturer frequently using the chalkboard to make points, draw diagrams, develop lists, or provide examples. The teacher may use the overhead projector like a chalkboard, by facing the class and writing information on the screen with a marker. The chalkboard provides a visual reinforcement for the student and enables the teacher to emphasize specific points in the presentation.

4. *Audiovisual lectures* rely on media, such as the slide projector, overhead projector, film projector, video, or pictures and drawings, to parallel the presentation. In the audiovisual lecture, the teacher may use prepared overhead transparencies with different colored sheets of acetate to depict important visual differences in the information presented. The use of media adds another dimension to the instructional process. The students can see examples of information presented during the lecture.

5. *Interactive lectures* provide for the opportunities to elicit questions from students, with discussion during the presentation. Students may interrupt the lecturer at appropriate times to clarify points or to ask questions. The lecturer may also stop the lecture and ask students to comment on what has been presented. There is a give-and-take between the teacher and students, with the students having a more active role in the learning process.

6. *Guided note-taking lectures* are usually used by instructors at the middle-school, junior high, or senior high-school levels. The instructor provides the students with an outline of the topics to be covered during the class. The outline could be on a dittoed sheet, written on the chalkboard, or placed on the overhead projector. The teacher points to the outline as key points are presented during the presentation.

7. *Demonstration lectures* find the teacher showing some type of prop or material to the students. The demonstration is used to reinforce and provide a concrete example for an abstract concept. A science lesson on geology could include a rock sample to provide examples of different strata found in the earth. The use of a demonstration lecture adds a strong visual element to the presentation (Freiberg 1987).

With which of the above approaches to lecture are you most familiar? Which approaches would be new to you? Would you see yourself using any of the above in your own future classroom setting? What are your feelings about the lecture method? What are some of the advantages and limitations of using this method of instruction? Let's start with the last question first. Any instructional method has its benefits and disadvantages. The following describes some of these advantages and limitations.

Advantages of the Lecture.   Teachers use the lecture method for the following reasons:

1. It provides a great deal of comfort for most teachers, particularly at the secondary levels, because it is the method experienced by most of us in our schooling.
2. It gives teachers a high degree of control over the pace, material, questions, organization, time, and flow of interaction in the classroom.
3. It enables the teacher to synthesize and summarize material to which the students may not have easy access.

4. It enables the teacher to provide the same material to all students at the same time.

5. It is economical for use with large groups of students.

6. It provides the students with the opportunity to sharpen note-taking and listening skills, and at the secondary level, prepares the student for the college classroom.

7. It enables the teacher to develop a sequence of learning that can build from basic facts to higher concepts.

Each of the above advantages are based on our own experiences as teachers, discussions with other teachers, and synthesis of the research on the lecture method conducted during the past fifty years (Atherton 1972; Freiberg 1985; Henson 1980; Hillocks 1981; and Smith 1978).

Limitations of Lecture. As with any instructional strategy, lecture also has limitations for the teaching-learning process. Some would argue that the limitations of the lecture method are caused by the inappropriate use of the method by the instructor. Knowing those limitations may assist you in avoiding these pitfalls:

1. The lecture may become boring if the teacher uses a pure lecture format without any opportunity for student participation.

2. The lecture may have limited benefit if the teacher presents only the same information that is available in the textbook.

3. The lecture method places the student in a passive, rather than active, learning role. A long lecture after lunch, for example, could cause the students to lose the ability to concentrate after a few minutes.

4. Unless the teacher stops frequently to ask and answer questions, she or he is generally unaware of the amount of learning taking place.

5. Because lectures are usually used with large groups of students, the lecture method rarely identifies the needs of the individual learner.

6. In practice, most lecturers emphasize facts and information rather than larger concepts.

Variability and student participation improve lectures.

7. Higher-level thinking skills are difficult to develop when the instructor dominates the talk and provides limited opportunities for student input.

The advantages and limitations of the lecture method should be considered when deciding to use this strategy in the classroom. The effectiveness of any instructional strategy is contingent on the ability of the teacher to know when a method is appropriate and how to use it correctly.

Questioning

After lecture, teacher questioning of students is the most prevalent instructional strategy in both elementary and secondary classrooms. Dating back to studies conducted from the turn of the century, questioning is a well-documented part of most teachers' instructional repertoire (Gall 1984). Questioning also includes the elements of discussion that teacher questions can elicit in the classroom.

In our everyday activities, people who ask questions are seeking information about that which they are unsure of or do not know. If you are lost in a new town, you ask for directions; as you complete a form, you ask questions about the procedures for completing required information. The classroom, however, is one environment in which the person who usually knows the information asks questions of individuals who may not know the information.

The teacher asks questions in the academic setting for many reasons. Think back to your own learning experiences in school and reflect on the reasons teachers ask questions. As a future teacher, why would you want to ask questions? One of the most important reasons for asking questions is to check for understanding.

Questioning is a way to check for understanding.

Checking for Understanding

Considerable information is presented in the classroom, and the teacher needs to determine if the information has been retained by students. Checking for understanding should take place throughout the lesson. The following steps are proposed by Rosenshine and Stevens for checking student understanding. We have added notes to each of their points to provide additional examples and explanations.

1. Prepare a large number of oral questions beforehand.

   [Note: These questions could be written on three-by-five-inch cards prior to the lesson.]

2. Ask many brief questions on main points, supplementary points, and on the process being taught.

   [Note: For teaching basic skills and concepts, questions calling for short answers are appropriate.]

3. Call on students whose hands aren't raised in addition to those who volunteer.

   [Note: Teachers tend to call on those students who have the correct answer. Varying the routines for questioning will stimulate all students to be thinking of their response and to be active members of the lesson.]

4. Ask the students to summarize the rule or process in their own words.

   [Note: Have each student state one fact or idea learned from the lesson.]

5. Have all the students write the answers (on paper or chalkboard) while the teacher circulates.

   [Note: The use of small, hand-held chalkboards, which may be made or purchased at a teacher supply house, could be used in elementary grades.]

6. Have all students write the answers and check them with a neighbor (frequently with older students).

   [Note: This activity could be done for a few minutes at the beginning or end of the period or lesson.]

7. At the end of a lecture/discussion (especially with older students) write the main points on the board and have the class meet in groups and summarize the main points to each other (1986, 384).

   [Note: Students could meet in groups of two, three, or four for a few minutes. Depending on the amount of time, the teacher could ask one student from each group to summarize the main points.]

By asking the questions, the teacher is having the students focus on the subject or material, and the entire class has the opportunity to hear the answers and think about the questions themselves.

Advantages of Teacher Questions. Querying students has a number of important advantages for teachers:

1. It enables the teacher to check for understanding.
2. At both the elementary and secondary levels it can promote reading comprehension.
3. If comparison, opinion, synthesis, and evaluation questions are used in the classroom, higher-level thinking skills will develop.

4. It provides the opportunity for oral communication in the classroom.

5. Combined with discussion, the teacher can assist students in their social environment.

Approximately 60 percent of teacher questions require students to recall facts or information. Twenty percent of the questions focus on higher-level thinking skills, and the remaining questions fall into the organizational or procedural category. Teacher questions that ask students to think serve a different purpose than questions that ask students to recall information. The key for a teacher is to balance both types of questions (Gall 1984).

Limitations of Questions. The use of teacher questions also has its limitations. One researcher (Dillon 1985) concluded that teacher questions inhibit discussion in the classroom. Teachers can misuse questions to limit dialogue by dominating the interaction, or they can use questions for classroom management rather than academic purposes, addressing students who are not paying attention. The following list provides some insight into the limitations of teacher questions. Suggestions are provided in the notes, we developed to assist you in modifying the limitations.

1. The teacher may ask the same students most of the questions.

[Note: For elementary students, drawing popsicle sticks from a can with a student's name on each stick allows the teacher to ask questions in a more random fashion. For upper-elementary and secondary classrooms, the teacher can have the students write their name on two three-by-five-inch cards. The teacher collects the cards and uses the "two decks" of cards to draw the student's names. Two decks are used to increase the chance that a student may be called on more than once.]

2. The questions may only be directed at factual recall and ignore higher-level questioning skills.

[Note: Writing the higher-level questions on cards in advance will ensure that higher-level questions are asked during the lesson. Classifying questions according to Bloom's taxonomy (see Chapter 7) helps assure that higher-order questions are included in the discussion.]

3. The students may become bored if the teacher does not try to vary the teacher-question routine.

[Note: Using a combination of volunteers and teacher-selection of students to answer questions will reduce boredom. Be sure to ask the question first; then call out the student's name.]

4. The use of questions can be time-consuming if you do not have the questions prepared in advance.

[Note: Incorporating questions into the lesson will provide you with more time to observe and interact with the class than will trying to think about the next question during instruction.]

5. Adequate wait-time needs to be provided for the students to answer the questions.

[Note: Mary Bude Rowe (1974) suggests that three to five seconds between the time the teacher asks a question and the next teacher statement will give students adequate time to respond. This is particularly important for higher-level questions.]

Being attentive to student responses to your questions is an important part of the teaching-learning process. Effective use of questions can lead to a more productive and interesting instruction.

In the first two strategies, the teacher spends a considerable proportion of time presenting information orally, asking students questions and waiting for them to respond. The third most prevalent strategy in the classroom is drill and practice.

Drill and Practice

Providing the opportunity for drill and practice enables students to learn through repetitive actions. Drill and practice are different sides of the same coin. Drill is a teacher-directed activity, while practice is usually an independent student activity. For our discussion, we will separate drill from practice, although in classroom settings, they are used in tandem.

Drill. The word drill is defined here as any action by the teacher to impart or communicate information by repetition. The type of drill should be consistent with the purpose of the lesson. Drill in spelling should be written by the students, while drill in learning a language should be oral. Drill is used for rehearsal to make a seemingly awkward and difficult skill easier and more automatic. Young children do not have effectively-developed rehearsal strategies. These rehearsal strategies develop as a child matures. Teachers can assist them in improving both their knowledge of a subject and their ability to rehearse by including such activities in the instruction. Role playing, reading and rereading parts of a play, asking questions in advance to help students simulate an event before it occurs—all are ways of rehearsing. As adults we have developed strategies for learning lists of information. In learning dates, times, and places we tend to go over these bits of information in our minds. In studying for a test, some adults highlight the key points as they read; others orally state the key points while studying; and others rewrite the key points from lecture notes or from the text. In each of these cases, the student has developed a rehearsal strategy for learning the information. In the elementary or secondary classroom, the most common form of rehearsal is drill.

Weinstein and Mayer (1986) report, in the review of the research on student-learning strategies, that most ten-year-olds move their lips when involved in a learning activity, but most five-year-olds do not. The ten-year-olds are exhibiting a rehearsal strategy, while the five-year-olds have not yet spontaneously developed rehearsal strategies.

Advantages of Drill. The use of drill in the classroom includes several important advantages.

1. Drill provides an efficient strategy when repetition is needed to learn the skill or task (for example, in learning lists, the alphabet, dates, or names).
2. It is an efficient strategy when memorization is needed to move information from short-term to long-term memory.

3. It is an effective means of moving groups of students to the same level of understanding.

4. It is an important strategy when students must learn basic information that will be used to assist in more complex tasks (for example, learning the "times" table to complete higher-level math skills or to learn the rules of spelling and grammar to be a more effective writer).

Limitations of Drill.   The fact that drill is used in most classrooms in the United States is an indication of its importance. Summaries of research also support the effectiveness of drill. However, many students complain that drill can be boring, and teachers complain that some students are reluctant to volunteer during the drill activities. The disadvantages of using drill include the following:

1. Drill can become boring when the same pattern of drill is used each time.

[Note: The teacher could change the pattern by using choral drill, then moving to flash cards for individual responses, and three-by-five-inch cards to provide all the students with equal opportunities to respond.]

2. Oral drill can allow some students to be ignored by the teacher if a systematic pattern is not used in calling on all students.

3. Drill can be used as a substitute for teaching content to students.

[Note: The teacher should spend time instructing, discussing, and providing examples of key concepts in the lesson before moving into a drill activity.]

4. Drill can be used for a too lengthy period, causing fatigue in younger students and boredom in older students.

[Note: For the elementary grades, three to five minutes of drill is appropriate, and for the secondary grades five to seven minutes is appropriate.]

The teacher directs the drill activity for the entire class. Some educators have begun to call this activity *guided practice.* (One discovers, that in the field of education, several different terms may be used for the same instructional functions.)

Drill helps solidify understanding.

Practice, which is the partner of drill, is usually conducted independently by the students at their seats. Practice provides students with the opportunity to apply—as individuals—the instruction presented by the teacher to the entire class.

Practice. Both drill and practice are important when students need to overlearn a skill to the point it becomes automatic. All sports require both drill and practice. For example, the skill of dribbling in basketball must be mastered first to enable the player to integrate it with the jump shot. In learning to play the piano, the student begins with simple notes for the right hand, then the left, and progresses to mastering all the possible individual notes. When the individual notes are mastered to the point of becoming automatic, the student is able to progress to using the notes in combination, playing chords and complex songs.

Classroom teachers also need to provide students the opportunities for mastery of basic skills before students move on to higher levels and more complex processes. Students need to master basic addition and subtraction skills before they study multiplication and division. Writing requires a knowledge of the topic, audience, and a plan for presenting the written information (Scardamalia & Bereiter 1986). A teacher can teach the basics of writing, but it is the opportunity to practice writing and receive feedback on the writing samples that provides the student with the opportunity to build on previous knowledge.

Seatwork. It is estimated that in grades one through seven, seatwork is the most common form of independent practice. Students working alone at their seats account for 50–70 percent of all instructional activities in the classroom (Rosenshine & Stevens 1986) and students may spend up to 90 percent of their mathematics activity time on paper and pencil seatwork activities (Burns 1986).

For seatwork to be effective, the teacher must prepare students for the independent activity. Having the entire class complete one or two examples of an activity will help students be more productive during their seatwork time. If possible, you should move around the room and monitor what students are doing. It is important to determine which students are completing the tasks correctly. Behavior problems will increase if students become frustrated with seatwork assignments. With twenty-five to thirty students in the classroom, it is necessary to spend a brief period of time with each student while you walk around and monitor their work. More time may be spent with those students who have a pattern of difficulty in the seatwork activity.

If students are doing seatwork while the teacher is in the reading circle, then a two to three minute period between reading groups could be used to provide additional assistance to students. As with any instructional function in the classroom, seatwork takes some prior thought and planning to be an effective strategy.

Student-Focused Strategies

Grouping

Unlike most other professions, teachers work with groups of people every day. While a physician examines an individual patient and a lawyer defends an individual client, a teacher's job is at once to teach the group and educate the individual.

We group students for many reasons, the least of which is to reduce the cost to society for educating the young. We can find at least five different types of groupings in schools. The following describes some of these grouping patterns.

1. *Mental Ability.* Students may be grouped according to their ability as measured by standarized tests, teacher-made tests, or teacher observations of academic work. Such a grouping is called *homogeneous*, because students who have similiar abilities are clustered together. When students are randomly assigned to a class, then the group is *heterogeneous*. In such groups students represent a wide range of abilities.

2. *Age.* Most public schools set ages for entry into school. For example, many school districts require a child to be six years of age by September 1 prior to entry into first grade. This enables the teacher to work with a group of students whose birthdays are within a year of each other. Most states require all students to stay in school until they are sixteen years of age. In some instances, students who have excelled in academic work are allowed to progress more rapidly than their peer group. In other instances, students who have lacked maturity for their age or failed several courses may lag behind their initial peer group. Both of these instances reflect the exception rather than the rule. Although exceptions are found in our nation's educational system, the norm for entering and leaving schools is relatively consistent from district to district and from state to state.

3. *Sex.* For years in the development of our educational and schooling system, girls were either excluded from schooling entirely or segregated from boys. Many parochial schools continue to group by sex; physical education classes in private schools often separate boys and girls and some have pairs of schools—one for males and one for females. Title IX legislation and public sensitivity have reduced such segregation of the sexes in most public school settings.

4. *Physical Ability.* With the passing of the federal Public Law 94–142, students, with disabilities must be placed in the least restrictive learning environments. Students with physical handicaps may be grouped into special classes for the handicapped or they may be mainstreamed into regular classrooms. The hearing impaired, deaf and severely handicapped may be grouped separately from each other. However, many wheel chair-bound students are in regular classrooms, and schools are required to provide ready access to such classes for them. Many deaf students are placed in heterogeneous classrooms where they are assisted by a translator or where they lip read oral communication.

5. *Language.* Each year nearly two million non-English-speaking immigrants settle in the large urban areas, mostly in the southwest and western parts of the United States. Bilingual classes and ESL classes (English as a Second Language) draw their students into groups based on language needs. ESL classes may consist of students among whom as many as twenty different native languages (from Portugese to Vietnamese) are spoken. The teacher is trained as an ESL teacher with instruction in English. The bilingual classroom is usually taught primarily in the students' first language. As students become more proficient in English, they may move to an ESL classroom or to a regular classroom.

The five types of groups reflect ways in which the class is formed, and the teacher generally has little control over the formation. District policy and federal and state laws determine the types of grouping allowed in most schools. The teacher, however, does have control over the types of groups to be formed within the classroom. Within the classroom the teacher may also group students for specific learning activities. In the elementary grades students are most often grouped for reading. Two, three, or four reading groups are formed, based on the like reading levels of students. In secondary schools, grouping is seldom found in the content areas within a class.

Why Groups? While the research clearly supports groups containing one teacher for every one to three students, because such ratios produce higher student gains (Bloom 1984), the cost of such a method is beyond what our society is willing to support. Therefore, one teacher is commonly assigned for every thirty students, in order to save money. Several states have reduced the ratios to one teacher for every twenty-two students in kindergarten through second grade to provide students in their early, formative years a greater opportunity for learning. The trend in schools during the last few years has been to reduce teacher to student ratios.

Grouping for Learning. Using small groups to facilitate student learning and to produce gains in achievement is supported in the research literature (Slavin 1980). The two most common reasons for grouping is for *peer tutoring* and *group problem solving* or investigation. Peer tutoring occurs when a more able student is paired with a less able student. The two students work together during the normally assigned seatwork time.

The problem-solving group, which usually consists of four students, is presented a problem related to the content area and given an opportunity to solve the problem using a set of specific steps. The guided-discovery activity discussed next in this chapter incorporates problem-solving groups.

The process of having students work together in small cooperative groups is important if your goal is to increase cooperation among the students, to develop social and verbal interaction skills, and to provide opportunities for group problem solving and decision making. As with the other teaching methods, grouping has its advantages and limitations. The advantages of grouping center around the increased opportunity students have to interact with other students to solve problems and work cooperatively. Grouping also provides greater variety for the teacher in classroom instruction.

Effective classrooms aren't always desks in straight rows.

Advantages of Grouping.

1. Grouping provides instructional variability for the learner and teacher.
2. Grouping channels—within an academic environment—the social needs of students to interact.
3. Grouping gives students a greater opportunity to participate actively in the learning process.
4. Grouping gives students the opportunity to solve problems with others.
5. Grouping allows students (when using cooperative groups of two or four) to cooperate—rather than compete—in the classroom.

Limitations of Grouping.

1. The teacher must be adequately prepared in advance to manage small group activities.
2. Without proper training, students may not know how to solve problems and work cooperatively.
3. Indirect learning takes more time than teacher-directed learning.
4. The more articulate students may dominate the small groups.
5. Some groups may complete their assignments earlier than others.

Why Teachers Don't Group. Grouping for certain learning tasks seems to diminish as students progress through the grade levels. Secondary teachers attending a workshop on instructional effectiveness commented recently that they enjoyed working in groups during the inservice session. It kept them motivated and provided for active participation. Yet one teacher, who has taught for fifteen years admitted, "I rarely use groups in my freshman English class." Her concern about grouping resulted from a lack of experience in using the strategy and an absence of information about grouping during her preparation to be a teacher.

If you want to develop a range of instructional methods, you need to begin to explore those methods with which you have had limited experience. If grouping is one of those methods, begin building this strategy into your practice lesson plans and simulated teaching experiences.

Guided Discovery

Discovery. The term *discovery* has numerous definitions. Depending on the particular journal, text, or decade, the definition of discovery in an educational context takes on a slightly different meaning. At times, educators have used the terms *inquiry, problem solving, inductive learning,* and more recently *critical thinking* to mean discovery. For our use, we are incorporating a synthesis of definitions (Dunkin & Biddle 1974) to define guided discovery as: the ability of students to discover for themselves, based on a set of learning experiences, rules, principles, and generalizations.

... *P*roblems are the stimulus to thinking.

John Dewey—1938
Experience and Education.

Resurgence of Discovery Learning. We talked about educational trends from the 1940s up to the present in Chapter 2. The trend of independent thought in the learner evolved from the writings of Rousseau in the eighteenth century and from the progressive education movement and John Dewey in this century. During the 1950s when the nation was focusing on the need to develop a lead in the space race, educators began to look for ways to provide the opportunity for higher-level thinking skills. Curriculum projects in science, mathematics, and the social studies were developed

Grouping students can be effective if they aren't just sharing ignorance.

to respond to the need for a new type of thinker. This trend began to peak by the late sixties and early seventies. A renewed interest in discovery learning has emerged again during the eighties. This may be in response to the technological challenges the United States faces from the world economic community.

Sample Projects. Projects like those in Highland Park, Illinois (Falkof & Moss 1984) and Shoreham, New York (Grennon 1984) and SummerMath for Teachers (Simon 1986) reflect this renewed emphasis on discovery learning. Many in the mathematics field express a concern about students' lack of higher-level conceptual understanding. According to Simon (1986), mathematics teachers are using exploration/discovery and group problem solving to address these concerns.

Teacher's Role. With the guided-discovery approach, the teacher plays a greater role in determining what the student will experience and learn. The teacher structures the experience or problem for students and provides a series of steps for students to follow to discover the principle, rule, or generalization (see Exhibit 9.1). In other forms of discovery, the teacher withdraws from the guiding role and simply provides materials for students to use in discovering new principles (some critics would say students flounder).

The difference between the discovery curriculums of the sixties and those of the eighties relates to the role of the teacher. In the eighties, the teacher plays a more direct role in guiding students. The following steps should be considered in developing a guided-discovery lesson.

Guided discovery is an opportunity to explore new ideas.

EXHIBIT 9–1   Steps in Guided Discovery

1. The teacher or facilitator presents a problem, question, or situation that is interesting or exciting and will provoke student questions.
2. The teacher, by asking the students to define or explain terms, enables the students to precisely define the problem, question, or situation to be studied.
3. The teacher aids the students in the formulation of specific questions that will focus the inquiry and facilitate the collection of data relevant to the problem.
4. The teacher guides students toward a variety of sources, including himself or herself and other students, that can provide the necessary data.

5. The teacher assists students in double checking the data by clarifying the students' statements or judgments about the problem.
6. The teacher creates an open, student-centered environment in which students are encouraged to develop alternative solutions to the problem.
7. The teacher helps students develop a number of solutions, from which they may choose, and provides an opportunity for feedback and revision. The solutions are tested as to their effectiveness in solving the problem.
8. The teacher guides students in developing a plan of action (Freiberg 1973).

Facilitating students' discovery of mathematical concepts requires far more than a laissez-faire approach, in which the teacher does little other than stay out of the way. Rather, this difficult and demanding form of teaching requires teachers to examine the cognitive structure of the concepts to be taught and then to create series of experiences that will offer students the opportunity to explore the domain and discover these concepts.

Simon 1986, 41.

The steps just described should be used as a checklist for providing a smooth transition for the lesson. The guided-discovery approach incorporates several methods of teaching. These methods include a presentation of the background for the material to be reviewed by the students, discussion of key points, and the formation of students into working groups. The guided-discovery approach is more difficult than most to manage because of the need to balance several different types of methods.

Advantages of Guided Discovery.   Guided discovery offers a number of advantages to teachers.

1. Students become more actively involved in the learning process.
2. Students can begin to understand the relationships between schooling and the everyday world.
3. Students are provided the opportunity to solve problems.
4. Students are provided an opportunity to work in groups.
5. The teacher feels more freedom in the instructional process.

Limitations.   Guided discovery often is limited by a number of disadvantages.

1. The teacher may have difficulty changing from the role of information giver to the more indirect role of guider of learning.
2. The students may not be prepared for their own changing roles—from passive listeners to active learners.
3. The time spent in the process of discovery may not equal, in the short term, the knowledge gained from the strategy.
4. The teacher may need to spend more time in preparing and planning for a guided-discovery lesson.
5. The students may discover information that is not relevant to the intended goal of the lesson.

Adequate preparation is the key to successful implementation of a guided-discovery lesson. Students should have had the opportunity—prior to a discovery lesson—to work in groups of two and four to solve simple problems together. As the guider of the lesson, you should have a clear picture of the goal of the lesson and how the classroom materials will provide the necessary experiences to encourage the discovery process.

Conclusion

The use of a variety of instructional strategies will allow you to provide the students with a range of stimuli throughout the lesson. Based on current research and practice, we have learned that varying your teaching methods will enable you to keep the lesson interesting and to create a higher degree of student involvement. Teaching methods are a means of delivering instruction. A solid understanding of the content is needed if the teaching process is to be effective. Combining a range of instructional activities with a systematic curriculum will give you and your students an effective teaching-learning cycle.

Building Reflective Inquiry Skills

Design a lesson using either the specific lesson-plan format your instructor uses or one of the formats described in Chapter 8. Include three different teaching methods in the lesson. Use this plan in a simulated teaching situation or in a real one if the opportunity presents itself. In developing the plan, ask yourself the following questions relating to the selection and use of the teaching methods:

1. What was my rationale for selecting the three teaching methods?

2. Which of the three methods do I feel the most comfortable using and why?

3. What level of participation am I seeking from my students?

4. How will the teaching methods increase the opportunity for student learning?

Explorations

Exploration 1
Exploring Other Strategies
This chapter presented the five instructional strategies (lecture, questioning, drill and practice, grouping, and guided discovery) that are used most often in classrooms. There are, however, numerous other instructional strategies that may be used for specialized situations. Strategies for laboratory settings, field trips, learning centers, gaming, simulations, computer assisted instruction and demonstrations are only a few of the possibilities. Several books have been written, during the past few years, that focus exclusively on general teaching methods. This exploration will provide you the opportunity to expand your repertoire of teaching methods by reviewing the books below.

Dulaney, Carole; Eggen, Paul; Kauchak, Donald & Jacobsen, David (1981). Methods for Teaching: A Skills Approach, Charles E. Merrill Publishing Company, Columbus, Ohio.

Hyman, Ronald T. (1968). Teaching: Vantage Points for Study, (2nd Edition) J. B. Lippincott Company, Philadelphia, PA.

Jones, A. S.; Bagford, L. W. & Wallen, E. A. (1979). Strategies for Teaching. Scarecrow Press, Inc., Metuchen, N.J. & London.

Select only the one or two additional strategies from the books that you feel would be helpful for future teaching situations. Consider the following in the selection of the strategies:

1. Will the strategies add to your repertoire of teaching methods?

2. Will you have an opportunity to practice these strategies during your field-experience activities or in simulated teaching situations?

3. Does the strategy increase your understanding for implementing a particular content or curriculum?

If you can answer yes to each of these questions, then proceed to read the strategies in depth. Consider the following questions in reading each of the strategies:

1. What are the advantages and disadvantages of using the strategy in the classroom?

2. Is the strategy applicable for all grade levels and content areas?

3. Is the strategy teacher-focused or student-focused?

4. How would you intergrate the strategy into a lesson plan?

Clearly, expert teachers use a variety of instructional strategies in their classrooms. Building your repertoire of strategies will assist you in expanding your instructional options.

Exploration 2
Guided Discovery/Lesson Check
If you have an opportunity to teach a lesson using a guided-discovery instructional strategy, check your lesson against the guided-discovery checklist provided in this chapter.

Exploration 3
Types of Groups
Ask an experienced teacher what types of groups she or he uses in the classroom. Ask how the groups are managed and what preplanning is needed to have the groups work effectively. Ask if cooperative grouping is used in the classroom.

References

Atherton, C. R. (1972). Lecture, discussion, and independent study methods revisited. *Journal of Experimental Education, 40*, 24–29.

Bloom, Benjamin S. (1984). The search for methods of group instruction as effective as one-to-one tutoring. *Educational Leadership, 41*, 4–17.

Burns, M. (1986). Teaching "what to do in arithmetic" vs. teaching "what to do and why". *Educational Leadership, 43*, 34–38.

Cuban, L. (1984). *How teachers taught. Constancy and change in American classrooms: 1890–1980.* New York: Longman.

Dewey, J. (1938). *Experience & education,* New York: Collier Books.

Dillon, J. (1985). Using questions to foil discussion. *Teaching & Teacher Education, 1*, 109–121.

Dunkin, M. & Biddle, B. (1974). *The study of teaching.* New York: Holt, Reinhart, and Winston.

Falkof, L. & Moss, J. (1984). When teachers tackle thinking skills. *Educational Leadership, 42*, 4–9.

Freiberg, J. (1973). *Inquiry approach* In W. R. Houston and Sarah C. White (Ed.) *Professional Development Modules*, Houston, Texas.

Freiberg, J. (1985). *Generic teaching strategies: Lecture.* Unpublished manuscript. University of Houston.

Freiberg, J. (1987). *Lecture—A universal teaching method.* In *Contributed Papers of Improving University Teaching: Proceedings of the Thirteenth International Conference*, Haifa, Israel (pp. 274–283) College Park: University of Maryland-University College.

Gall, M. (1984). Synthesis of research on teacher's questioning. *Educational Leadership, 42*, 40–47.

Grennon, J. (1984). Making sense of student thinking. *Educational Leadership, 42*, 11–16.

Henson, K. T. (1980). What's the use of lecturing? *The High School Journal, 64*, 115–119.

Hillocks, G., Jr. (1981). The response of college freshman to three modes of instruction. *American Journal of Education, 89*, 373–395.

Leinhardt, G. (1986). Expertise in mathematics teaching. *Educational Leadership, 43*, 28–33.

Rosenshine, B. & Stevens, R. (1986). Teaching functions. In M. C. Whittrock (Ed.), *Handbook of research on teaching.* (3rd Edition), New York: Macmillian.

Rowe, M. (1974). Wait-time and rewards as instructional variables, their influence on language, logic, and fate control: Part 1 Wait time. *Journal of Research in Science Teaching, 11*, 81–94.

Scardamalia, M. & Bereiter, C. (1986). Research on writing composition. In M. C. Wittrock (Ed.), *Handbook of research on teaching.* (3rd Edition). New York: Macmillian.

Simon, M. (1986). The teacher's role in increasing student understanding of mathematics. *Educational Leadership, 43*, 40–43.

Slavin, R. (1980). Cooperative learning. *Review of Educational Research*, 50, 315–342.

Stallings, J. & Mohlman, G. (1981). *School policy, leadership-style, teacher change and student behavior in 8 secondary schools.* Prepared for the National Institute of Education, La Handa, CA: Stallings Teaching and Learning Institute.

Smith, I. K. (1978). Teaching with discussion: A review. *Educational Technology, 28*(11), 40–45.

Weinstein, C. & Mayer, R. (1986). The teaching of learning strategies. In M. C. Whittrock (Ed.) *Handbook of research on teaching* (3rd Edition). New York: Macmillan.

Creating Effective Classroom Management

OBJECTIVES

By the end of this chapter, you will be able to:

1. Define classroom management.
2. Describe your management values for the classroom.
3. Describe how to use time effectively in the classroom.
4. Discuss rules and procedures for the first day and weeks of school.
5. Discuss several perspectives of classroom management.
6. Identify strategies for preventing and stopping inappropriate behavior.

KEY WORDS AND CONCEPTS

Consequences and rewards in the
   classroom
First days and weeks of school
Historical perspectives on classroom
   management
Linking effective instruction with class-
   room management
Off-task and on-task student behaviors
Prevention and intervention
Rules and procedure development
Stopping inappropriate behavior

The Importance of Management

Management is at the heart of any effective organization. An effective manager is someone who coordinates and orchestrates activities to meet specific goals and objectives. Today's classrooms, more than ever, need effective managers. The expectations by parents and the public for both students to achieve and for teachers to keep order is greater today than in any other time in recent history. Classroom management is a skill which enables the teacher to instruct and the students to learn. Without effective management, the learning process is disrupted and the teacher turns to reprimanding or disciplining students for interfering with instruction.

Teachers need the same management skills as a civil engineer or a television news director. The Tucson Education Association (1986), in an extensive review of jobs comparable to teaching, identified civil engineers and television news directors as having the same on-job, decision-making demands as teachers. The classroom teacher has also been compared to a business executive with an ongoing list of decisions, responsibilities and actions required on a daily basis (Berliner 1982).

Classroom teachers manage numerous details during the course of a day. The following is a representative sample of only a few of the major actions taken by teachers each day. The range of activities includes the following:

- planning and preparation for teaching,
- continuous interaction with students,
- implementation of lessons,
- organization of time and materials,
- movement of students through different activities,
- establishment of order, and
- the creation of an environment for learning, which at times may include disciplining students who disrupt the learning process.

In many instances, classroom management and discipline are used interchangeably. As we will see, management is more than discipline, and teaching is more than management. Although effective classroom management does not guarantee outstanding teaching, most effective teachers are also effective classroom managers.

Defining Classroom Management

Based on the research of Edmund Emmer and Carolyn Evertson, classroom management is described as consisting of:

> [1] teacher behaviors that produce high levels of student involvement in classroom activities, [2] minimal amounts of student behaviors that interfere with the teacher's or other students' work, and [3] efficient use of instructional time. (Emmer & Evertson 1981, 342)

The definition has three distinct components, which we have highlighted with corresponding numbers [1], [2], and [3]. We will disuss each of the three elements and provide examples for your analysis.

Classroom management consists of: [1] teacher behaviors that produce high levels of student involvement in classroom activities;

Active Involvement. The first part of the definition emphasizes the need for the teacher to actively involve the students in the instructional process. Students who are actively learning will have fewer opportunities to be off-task or misbehave. Keeping the students on-task is an important aspect of both instruction and management. Students who are on-task are actively engaged in the assignment presented by the teacher. The students are not looking out the window, resting their head on the desk behind an open textbook, talking, or doodling. The students are engaged in the task at hand.

The management of instruction and of students is interrelated with teaching activities. Chapters 8 and 9, which discuss instructional delivery and instructional design, provide plans and examples for keeping students on-task by engaging and motivating the learner.

Classroom management consists of: [2] minimal amounts of student behaviors that interfere with the teacher's or other students' work;

Minimal Disruptions. The second part of the definition of classroom management focuses on the need for creating an orderly environment for learning. The teacher is not prevented from teaching nor are the students prevented from learning. Small infractions, like chatting during instruction, can ripple through the classroom to cause major distractions in the learning climate.

Effective teachers minimize disruptions by capturing student attention.

Jacob Kounin (1970) first described the "ripple effect," the effects of misbehavior by a few students on the entire class. The ripple effect looks much like a stone that is dropped into a still pool of water. The stone causes a series of expanding concentric circles. Within the classroom, a misbehavior by one student may ripple throughout the classroom to other students. Kounin recommends that the teacher "desist" the misbehavior before it begins to ripple throughout the classroom.

As a student in school, how many times have you seen a minor infraction, like whispering in class by two students during instruction, suddenly become a tidal wave of talking. The teacher needs a workable plan for managing the classroom, but any plan will falter if the teacher is not consistent. If the teacher expects the students to listen during instruction (which is a reasonable expectation), the teacher must be consistent in enforcing that rule. The sooner the misbehavior is desisted, or ended, the better. Analyzing the problem of misbehavior becomes more meaningful when you can practice your responses to some potentially disruptive student behaviors in a nonthreatening situation.

Disruptions.   Most disruptions occur during the first five minutes of class, during transitions from one activity to another, and at the end of the class period. Preventing problems from occurring in the classroom is a key element to classroom management. Most effective classroom management is a combination of good organization, preparation, consistency of actions and feedback, clarity of expectations and directions, and an understanding of the students—both as individuals and as a group. Discipline problems occur only when the prevention strategies break down or if the teacher never had them adequately in place. Communicating expectations becomes a key element in the development of a management plan for the classroom. Exploration 1 is an activity that will have you focus on those values that you hold to be important in the establishment of classroom management for your future classroom. The management values activity will give you an opportunity to identify the values that you feel are the most important in the classroom.

Today, teachers from kindergarten through grade twelve are faced with a wide range of management and discipline problems that, left unchecked, may hinder and frequently prevent students from learning. In the study cited by Walter Doyle (1979) of first and fifth graders, teachers made conduct statements to students nearly 16 times per hour, which accumulated to 87 times a day or approximately 16,000 times a year. Although teacher statements regarding student behavior is an ongoing occurrence, most student misbehaviors are relatively minor, with student talking during instruction and tardies being the most common problems.

Student Perceptions.   Students also have concerns about discipline in the classroom. The information reported from a national sample (see Tables 10.1 and 10.2) reflect high school students' perceptions and self-reports about discipline in their schools. The data were compiled by the U.S. Department of Education, National Center for Education Statistics, *High School and Beyond Study* in 1984. Did any of the results surprise you? What would you conclude about our high schools from the data?

TABLE 10.1   High School Seniors' Perception of School Discipline and Behavior Problems

	Percent of Students Indicating "My School Has A Problem With:"				
Characteristic	*Class Cutting*	*Poor Attendance*	*Student Fighting*	*Threats or Attacks on Teachers*	*Percent of Students Who Do Not Feel Safe At School*
All students	65	54	29	5	7
Student characteristics:					
Sex:					
Male	61	51	30	6	8
Female	68	57	29	4	6
Race/ethnicity:					
White, non-Hispanic	64	53	27	4	5
Black, non-Hispanic	68	56	39	12	12
Hispanic.	63	56	34	8	10
Asian or Pacific Islander	63	45	21	5	10
American Indian/Alaskan Native . . .	59	51	25	4	9
Socioeconomic status group: [1]					
Low.	68	61	38	8	10
Low-middle	68	59	34	6	7
High-middle	69	57	30	5	6
High.	66	49	22	3	5
Test performance group: [2]					
Low.	62	55	38	10	13
Low-middle	68	60	33	5	7
High-middle	67	55	26	3	5
High.	63	46	19	2	3
High school program: [3]					
Academic	64	49	24	3	4
General	72	63	35	6	7
Vocational	71	62	37	8	9
School characteristics:					
Control:					
Public.	68	57	31	6	7
Catholic	27	18	13	2	4
Other private.	39	25	9	1	4
Community type:					
Urban.	69	57	31	8	10
Suburban	66	53	27	4	6
Rural	60	54	31	5	7

1. Socioeconomic status was measured by a composite score on parental education, family income, father's occupation, and household characteristics.

2. Test performance was measured by a test battery administered as part of the High School and Beyond Study.

3. High school program as reported by student.

Source: U.S. Department of Education, National Center for Education Statistics, High School and Beyond Study, unpublished tabulations (September 1984).

Because school tends to reflect our society (as we noted in Chapter 2), violence in society unfortunately finds its way into the schools. In the past few years, school board members and district administrators have taken a much tougher stand against all forms of disorder through stronger school and classroom discipline policies and practices.

Classroom management consists of: [3] efficient use of instructional time.

TABLE 10.2 High School Seniors' Self-Reports of Discipline and Behavior Problems

	Percent of Students Who Reported They Had:					
Characteristic	Cut Classes	Attended Class Without Homework Completed	Disciplinary Problems	Been Suspended for Academic Reasons	Been Suspended For Disciplinary Reasons	Been in Serious Trouble With The Law
All students	42	28	14	4	12	5
Student characteristics:						
Sex:						
Male	46	35	18	6	17	8
Female	38	21	10	2	8	2
Race/ethnicity:						
White, non-Hispanic	42	28	12	3	12	5
Black, non-Hispanic	36	25	18	6	13	5
Hispanic...........	43	32	20	8	14	7
Asian or Pacific						
Islander	42	24	15	6	7	4
American Indian/						
Alaskan Native	52	31	19	5	12	12
Socioeconomic status group: [1]						
Low	37	32	18	6	14	5
Low-middle	40	30	14	4	13	4
High-middle	44	29	13	4	12	5
High..............	44	26	12	3	11	4
Test performance group: [2]						
Low	42	32	21	8	15	7
Low-middle	43	29	15	4	15	5
High-middle	44	27	12	2	12	4
High..............	37	23	9	1	7	3
High school program: [3]						
Academic..........	37	22	9	2	8	2
General	47	36	16	5	15	5
Vocational	41	33	17	6	14	6
High school characteristics:						
Control:						
Public...........	43	28	14	4	12	5
Catholic	24	26	11	4	11	3
Other private	43	24	14	2	14	5
Community:						
Urban...........	46	26	16	5	11	5
Suburban	43	29	13	4	13	5
Rural	37	28	14	4	12	5

1. Socioeconomic status was measured by a composite score on parental education, family income, father's occupation, and household characteristics.

2. Test performance was measured by a test battery administered as part of the High School and Beyond survey.

3. High school program as reported by student.

Source: U.S. Department of Education, National Center for Education Statistics, High School and Beyond Study, unpublished tabulations (October 1984).

Efficient Use of Time. The third and final element of the classroom management definition by Emmer and Evertson emphasizes the need for effective use of instructional time. A great deal of time is wasted during the instructional day. Effective classroom managers provide up to 90 minutes of instruction per day more than do ineffective teachers (Stallings 1980).

Given 180 days in the school year, that could equal up to 9 weeks of instruction. Add to this the time lost at the beginning and end of the school year and before and after major holidays, the amount of time lost for instruction is significant.

Time is lost, for example, at the beginning of the period if the teacher takes role while the students wait for their names to be called. A more efficient approach to maximizing the use of time could include the following procedure: *As the students enter the room, they read an assignment the teacher has written on the board or a written review the teacher has placed on each student's desk. The teacher takes role or answers individual questions while the class works.*

Examples of how two teachers use time in the classroom are presented in Case Studies A and B (Exhibits 10.1 and 10.2.) These case studies are based on verbatim transcripts received as part of a research study conducted by Emmer, Evertson, Sanford, Clements, and Worsham (1981). On the exhibit itself, using the space to the right of the transcript, or on a separate piece of paper, make notes regarding the effective use of time by each teacher. The researchers have conducted their own analysis, which is provided in the Appendix at the conclusion of this chapter. Note how closely your own analysis matches the expert's view of the two situations.

EXHIBIT 10.1   Case Study A

Your Comments

Teacher tells class to open math books to Page 148. Noise begins immediately. Teacher says, "Jose, I need your attention." (Actually, she needs the attention of the whole class, but Jose was very visibly not paying attention and climbing around under his desk.) The teacher starts to explain some of the problems in the math book. Jennifer and Michael decide they need to sharpen their pencils while the teacher is going over the instructions and they do so.

The teacher doesn't say anything about it and lets them both do it. The teacher asks a question and gets all kinds of call-outs in reply—some of them completely off base.

She makes no comment about this. The teacher is still having to tell those who haven't been paying attention what page they are on. She has already said this about ten times to various individuals. The teacher gets frustrated by the noise and inattention.

So she decides to stop and sit quietly, hoping that they will be quiet and listen to her. The noise and call-outs continue, and if the students are even aware that the teacher has stopped the lesson, they give no indication. After four minutes (while 20 of the students are talking and fooling around and three are waiting for the teacher to resume) the teacher says, in a slightly upset voice, "I can't talk above the noise and I won't even try."

<u>Students settle down a little bit but the majority still do
not give her their attention as she continues the lesson.
She resumes, but is continually interrupted by the noise.</u>
Two students have a brief fight in the back of the room,
but she appears not to notice. Teacher tells one student
loudly to sit down. He does so, but has still not opened his
math book and she makes no comment on this. Another
student gets up to look at the spelling spirals. Less than
half of the class is listening and doing the problems with
the teacher. The teacher has done nothing to remedy the
situation. One student comes up to the teacher while she
is talking and asks a question. She says rather loudly, "we
are doing math now. I don't have time for that sort of
thing." Several students are up and roaming around. Two
boys are playing with a wet paper towel. One is loudly
slapping it in his hands as he wanders back to his seat.
The teacher says nothing. Instead she tells the class that
she expects them to have all the math problems down on
their papers. Noise continues while some of the students
scramble to get to work on the lesson that has now been
going on (or has been trying to go on) for the last twenty
minutes. Five minutes later she collects the students' math
spirals. It is now dead time for the students for the next six
minutes. One student gets up and switches on the overhead projector without permission. Then three more students join him in fooling around with it. The teacher then
tells them to sit down. The noise continues, and none of
the students are paying attention to the teacher. The
teacher just stands watching the class, saying and doing
nothing.

Your Comments

Source: Emmer, E., Evertson, C., Sanford, J., Clements, B., & Worsham, M. (1981). Organizing and
managing the elementary school classroom. Austin: University of Texas at Austin, R & D Center for
Teacher Education.

EXHIBIT 10.2   Case Study B

Your Comments

It is the morning of the first day, and the students are arriving at the room individually and in small groups. Two
boys enter the room "goofing off." The teacher says in a
pleasant but firm voice, "Okay, guys, quit fooling around."
They comply, get their nametags, and take their seats
quietly. . . .

. . . Later in the morning a student bangs his chair
noisily on the floor. <u>The teacher immediately tells him, "Be
quiet, please."</u>

. . . It is time for a break to get drinks of water in the
hall, and the teacher has told the class they will line up by
tables. Jimmy, however, immediately jumps up. <u>"What did
I say, Jimmy?"</u> No reply, he sits. <u>"Jimmy?"</u> Jimmy responds,
"Huh?" The teacher states firmly, <u>"It's 'Sir' in this room, not
'huh'."</u> The teacher doesn't need to specify that Jimmy
must sit down and wait for his table to be called. Jimmy knows this is what he was called down for. (This is
probably why he did not respond to the initial question.)

. . . Jeffery starts talking to the students at his table. The teacher says, "Jeffery, I'd like you to move to this table," pointing to one in the center of the room. "There's been too much talking at this table this morning," referring to his present table.

. . . The teacher directs the students to look at a sign posted at the back of the room. It has "Leaders" written on it, and one student calls out, "Leaders!" The teacher replies, "Yes, but in this class we don't call out answers, we raise our hands." He asks what leaders do and calls on various students with raised hands.

. . . Toward the end of the morning two students begin fooling around and one of them shouts out. The teacher tells him, "Excuse me, would you turn around and face front." He does so, and the fooling around stops.

These are the disruptive incidents that occurred in the first four hours of the first day. Each time, the teacher stepped in immediately and firmly, but not harshly. On the third day another observer commented, "This class is already molded in terms of management and procedures. . . . This teacher has good rapport with his students."

Source: Emmer, E., Evertson, C., Sanford, J., Clements, B., & Worsham, M. (1981). Organizing and managing the elementary school classroom. Austin: University of Texas at Austin, R & D Center for Teacher Education.

Your Comments

Perspectives of Classroom Management

In addition to the research perspectives described by Emmer and Evertson and others in the definition of classroom management, two other perspectives will be presented in this chapter—an historical perspective and a psychological perspective. The historical perspective will be addressed from the viewpoint of a school principal. The psychological perspective will be presented from the viewpoint of two different philosophies of human behavior.

Historical Perspective

Much has been written during the last twenty years about classroom management and discipline. Kounin's (1970) work seems to be a benchmark for the recent researchers (Emmer & Evertson 1981). However, school and classroom management has been researched, discussed, and debated in print at least since the time of compulsory education. In a classic book for school administrators, *The Management of a City School*, Arthur C. Perry identifies numerous teacher traits and management skills which he feels lead to an effective teacher:

1. *A calm and quiet manner.* Quiet begets quiet. The teacher's self-control impresses pupils with the feeling that the teacher has inexhaustible reserve, so that it would be useless for them even to attempt to fathom it.

2. *Firmness and decision.* These are in no way inconsistent with kindness and kindliness. Pupils respect the firm hand and the decisive will.

3. *Industry and energy.* The spirit of work is contagious. The working teacher has working pupils.

4. *Cheerfulness.* Work is not related to solemnity. A cheerful spirit will induce productive work where a "soured" disposition can, at best, get only time service.

5. *Sympathy.* By this is meant the deep, true sympathy with boy- and girl-nature; no "mollycoddling," but a sincere desire to get the pupil's viewpoint, to appreciate his problems, to get into his life, and to help him to help himself.

6. *Vigilance.* The alertness of the eye, ear, and trained perceptions will permit little that occurs in the class to escape notice. On the other hand, good judgment as to what to recognize and refer to on the moment, and what to stow away in memory to be drawn upon later if needed, must be ever present.

7. *Fairness and justness.* The pupils forgive almost anything else in a teacher but unfairness or partiality.

8. *Order, system and neatness.* These virtues of the teacher reflect themselves in corresponding virtues in the pupils.

9. *Scholarship.* This alone will not discipline a class, but the teacher who has it may with it command the respect of her pupils, and this respect is the best foundation upon which to rear the superstructure of class control.

10. For most new teachers, however, mere emphasis of these positive principles is insufficient and must be supplemented by continual cautions as to "what not to do." For instance, they must be warned against:

    a. *Not working pupils enough.* It is more difficult to do nothing than to do something; particularly, it is more difficult to make pupils do nothing than to make them do a specific something.

    b. *Not maintaining good order at the start.* The teacher passes over the early infractions with the thought, if she thinks about it at all, that she will discipline when there is something more serious to consider.

    c. *Not having a carefully planned system for the changing of activities.* Good teaching method carries the class along nicely during the lessons, but the "between times" are bothersome. The teacher must learn both to merge one exercise into another so that there are few "breaks," and also to plan the inevitable breaks, e.g., the distribution of materials, the changing of seats, the dismissals, etc., so that they may be executed without confusion.

    d. *Giving unnecessary directions and orders.* It is far better to give one carefully thought out, rational order and see that it is obeyed by all, than to give half-a-dozen different and probably conflicting directions in the same time.

    e. *Threatening.* The quiet teacher who gives orders and tacitly but clearly expects them to be obeyed, leaves the pupils to "guess" what will happen to them in case of disobedience, until such disobedience occurs, when the punishment comes surely, promptly and unmistakenly.

    f. *Scolding and using sarcasm and epithets.* Very rarely, indeed, should the teacher use these weapons, and then only as a deliberate and judicial punishment.

g. *Driving the willful child into obstinacy.* Instead of avoiding conflict, she is apt to think it her duty to raise issues and "conquer" the pupil's will.

h. *Assigning school exercises as punishments.* The wrong of doing this needs no demonstration, yet it is a mistake made by nearly every new teacher.

i. *Punishing a group for the offense of an individual.* Far better is it to let a dozen guilty pupils escape than to punish them and with them a single innocent pupil. (Perry 1908, 262–265)

What are your thoughts about the author's insights? Current research supports many of Perry's ideas, which were articulated over *eighty years ago*. Why do you think classroom management remains a difficult task today?

Psychological Perspectives

The development of theories about classroom management are derived in part from the field of psychology. The two most prevalent theories of psychology related to classroom management are based on the works of B. F. Skinner and Carl R. Rogers. Neither Skinner nor Rogers have proposed programs or models for classroom management; however, many of the current approaches to classroom management build upon their works.

Reinforcement.   B. F. Skinner (1957) described human behavior as resulting from the environment. If the environment can be controlled through reinforcement, then the individual's behavior can be shaped or changed. Students exhibit a range of behaviors in the classroom. For example, when the teacher asks a question of the class, some students raise their hands while other students shout out the answer. Both behaviors are operant in that they are natural for students at that time. The teacher wants the students to raise their hands rather than shouting out the answer and disrupting the question-and-answer period. Using the principle of reinforcement, the teacher would recognize only those students with their hands raised. Reinforcement increases the likelihood that a particular behavior will continue in the future. In this case, the teacher is reinforcing the behavior of the students who are raising their hands. Ignoring the students who shout out the answers will lessen the reinforcement for this behavior and reduce the likelihood of its occurrence. However, many teachers make the mistake of recognizing the students who shout out the answers and, therefore, reinforce the shouting-out behavior while reducing the likelihood that the other students will continue to raise their hands.

Behavior Modification.   Skinner's psychological ideas were translated into educational practice in the early 1970s, through the concept of behavior modification. If the teacher can control the classroom environment, then the behavior of the students could be modified to fit a standard of behavior. Many of the reinforcers used to modify student behavior include rewards for appropriate behavior and consequences, or punishment, for inappropriate behavior. Some elementary and middle-school teachers use stickers, happy faces, treats, and other tangible rewards to reinforce appropriate behavior in the classroom. Consequences for inappropriate behavior may include loss of free time, staying after school, or moving a student to another chair in the back of the room. High school teachers who use behavior modification principles tend to emphasize nontangible rewards like praise or providing leadership roles in the classroom. As consequences for inappropriate behavior, high school teachers usually emphasize detention after school and the threat and use of suspension for severe behavior problems. Although the number of states that legally allow corporal punishment has diminished during the last ten years, some states, particularly in the south and southwestern parts of the United States, legally allow teachers or principals to spank, "pop," or paddle students who are disruptive. States that do allow corporal punishment usually require the written permission of the parents.

The following is a description of how rules, consequences and rewards could be implemented in the classroom from a Skinnerian, or behavior modification, perspective. These examples and discussions are based on an article entitled *Consistency: The Key to Classroom Management*, which is listed in the reference section.

Establishing Rules

An effective manager establishes the most important rules (limited to five or six) and procedures needed for the class to function effectively. Just as street lights are used to give each motorist an equal opportunity to enter and leave an intersection, classroom rules are needed to establish equal opportunities for each student to learn.

The students look to the teacher as a role model. A teacher who is consistent in reinforcing the class rules will be able to provide the students with more opportunities to learn with fewer disruptions. The need to be consistent is not a one-time effort. Although the research presented here supports the position that the better managers establish rules on the first day and teach them each day for the first month—consistency is needed every day school is in session.

Rules. The rules the teacher establishes should be stated in the positive. For example, "Bring pen, books, and paper to class," "Raise your hand," "Keep hands and feet to yourself," and "Walk in the classroom." "Don't run" is an example of the last rule stated in the negative. It tells the student what not to do, but fails to redirect inappropriate behavior. It is important that the expectation levels be directed toward what the student should be doing. The rules should be posted in plain view of all students.

Three Approaches. Establishing rules during the first days of school provides a framework for the students. Rules act as a guide for what is acceptable and unacceptable behavior in the classroom. Allowing students to contribute to the development of the rules encourages student participation. Teachers who involve their students in the development of the rules find greater involvement and fewer disruptions during class. Some teachers have the students sign the posted rules as a type of group contract.

Many teachers have a set of rules in mind when they meet their students for the first time. There are at least three ways in which a teacher can establish rules for the class:

1. The teacher prepares the rules and brings them to class the first day. Time is spent reviewing and explaining the rules.
2. The teacher has established the rules in his or her own mind but spends the first part of the class having the students discuss the needs for rules and procedures; then, as a group the teacher and the students create five or six rules for the class.
3. The teacher presents three or four rules that she or he believes are important and permits the class to add two or three rules to the list that they believe are needed.

Regardless of the procedure used to establish rules for the classroom, the key to maintaining them is the ability of the teacher to "teach" and then practice the rules with the students as if he or she were teaching a math, science, or English lesson.

In Elementary Schools. On the first day of school, elementary teachers (K–5) often have their students practice lining up and walking to the cafeteria prior to lunch so they will know what to do. They practice going to the restroom, receiving a hall pass, and other procedures for movement inside or outside the classroom. At the upper elementary-school levels, for example, the teacher may also have the students practice lining up, passing in papers, or using the pencil sharpener.

In Secondary Schools. At the secondary level, the teacher would present a written list of the rules to the class once one of the above three procedures for establishing rules has been accomplished. Many secondary teachers post the rules in the classroom. Teaching and discussing the rules is also important for the secondary classroom. The teacher may begin a discussion of rules in general, using questions like these: Are there rules in everyday life? What would a football game or other sporting event be like without rules? Why were rules established for sports? What is the purpose of traffic signals or railroad crossing signs? What is the purpose of a legal system for the society? From a general description of the rules, the teacher and class could then discuss the specific rules for the classroom.

During early field experiences in the schools, you may want to ask the teacher if she or he established any particular rules for the classroom. Notice if they are posted or, at some point, distributed to the students. During your student-teaching experience, awareness of the written and unwritten rules of the classroom may play an important part in your own understanding of the limits previously established for the students by your cooperating teacher.

The teacher can prevent many problems by begining the instructional activities quickly and by anticipating misbehavior and heading it off before it begins. However, once a student misbehaves, some form of intervention is necessary.

Consequences

Teachers need to set limits for students' behavior and provide some consequences for inappropriate behavior. The most common consequences for inappropriate behavior include the use of verbal reprimands, additional assignments, detention, or corporal punishment. It seems to defeat the purpose of school to use academic work or staying after school as a punishment. Corporal punishment may lead to greater problems of aggressiveness in the future. Verbal reprimands have a point of diminishing returns. After a while, the teacher may find himself or herself yelling at the students.

The teacher could establish a hierarchy of five or six consequences for breaking classroom rules. The teacher may keep a notebook and list any rules a student breaks during class time. This procedure could be used to establish a behavior grade, which many school districts require for report cards. Students may be asked to write down the rules that they broke, or they may be asked to send a note home explaining the problems that occurred in class and disrupted the teaching-learning process. Consequences should fit the infraction. Prevention is the key to effective management. An overreliance on consequences can lead to a fearful learning environment. It is important to create a balance between rules, consequences, and rewards.

Both the rules and the consequences must be applied equally to all students in the classroom. Any management plan should be sent home to the parents; it has been our experience that early parental involvement is an important element in successful classroom management.

Reinforcement

The teacher as a role model is particularly important at the elementary school level. It is important for the teacher to prevent inappropriate student behavior. However, it is equally crucial to provide positive models of appropriate student behavior. Praising a student for doing her or his work may seem simplistic, but the results are highly effective. For example, one of the authors observed a fifth-grade class going from their classroom to the cafeteria. The thirty students had to pass by fifteen classes still in session. Three male students began making loud noises. Typically, the teacher would have yelled at the students to be quiet. The results would have been unpredictable, but it is certain that more noise would have been generated by the teacher's reprimand. The teacher, however, handled the situation by stating, "I like the way John, Linda, Jeffery, and Jose are walking quietly in the hall." All three disruptive students suddenly became quiet. Through positive praise of others, the teacher was able to establish positive expectations and appropriate behavior in the halls.

Rewards. Over the years, teachers have used a variety of methods to reinforce or reward appropriate student behavior. Some of the ideas are best described by the following examples:

1. Mrs. Jones, who teaches in an inner-city school, had a glass jar and marbles near her desk. When she felt the class was working well on tasks, she would call out the names of two or three students and drop a marble in

the jar. She felt the class needed to earn their reward and the jar of marbles was her way of reinforcing the students. The more appropriate the behavior of individual students, the greater the number of marbles the entire class received. Inappropriate student behavior limited the number of marbles placed into the jar, but the class always kept the marbles they had previously earned. Students earned a reward when the jar was filled. Marbles were never removed from the jar. Mrs. Jones asked the students, in a short survey, what they considered to be a good reward. Their responses included: more story-telling time, ten minutes of free reading time, awards for good conduct, good citizen awards, a popcorn party on Friday afternoon, "super student" buttons, guest speakers, field trips, a picnic during regular lunch time, special art projects, and listening to music.

The ideas surprised the teacher because of their intrinsic value. The teacher was very pleased with the results and with the positive climate that began to develop in the classroom.

2. Mr. Clark, who taught talented and gifted students, used a check chart for his ninth-grade class. Each check equaled five points toward a reward on Friday. He was impressed by the cooperation of the students in working toward the goal of two-hundred points each week.

3. Miss Smith, a first-grade teacher, used a puppet to explain her classroom rules to the students. She also used the puppet to drop pennies in a jar. Spending extra time talking to the puppet was the favorite reward for most of her students.

4. Mr. Blaire, who taught sixth grade, used a chart with the students' names printed in five-inch letters. The students started each day with the letter A next to their names. If a student misbehaved once, the A was replaced by a B. The second infraction caused the student to have the B replaced with a check mark (the first check had an immediate consequence). Each A that remained by lunch equaled one point. All As that remained by the end of the day equaled five points. If 25 of the students had As, then the class earned 125 points for the day plus any points for As before lunch. The students needed 500 points to receive their reward at the end of the week.

Teachers, principals, and outside observers have reported that the positive climate created by selected verbal praise and a reinforcement system has reduced the number of management problems.

The use of behavior-modification techniques in the classroom come with some cautions. The use of a reward and ignore system (as some teachers call it) in the classroom has limitations:

1. Students may become overly dependent on the rewards for appropriate behavior.
2. The teacher role as controller may not match the philosophy of the teacher.
3. The expenses to the teacher who uses tangible rewards may be high.
4. The system may not foster self-reliance and independence in the student.

5. It is not consistent with democratic principles of free choice, expression, and independence.

While some educators developed classroom-management programs based on the work of B. F. Skinner, other educators followed the path of Carl Rogers, who emphasized the need for self-directed actions on the part of the individual.

Freedom to Learn.   Rogers talked about the relationship between his philosophy and its applications to students in schools (although not specifically to classroom management). In *Freedom to Learn* he states:

> When we put together in one scheme such elements as prescribed curriculum, similar assignments for all students, lecturing as almost the only mode of instruction, standard tests by which all students are externally evaluated, and instructor chosen grades as the measure of learning, then we can almost guarantee that meaningful learning will be at an absolute minimum. (Rogers 1969, 5)

Rogers is concerned about the self-concept of the student and about providing meaningful learning experiences. Rogers sees the teacher's role as facilitative rather than authoritative. In his view, the teacher is to establish self-discipline in the student rather than to modify or to control student behavior through punishment or other external means.

The classroom management programs of Haim Ginott, who wrote *Teacher and Child* (1972), were concerned with the self-concept of the child and the need for teachers to communicate with students humanely. Ginott's ideas about communicating with students is summarized here by C. M. Charles (1981). (Note: Information in parentheses was added by the authors.)

1. Send sane messages, addressing the situation rather than the child's character;
2. Express anger appropriately (without demeaning the student);
3. Invite cooperation (rather than demanding cooperation);
4. Accept and acknowledge student feelings (rather than ignoring or rejecting their feelings);
5. Avoid labeling students—it is disabling;
6. Correct students by directing them appropriately;
7. Be brief when correcting students;
8. Be models of humane behavior. (Charles 1981, 79)

Ginott states, "The essence of discipline is finding effective alternatives to punishment. . . . whatever generates hate must be avoided. Whatever creates self-esteem is to be fostered" (Ginott 1972, 147–148). He emphasizes the need to create a positive climate for learning through effective modeling by the teacher. The students attend to both the teacher's words and actions. However, if there is a discrepancy between the two, students will respond to the teacher's actions as a model for their own behavior. Ginott quotes an experienced teacher, who is reflecting on his actions as a model for the students in the classroom.

. . . I have become aware of a personal paradox: I often use tactics similar to those that I try to eradicate in my pupils. I raise my voice to end noise. I use force to break up fighting. I am rude to a child who is impolite, and I berate a child who uses bad language. (p. 149)

Ginott envisioned in 1972 that new technologies and means of instruction would be created in the next few decades to change the learning opportunities of children. "One function, however, will always remain with the teacher: to create the emotional climate for learning. No machine, sophisticated as it may be, can do this job" (p. 16). Other psychologists also saw the classroom as a place for the teacher and students to work together to build a cooperative learning environment based on mutual needs.

William Glasser, in his book *Control Theory in the Classroom* (1986), explains that students are rational beings who can control their behavior. "Even if the student's life away from school is bleak, and miserable, he will work if what he finds in school is satisfying" (p. 27). The goal of school, according to Glasser, is to enable students to make good choices about their behavior and actions in the classroom and in life and understand the consequences for inappropriate behavior. He feels classroom rules are important and should be enforced. The development of the rules should involve the students, and problems arising from enforcing the rules could be resolved through classroom meetings. During the classroom meetings, the teacher and students would discuss problems arising from disruptions or other management concerns.

Mistaken Goals. Rudolf Dreikurs' ideas appear in several books (which are listed in Exploration 2), the most recent of which is *Maintaining Sanity in the Classroom* (1982), which is a revision of an earlier book *Maintaining Sanity in the Classroom: Illustrated Teaching Techniques* (1971).

Dreikurs (1982) and his associates see misbehavior by students as the result of four mistaken goals:

1. to gain undue attention
2. to seek power
3. to seek revenge or to get even
4. to display inadequacy (real or assumed). (p. 14)

The child may be unaware of these goals until it is brought to his or her attention. Dreikurs suggests that the teacher respond to the different behaviors by reflecting the behavior back to the student. For example, a child seeking to gain undue attention could receive the following teacher response: "Could it be that: You want me to do more with you?" (p. 29). In responding to a student seeking revenge, the teacher, according to Dreikurs, could respond: "Could it be that: You want to make me feel bad?" (p. 29). Dreikurs provides a series of responses to students whose behavior could be as a result of one of the four mistaken goals.

Dreikurs talks about three types of teachers: autocratic, permissive, and democratic. He believes that the autocratic teacher forces students to obey, at times creating problems that did not exist. The permissive teacher creates problems when no consistent limits are established for the daily operations of the classroom. The democratic teacher, he believes, is the most effective manager because the teacher becomes the leader in the classroom, acting by example and inviting student participation through effective decision making. Rules and consequences are part of everyday life and, therefore, should be part of the classroom. Freedom in the classroom carries with it responsibility, which is at the heart of a democratic society.

Many effective classroom managers combine elements from both the Skinnerian and the Rogerian philosophies. The approach you select is less important than the need to be consistent with your actions and behaviors. The dynamics in the classroom are constantly changing; the ability to be consistent and communicate effectively are key ingredients to successful teaching.

The management programs discussed above reflect different philosophies. Effective classroom managers are also effective communicators. Teachers communicate their expectations about appropriate and inappropriate behavior, academic work requirements, and the general climate of the classroom. Teachers communicate expectations both verbally and nonverbally. Expectations are an extension of what a teacher values. We will review what many teachers express as important management values for their classrooms.

Communications

Teaching is more than providing information to groups of students. The task of the teacher is to create a climate in the classroom that is conducive to learning and teaching. The climate is created by both the teacher and the students, but the teacher has the responsibility to organize the work and time and to manage the flow of interaction in the classroom. Instructionally, the teacher needs a vision of what is to come—in the next five minutes, at the end of the period or day, at the end of the week or unit, and at the end of the school year. This vision, as we have discussed in Chapter 8, is made up of goals and objectives. Having clear goals and objectives is the first step in creating expectations of what is needed for students to function effectively in the classroom.

Expectations

Expectations are created through our words, deeds, and actions. Teachers communicate expectations to the students through verbal and nonverbal means and by the way in which they organize the classroom environment. Students also have expectations about the classroom environment. Senior high-school student perceptions and self-reports of the discipline and behavior problems in the schools reported in Tables 10.1 and 10.2 reflected student concerns about discipline in our schools. The basis of these concerns actually begins with the organization and effectiveness of the classroom. When secondary students were asked about their expectations for classroom organization, they identified the following:

1. How soon after entering the classroom are students informed of the day's assignments?

"She may be expecting too much of us."

2. Are the students told the kind, amount, and quality of work that is expected during the period?
3. Is the work assigned in such a way that, for each period, students know the goal and can have a feeling of accomplishment?
4. Do students know how materials are distributed in class and what materials they must bring to class? Are the penalties for not having them clear?
5. What procedures are established for students to receive feedback for their work during the period?
6. Do students know where to sit, what group they are in, when to work alone, and when to work with a group?
7. Are students aware of the teacher's expectations regarding their behavior? (Stallings 1987)

Expectations are not unique to the teaching profession. We have expectations for physicians, lawyers, accountants, dentists, nurses, engineers, and other professionals. Chances are that you would not return to the office of a physician that had a dirty waiting room or that had a receptionist who did not acknowledge your arrival or who had no system for determining who is next. The skills of the physician might be oustanding, but the lack of organization would deter you from returning. In such a case, the physician will lose patients and money, just as the teacher may lose the interest and attention of students and potentially lose order in the classroom. The teacher can communicate several areas of expectations to the students. The following list is derived from a survey conducted during workshops on classroom management over the last ten years by one of the authors, who used a management values activity adapted from Rick Curwin and Barbara Fuhrmann (1975). (See Explorations 1.) The items most often cited by both elementary and secondary teachers include: purposefulness, respect, orderliness, fairness, safety, and caring. We will discuss each of these areas and describe how you can develop workable expectations for your students.

Purposefulness. The first of these management values is purposefulness. The teacher communicates purpose by providing the students with a framework for what is to be accomplished in the lesson (for elementary students) or for the period (for secondary students). Explaining, or writing on the chalkboard, what the students will learn provides the students with a sense of direction for the lesson. The teacher's role is to have all materials ready and be well prepared for the lesson. Starting immediately after the bell rings also creates a sense of purpose. Knowing the purpose for the lesson provides the students with a direction.

Respect. In years past, respect was accorded teachers as a matter of position. The 1960s and early 1970s saw many of the established institutions, including schools, challenged by school-age and college youth. Respect for teachers was no longer a given, but something that had to be earned, each and every year, by the teacher. Many veteran teachers express the importance for the teacher to respect the students and the students to respect each other. Showing mutual respect is deemed important by many experienced teachers in the development of a positive learning environment.

Orderliness. Order is a necessary ingredient for teaching. Students shouting out answers, moving around the room while the teacher is instructing, passing notes, making noises, or challenging the teacher are a few examples of elements of disorder. Creating order requires the teacher to establish certain rules and procedures that will enable all students to have an equal opportunity to learn by eliminating distractions and intrusions into learning time.

Fairness. The ability of the teacher to respond equitably to all the students in the classroom is an important element in developing a positive working relationship. Students can tolerate many conditions in the classroom, but injustice is an area that creates conflict between teacher and students. Calling on the same students; smiling, praising and giving rewards to only a select few in the classroom; believing one student over another in a dispute; and using the same students for leadership positions in the class are a few examples of what students feel are unfair behaviors. Teacher actions are constantly being observed by the students. Demonstrating fairness will enhance the ability of the teacher to create a positive learning environment.

Safety. Creating a safe classroom environment is the responsibility of the teacher. Students need to feel safe and secure in the classroom if they are to be productive learners. Three areas that cause students to feel unsafe include: ridicule by either the teacher or other students; destruction of students' work by other students; and fights in the classroom. In each of these three areas, it is the responsibility of the teacher to establish clear expectations about what is appropriate and inappropriate behavior for the classroom. The teacher needs to respond quickly, fairly, and firmly when one student ridicules another student in class. If the teacher establishes, through words and actions, that it is inappropriate to "make fun" of others,

Maintaining student interest and task orientation are major challenges in classroom management.

the students will begin to respond accordingly. A teacher who is aware of what is going on in the classroom will prevent the destruction of property or fighting in the class.

Caring.   The folklore about not smiling until Christmas is, in fact, just one of the many myths about teaching. Effective teachers smile more, give more specific praise, and use eye contact more than less-effective teachers. Stallings (1975) indicates that the reading gain scores for third graders who entered school with less scholastic ability reflected more improvement with teacher support and praise than did the scores of students who entered with higher scholastic ability. Aspy and Roebuck (1977) report, in a book entitled: *Kids Don't Learn From People They Don't Like*, that empathy (the ability of the teacher to reflect the student's feelings) and genuineness (the words and statements of the teacher are consistent with the actions) had produced significant gains in academic outcomes. Caring teachers take the extra step to ensure that the students feel good about what they are achieving in the classroom.

Nonverbal

Nonverbal communication is a powerful means of transmitting information to the students. If there is a discrepancy between a verbal statement and a nonverbal look or gesture, the students will usually respond to the nonverbal information. The tone of the teacher's voice, a look or stare, the position of the body when the teacher gives a direction—all provide the students with information about what is expected.

Nonverbal Interaction.   Teacher-student interaction exists at both the verbal and nonverbal levels. The teacher may praise both verbally and nonverbally. Some of the praise in the classroom can be communicated nonverbally. A teacher may smile at the student who answers correctly or nod to indicate that the student is on the right track. A gesture of the hand could communicate encouragement. The teacher may also communicate negative feelings nonverbally. The tone of an angry teacher communicates displeasure. A frown or stare may cause students to stop a specific behavior. Teachers may use other forms of nonverbal communications to manage the classroom environment.

Nonverbal Management. The teacher can use any of three key nonverbal strategies at any level to desist misbehavior.

1. Physical proximity—the teacher moves about the room during instruction and seatwork. The students are less likely to engage in minor infractions (like talking) if they see the teacher actively monitoring their academic work and behavior.
2. Eye contact—the teacher needs to keep eye contact with the class at all times. If the class is doing seatwork, the teacher should go to the students if they have questions rather than have the students come to the teacher's desk. Two or three students in front of the teacher's desk will prevent a total view of the classroom.
3. Silence—combining eye contact with silence will allow the teacher to look at a student or students who, for example, are talking during instruction. In most cases, when the teacher stops talking, the offending students will look up to the stare of the teacher.

Communication, both verbal and nonverbal, is important to a successful classroom. Teaching is a very public occupation. The students are constantly watching the teacher's actions and decisions. First impressions are, in fact, important. These impressions are created from the first day of school when the students walk into your classroom. Student impressions are created from the patterns of communication which occur in every classroom. Establishing the patterns of communication begin on the first day and continue throughout the school year.

Setting the Stage

Regardless of how many years one teaches, the first day of the school year is always a new adventure. The classroom context and dynamics created by teacher-student and student-student interactions within the classroom environment create uniquely different patterns from year to year. A teacher who has had few management problems one year should not be surprised if the new class begins to test the limits for acceptable behavior in early September.

A critical management activity at the beginning of the year is teaching the students the classroom rules and procedures. The first few weeks see effective managers spending time each day reinforcing classroom rules and procedures—"helping students learn how to behave in their classroom" (Emmer & Evertson 1981). The establishment of rules at the beginning of the school year is important because rules are the means by which teachers convey their expectations of appropriate behavior to students. A number of other researchers have looked at effective classroom managers and concluded that they establish and reinforce rules from the very first day of school (Buckley 1977; Jackson 1968; Sarason 1971; Tikunoff et al. 1975). In Emmer and Evertson's (1981) review of the research literature on classroom management, the use of a system of consequences for inappropriate behavior and rewards for appropriate behavior has been linked to improved student achievement and reduced student disruption in class.

A Case Study of Three Teachers

In a case study of three teachers from a low socioeconomic junior high school (Sanford & Evertson 1981), the importance of establishing both clear management expectations the first day and consistency of action throughout the year seemed to be the difference between a disruptive and nondisruptive environment. As Table 10.3 would indicate, Teacher A began and ended the year with a low level of disruption. Teacher B began the year with a high level of disruption and concluded with the highest level of the three teachers. Teacher C began with a relatively low level of disruption. However, the number of disruptions by the end of the year were $2\frac{1}{2}$ times greater. The deterioration in Teacher C's management, according to Sanford and Evertson, stemmed from a lack of consistency in enforcing rules and standards of conduct in the class. "Without continuing, consistent maintenance of classroom management systems established in the first days, a productive classroom climate may deteriorate rapidly" (Sanford & Evertson 1981, 38).

The researchers found that Teacher A spent more time during the first days and weeks of school establishing rules and procedures than did either Teachers B or C. Teacher A also had greater clarity in giving directions, provided consistent enforcement and feedback to the students for appropriate behavior, and knew the students as individuals. The first days of school are critical to the establishment of rules, procedures, and general expectations for classroom operations.

Students during the first week usually present few discipline problems for the teacher. However, the solid line in Figure 10.1 presented by Walter Doyle (1979, 9) indicates that misbehavior gradually increases from the first days of school until a critical point is attained. Effective response by

TABLE 10.3 Comparison of Mean Inappropriate Behavior in Three Teachers' Classes

	Beginning of Year	Middle of Year	End of Year
Teacher A	1.50	1.25	1.33 *
Teacher B	3.50	3.67	4.75
Teacher C	2.00	4.00	4.50

Source: Sanford & Evertson, 1981, p. 34.

Note:* This figure is the mean rating obtained in another class taught by Teacher A. No data are available for this class of Teacher A, end of year, because a student teacher took over the class.

Scale: 1 = no inappropriate behavior; 5 = high degree of inappropriate behavior.

FIGURE 10.1
The Rhythm of the Be-
ginning of the Year

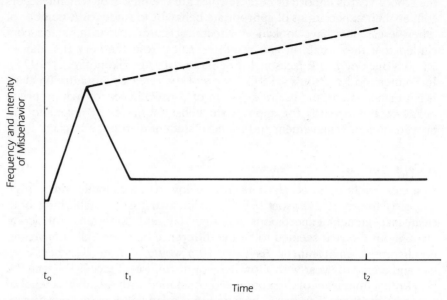

Source: Adapted from W. Doyle. "Making Managerial Decisions in Classrooms," in
Classroom Management. The Seventy-eighth Yearbook of the National Society for the Study
of Education. Part 2, ed. D. L. Duke (Chicago: University of Chicago Press, 1979), p. 51.
Reprinted with permission.

the teacher to the challenges during the first few weeks may determine the
direction of the entire school year. The testing of the behavior limits by the
students will become more serious as additional students participate in the
infractions. The broken line in the figure indicates a lack of control of the
learning environment by the teacher (Doyle 1979). The teacher needed to
be prepared with a management plan at the beginning of the school year
that would include both prevention and intervention strategies.

Fifteen Thousand Hours

An extensive review of education at the secondary level and its effects on
students in England is reported in *Fifteen Thousand Hours* (Rutter,
Maughan, Mortimore, Ouston & Smith 1979). Their review seems to establish a clear direction of the general nature of classroom management
across geographic boundaries for both effective teaching and successful
schools.

The results reported in *Fifteen Thousand Hours* (Rutter et al. 1979)
support the findings of other studies on classroom and school management,
both in Britain and in the United States.

1. The particular rules and approaches to discipline may be less important
than the existence of some generally recognized and accepted set of
standards. (p. 121)

2. While the links between punishment and outcome are rather variable,
those between rewards and outcome were more consistent. All forms of
reward, praise, or appreciation tended to be associated with the better
student outcomes. (p. 123)

3. The absolute levels of praise observed in lessons were rather low; the
average across all schools being only three or four instances of positive

comment by teachers in any one lesson. However, in those schools where staff took more opportunities to praise pupils' work, outcomes were substantially better with respect to both behavior and delinquency. (p. 123)

4. The findings suggest that there are likely to be benefits in ensuring that a high proportion of pupils have opportunities to hold some kind of post of responsibility... Schools with a higher pupil participation in these activities had significantly better behavioral and academic outcomes. (p. 130)

5. Children's classroom behavior was much better when the teacher had prepared the lesson in advance, so that little time was wasted at the beginning in setting up apparatus or handing out books and papers; when the teacher arrived on time at the start of the lesson; and when, if the lesson was planned as class-oriented, the teacher mainly directed attention to the class as a whole. (p. 184)

6. One of the hallmarks of successful class management was keeping pupils actively engaged in productive activities rather than waiting for something to happen. (p. 184)

7. Probationary teachers were notably less successful in coping with their classes than their more experienced colleagues. (p. 186)

8. Children had better academic success in schools where homework was regularly set and marked, and where the teachers expressed the expectation that a high proportion of the children will do well in national examinations. (p. 188)

11. Outcomes tended to be better when both the curriculum and approaches to discipline were agreed and supported by the staff acting together. (p. 192)

12. The particular rules which are set and the specific disciplinary techniques which are used are probably much less important than the establishment of some principles and guidelines that are both clearly recognizable and accepted by the school as a whole. (p. 192)

Conclusion

Effective classroom management is an important step toward successful teaching. Unfortunately, it usually represents the only step. Teachers are unable to direct their concerns to student well-being when they are preoccupied with professional survival. Some educators may believe that rules, consequences, and rewards are unnecessary and even inhibit freedom. In fact, the opposite is true—freedom has rules, consequences, and rewards in everyday life. Freedom requires structure and responsibility, while license elicits neither. If students are to become responsible adults, they must be provided with the opportunity to see positive role models early in their development, both at home and in school. As A. S. Neill stated in his book, *Freedom Not License*! (1966, p. 9), "In the disciplined home, the children have no rights. In the spoiled home, they have all the rights. The proper home is one in which children and adults have equal rights." The same could be said for the classroom and the school. Teachers, administrators, and students need to share equally in both the rights and responsibilities of the school and classroom (Freiberg 1983).

Classroom management is an area that is always a part of an effective teacher's repertoire. Thinking about how you manage your time in the classroom, the relationship between management and instruction, and how to communicate expectations to your students is an ongoing process, which should begin early in your professional experiences.

We explored different perspectives to managing classrooms based on one's view of human behavior. Both research and practice clearly suggest that several approaches to classroom management are possible. The key to becoming an effective classroom manager is to draw upon the ideas presented in this text that match your own values. The frame of reference for teaching you have now will evolve through your professional-development experiences. The skills you acquire through your readings, field experiences, and your first years of teaching will require adjustments in order for you to respond effectively to the needs of your perspective students. Being a reflective teacher requires ongoing inquiry into how I can become a better teacher.

Building Reflective Inquiry Skills

This section is designed to increase your understanding of classroom management and to provide an opportunity to analyze a brief teaching transcript and interpret the actions of the teacher vis-à-vis what you have learned from the chapter.

Management Analysis
Look at the following transcript of a teacher from a study conducted by researchers (Emmer, Evertson, Sanford, Clements & Worsham 1981) at the University of Texas R & D Center. Under the Comments column, identify those elements of the management procedures that you consider to be either effective or ineffective. After you have completed your analysis,

compare your analysis with that of the research group, which is located on page 247. Discuss your analysis with the instructor and class members. Respond either individually or as a group to the following questions:

1. In what areas did you agree or disagree with the researchers?

2. In what areas did you agree or disagree with each other?

3. What new insights have you gained from analyzing the transcripts?

4. What changes would you make if you were the teacher in the classroom?

Your Comments

When the tardy bell rings, students are still coming into the room, getting copies of a book on some shelves at the front of the room. Teacher tells the class that she has an announcement to make. She says if their spelling is not finished, they should do that first, and then join in with the reading later on. Teacher then says, "Roger, I think that means you." Teacher reminds the class that the bell has rung and adds that the class will not get to see the movie of the book they are reading if they have not reached page 275 before tomorrow, so they had better get quiet. When students don't get quiet, Teacher says that she has heard this class be quieter than this and so she knows they can do it. She waits about 10 seconds at the front of the room until the noise has subsided a little. She tells the class they have to stay in 10 seconds after class. She adds that today's lesson will be enjoyable if they will settle down.

Teacher then begins to review what has happened in the book Dr. Jekyl and Mr. Hyde up to this point. Janey gets up to go to the pencil sharpener. Teacher says that she doesn't need a pencil. Janey protests that she is finishing her spelling. Teacher tells Janey that the next time she should follow the rule and sharpen her pencil before the bell.

Teacher continues with her review, occasionally calling on one or two students at random to answer questions. She notices Donna talking to her neighbor and says, "Donna, if I hear another word out of you, you're going to the office." Teacher asks a few more questions calling on students with their hands raised, but also allowing call-outs.

When the call-outs get too loud, Teacher says, "You are disturbing me. I can't think when I am babysitting. You all are too old for this." At this point, Teacher begins to read from the book, beginning where they had left off on page 253. She sees Donna asking her neighbor a question, goes to desk, and writes out a referral slip for Donna. Teacher tells Donna she will send her to the office the next time she sees her talking. Teacher again begins to read, hears some whispering and stops. She notices Barry with his feet in the chair in front of him and tells him to sit up straight. He gets up and moves to a chair at the back of the room. Teacher tells him to read where she left off.

Barry begins to read. Johnny and Allen start to snicker. Teacher ignores this. The snickering starts to spread as Barry reads. When teacher notices Donna is snickering also, she tells her to go to the office. Donna shrugs, gets up, and leaves the room, not at all contrite. Teacher turns to the class and says, "Let that be a lesson to you all." Roger goes up to the teacher, and the teacher says, "Don't ask questions about spelling now." He returns to his seat after picking up a book from the front shelves. Once at his seat, he wads up the paper and tosses it under his desk. Teacher calls on other students to have them read. After about five minutes, Donna returns to the room to get a referral slip which the teacher had forgotten to give to her when she left. Donna leaves again and the students start to snicker again. Teacher tells the students they are really being bad today and warns that they will not get through with the reading if they do not settle down.

Teacher is very complimentary of most students after they have read. However, by accident, she sometimes calls on students who say they are working on spelling. About one-third of the class is still working on spelling exercises.

About a minute before the bell rings, the Teacher tells the students to pass in the books. (They finished reading through page 260.) Quite a few students get up and take their books to the shelves rather than passing them to the front. Teacher reminds the students that they are to meet in the auditorium tomorrow to see the movie <u>Dr. Jekyll and Mr. Hyde.</u> When the bell rings, she smiles at the class and says, "Have a nice day." Students get up and rush out.

Source: Emmer, E., Evertson, C., Sanford, J., Clements, B., & Worsham, M. (1981). Organizing and managing the junior high classroom. Austin: University of Texas at Austin, R & D Center for Teacher Education.

Explorations

Exploration 1
Management Values in the Classroom*
Below are twelve qualities that might be displayed in various ways in a classroom. In your ideal classroom, how would you rank them? Place a 1 next to the quality you most value in a classroom, 2 next to the second most valued, and so on through 12, which will represent the quality you value least in relation to the others. Although you may feel all the statements are important, you will need to set priorities in the classroom. After you complete the rankings, join a group of three to four other students and try to reach a consensus on a ranking for the first and last value statements.

_____ freedom	_____ orderliness
_____ self-direction	_____ creativity
_____ quiet	_____ respect
_____ laughter	_____ equality
_____ safety	_____ fairness
_____ purposefulness	_____ caring

Most elementary teachers who completed this activity in the 1980s selected caring for their first choice and quiet for their last choice. Most secondary teachers selected respect or purposefulness and safety as their first choices and freedom as their last choice.

The key to this activity is that you defined the qualities for yourself. Freedom for some may mean responsibility, while for others it may represent license. Once you determine what is important for you in the management of the classroom, then the communication of these values to your students becomes the next step. This activity is one of the building blocks for the development of rules and procedures for the classroom.

---

*The Management Values in the Classroom was developed by Richard Curwin and Barbara Fuhrmann (1975) from their book entitled, Discovering Your Teaching Self: Humanistic Approaches To Effective Teaching. Used by permission of the authors.

Exploration 2
Listed below are several textbooks on classroom management. Use this list as a resource for further reading. Review one book or chapters within several books that may build upon an area of interest to you. Discuss the material with another student either during or after your education class. Consider the following questions in your discussion:

1. What viewpoint(s) does the author take on human behavior?

2. What concepts does the author discuss?

3. What skills does the author present?

4. How do the viewpoints of the author compare with your own perspectives of classroom management?

5. What are some questions that have been raised as a result of your readings?

List of Textbooks

Dollar, B. (1972). *Humanizing classroom discipline: A behavioral approach.* New York: Harper & Row.

Dreikurs, R. (1968). *Psychology in the classroom* (2nd ed.). New York: Harper & Row.

Dreikurs, R. & Cassel, P. (1972). *Discipline without tears* (2nd ed.). New York: Hawthorn Books.

Duke, D. L. & Meckel, A. M. (1984). *Teachers' guide to classroom management.* New York: Random House.

Gnagey, W. J. (1981). *Motivating classroom discipline.* New York: Macmillan.

House, E. R. & Lapan, S. D. (1978). *Survival in the classroom: Negotiating with kids, colleagues, and bosses* (abridged edition). Boston: Allyn & Bacon.

Leinlech, J. K. (1979). *Classroom management.* New York: Harper & Row.

Long, J. D. & Frye, V. H. (1981). *Making it 'til Friday: A guide to successful classroom management* (2nd ed.). Princeton: Princeton Book Co.

Madsen, C. H., Jr. & Madsen, C. K. (1981). *Teaching/discipline: A positive approach for educational development* (3rd ed.). Boston: Allyn & Bacon.

References

Aspy, D. N. & Roebuck, F. N. (1977). *Kids don't learn from people they don't like.* Amherst, MA: Human Resource Development Press.

Berliner, D. (1982, March). *The executive functions of teaching.* Paper presented at the Wingspread Conference on Relating Reading Research to Classroom Instruction, Wingspread, Racine, WI; and at the meetings of the American Educational Research Association, New York City, NY.

Buckley, P. (1977). *An ethnographic study of an elementary school teacher's establishment and maintenance of group norms.* Unpublished doctoral dissertation, University of Houston.

Charles, C. M. (1981). *Building classroom discipline from models to practice.* New York: Longman.

Curwin, R. L. & Fuhrmann, B. S. (1975). *Discovering your teaching self: Humanistic approaches to effective teaching.* New Jersey: Prentice-Hall.

Doyle, W. (1979). Making managerial decisions in classrooms. In D. L. Duke (Ed.), *Classroom management: The seventy-eighth yearbook of the National Society for the Study of Education* (part 2). Chicago: University of Chicago Press.

Dreikurs, R., Grunwald, B. B. & Pepper, F. C. (1971). *Maintaining sanity in the classroom: Illustrated teaching techniques.* New York: Harper & Row.

Dreikurs, R., Grunwald, B. B. & Pepper, F. C. (1982). *Maintaining sanity in the classroom: Classroom management techniques* (2nd ed.). New York: Harper & Row.

Emmer, E. & Evertson, C. (1981). Synthesis of research on classroom management. *Educational Leadership, 1*, 342–7.

Emmer, E.; Evertson, C.; Sanford, J.; Clements, B. & Worsham, M. (1981). *Organizing and managing the elementary school classroom.* Austin, TX: University of Texas at Austin, R & D Center for Teacher Education.

Emmer, E.; Evertson, C.; Sanford, J.; Clements, B. & Worsham, M. (1981). *Organizing and managing the junior high classroom.* Austin, TX: University of Texas at Austin, R & D Center for Teacher Education.

Freiberg, H. J. (1983). Consistency: The key to classroom management. *Journal of Education for Teaching, 9,* 1–15.

Ginott, H. (1972). *Teacher and child.* New York: Macmillan.

Glasser, W. (1986). *Control theory in the classroom.* New York: Harper & Row.

Jackson, P. (1968). *Life in classrooms.* New York: Holt, Rinehart and Winston.

Johnson, L. V. & Bany, M. A. (1970). *Classroom management: Theory and skill training.* New York: Macmillan.

Kounin, J. (1970). *Discipline and group management in classrooms.* New York: Holt, Rinehart and Winston.

Neill, A. S. (1966). *Freedom not license.* New York: Hart.

Perry, A. (1908). *The management of a city school.* New York: Macmillan.

Rogers, C. R. (1969). *Freedom to learn.* Columbus, OH: Merrill.

Rutter, M., Maughan, B., Mortimore, P., Ouston, J., & Smith, A. (1979). *Fifteen thousand hours.* Cambridge, MA: Harvard University Press.

Sanford, J. & Evertson, C. (1981). Classroom management in a low SES junior high: Three case studies. *Journal of Teacher Education, 32*(1), 34–48.

Sarason, S. B. (1971). *The culture of the school and the problem of change.* Boston: Allyn & Bacon.

Shedd, J. B. & Malanowski, R. M. (1985). *From the front of the classroom: A study of the work of teachers.* Ithaca, NY: Organizational Analysis and Practice, Inc.

Skinner, B. F. (1957). *Verbal behavior.* New York: Appleton-Century-Crofts.

Stallings, J. (1975). *Implementations of child effects of teaching practices in Follow Through classrooms. Monograph of the Society for Research in Child Development, 40* (Serial No. 163).

Stallings, J. (1987). *Effective use of time training materials* Workshop II pp. 23–24. Unpublished Materials.

Tikunoff, W., Berliner, D. & Rist, R. (1975). *An ethnographic study of the forty classrooms of the beginning teacher evaluation study—known sample.* San Francisco: Far West Laboratory for Educational Research and Development.

Case Study A—Elementary

Teacher tells class to open math books to Page 148. Noise begins immediately. Teacher says, "Jose, I need your attention." (Actually, she needs the attention of the whole class, but Jose was very visibly not paying attention and climbing around under his desk.) The teacher starts to explain some of the problems in the math book. Jennifer and Michael decide they need to sharpen their pencils while the teacher is going over the instructions and they do so.

The teacher doesn't say anything about it and lets them both do it. The teacher asks a question and gets all kinds of call-outs in reply—some of them completely off base.

She makes no comment about this. The teacher is still having to tell those who haven't been paying

Researchers' Analysis

The teacher should have stopped all activity and reminded students of the rule for no talking when the teacher is working with the class. Instead, she goes after one student, when many are being inattentive.

The teacher should stop students and require that they wait.

The teacher should require that hands be raised. Now would be a good time to rehearse this.

attention what page they are on. She has already said this about ten times to various individuals. The teacher gets frustrated by the noise and inattention.

So she decides to stop and sit quietly, hoping that they will be quiet and listen to her. The noise and call-outs continue, and if the students are even aware that the teacher has stopped the lesson, they give no indication. After four minutes (while 20 of the students are talking and fooling around and three are waiting for the teacher to resume) the teacher says, in a slightly upset voice, "I can't talk above the noise and I won't even try."

Students settle down a little bit but the majority still do not give her their attention as she continues the lesson. She resumes, but is continually interrupted by the noise. Two students have a brief fight in the back of the room, but she appears not to notice. Teacher tells one student loudly to sit down. He does so, but has still not opened his math book and she makes no comment on this. Another student gets up to look at the spelling spirals. Less than half of the class is listening and doing the problems with the teacher. The teacher has done nothing to remedy the situation. One student comes up to the teacher while she is talking and asks a question. She says rather loudly, "We are doing math now. I don't have time for that sort of thing."

Several students are up and roaming around. Two boys are playing with a wet paper towel. One is loudly slapping it in his hands as he wanders back to his seat. The teacher says nothing. Instead she tells the class that she expects them to have all the math problems down on their papers. Noise continues while some of the students scramble to get to work on the lesson that has now been going on (or has been trying to go on) for the last twenty minutes. Five minutes later she collects the students' math spirals. It is now dead time for the students for the next six minutes. One student gets up and switches on the overhead projector without permission. Then three more students join him in fooling around with it. The teacher then tells them to sit down. The noise continues, and none of the students are paying attention to the teacher. The teacher just stands watching the class, saying and doing nothing.

Source: Emmer, E.; Evertson, C.; Sanford, J.; Clements, B. & Worsham, M. (1981). Organizing and managing the elementary school classroom. Austin: University of Texas at Austin, R & D Center for Teacher Education.

Researchers' Analysis

The teacher should stop all student activity and require that all books be open. The teacher should be actively involved in settling the children, not passively waiting.

The lesson should not be continued unless students are attending. Things are so far gone at this stage that progress in the lesson will be impossible without more drastic intervention. The teacher may need to separate some children or enforce a "quiet time", perhaps with heads down on desks.

This lesson is not just an isolated event. It is symptomatic of a general inability to gain student cooperation. The time to do that is early, rather than later in the lesson. The teacher simply didn't stop inappropriate behavior quickly enough. She let it build up until it forced her to terminate the lesson prematurely.

Case Study B—Secondary

It is the morning of the first day, and the students are arriving at the room individually and in small groups. Two boys enter the room "goofing off." The teacher says in a pleasant but firm voice, "Okay, guys, quit fooling around." They comply, get their nametags, and take their seats quietly. . . .

. . . Later in the morning a student bangs his chair noisily on the floor. The teacher immediately tells him, "Be quiet, please."

. . . It is time for a break to get drinks of water in the hall, and the teacher has told the class they will line up by tables. Jimmy, however, immediately jumps up. "What did I say, Jimmy?" No reply, he sits. "Jimmy?" Jimmy responds, "Huh?" The teacher states firmly, "It's 'Sir' in this room, not 'huh'." The teacher doesn't need to specify that Jimmy must sit down and wait for his table to called. Jimmy knows this is what he was called down for. (This is probably why he did not respond to the initial question.)

. . . Jeffery starts talking to the students at his table. The teacher says, "Jeffery, I'd like you to move to this table," pointing to one in the center of the room. "There's been too much talking at this table this morning," referring to his present table.

. . . The teacher directs the students to look at a sign posted at the back of the room. It has "Leaders" written on it, and one student calls out, "Leaders!" The teacher replies, "Yes, but in this class we don't call out answers, we raise our hands." He asks what leaders do and calls on various students with raised hands.

. . . Toward the end of the morning two students begin fooling around and one of them shouts out. The teacher tells him, "Excuse me, would you turn around and face front." He does so, and the fooling around stops.

These are the disruptive incidents that occurred in the first four hours of the first day. Each time the teacher stepped in immediately and firmly, but not harshly. On the third day another observer commented, "This class is already molded in terms of management and procedures. . . . This teacher has good rapport with his students."

Source: Emmer, E.; Evertson, C.; Sanford, J.; Clements, B. & Worsham, M. (1981). Organizing and managing the elementary school classroom. Austin: University of Texas at Austin, R & D Center for Teacher Education.

Researchers' Analysis

From the beginning, this teacher is pleasantly setting firm limits and getting good results.

Being quiet with chairs is an important precedent.

The teacher is establishing that he expects all students to listen and follow directions, and to answer his questions.

The teacher has let the class know he is aware of individual and group misbehavior, and the he will act on that.

Consistently stop those terrible call outs from the start.

Consistently setting limits from the beginning is critical.

Building Reflective Inquiry Skills

Classroom Management

When the tardy bell rings, students are still coming into the room, getting copies of a book on some shelves at the front of the room. Teacher tells the class that she has an announcement to make. She says if their spelling is not finished, they should do that first, and then join in with the reading later on. Teacher then says, "Roger, I think that means you." Teacher reminds the class that the bell has rung and adds that the class will not get to see the movie of the book they are reading if they have not reached page 275 before tomorrow, so they had better get quiet. When students don't get quiet, Teacher says that she has heard this class be quieter than this and so she knows they can do it. She waits about 10 seconds at the front of the room until the noise has subsided a little. She tells the class they have to stay in 10 seconds after class. She adds that today's lesson will be enjoyable if they will settle down.

Teacher then begins to review what has happened in the book Dr. Jekyll and Mr. Hyde up to this point. Janey gets up to go to the pencil sharpener. Teacher says that she doesn't need a pencil. Janey protests that she is finishing her spelling. Teacher tells Janey that the next time she should follow the rule and sharpen her pencil before the bell.

Teacher continues with her review, occasionally calling on one or two students at random to answer questions. She notices Donna talking to her neighbor and says, "Donna, if I hear another word out of you, you're going to the office." Teacher asks a few more questions calling on students with their hands raised, but also allowing call-outs.

When the call-outs get too loud, Teacher says, "You are disturbing me. I can't think when I am babysitting. You all are too old for this." At this point, Teacher begins to read from the book, beginning where they had left off on page 253. She sees Donna asking her neighbor a question, goes over to desk, and writes out a referral slip for Donna. Teacher tells Donna she will send her to the office the next time she sees her talking. Teacher again begins to read, hears some whispering and stops. She notices Barry with his feet in the chair in front of him and tells him to sit up straight. He gets up and moves to a chair at the back of the room. Teacher tells him to read where she has left off.

Researchers' Analysis

Teacher does not enforce rule for being in class on time.

Teacher creates a monitoring problem by having class members working on different things.

This threat is unreasonable.

She announces that the class has earned a penalty. This is acceptable only if the teacher follows through.

Teacher is not aware of who is working on spelling.

Teacher allows Janey to get away with breaking an established rule.

This threat is too extreme.

Teacher calls on some students with their hands raised, but also allows call-outs.

The teacher should have stopped inappropriate call-outs when they started. She finally gets annoyed and badgers the students.

Again, Teacher threatens Donna but does not follow through.

Barry begins to read. Johnny and Allen start to snicker. Teacher ignores this. The snickering starts to spread as Barry reads. When teacher notices Donna is snickering also, she tells her to go to the office. Donna shrugs, gets up, and leaves the room, not at all contrite. Teacher turns to the class and says, "Let that be a lesson to you all." Roger goes up to the teacher, and the teacher says, "Don't ask questions about spelling now." He returns to his seat after picking up a book from the front shelves. Once at his seat he wads up the paper and tosses it under his desk. Teacher calls on other students to have them read. After about five minutes, Donna returns to the room to get a referral slip which the teacher had forgotten to give to her when she left. Donna leaves again and the students start to snicker again. Teacher tells the students they are really being bad today and warns that they will not get through with the reading if they do not settle down.

Teacher is very complimentary of most students after they have read. However, by accident she sometimes calls on students who say they are working on spelling. About one-third of the class is still working on spelling exercises.

About a minute before the bell rings, the Teacher tells the students to pass in the books. (They finished reading through page 260.) Quite a few students get up and take their books to the shelves rather than passing them to the front. Teacher reminds the students that they are to meet in the auditorium tomorrow to see the movie <u>Dr. Jekyll and Mr. Hyde</u>. When the bell rings she smiles at the class and says, "Have a nice day." Students get up and rush out.

Source: Emmer, E., Evertson, C., Sanford, J., Clements, B. & Worsham, M. (1981). Organizing and managing the junior high classroom. Austin: University of Texas at Austin, R & D Center for Teacher Education.

Researchers' Analysis

Teacher appears arbitrary and inconsistent. She allows a number of students to snicker at Barry but punishes Donna.

Class is interrupted because Teacher in her haste to get rid of Donna forgot to give her the referral slip.

These students received only a warning for the same behavior for which Donna was sent to the office.

Teacher is not monitoring and does not know who is working on spelling still and who is goofing off.

Teacher does not follow through on the penalties she threatened students with earlier in the period. She is going to allow the students to see the movie even though they did not read as much as she told them they had to. Neither did she keep them 10 seconds after the bell as she said she would.

CHAPTER ELEVEN

Measurement and Evaluation

OBJECTIVES

By the end of this chapter, you will be able to:

1. Distinguish between terms such as measurement, assessment and evaluation; formative and summative evaluation; and direct and indirect measurement.
2. Describe achievement and aptitude tests.
3. Interpret scores from norm- and criterion-referenced achievement tests.
4. Discuss ways to assess behavioral, expressive, problem-solving, and attitudinal objectives.
5. Describe essay, short-answer, completion, multiple-choice, true-false, and matching tests.

KEY WORDS AND CONCEPTS

> Achievement tests
> Aptitude tests
> Age equivalent
> Criterion-referenced tests
> Direct and indirect measurement
> Evaluation
> Formative and summative evaluation
> Grade equivalent
> Intelligence tests
> Measurement
> Measurement error
> Norm-referenced tests
> Precision of measurement
> Standardized tests
> Table of specifications

Using Measurement and Evaluation in Making Decisions

"*Y*ou can't measure the effects of what I do."

"Why not?"

"They're intangible."

"Oh? Why should I pay you for intangible results?"

"Because I've been trained and licensed to practice."

"Hmm . . . all right. Here's your money."

"Where? I don't see it."

"Of course not . . . It's intangible."

Robert Mager, *Developing Attitude Toward Learning*, 1984, 79.

Teachers make many evaluative decisions. Should Mary be referred for special education? Who should be in the annual play? Which students should represent the school in the math competition? What resources should be used in instruction? Should Johnny pass? How can I best organize my daily schedule? Each of these decisions requires some form of evaluation. Some are related to students, some to curriculum, some to organization, and some to interpersonal relations.

Some of these questions require the analysis of test data, some require speculation about the situation, and some require the collection of information. While the decisions identified here generally are important and require thought and data collection, many decisions of teachers are made quickly during the course of instruction and on the basis of professional judgement. In this chapter, we will explore some basic ideas about evaluation and a related but different concept—measurement.

Importance of Evaluation

Although some teachers view their students as merging into a homogeneous "history class," most recognize that each student is different from the rest. A century of research has provided ample documentation of individual differences in every dimension—physical, social, emotional, and intellectual. Recognizing that there are differences and discovering specifically what these differences are, however, are two different levels of professional competence. Many teachers verbalize about individual differences; fewer identify and act upon such information. An underlying philosophical position taken by the authors is that we must evaluate as many relevant factors as feasible in making decisions. This is a major part of reflective inquiry.

Evaluation is not an end in itself; it is a means to more effective teaching. Too often evaluation is delayed until the end of an activity or course. This terminal evaluation of the product of action permits a review of the experience, but it in no way improves the experience. Evaluators refer to this as *summative evaluation*. It is completed at the end of the program and typically assesses what the student has learned from the total program. Standardized achievement tests, final examinations, and course evaluations are illustrative of such formal instruments. They are vital to the modern educational program but are only one part of evaluation.

Effective evaluation implies not only summative evaluation, but also ongoing or process evaluation. This type of evaluation is used by teachers to help formulate strategies to use in the classroom and is referred to as *formative evaluation*. Diagnostic tests, which inform the teacher of specific concepts or information not understood by students, is an example of formative evaluation. For example, a spelling teacher may give a test on Monday of the words to be learned that week in order to know which of those need to be emphasized in instruction; then on Friday, the actual test is administered.

Effective instructors also use many informal assessments as they note students' changes in facial expressions, questions asked or answers given, and manual dexterity. These assessments are employed during the course of teaching and, in turn, modify teaching strategies. Evaluation is more effective when it is continually employed rather than fragmentary or spasmodic and when both formative and summative evaluation are used.

Evaluation and Measurement

Many persons have mistakenly regarded evaluation as a synonym for measurement. Two illustrations may clarify the distinction between these two terms. We can *measure* the width of a classroom door using a ruler or other linear measuring device. This measurement can be described in linear units (The door is 3 feet 2 inches wide). We *evaluate* whether the door is wide enough for the purposes for which it is to be used. The evaluation utilizes other measurements and subjective judgements, and their interrelationships (for example, size of students, number to use door, purpose for its use, and its placement in the school plant). Generally, measurement describes one dimension or aspect of a situation, while evaluation considers a number of measurements in broader perspective. Measurement is fact-oriented; evaluation is decision-oriented.

We may measure the spelling achievement of students by administering a spelling achievement test. We evaluate these data when we compare them with other data (for example, student ability, change in achievement) and develop teaching strategies based on all available information. We evaluate when we consider the relative importance of this information in the total situation for a given learner (for example, the learner's social maturity, acceptance of responsibility, initiative). Thus a measure of 46 might be highly commendable for one student and inadequate for another.

Measurement is generally concerned with the *quantitative* aspects of the situation while evaluation deals also with *qualitative* aspects. The score a student makes on a mathematics test is a measurement of his or her ability; judging the adequacy of such a score is evaluation. Evaluating that adequacy might include such factors as the student's ability, scores of other students, and standards established by the school district, the state, or test makers.

When evaluating, teachers base their conclusions on value judgments in terms of standards previously established and factors considered relevant. Analyzing as many relevant factors as possible is imperative as you develop your ability as an educational decision maker. It is our hypothesis that your effectiveness as a fledgling teacher will be enhanced through the development of increasingly sophisticated and precise methods of measurement and evaluation.

Properties or Characteristics Measured

Yardsticks, achievement tests, automobile odometers, scales, stop watches, and other measuring devices are basically extensions of our senses. With them, data can be collected and described with greater precision, reliability, and objectivity than if our five senses alone were used. We can describe the length of a room more precisely if we measure it with a yardstick rather than estimate it with our vision. Likewise, an achievement test provides a more accurate estimate of a child's true achievement than casual observation.

When we describe a stick as seven inches long, we actually are referring to a *property* or *characteristic* of the stick (its length), not to the stick itself. An intelligence quotient (I.Q.), achievement score, or psychological profile is a descriptor or characteristic of a person, not the person. This is an important distinction for teachers.

Some measures are *direct*, because they use measuring tools that are closely aligned to the observable physical characteristic being measured (ruler and stick, for example). Other measurements are *indirect*; that is, the measuring instrument is not of the same nature as the attribute measured. Temperature is measured by observing the expansion of mercury in an enclosed tube. Time is another attribute that is measured indirectly; watches have mechanical works or electric impulses that establish a regular rhythm with numerals or movements of hands to denote changes in time.

Psychological and educational tests and measurements are indirect. We *infer* intelligence or achievement by the number of questions answered correctly during a specified time period. We infer dogmatism or locus of control or other psychological characteristics by responses people make to questions, statements, or situations. As you work with such instruments, it is important to understand their uses and their limitations.

Measurement and Precision

Measurement can be made with varying degrees of precision. For example, if we measure the pencil in Figure 11.1 with a ruler divided into one inch segments, we would estimate its length to be four inches to the nearest

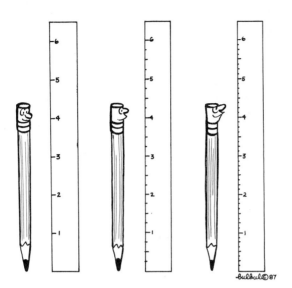

-bulbul©87-

FIGURE 11.1
The exact length
of the pencil can never
be known, but with more
precise measuring
instruments, a closer
approximation can
be found.

inch. If we measure that same pencil with a ruler marked by half inches, we would note that it is $4\frac{1}{2}$ inches long to the nearest half inch. If the ruler were divided into fourths of an inch, our estimate would be $4\frac{1}{4}$ inches; into eighths—$4\frac{3}{8}$ inches; and if into ten-thousandths of an inch, 4.3576. But none of these measurements is an exact expression of the length of the pencil.

The precision of measurement can be increased by using a more precise measuring instrument (such as a micrometer) and more careful measuring procedures, but the measurement is always an estimate of the length of the pencil. Therefore, as we describe the pencil as being four inches long to the nearest inch or $4\frac{3}{8}$ inches long to the nearest eighth inch, we denote to the reader the precision of our measuring instrument; that is, the margin of *error* between the assumed real length of the pencil and its measured length.

Measuring the length of a pencil is a relatively simple task. We know exactly what we are measuring (a pencil). We can readily identify the dimension or attribute being measured (length). We have available a reliable measuring tool (ruler) and standard procedures for using it. Measuring psychological dimensions of human personality is far more complex. It is often difficult even to identify such human characteristics as ability, achievement, or performance.

For example, what is intelligence? What are the dimensions of intelligence? To what extent does each of the identified dimensions contribute to the individual's total intelligence, and what is its relation to other dimensions? How is intelligence measured? Today, psychologists use intelligence tests, mental maturity tests, and other aptitude scales. In the past century, as people became interested in intelligence or innate ability, a number of interesting approaches were used. Some psychologists believed intelligence to be related to the size of the brain, the angle of the jaw to the face, the ratio of the maximum width of the skull to its length, or the circumference of the head. For an interesting account of this, see Stephen Jay Gould, *The Mismeasure of Man.*

Intelligence testing has developed rapidly in the past seventy-five years since Alfred Binet began testing French children to determine which ones had the ability to read and be successful in school. While improving, intelligence tests are only *estimates* of intelligence—and perhaps only one kind of intelligence—and should be interpreted with caution.

I.Q. tests are developed indirectly. A person whom others judge to have high intelligence responds in one way to a question, while a person whom others judge to have low intelligence responds in another. The question is then said to *discriminate* between high and low intelligence; a series of such questions becomes an "intelligence test." The dilemma we face, however, is whether or not we are measuring all of the dimensions that are inherent in intelligence. Are there others not yet identified, or which we are unable to measure with our crude tools? Further, such tests may not be valid for all children. Children who have handicaps may not handle a pencil rapidly enough to meet time constraints (at issue is not their ability to think, but their ability to act). Students from low-income homes may be disadvantaged on the test because of lack of life experiences rather than lack of ability. On a recent test, several students living in a poor neighborhood of a central city circled the word "dog" upon seeing a picture of a cow. They had never seen a cow.

Validity and Reliability

Two terms are used in education to describe the worth of a testing instrument: validity and reliability. *Validity* refers to the extent to which a measuring instrument measures what it is supposed to measure. On the surface this sounds quite simple. Obviously, we would never use gallon containers to measure the width of a book. However, in psychological measurement, identifying the factor to be measured or selecting appropriate instruments is not always so easy. The most obvious examples of this difficulty can be drawn from personality tests wherein interpretations must be based on technically written descriptors that often vary from more common uses of the language. Even the validity of achievement tests must be considered. A standardized economics achievement test that measures concepts unrelated to the curriculum is not a valid indication of achievement for a particular group of students.

The second term used to describe the worth of a measuring instrument is *reliability* or consistency. The extent to which a particular instrument yields similar results each time it is administered is important. If a test were given to a student three days in succession, and each day quite different results were obtained, the value of the measurement would be nil or at least questionable.

Each time we measure the length of a pencil we are apt to obtain varying readings with our ruler (this is particularly true of more precise measurements). A scientist may, for example, take many measurements of a phenomenon and find the average of these readings—thus increasing precision. Each time a person responds to most educational measurements, he or she is likely to do so in a slightly different way. The scores vary. The variance of scores yielded by a test from an individual through repeated measurements is used to estimate the precision of the instrument and is known as the *standard error of measurement*. A test is said to be more reliable if its variance is less; that is, if it consistently yields the same results. This error term is similiar to the distinction between the actual length of the pencil and the measured length.

Measurement errors may be due to the instrument, the process used in measuring, and/or the attribute being measured. Carefully developed standardized instruments tend to be more stable than teacher-made tests and thus more reliable; their standardized procedures for administration produce more consistent scores over time. Finally, some attributes of people are more stable than others. Reliability typically is reported on a scale from .00 to 1.00, with .65 considered a good reliability coefficient for ratings of a program but low for achievement tests.

The perception of standardized tests by prospective teachers tends to be at one of two extremes. At one extreme are those teachers who consider the results infallible. In their view, if something can be tested and described in quantitative terms, the results must be accurate and true. They tend to ignore the factors influencing the worth of the test, factors previously discussed in this chapter.

At the other extreme are those who discredit all tests as being unreliable and useless. They overemphasize the points made in our discussion. Neither of these points of view is defensible. Tests and other assessment instruments have weaknesses inherent in them, but they have made a tremendous contribution to educational progress and are an increasingly important part of schools. The years ahead promise even more valuable instruments to aid the teacher.

Assessing Instructional Objectives

In Chapter 8 we discussed four types of instructional objectives: behavioral objectives, problem-solving objectives, expressive objectives, and attitudinal objectives. In this section we will consider how teachers may assess student's work on academic tasks as defined by these various types of objectives.

Assessing Behavioral Objectives

As you will recall from our earlier discussion, behavioral objectives are written as a sentence containing three statements: 1) a specification of the evaluation conditions, 2) the behavior that a student is expected to exhibit, and 3) the conditions for evaluating whether or not the task has been accomplished. If you have specified the evaluative conditions, then making a decision about whether or not the student has satisfactorily completed the task requires some form of assessment.

This assessment can take several forms. Although some form of paper and pencil test is most often used, it is not the only method of assessment. Consider, for example, using laboratory exercises, written descriptions, physical performance exercises, oral presentations, cooperative group assignments, and classification tasks. The appropriateness of the process is determined by the nature of the skill or competency specified in the instructional objective.

1. Given 20 2-digit problems with sums less than 100, the student will correctly add 18.
2. Given a list of terms, students will use each term correctly in a written sentence without the use of a dictionary.
3. The student will label in writing each of the five major components on a diagram of a plant cell.
4. When asked ten questions in Spanish, the student will orally answer at least nine, completely and correctly, in English.
5. The student will classify thirty assorted objects into sets of wood, glass, plastic, metal, leather, and clay with no errors.

Assessment of the first three objectives requires paper and pencil responses, but of different dimensions. The first requires the student to write the sums of addition problems; the second to write out sentences; and the third to label a diagram. The response mode for the fourth objective is oral while the fifth requires the grouping of objects.

What is important is the correct matching of the assessment to the expected behavior identified in the objective. Kibler, Cegala, Barker, and Miles (1974, 121–22) illustrated this using objective 3 above. Consider the appropriateness of the following test item for this objective.

> **Test Item for Objective 3.** Below is a diagram of a plant cell. Describe how each component of the plant cell contributes to the life of the plant and how each component interacts with other components in the cell.

While the objective calls only for students to label the major components of the plant cell, this test item requires that they describe the interrelationship and function of each component. A more appropriate test item would be consistent with the conditions in the objective.

> **Alternate Test Item for Objective 3.** Below is a diagram of a plant cell. Label each of the five major components of the cell.

Behavioral objectives are the most common bases for tests in education, but test items should be consistent with the intent and structure of each.

Assessing Problem-Solving and Expressive Objectives

In Chapter 8 we discussed five criteria for evaluating problem-solving objectives.

1. Did the student arrive at a solution that met all of the specified conditions?

Every year there is a national contest for students known as the Olympics of the Mind. In this contest students from secondary schools compete to solve difficult problems such as building "cars" that are powered by the

Formative evaluation often takes place during instruction.

wind or paper structures that can hold heavy objects. The students are judged on whether or not they have met all of the conditions for the task and then whether or not they have produced a superior product that meets the challenge set by the task. These two elements are an important part of any evaluation: meeting the criteria and producing a superior product within the confines of the criteria.

In your classroom the task could be a written assignment such as a play or a story or a proposed explanation of why some physical event occurs. As long as you specify the criteria students must meet when you make the assignment, you can then give them freedom to write in any way they choose—alone or with a small group. The task also may be a construction assignment, an art project, or a dramatic performance, but the criteria for working through the assignment must be specified in advance.

2. Did the student work through the problem without deviating from the specified conditions, even though no solution was reached?

Your students may not solve some of the problems you pose for them; this may be perfectly all right if you can judge whether or not they were actively attempting to solve the problem. To help you make this judgment you may wish to rely on an *observation record* that permits you to record each student's progress—a series of small tasks that lead to the final task (which may be a logical progression, but more likely are not sequential and include leaps, errors, and guesses) or a *written journal* in which the students record their progress through the activity.

The last three indicators for problem-solving objectives are also useful guidelines for evaluating expressive objectives.

3. How would you describe the quality of the work?

An expressive objective has no specified outcome. As we discussed in Chapter 8, one important aspect of learning is simply having an opportunity to experience a trip to the zoo, to see a play, to draw a picture, to write a poem, or to perform in creative improvisation. Although there *are* outcomes associated with expressive objectives, these outcomes result from the student's own experience, not the teacher's predetermined and structured specification.

However, that does not mean that expression cannot be evaluated, nor does it mean that expressive activities are chaotic experiences with no structure or form. One way to begin to evaluate expressive activities (as well as another way of evaluating problem-solving activities) is to *describe* what the student has done and to ask other students to describe the results of the activity. You can then move the discussion toward what is especially effective about the work (or the process) and what needs more attention.

For example, consider a student who designs a poster for Fire Prevention Week. The student has conformed to specifications related to size, media, and theme. How then does one move beyond that to evaluate the poster? One can begin to describe the poster in terms of balance, color, detail, line, and implied meaning. Such a description could be compared to other students' works. Thus the students would not only receive feedback on their work, they would also receive a mini art lesson on learning to look at pictures.

4. How would you describe the quality of the process the student used to solve the problem?

The same procedures are used for describing the process a student uses to solve a problem or to express an idea. The students can take notes on their own attempts to solve a problem (or you can take notes as they work through a problem), and those notes can then become the basis for a discussion of effective and less effective problem-solving strategies. This debriefing process is a vital element in activities that involve simulation and role playing, but it is also important in mathematics problem solving and in problem solving in the physical and social sciences.

When evaluating expressive objectives, it is equally important to describe how the student created an expression that communicated (or failed to communicate) the experience to others. Were the choices of words compelling? Did the student use appropriate gestures? What did vocal inflection imply? Was the use of form and color pleasing, disturbing, boring?

5. What did the student learn from the experience?

This category is perhaps the most important of all—and the most elusive, for we have to rely on the student's ability to report and to discuss what the experience or the activity meant individually. This involves an evaluation assignment that permits students to talk about the experience or to write about it. It is a record of the students' impressions, not a record of demonstrated ability. Such a record is a qualitative document that captures the students' abilities to express their thoughts and feelings and is, in itself, an expressive activity.

Assessing Affective Objectives

One of the greatest challenges in student assessment is the measurement of their changes in attitude. While most educators generally agree that student attitudes are a vital component of school learning, they don't always agree on how to assess those changes.

The problem with assessing attitudinal change is that we make major inferences of *internal* attitudinal states from *external* behavior. That is, we infer that a student has a poor attitude about the study of English when he or she—

► skips English class as often as possible;
► fails to complete homework in English on a fairly regular basis;
► volunteers negative comments ("Boy, is this dumb." "How come we gotta study English anyway?" "I don't need no more English!");
► or any of a number of other behaviors which would lead us to believe that the student has a less than positive attitude toward the study of English.

How should the teacher assess attitudinal change? The first step is to be clear about the types of behaviors we want to foster among students, behaviors we believe to be indicative of positive attitudes.

Mager (1984) suggests that the easiest means of assessing student attitudes is to begin by stating what you would like to see them doing if their attitudes were positive. For example, a history teacher might specify the following objective and indicators.

Students will demonstrate a positive attitude toward the study of history by—

► volunteering positive comments about the content of lessons;
► voluntarily continuing discussions in halls, cafeteria, and elsewhere about topics that were initiated in class;
► making comments about news items appropriate to the topic(s) under study;
► voluntarily reading books on historical topics when given a choice of reading assignments.

The key, operant term here is *voluntary*. When working in the affective domain, we can be more confident in our observations if we are careful to specify that what is sought is voluntary compliance. Why? The reason is simple.

If the history teacher were to *require* students to report on news items relevant to an historical topic under discussion, that would probably be a good learning activity to help students bridge the gap between history lessons and the world in which they live. But if students do those required reports on contemporary news items, can the teacher then infer that their attitudes toward history are becoming more positive? Not necessarily. Their attitudes toward getting good grades, or at least not receiving a lower grade because they failed to do the assignment, would probably be a stronger driving force and a more accurate inference on the part of the teacher.

On the other hand, if students volunteer things *above and beyond* the minimum required for a grade, the teacher can infer with some degree of confidence that their attitudes toward history are becoming more positive. And if the usually negative student described earlier actually started coming to class regularly, volunteering positive comments about history, and doing *at least* the minimum required, the teacher can likely infer that positive changes in that student's perceptions of the study of history are taking place.

A caution must be offered here, though, regarding the use of voluntary behavior as a fully valid indicator of having achieved effective objectives. Some students may reflect a positive attitude to get better grades, to please the teacher, or for reasons other than their positive attitude toward the subject matter. The teacher who is a perceptive observer of human behavior will take care to treat observations as tentative hypotheses, to be tested with additional data, and not simply taken at face value. The key to assessing student development in the affective domain is noting voluntary behavior that you are willing to accept as evidence of attitudinal changes.

Assessment is a direct result of, and is linked to, the goals and objectives of instruction. Test and assessment instruments may result in interesting findings, but if they do not provide feedback on the effectiveness of instruction, they are not useful.

Measuring Student Progress

Using multiple and varied techniques and instruments for measuring student progress is an important aspect of evaluation. Some are in the form of tests, others include more subjective observations, rating scales, and interviews. Some are available commercially while others are prepared by individual teachers.

Commercial Instruments

Most school systems utilize a continuing program of student assessment which extends from kindergarten through high school. Generally included are tests of student ability and achievement. These are administered periodically as the student progresses through the grades, with the results recorded in a cumulative record folder. As a teacher, you will find these results to be very useful.

Many of the instruments employed are standardized tests. That is, the procedures for administering, scoring, and interpreting the tests have been systematized through an extensive process. After the objectives and population for a standardized test have been identified, numerous potential test items are written, evaluated, and rewritten. These items are administered to an experimental population, and ambiguous items or those that do not discriminate between high and low scoring individuals are eliminated. The resulting set of items that effectively test the objectives are formed into a test. Specific procedures and directions are written, and the test is administered to hundreds of students. This population is carefully selected so that it is as representative as possible of the general population for which the test is designed.

Based on the raw scores obtained in the testing program, norms are derived for analysis and comparison. The test norms describe the relationship of a particular score to other scores obtained. They are descriptions of what *is*, not what *should be*. Some norms are expressed in "grade equivalents," "age equivalents," "percentiles," and "stanines." These will be explored later in this chapter in the Reflective Inquiry section.

*M*istakes can serve an infinitely more useful function in learning than correct answers memorized and reproduced for the examination.

Daniel Tanner, *Using Behavioral Objectives in the Classroom*, 1972, 24.

Test norms should not dictate the needs of a curriculum, however. They are measures of comparison and must be interpreted in terms of the local situation and the many other interrelated factors. Insecure teachers have, at times, attempted to teach the content of a standardized test. They rationalized that if the items were important enough to be included on the test, they are important enough to be taught. This procedure destroys the value of the test norms and violates every known principle of teaching. The instructional program must be built on significant goals for a specific group of students and not on the content of standardized tests. However, the content of the test must reflect previously set goals of instruction. Consider Exhibit 11.1 and its implications for teaching and testing.

EXHIBIT 11.1   Teaching and Testing

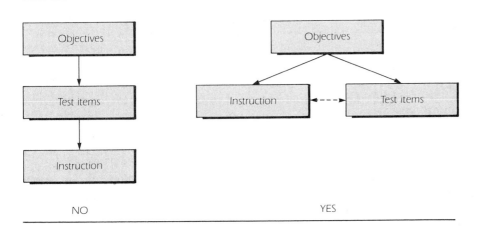

Exhibit 11.1 illustrates proper and improper use of tests in instruction. In the sequence on the left, instruction is based on test items, while on the right, both the test and instruction are based on objectives. However, do not infer from this that teachers should not prepare students to feel confident in taking tests and to develop test-taking skills. Teachers often administer practice, timed tests during which they teach students how to mark test items, how to use machine-scorable answer sheets, how to work during timed tests, and how to prepare psychologically for the test.

Many excellent commercial tests are available to appraise student characteristics. Identifying and selecting appropriate specialized instruments usually is done in cooperation with specialists in the school district. Some instruments must be administered and interpreted by specially trained personnel, while others can be used by classroom teachers who carefully follow the outlined procedures. While teachers do not often select the standardized tests to be used in the school district, it is useful to know what is available. Brief descriptions and critical reviews of many testing instruments may be found in Buros (ed.), *Eighth Mental Measurements Yearbook* (1978). Here are some factors to consider in selecting a test: Does it meet my needs? What facilities and equipment are required? What does the test cost? How easy is it to administer and score? Are special skills and competencies needed to administer the test?

Two major categories of commercial tests are used in schools. *Aptitude* tests provide an estimate of future success. *Achievement* tests provide an estimate of the student's current knowledge in a particular subject or field.

Aptitude Tests. Aptitude tests are used to predict future success; either generally—as measures of intelligence—or in a particular area. Intelligence tests such as the individually administered *Stanford Binet* or the group-administered *Otis-Lennon School Ability Test* provide information on general ability or intelligence. A score on the Otis-Lennon "is an index of the pupil's relative ability, in comparison with pupils of similar chronological age regardless of grade placement, to deal with abstract relationships involving the manipulation of ideas expressed in verbal, numerical, figurative, or symbolic form (Otis & Lennon 1982, 16). While the Otis-Lennon yields a single score, the *Differential Aptitude Tests* include several scores, including verbal reasoning, numerical ability, abstract reasoning, clerical speed and accuracy, mechanical reasoning, space relations, spelling, and language usage.

The *Test of Cognitive Skills* is an ability test designed to assess student's academic aptitude in four areas and thereby predicts level of success in school. The four areas are (1) *sequences*, which measures the ability to recognize patterns in figures, letters, or numbers; (2) *analogies*, which tests ability to recognize relationships among subjects, people, scenes, and geometric figures; (3) *memory*, which measures ability to recall previously presented material; and (4) *verbal reasoning*, which measures ability to reason logically and discern relationships between pictures and words.

Scores from aptitude or ability tests are often misused and misinterpreted. Intelligence is assumed to be a definite, specific, unchangeable factor that has accurately and precisely been measured and described in "I.Q. units." For example, it has been said that, "The student with an I.Q. of 98 is below average, while the one with 105 is above average." In truth, the two students may be equally intelligent or the rating might be reversed from that suggested by these scores, but because of measurement error, these particular scores were obtained.

The standard error of measurement is greatest when the measuring instrument for intelligence is a written test administered to a group of students. We would caution that although group-administered intelligence test results suggest a general level of ability, they do not do so with high precision. They are better predictors of students at the top and bottom of the range than those near the center. This is perhaps one reason why schools are generally reluctant to share these data with parents, for such data are so often misinterpreted and misunderstood.

Some aptitude tests are designed for special purposes. A kindergarten or first-grade teacher may use aptitude tests to determine whether a child might profit from formal instruction in reading (referred to as reading readiness tests). A secondary mathematics teacher may identify, before instruction begins, those students who are likely to achieve relative success in algebra and those who are likely to encounter difficulties. A high-school teacher or counselor may use them to forecast the probability of success of a student in college. While useful, results of such aptitude tests must be used in conjunction with other data. They provide *information* for decision making, not *decisions*.

Achievement Tests.   Achievement tests are the most commonly used commercial instruments in schools today. They provide an estimate of the knowledge of students in various subject fields. Such tests provide an objective, external criterion—independent of teacher judgement—that permits teachers to compare a class or individual with a representative group. Most achievement tests are part of a battery of tests, administered at successive grade levels, that make possible the examination of rates of student growth over time. Some batteries have standardized scores across subject fields so that it is possible, for example, to compare student achievement in mathematics and reading. Finally, when new students transfer to a school, achievement tests provide a benchmark of their achievement and often a guide for placement of the student at the correct level.

Achievement tests include subtests to help identify specific strengths and weaknesses of students. The *SRA Achievement Series*, for example, includes eight levels of tests from kindergarten through grade twelve. Reading and mathematics tests are available for grades K–12; language arts—grades 2–12; social studies, science, and use of reference materials—grades 4–12; and the survey of applied skills—grades 9–12.

Subscales are based on the curriculum at each level; thus they vary according to the level of the test. Reading tests include vocabulary and comprehension subscales on all but the lowest level; visual discrimination is tested only at the first level; auditory discrimination only in the first two levels; and letters/sounds only in the lowest three levels. Mathematics subtests include concepts, computation, and problem solving (the latter not tested until the fifth level). Language arts tests begin at the third level (for grade two) and include three subtests: mechanics, usage, and spelling. Other achievement tests on the market have similar scales and subscales.

Achievement tests are administered typically by the classroom teacher, collected by schools, and forwarded to the school district central office or the testing agency for scoring. The computer-generated profiles that are returned usually provide information on the performance of individual students and the class on each of the skills and subskills.

Norm- and Criterion-Referenced Achievement Tests.   Some achievement tests are norm-referenced. Their scores usually are reported so as to indicate the relative position of a student or a class in comparison with a nationally-normed reference group. When a student's score is at the fortieth percentile, it means that she or he scored as well as or better than 40 percent of those in the national group used for norming the tests and that 60 percent of the persons in the norm group scores as well as or higher than this student. Norm-referenced tests rank learners, provide a comparison of relative achievement, and foster competition with others.

Table 11.1 includes percentiles for students in the fifth grades in two elementary schools and for the school district as a whole. In addition to these group norms, each child in the fifth grade would have an individual percentile score. As you examine this table, what would you conclude about vocabulary achievement in the district and in the two schools? In which areas did students score highest? Lowest? How would you compare the two schools?

TABLE 11.1   Nationally-Normed Percentiles for the Fifth Grades in Two Schools and the District

Subtest	Total District	School A (n=109)	School B (n=83)
Vocabulary	50	55	41
Comprehension	52	53	42
Total Reading	51	53	41
Spelling	53	60	52
Language Mechanics	53	60	47
Language Expression	53	58	50
Total Language	52	58	46
Math Computation	59	61	55
Math Concepts & Appl.	51	53	58
Total Math	55	55	54
Total Battery	51	52	47
Reference Skills	53	54	55

Percentiles from the *Comprehensive Tests of Basic Skills*

EXHIBIT 11.2   Criterion-referenced Scores for Fifth Grade of School A on TEAMS test

TEXAS EDUCATIONAL ASSESSMENT OF MINIMUM SKILLS
SUMMARY REPORT

REPORT DATE: MAY 1986

ALL STUDENTS

DATE OF TESTING: FEBRUARY 1986

CAMPUS:
DISTRICT: A

GRADE: 05

BASIC SKILLS AREAS	OBJECTIVES	MASTERING NUMBER	MASTERING PERCENT	NOT MASTERING NUMBER	GROUP CHARACTERISTICS		
M A T H E M A T I C S	1. PLACE VALUE	80	92	7	TOTAL ENROLLMENT	97	
	2. EQUIVALENT FRACTIONS	80	92	7	Number Not Tested	10	
	3. DECIMALS (+,–)	78	90	9			
	4. MULTIPLICATION	85	98	2	The following data are based on	NUMBER	PERCENT
	5. DIVISION	61	70	26	NUMBER OF STUDENTS TESTED	87	100
	6. WORD PROBLEMS (+,–)	62	71	25			
	7. WORD PROBLEMS (x,÷)	69	79	18	ETHNIC COMPOSITION		
	8. WORD PROBLEMS (DECIMAL)	76	87	11	American Indian or Alaskan Native	0	0
	9. MEASUREMENT UNITS	70	80	17	Asian or Pacific Islander	0	0
	10. GRAPHS	57	66	30	Black	11	13
	11. PERIMETER OR AREA OF POLYGONS	77	89	10	Hispanic	51	59
	STUDENTS TESTED: 87 TOTAL MATHEMATICS:	78	90	9	White	25	29
					FREE/REDUCED PRICE MEAL PROGRAM	61	70
R E A D I N G	1. MAIN IDEA	61	70	26	CHAPTER I REGULAR PROGRAM	15	17
	2. CONTEXT CLUES	64	74	23			
	3. SPECIFIC DETAILS	67	77	20	CHAPTER I MIGRANT PROGRAMS		
	4. SEQUENCING OF EVENTS	55	63	32	Remedial Mathematics Program	0	0
	5. DRAWING CONCLUSIONS	48	55	39	Remedial Reading Program	0	0
	6. FACT, OPINION	69	79	18	Remedial Writing Program	0	0
	7. CAUSE-AND-EFFECT	64	74	23	Eligible but does not participate	0	0
	8. PARTS OF A BOOK	79	91	8	Neither eligible nor participating	87	100
	9. GRAPHIC SOURCES	67	77	20	LIMITED ENGLISH PROFICIENCY	5	6
	STUDENTS TESTED: 87 TOTAL READING:	73	84	14	BILINGUAL / ESL PROGRAMS		
					Bilingual Program	0	0
W R I T I N G	1. CAPITALIZATION	80	92	7	English as a Second Language Program	0	0
	2. PUNCTUATION	76	87	11			
	3. SPELLING	80	92	7	SPECIAL EDUCATION		
	4. CORRECT ENGLISH USAGE	81	93	6	Learning Disability	0	0
	5. SENTENCE STRUCTURE	79	91	8	Emotionally Disturbed	0	0
	6. PROOFREADING	79	91	8	Speech Handicapped	0	0
					Visually Handicapped	0	0
	7. DESCRIPTIVE WRITTEN COMPOSITION				Other handicapping condition	0	0
	RATING: 4 3 2 1 0				Non-special education students	87	100
	NUMBER: 1 22 51 13 0						
	PERCENT: 1 25 59 15 0				GIFTED/TALENTED PROGRAM	0	0
					PASS/FAIL SUMMARY		
	MULTIPLE CHOICE SUB-TEST:	79	91	8	Passed all three tests	57	66
	WRITTEN COMPOSITION SUB-TEST:	74	85	13	Failed one test only	21	24
					Failed two tests only	6	7
	STUDENTS TESTED: 87 TOTAL WRITING:	68	78	19	Failed all three tests	3	3

Criterion-referenced tests are based on specific objectives and acceptable criterion levels, foster competition with self, and are useful for diagnosis. For example, a test may include five questions related to a particular objective, and the criterion may be set at three questions. Students answering three questions correctly pass; those with fewer than three correct answers fail. For each objective, an individual either passes or fails. When a teacher receives feedback about a class, the analysis shows the percent of students in that class who passed. The comparison is based on the objective, while in norm-referenced tests, the comparison is with other students. This distinction is important; both types of achievement tests are needed.

The feedback for all fifth-grade students in School A on a criterion-based achievement battery, the *Texas Educational Assessment of Minimum Skills*, is illustrated in Exhibit 11.2. Several notes should help in reading these analyses.

On the left side of the report are listed three basic skills areas—mathematics, reading, and writing. Several objectives are tested in each area; for example, there are eleven in mathematics. Four questions were included on the test for each objective, with mastery defined as correctly answering at least three. Of the 87 students who were tested, 80 mastered objective 1, place value, and 7 did not master this objective. To master the entire mathematics area, students must have correctly answered 27 of the 44 questions. Seventy-eight students met this criterion and thus mastered the mathematics area. Note that the criterion levels (3 of 4 correct items for each objective and 27 of 44 for mathematics) are arbitrarily set in advance and that students either meet the criterion and pass (that is, achieve mastery) or fail to pass.

For mastery of the reading area, 22 correct responses out of 36 questions (9 objectives times 4 questions per objective) were required. Writing consisted of two subtests—multiple-choice (6 objectives) and a written composition. To master writing, the student must have correctly answered 16 of the 24 multiple-choice questions and scored either a 2, 3, or 4 on the written composition. The number and percent of students for each rating are listed as well as the percent of students mastering each of the two subtests.

Characteristics of the group are listed on the right side of the report. Through federal programs, some students receive lunch, either free or at reduced prices. Chapter 1 refers to the number of students in the fifth grade who were eligible, because of poverty, for special instruction. It is a federally-supported program to provide compensatory education for low-income students. Limited English proficiency refers to the number of students whose English is poor; bilingual and ESL (English as a Second Language) are programs provided for such students. Finally, at the botton of the page is a summary of the success of this group of fifth graders on the test. Two-thirds of them passed all three tests (57 students), while only three failed all three tests.

In mathematics, which objective did the greatest number of students master? Which did the fewest students master? How many students failed to master this objective? If you were the teacher, what objectives in the three areas would you identify as needing the greatest emphasis in reteaching? Compare the results of this criterion-referenced test with those on the norm-referenced test reported in Table 11.1. What observations about them would you make?

Teacher-Prepared Instruments

Commercially produced instruments are not, can not, and should not be used in measuring all aspects of a school program. Although teacher-prepared instruments may not be as carefully designed as commercial ones, they have the advantages of being focused for a specific group of students, covering a specific subject area, and being narrow in scope. Teachers can also utilize techniques of informal observation generally not part of commercial tests, and such techniques and instruments can be continually employed. Some of the evaluative information and techniques available to the teacher include autobiographies, observational records, sociograms, case studies, interviews, conferences, anecdotal records, informal tests and inventories, role-playing situations, parent conferences, samples of manual dexterity skills (for example, handwriting, physical education, industrial arts).

Constructing Assessment Instruments

All teachers make tests; but not all make good tests. This task is not as simple as the uninitiated might suppose. Prospective teachers are not expected to be experts in test construction, but they should know basic testing principles. Suggestions in this section are designed to assist you in making better testing instruments.

Tests are constructed to measure representative knowledge, performance, or behaviors. Since tests do not measure all possible areas in the domain being tested, we infer that students' responses to the sample are indicative of their responses to the total domain. This implies that sample test items are drawn in such a way as to be representative of the whole.

Two general principles in designing tests should be considered. First, sample test items should be drawn from various parts of the content to be tested, not solely from one portion or segment. Second, the greater the number of test items, the more accurate the results are likely to be.

To assure tests that are representative, some teachers rely on the development of a table of specifications. They first identify the important dimensions in the test. This usually entails two types of information: a description of the important subject matter content and an identification of the kinds of responses expected of students. A third-grade teacher listed, for the first type of information, addition and subtraction of whole numbers and for the second type, facts, problems, and applications. These were placed on two axes of a table of specifications; then the approximate number of items in each area to be tested were filled in to reflect the weighting for that category. The completed table of specifications is illustrated below.

The teacher determined that subtraction should be emphasized more than addition, that a 25-item test was long enough, that facts should make up nearly half of the test, and that application questions, which would take longer to complete, should make up only 20 percent of the test.

In this way, the sample of test items was more likely to reflect the total subject matter being tested. The length of the test was long enough to be relatively reliable but not so long as to be tiring for third graders. Most textbook series and school district curriculum guides provide questions and

TABLE 11.2   Table of Specifications

Content	Type Of Test Item			
	Facts	*Problems*	*Applications*	*Total*
Addition	6	2	2	10
Subtraction	6	6	3	15
Total	12	8	5	25

problems to be used in teacher-made tests; thus, teachers rarely have to formulate tests from scratch.

Power tests are tests with no time limits, so students are able to demonstrate all they know without being penalized if they are slow responders. *Speed* tests, on the other hand, have tightly defined time limits.

Nine further suggestions for writing good test items are summarized in the following list.

1. Each item should be written to test a particular instructional objective.
2. Test only the more important factors, avoiding the inconsequential or trivial.
3. Keep the reading difficulty level of the test low in relation to that of the class.
4. Eliminate ambiguous questions and directions.
5. Be sure each item has one—and only one—best or correct answer.
6. If a question is based on opinion or authority, state whose authority or opinion.
7. Try to avoid using expressions that may have different meanings for different students.
8. Avoid questions that provide cues to the correct response of other questions.
9. Before administering, be sure the instrument can be scored and the information synthesized.

Test items may be classified as *supply* and *selection* questions. With supply items, the student furnishes the response. Types of supply items include essay questions, short-answer items, and completion questions. In selection items, the student need only select a response from two or more alternatives. Selection questions include multiple-choice, true-false, and matching items.

Essay Questions.   The primary purpose of the essay question is to test students' ability to do creative or reflective thinking, organize knowledge about the solution to a problem, and express their responses in writing. Questions should be so stated that the response can be focused. They should be concise and explicit, calling for relatively brief rather than lengthy responses. Terms such as *explain, contrast, illustrate,* or *compare* elicit sharper responses than instructions such as "tell all you know about" or "review." Being explicit may require additional questions, but the results are far more satisfactory.

Essay questions are particularly appropriate if questions require the student to write a summary, compare two phenomena, apply information to various problems, make decisions and explain why, discuss cause-effect relationships, evaluate ideas and relate ideas in a coherent manner, and/or make comparisons. They are less effective for measuring knowledge of factual material. Scoring is difficult and less reliable than objective tests, since the answers include varying degrees of factual material organized in varying degrees of coherence and expressed with varying degrees of articulateness.

In writing essay questions, (1) phrase each question in such a way that the task is clearly indicated; (2) specify the expected length of the response or give a time limit; (3) prepare—in advance—an outline of major points expected in student answers and a scoring guide; (4) evaluate all answers to one question before analyzing the next question; and (5) avoid "halo effects" by evaluating answers without prior knowledge of student names. Written comments by the teacher as to how the paper could be improved are far more beneficial than letter or numerical grades.

Poor: Discuss the events leading up to the American Civil War in 1861.
Better: Compare the economic conditions of the North and the South at the beginning of the American Civil War.

Poor: Why did Columbus seek help from Queen Isabella?
Better: What factors and events led Columbus to seek support from the Spanish Court for his first voyage?

In contrast to essay tests, objective tests are highly structured; they present the student with a definitive task that limits the response that can be made. Students must demonstrate specific knowledge and are not free to redefine the problem or organize responses of their choosing. Scoring objective tests is quicker, easier, and more accurate than essay tests. Several types of objective tests are discussed in the following paragraphs.

Short-answer Questions. These test items usually are stated in the form of a question which is to be answered by a brief statement. They may be used effectively to test knowledge of terminology, basic ideas, and principles; interpretation of data; generalized notions; and recall of simple facts. The test question should be so stated that the response is brief and unambiguous.

Short-answer questions are relatively easy to construct. Because students supply the answer and thus cannot rely on partial knowledge or guessing to choose the correct answer, the possibility of guessing is reduced. They are, however, unsuitable for assessing complex learning outcomes and are difficult to score, since a variety of answers of varying degrees of correctness may be considered for partial or total credit.

Here are two suggestions for writing short-answer questions: first, word the question so as to elicit a brief and concise answer; second, when the answer is to be expressed in numerical units, indicate the type of answer desired.

Poor: What is the role of white blood cells in the body's defense system?
Better: Provide illustrations of the following phenomena in relation to white blood cells: (a) bacterial invasion, (b) blood coagulation, and (c) antibody activity.

Poor: Where does the President live?
Better: What is the name of the home of the President of the United States?

Completion Statements. These items require the student to complete a statement or fill in blanks in which one or more words have been omitted rather than respond to a question. They are appropriate whenever an objective specifies the student be able to name, list, or supply the answer or when the student is supposed to have memorized certain terms, names of persons, dates, or symbols.

This type of test question is probably the most misused by teachers. Frequently, a statement is abstracted directly from the textbook, a key word or phrase deleted, and the student expected to recall the missing information. This, in effect, requires a knowledge of exact wording from a source rather than broader general understanding, and could lead to an emphasis on memorization.

Some suggestions for improving completion questions include the following: (1) have only one blank in each statement; (2) omit key words or phrases rather than minor details; (3) do not select direct quotations from the textbook, lecture, or other source; and (4) have all blanks be of the same length.

Poor: _____ , _____ , _____ , and _____ were President during times of peril.
Better: Four persons who were President of the United States at the beginning of major wars were _____ , _____ , _____ , and _____ .

Poor: All eclipses involve _____ .
Better: When some of the light from the sun to the earth is blocked by the moon, a(n) _____ is said to occur.

Multiple-choice Questions. As a college student, you are no doubt well acquainted with this type of question, for it is perhaps the most used and useful device for testing knowledge and understanding. An incomplete statement or question, called the "stem," is followed by several alternate responses, only one of which is correct. Incorrect responses are called "distractors." Students may be asked to select the one right response among distractors, the one incorrect response among correct distractors, or the most appropriate or best answer from several possibilities. These questions have been used for making fine distinctions by asking for the "most important reason," "principle cause," or "best explanation."

Multiple-choice questions are more reliable because scoring is objective. Several alternative responses reduce the impact of guessing. Using a number of plausible alternatives makes results amenable to diagnosis (that is, the nature of incorrect alternatives provides clues to factual errors and misunderstandings).

Multiple-choice questions, like all objective items, are not well-suited to problem-solving ideas. In constructing items, locating a sufficient number of incorrect but plausible distractors is often difficult.

Here are some suggestions for improving questions of this type: (1) include as much of the statement as possible in the stem; (2) provide four or more alternative answers for each question; (3) use the same number of alternative responses throughout the test; (4) write all distractors as plausible completions of the stem; and (5) make all responses grammatically correct completions of the stem.

A variation of the multiple-choice test is the multiple-response test. While multiple-choice items include a single best answer, multiple-response items can include several correct answers. Such items require greater knowledge by students and provide a way to extend test complexity.

Poor: In the story, Betty's favorite flower was a
a. orchid
b. tulip
c. rose
d. iris

Better: In the story, Betty's favorite flower was
a. an orchid
b. a tulip
c. a rose
d. an iris

Poor: The Constitution of the United States
a. was written by George Washington
b. provides for the separation of powers
c. does not mention education
d. was written in 1776

Better: The Bill of Rights in the Constitution protects which of the following?
a. the right of states to tax their citizens
b. freedom of the press
c. the freedom of citizens from high interest rates
d. all of the above

True-false Questions. True-false questions are declarative statements which the student judges to be true or false. They are relatively easy to construct and score and are capable of sampling a large amount of subject matter without using extensive student testing time. Because the student has one chance in two of making a correct response, this type of question encourages guessing. Alternative forms of true-false questions include right-wrong, correct-incorrect, yes-no, fact-opinion, and agree-disagree.

Here are some suggestions for improving true-false items: (1) in writing true-false questions, draw up a list of significant true statements, then reword about half of them to make them false; (2) use wording that differs from the textbook, class discussion, or other source; (3) include only one idea in each question; (4) construct statements that are definitely true or definitely false; (5) avoid the use of negatives and especially double negatives; and (6) avoid specific determiners such as *all, always, definitely, never,* and *undoubtedly* (usually contained in false statements) or *frequently, may, most, possibly,* and *sometimes* (typically contained in true statements).

Poor: T or F The Vietnam War was the cause of the unrest of young people during the 1960s.

Better: T or F U.S. involvement in the Vietnam War began with the introduction of U.S. military advisors into the area during the 1950s.

Poor: T or F All instruction should be introduced with an advanced organizer.

Better: T or F According to D. P. Ausubel, instruction is enhanced when preceded by an advanced organizer.

Matching Questions. The matching test is usually composed of two parallel columns, with each word or symbol in one column matched to a word, sentence, or phrase in the other column. Students are expected to match the correct pairs of items. Matching is appropriate when measuring a large amount of related factual information and when testing associations. Here are some suggestions for writing matching questions: (1) include no more than ten to twelve items in either column; (2) have a greater number of items in the column from which the items are to be selected than in the other column; (3) include homogeneous materials in each set of columns; (4) use consistent grammatical style for all items; and (5) have all items in columns on the same page.

Match the correct statements

Poor

Shakespere	contraction of blood vessels
Alvin Toffler	inventor of incandescent bulb
Thomas Edison	English playwright
smoking	The Declaration of Independence
Thomas Jefferson	The Third Wave

Better

_____ a.	Habitable	1.	Pluto
_____ b.	Many moons	2.	Saturn
_____ c.	Smallest planet	3.	Venus
_____ d.	Slowest rotation	4.	Mercury
_____ e.	Farthest from sun	5.	Earth
_____ f.	Satellite of the earth	6.	Jupiter
_____ g.	Largest planet	7.	Mars
_____ h.	Closest to sun	8.	Neptune
		9.	Uranus
		10.	None of these

Constructing Inquiry Instruments

At times, obtaining information about a person's attitudes, interests, and perceptions of events or ideas is appropriate. To inquire is to ask, and these instruments ask students to make judgments and to respond to questions. The instruments take the form of questionnaires, interviews, sociometric devices, and rating scales.

Questionnaires. Questionnaires are commonly used and, typically, poorly constructed. A well-constructed questionnaire contains a list of questions to which students can easily respond. Questionnaires yield perceptions rather than evidence of reality, knowledge, or events. Here are some suggestions for improving questionnaires: (1) clarify, in the directions, the purpose for which information from the questionnaire will be used; (2) convince the reader that the data are important; (3) write short questions at the reading level of students; and (4) avoid questions that are interesting but not germane; many questionnaires request information that, later, the teacher neither analyzes nor uses.

Interviews. Interviews provide information about opinions, interests, self-perceptions, and knowledge. Information of a highly personal nature can be more readily obtained through interviews. The results are subjective, and interviews take considerable time. Here are some ideas for improving interviews: (1) establish rapport in the early phase of the interview; (2) ask easier and less personal questions early in the interview; (3) plan and structure the interview—write out questions and check wording; and (4) be nonjudgemental, factual, and objective when asking personal questions and reacting to responses.

You may wish to refer to the Reflective Inquiry section of Chapter 1 for further information on interviewing skills. A sample set of interview questions, usually called an *interview protocol* is found in Exhibit 11.4.

EXHIBIT 11.3   Examples of Items From Questionnaires

1. In your opinion, what is the most important subject in school?
2. Why do you think the following rules were established?
3. What was the most difficult part of the chapter for you? Why?
4. If a storm hit, what would you do?

EXHIBIT 11.4   Sample Interview Protocol

Purpose: To interview a teacher about her/his schedule of activities during a day.

1. Could you describe what you did yesterday, beginning with the time you arrived at school?
2. In what ways was yesterday different from other days?
3. What was the most interesting thing you did yesterday?
4. What was the most difficult?
5. How did you feel about it?
6. Could you tell me more about _____? (These probes are for obtaining additional information about something said earlier).
7. Thank you for your time and candor. I have learned so much, and appreciate it.

Rating scales. Rating scales permit educators to make judgements about the degree to which a person exhibits a characteristic or behavior, about the quality of a situation, or about the extensiveness of concepts. In each case, a scale is used to indicate the quality, quantity, or level of the phenomenon being judged. The scale represents a continuum from high to low, from best to worse, or from definitely agree to definitely disagree.

Scales define the full range, not just the ideal (for example, a scale for meat might be *raw-charred* or *tender-tough*; economics of individuals, *rich-destitute*; or students talk, *always-never*). Scales may include descriptions only at the extreme ends of the continuum and spaces between, or they may contain several descriptive words or phrases. They may have five options or seven options, but sometimes they will have an even number of options to eliminate the middle, or neutral, option.

The advantages of rating scales are (1) simplicity of construction; (2) ease of interpretation; and (3) ease of translation into numerical analysis. Disadvantages include (1) lack of reliability among raters; (2) difficulty in judging abstract concepts, and therefore in establishing validity; and (3) subjectivity, possibly resulting in biases and halo effects. Several different kinds of scales are illustrated in Exhibit 11.5.

EXHIBIT 11.5 Examples of Rating Scales

Illustrative Semantic Differential Scales:

Good	___	___	___	___	___	___	___	Bad
Sharp	___	___	___	___	___	___	___	Dull
Important	___	___	___	___	___	___	___	Unimportant

Often a five-point scale is drawn, but the points can have different meanings. Several alternate meanings can be given to the following five-point scale.

| 1 | 2 | 3 | 4 | 5 |

1 - Always true
2 - True most of the time
3 - True about half of the time
4 - Seldom true
5 - Not true

1 - I am in complete agreement with the statement.
2 - I generally agree with the statement, but with reservations.
3 - I am undecided. I can think of arguments for and against the statement.
4 - I tend to disagree, but feel that something might be positive about the statement.
5 - I disagree with the statement without reservation.

1 - Strongly disagree
2 - Disagree
3 - Undecided
4 - Agree
5 - Strongly agree

1 - Always
2 - Usually
3 - Sometimes
4 - Seldom
5 - Never

1 - Much more than he does now
2 - A little more than he does now
3 - The same as he does now
4 - A little less than he does now
5 - Much less than he does now

Testing as a National Movement

The public has turned more and more to test results to find out about the status of its schools. Testing teachers in an effort to assure that quality persons are entering the teaching field has become a national movement.

Testing at various intervals during a student's school career and as a requirement for graduation is common practice. In 1984, 23 states used, or expected to use, minimum-competency testing for high-school graduation, and another 16 states used it for other purposes. The following chart, Exhibit 11.6, portrays the pattern of states that require tests for high-school

EXHIBIT 11.6   States Requiring Tests for High School Graduation

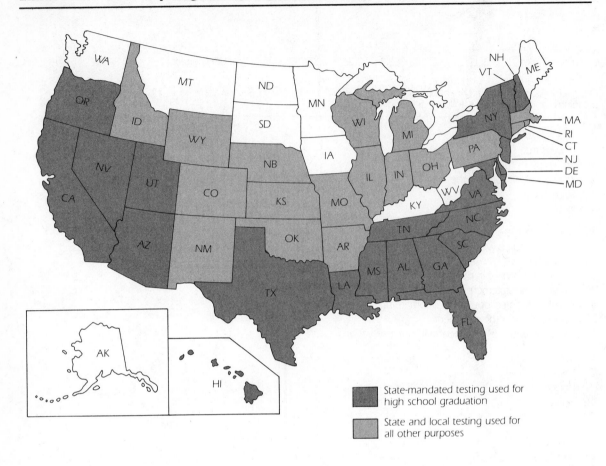

State-mandated testing used for high school graduation

State and local testing used for all other purposes

graduation. Table 11.3 provides details on the patterns of testing for several purposes, including promotion, graduation, early exit from school, and remediation. How many states relied on tests in 1984? What tests were required in your state? What has happened relative to testing students and teachers in your state since 1984?

TABLE 11.3   Testing Requirements in the United States

States Using Minimum-Competency Testing	Government Level Setting Standards	Grade Levels Assessed	Expected Uses					First Graduating Class Assessed
			Grade Promotion	High School Graduation	Early Exit	Remediation	Other	
Alabama	State	3, 6, 9, 11		X		X	X	1985
Arizona[1]	State/local	8, 12	X	X				1976
Arkansas[2]	State	3, 4, 6, 8	X			X	X	
California	State/local	4–11, 16 yr. old +	X	X	X	X		1979
Colorado	Local	9, 12		Local option				
Connecticut........	State	4, 6, 8				X	X	

TABLE 11.3 Testing Requirements in the United States

States Using Minimum-Competency Testing	Government Level Setting Standards	Grade Levels Assessed	Expected Uses					First Graduating Class Assessed
			Grade Promotion	High School Graduation	Early Exit	Remediation	Other	
Delaware	State	1–8, 11		X			X	1981
Florida	State/local	3, 5, 8, 11	X	X	X			1983
Georgia	State	1–4, 6, 8, 10+		X				1985
Hawaii[3]	State	3, 9–12		X		X	X	1983
Idaho	State	8+				X	X	1982
Illinois	Local	Local option					Local option	
Indiana	Local	3, 6, 8, 10				X	X	
Kansas[4]	State	2, 4, 6, 8, 10					Local option	
Louisiana[5]	State	2, 3, 4, 5, 11	X	X		X	X	1989
Maryland	State	3, 5, 7, 8, 9		X		X	X	1982
Massachusetts	Local	Local option					X	
Michigan	State	4, 7, 10				X	Local option	
Missouri	State	8–12					X	
Mississippi	State	3, 5, 8, 11		X			X	1987
Nebraska	Local	5+					X	
Nevada	State	3, 6, 9, 11		X		X		1982
New Hampshire[6]	State	4, 8, 12	Local option	Local option			Local option	
New Jersey	State	9–12		X		X	X	1985
New Mexico	State	Local option, 10–12					X	1981
New York	State	3, 5, 6, 8–12				X		1979
North Carolina	State	(1–3, 6, 9), 11		X			X	1980
Ohio	Local	Local option					Local option	
Oklahoma	None	3, 6, 9, 12					X	
Oregon	State/local	Local option		X				1978
Pennsylvania	State	3, 5, 8				X		
South Carolina[7]	State	K–3, 6, 8, 11	X	X		X	X	1990
Tennessee[8]	State/local	4–6, 8, 9–12		X		X	X	1982
Texas[9]	State	1, 3, 5, 7, 9		X		X		1986
Utah	State/local	Local option, 11, 12		X		X		1980
Vermont	State	1–12		X			X	1981
Virginia	State/local	K–6, 10–12		X			X	1981
Wisconsin	Local	1–4, 5–8, 9–10		Local option		X		
Wyoming	Local	Local option				X		

[1] Legislation in 1983 calls for Arizona to develop a minimum course of study and criteria for high school graduation standards and for grade-to-grade promotion criteria. Local school districts are to implement standards.

[2] In 1987, a minimum competency test will be administered for 8th grade promotion.

[3] For high school graduation requirements, students have 3 options: paper-pencil test; performance test; or course. First time taken (grade 9) must be paper-pencil test.

[4] The Kansas Minimum Competency Assessment (MCA) was reestablished by 1984 legislative action (S.B. 473). The MCA will be in effect 1984–85 through 1988–89.

[5] Louisiana will add 8th grade beginning with 1986–87 school year and will implement a graduating test for 11th graders in 1987–88.

[6] New Hampshire requires that students be tested in elementary, middle and high school. Some local districts test at grades other than 4, 8 and 12.

[7] The South Carolina Education Improvement Act of 1984 specifies that the 11th grade test being used to gather baseline data will be replaced in 1985–86 school year with an exit exam in the 10th grade. All students graduating in 1990 and after must pass the exam.

[8] Local districts in Tennessee must test students in grades 4 or 5 or 6, and 8 for remediation purposes.

[9] Requirements described above become effective in 1985–86 school year.

NOTE: Some States recorded dates for first high school graduating class to be assessed, but did not record expected use for high school graduation. Tabulation excludes District of Columbia.

Source: Education Commission on the States, Department of Research and Information, *Clearinghouse Notes,* "State Activity—Minimum Competency Testing," December 1984; and U.S. Department of Education, National Center for Education Statistics, unpublished tabulations (January 1985).

Conclusion

Just as instruction is based on objectives, so also are assessment and evaluation linked directly to objectives. The process of measurement and evaluation is vital to the teacher in the modern school. Testing has become commonplace. State legislatures and school boards are establishing standards for high school graduation and beginning to do so for promotion from grade to grade. They are relying, not just on the number of credits passed by students and the grades given by teachers, but on externally developed and administered standardized tests.

Almost every school district regularly assesses students. These programs typically include batteries of achievement tests about every three years, interspersed with aptitude tests and other special purpose tests. Most school districts have a testing and research department in the office of the superintendent of schools.

In addition, teachers are increasingly relying on testing and other assessment instruments to support their evaluations and reports to parents. Many of these are teacher made, but most are derived from teacher's editions of textbooks or from special materials to support instruction.

While our society runs pell-mell toward greater and greater assessment of more and more people and more deeply and in ever-increasing areas, people (including most educators) are increasingly concerned about being tested themselves. While being forced to rely more heavily on student evaluation themselves, teachers tend to express reservations about results of tests.

Building Reflective Inquiry Skills

Studying Results of Achievement Tests

Understanding and interpreting achievement-test results is a complex and technical process that can only be introduced at this time. However, several terms, concepts, and criteria will help make results more interpretable.

Several terms are used to describe the relative standing of an individual student or a group of students (class, school, or school district) with respect to the scores of those students on which the test was normed. The norm group is a relatively small group of students who are selected as representative of the population of students in the United States.

Grade equivalent (GE) compares scores according to grade level. A GE of 3.6 is a score equivalent to the average made by students in the third grade, sixth month of school.

Age equivalent compares scores according to age; 12.4 is applied to a score equivalent to the average made by students who are twelve years, four months of age.

Percentile indicates a student's rank in terms of the percentage of individuals who rank at or lower on this measure. A student with a percentile rank of 70 scored as well as or better than 70 percent of students in the norm group.

Stanine is a type of standard score derived by distributing scores into nine parts (standard nines). Stanine 5 is in the middle and includes the middle 20 percent of scores. Stanines 1–4 are lower (1 lowest) and 6–9 higher (9 highest). Using stanines provides broader bands or sets of scores, which are often more readily understood.

Several statistics are used with achievement tests; some are defined and illustrated below. The first three describe the central tendency of a distribution of scores, while standard deviations describe how widely dispersed scores are.

Mean is the most commonly used measure of central tendency. The mean (also referred to as the arithmetic average) is computed by adding all scores and dividing the total by the number of scores.

Median is the middle of a distribution of scores; it divides the scores into two equal halves and is the same as the fiftieth percentile. The median is determined by counting the number of scores to find the middle.

Mode is the score that occurs most frequently in a distribution of scores. To find the mode, determine which score is found most often in the distribution (can be more than one score if there is a tie).

Standard deviation (SD) describes the extent to which scores are spread out from the mean; a standard deviation of 8 tells us that the scores are more widely dispersed than those with a standard deviation of 5. Standard deviations are based on a normal distribution of scores (sometimes referred to as the bell curve), with the mean occurring at the fiftieth percentile. They may be negative or positive, with negative SDs below the mean and positive SDs above the mean.

About 68 percent of students score between -1 SD and +1 SD; only one in a thousand scores -3 SD or +3 SD. Test scores often are described in terms of mean and standard deviations. SAT scores, for example, were set at a mean of 500 and a SD of 100; thus a score of 600 equals the eighty-fourth percentile (mean plus one SD or 500 plus 100), while a score of 700 (+2 SD) is at the 97.7 percentile. The mean for the Stanford Binet is 100 (average intelligence) and the standard deviation is 15. Thus, a score of 115 is greater than that of 84.1 percent of people (50 percent below the mean plus 34.1 percent).

Understanding Tests

To understand the results of a test, you need to examine three sets of materials. The first is the test itself. What questions are asked? Upon what concepts are the questions based? How are the questions stated? How might potential responses be written?

Second, examine the test manual. This will include information such as the norming procedures and results, directions for administering the test, major concepts tested, and interpretation of results. Manuals often are written in technical language; time spent probing the meaning of terms and concepts as you study the manual will help you understand the construction and use of the test. For example, if you teach bilingual students, and the norm-group composition was quite different, you probably would search elsewhere for an appropriate set of test norms.

Third, examine the test answer sheet that students complete. What does it look like? What information is requested and how are students expected to respond? Sometimes it helps to take a test yourself in order to identify potential problems in advance.

A major trend sweeping our nation is the rapid increase in testing—testing at all levels. Understanding test procedures, terminology, concepts, and implications can be of valuable assistance for you as a teacher.

EXHIBIT 11.7   The Normal Curve

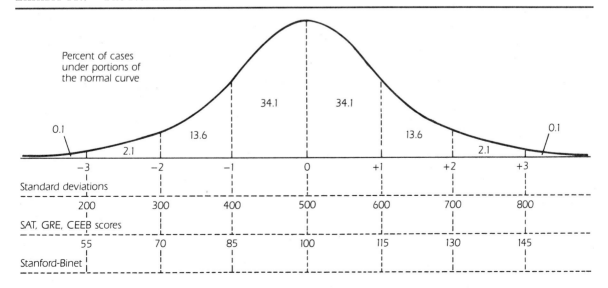

"Whatjaget?"
Grades are an important
aspect of life in schools.

Explorations

Exploration 1
Analyzing Achievement Tests
Examine several achievement tests. How are they
constructed? What directions are given for administration? What differences do you find among them?

Exploration 2
Designing Assessment Instruments
Select a curriculum guide or textbook; then select
three objectives and design appropriate testing instruments for them.

Exploration 3
Grading Papers: A Precise Practice?
Grade Jeri Gunwhite's paper (Exhibit 11.8). Each of
the ten problems is worth ten points. Then assign a
letter grade of A, B, C, D, or F. Finally, after you have
graded the paper, compare your assessment with
those of other prospective teachers. What factors did

you consider in your assessment? To what extent do
grades vary? Why? What are the implications of this
exercise for you as a teacher?

Exploration 4
Analyzing Criterion-Referenced Test
Results
Earlier in this chapter, you examined criterion-referenced and norm-referenced achievement scores for
a fifth grade in School A (Exhibit 11.2). The criterion-
referenced test report in Exhibit 11.9, page 280, is for
a fifth grade in another school in the same school
district. What difference do you note between the
two fifth grades? As a teacher, what concepts
would you emphasize in instruction? Norm-referenced scores for this same fifth grade are included in
Table 11.1. What observations would you make
about achievement, given these two reports?

Exhibit 11.8   Grading Involves Decisions

EVALUATION:

> Instructions: Grade this pupil's paper. With ten problems, each is worth ten points. Then give him a letter grade of A, B, C, D, or F.

Mathematics Test
Fifth Grade

Name _Jeri Gunewhite_   Score _____   Grade _____

1. $7.42
    2.58
    1.50
    6.39
    ―――
    17.89

2.   74
     829
    3596
     283
    ―――
    4882

3. 83 + 746 + 526 = 1373

       83
      764
      526
     ――――
     1373

4. 419 + 63 + 8 + 637 = 1172

      419
       63
        8
      637
     ――――
     1127

5.   1437
      418
      356
       70
      593
     ――――
     1447

6. 621 boxes
    538 boxes
    497 boxes
    ―――――
    1656

7.   5¼
     6¼
      3
    ――――
    14 $\frac{2}{4}$

8. $5.28
    3.49
    1.98
    6.37
    ―――
    $17.12

9. 3.59 + .8 + .48 =

    3.59
     .8
     .48
    ――――
    4.87

10. 17¾ = 17 $\frac{12}{16}$
     3½ = 3 $\frac{8}{16}$
     9⅜ = 9 $\frac{6}{16}$
     ―――――――――――
            24 $\frac{26}{16}$ = 30 $\frac{10}{16}$
                       = 30 $\frac{5}{8}$

EXHIBIT 11.9   Criterion-referenced Scores for Fifth Grade of School B on TEAMS test

TEXAS EDUCATIONAL ASSESSMENT OF MINIMUM SKILLS
SUMMARY REPORT

ALL STUDENTS

REPORT DATE: MAY 1986

DATE OF TESTING: FEBRUARY 1986

CAMPUS:
DISTRICT: B

GRADE: 05

BASIC SKILLS AREAS	OBJECTIVES	MASTERING NUMBER	MASTERING PERCENT	NOT MASTERING NUMBER	GROUP CHARACTERISTICS		
M A T H E M A T I C S	1. PLACE VALUE	99	83	20	TOTAL ENROLLMENT	124	
	2. EQUIVALENT FRACTIONS	86	72	33	Number Not Tested	2	
	3. DECIMALS (+,−)	108	91	11			
	4. MULTIPLICATION	102	86	17	The following data are based on NUMBER OF STUDENTS TESTED	NUMBER	PERCENT
	5. DIVISION	80	67	39		122	100
	6. WORD PROBLEMS (+,−)	62	52	57			
	7. WORD PROBLEMS (×,÷)	77	65	42	ETHNIC COMPOSITION		
	8. WORD PROBLEMS (DECIMAL)	107	90	12	American Indian or Alaskan Native	0	0
	9. MEASUREMENT UNITS	72	61	47	Asian or Pacific Islander	1	1
	10. GRAPHS	74	62	45	Black	8	7
	11. PERIMETER OR AREA OF POLYGONS	93	82	21	Hispanic	17	14
	STUDENTS TESTED: 119 TOTAL MATHEMATICS:	97	82	22	White	96	79
					FREE/REDUCED PRICE MEAL PROGRAM	17	14
R E A D I N G	1. MAIN IDEA	95	81	23	CHAPTER I REGULAR PROGRAM	0	0
	2. CONTEXT CLUES	101	86	17			
	3. SPECIFIC DETAILS	96	81	22	CHAPTER I MIGRANT PROGRAMS		
	4. SEQUENCING OF EVENTS	74	63	44	Remedial Mathematics Program	0	0
	5. DRAWING CONCLUSIONS	87	74	31	Remedial Reading Program	0	0
	6. FACT, OPINION	104	88	14	Remedial Writing Program	0	0
	7. CAUSE-AND-EFFECT	83	70	35	Eligible but does not participate	0	0
	8. PARTS OF A BOOK	113	96	5	Neither eligible nor participating	122	100
	9. GRAPHIC SOURCES	105	89	13	LIMITED ENGLISH PROFICIENCY	0	0
	STUDENTS TESTED: 118 TOTAL READING:	112	95	6	BILINGUAL / ESL PROGRAMS Bilingual Program	0	0
					English as a Second Language Program	0	0
W R I T I N G	1. CAPITALIZATION	110	93	8	SPECIAL EDUCATION		
	2. PUNCTUATION	104	88	14	Learning Disability	6	5
	3. SPELLING	111	94	7	Emotionally Disturbed	0	0
	4. CORRECT ENGLISH USAGE	108	92	10	Speech Handicapped	0	0
	5. SENTENCE STRUCTURE	112	95	6	Visually Handicapped	0	0
	6. PROOFREADING	90	76	28	Other handicapping condition	0	0
	7. DESCRIPTIVE WRITTEN COMPOSITION				Non-special education students	116	95
	RATING: 4 3 2 1 0 NUMBER: 0 6 49 63 0 PERCENT: 0 5 42 53 0				GIFTED/TALENTED PROGRAM	5	4
	MULTIPLE CHOICE SUB-TEST:	100	85	18	PASS/FAIL SUMMARY Passed all three tests	44	36
	WRITTEN COMPOSITION SUB-TEST:	55	47	63	Failed one test only	52	43
	STUDENTS TESTED: 118 TOTAL WRITING:	46	39	72	Failed two tests only	18	15
					Failed all three tests	4	3

References

Buros, O. K. (ed). (1978). *The eighth mental measurements yearbook.* Highland Park, NJ: Gryphon Press.

CTB/McGraw-Hill. (1982). *Comprehensive tests of basic skills.* Monterey, CA: CTB/McGraw-Hill.

CTB/McGraw-Hill. (1982). *Test of cognitive skills.* Monterey, CA: CTB/McGraw-Hill.

Gould, S. J. (1981). *The mismeasure of man.* New York: W. W. Norton.

Kibler, R. J., Cegala, D. J., Barker, L. L. & Miles, D. T. (1974). *Objectives for instruction and evaluation.* Boston: Allyn and Bacon.

Mager, R. F. (1984). *Developing attitude toward learning.* Belmont, CA: Lear Siegler/Fearon.

Otis, A. S. & Lennon, R. T. (1982). *Otis-Lennon school ability test; Manual for administering and interpreting.* New York: The Psychological Corp.

Plisko, V. W. & Stern, J. D. (1985). *The condition of education, 1985 edition.* Washington, DC: U.S. Government Printing Office.

Science Research Associates. (1978). *SRA Achievement Series.* Chicago: Science Research Associates.

Tanner, D. (1972). *Using behavioral objectives in the classroom.* New York: Macmillan.

Texas Education Agency. (1985). *Texas educational assessment of minimum skills.* Austin: Texas Education Agency.

Reflecting on the Contexts and Challenges of Teaching

CHAPTER TWELVE

Governmental Influence on Schools

OBJECTIVES

By the end of this chapter, you will be able to:

1. Identify the relationships among local, state, and federal educational agencies, including the agencies' effects on teachers.
2. Describe the role of the judiciary in education and discuss major court cases affecting schools and teachers.
3. Discuss school funding in the United States.
4. Discuss the ways in which educational decisions are made.

KEY WORDS AND CONCEPTS

Brown v. *Board of Education*
Chief state school officer
Civil Rights Act of 1964
Constitutional amendments
Due process
Formula and equalization funding
Line and staff administrators
Property and liberty interests
Public Law 94–142
Student rights
U.S. Department of Education
Teacher rights and responsibilities

Schools and teachers are affected by many governmental decisions that result from legislation, regulations, and court decisions made at local, state, and federal levels. Recently, we walked through a school and noted several examples of such requirements.

▶ Ramps had been built in the school and restrooms renovated to accommodate persons with physical handicaps.

▶ A two-hour conference was in process to determine what and how to teach a special education student. Attending the conference were the principal, regular classroom teacher, parents, special education resource room teacher, and counselor.

▶ Some students were served free breakfast and lunch.

▶ Students had been transported to school by bus from the other side of town.

▶ The principal was female.

▶ No prayer was offered at the beginning of the day.

▶ The vocational teacher was paid slightly more than other teachers.

▶ A white teacher was assigned to a school with predominantly black students.

▶ A special bilingual class with a certified bilingual teacher was organized for twenty students.

▶ Students had just completed a state-wide achievement test.

Your life as a teacher will be influenced by actions and decisions sometimes made far from you. Requirements such as those illustrated above affect how and what you teach, what you do, and the environment in which you teach. Some of those requirements resulted from federal legislation, others from court decisions, state regulations, and local school district policies. Schools are not isolated entities, but parts of more extensive organizations. Understanding these often complex interrelationships can help you be more successful as a teacher.

The roles, visibility, and organization of schools in America have evolved over the past three hundred years into institutions that are uniquely American. Until about 1835, schools were essentially a voluntary local concern. With the beginning of the public school movement and lasting through the latter part of the nineteenth century, schools were primarily the responsibility of state agencies and local school districts. The federal government exercised a minor role in school matters until about the time of World War II, but in the past forty years federal activity and funding have increased enormously, expanding national influence on educational practice. Nonetheless, education is still predominantly a responsibility of the states.

This is in contrast to education in many other countries, where public schools are under the direct control of a central authority in the nation's capital. In such countries, the person in charge of education often is an influential member of the national government's cabinet. Decisions originated in the Ministry of Education, for example, are conveyed to all schools across the country. Standards for admitting students and graduating them, textbooks to be used, content of the curriculum, and teacher employment are but some examples of policies that are under central control. The

United States has no such national system, although major changes are currently being made in education that, in the future, could affect the balance of control among local, state, and federal agencies.

In this chapter, we will explore the organization of education in America; the influence of federal, state, and local agencies on education; the impact of the judicial system on teachers and schools; and how schools are funded and decisions about them are made.

Federal Role in Education

The Constitution of the United States is silent on the education of its citizens, even though education was important to its framers. Having been schooled themselves in national educational programs or having observed closely the results of such systems in Europe, those who drafted the Constitution pressed for local control. By not referring to education, the Constitution left responsibility for it to each of the states and to local communities via the Tenth Amendment: "The powers not delegated to the United States by the Constitution, nor prohibited by it to the States, are reserved to the States respectively, or to the people."

The federal government has extended its role and responsibility for education during the past forty years. Along with its increased interest and rapidly accelerating funding, especially during the 1960s and 1970s, the federal government has exercised greater control. The U.S. Office of Education, which had been part of the Department of Health, Education and Welfare, was elevated in stature in 1979 to cabinet-level status in the government—becoming the U.S. Department of Education.

The shift toward greater federal concern for education is derived from three sources. The first source is the increased mobility of people today. With more than one-fourth of the population moving each year (and a far greater proportion in some communities), and with the trend toward migration to southern "sun belt" states, a greater number of citizens are concerned with the equality of education across the country. The federal government is viewed as the only agency with power to regulate education in all states.

Second, decisions of the courts, particularly the Supreme Court, have led to more federal regulations. Federal agencies have become far more active in determining how and under what conditions schools function. Schools have been pressed to respond to new federal legislation and regulations and to court decisions related to desegregation, equal educational opportunity, and student rights. In so doing, school policies and procedures have become more nearly uniform.

Third, communication with all parts of the world has improved. Reports of athletic contests, disasters, and news events are almost instantly available anywhere in the country. So too are educational ideas. The jet has made transportation of educators to conferences and to other school programs readily accessible. As a result of improved communication and transportation with all parts of the world, waves of educational reform seem to sweep the nation—appointment of select task forces and commissions to recommend ways to improve education, nontraditional educational programs, emphasis on basic skills in the curriculum, testing for high school graduation, and teacher competency testing. The result is the increasing similarity among schools across America amid increasing diversity of its people.

Influence of Federal Legislation

Congress relies heavily on its committees for analysis and careful consideration of proposed legislation. In the House of Representatives, the Education and Labor Committee is responsible for reviewing education bills. In the Senate, the Education, Arts, and Humanities Subcommittee of the Human Resources Committee considers educational legislation. In both houses of Congress, strong appropriations committees review educational requests for funding along with those of all other governmental agencies. What is evident in the names of these congressional committees is that education is but one of their missions, and can be a low priority. However, a number of influential laws have been passed by Congress that have greatly influenced educational practice.

Categorical Legislation. With few exceptions, federal legislation has been *categorical* in nature; that is, funding that accompanied new programs has been allocated for a specific purpose rather than for general support of schools. Categorical legislation has responded to areas of national need. Shortly after the Soviet Union launched the world's first earth-orbiting satellite, Sputnik I, on October 4, 1957, the United States' wounded national pride sought the source of the problem. The answer: scientists of sufficient stature had not been educated in American schools. The solution: enact the National Defense Education Act to implement massive curriculum-development and teacher-training programs in science, mathematics, and foreign language.

Improving schools in poverty areas was viewed as a way to regenerate the deteriorating core of cities as poverty sapped the economic strength of the nation. As President Lyndon Johnson declared a "war on poverty," the Elementary and Secondary Education Act of 1965 promoted compensatory educational programs for economically disadvantaged youth in an attempt to break the persistent cycle of poverty and to support desegregation in schools.

Other disadvantaged groups were the basis for legislation. Just as children from poor families were educationally disadvantaged, so too were handicapped children and adults, minorities, and women. For each group, legislation was enacted to break the bonds that inhibited development of that group's full potential and ultimately limited the potential of the nation.

[M]ost federal incursions into the traditional preserve of the states and local districts have been attempts to use schools to help resolve "non-educational" social or economic concerns. Few programs emanated from Washington with the simple objective of improving the quality of education (Sergiovanni, Burlingame, Coombs & Thurston 1980, 162).

EXHIBIT 12.1   Important Federal Legislation in Education

1917: Smith-Hughes Act
Supported secondary-school training in agriculture, home economics, and industrial education.

1958: The National Defense Education Act
Supported programs in science, mathematics, foreign languages, and guidance.

1964: Economic Opportunity Act
Outlined the war on poverty, including teacher retraining and remedial education for students.

1964: Civil Rights Act
Enforced desegregation of schools.

1965: PL 89–10, Elementary and Secondary Education Act
Designed to improve all education, with primary aid to schools having students from low income families.

1972: Title IX of Education Amendments of 1972
Prohibited sex discrimination in any educational program receiving federal assistance.

1972: Emergency School Aid Act
Provided funds on a competitive basis to schools to eliminate minority group isolation.

1975: PL 94–142, Education for all Handicapped Children Act
Mandated that all children with handicaps receive a free, appropriate public education, no matter how severe their handicaps.

Several of the most influential of the bills passed by Congress are summarized in Exhibit 12.1. Two deserve further consideration. In 1965, Congress passed Public Law 89–10, a comprehensive bill to improve elementary and secondary education. The various sections (called Titles) of the Elementary and Secondary Education Act (ESEA) provided support in a variety of areas. Title I provided aid to local districts and states to support special programs for low income and educationally deprived children. Title II, originally a right-to-read program, was expanded in 1978 to the Basic Skills Improvement Program. Title III encouraged schools to initiate innovative practices. Title VII funded programs in bilingual education for students with limited proficiency in English.

In 1981, Congress passed the Education Consolidation and Improvement Act (ECIA) to replace ESEA. The new act reduced funding for these programs, simplified Title I as Chapter I, ECIA, and consolidated over thirty of the smaller ESEA programs into block grants to state and local agencies as Chapter II, ECIA.

In 1975, Congress passed Public Law 94–142 "to insure that handicapped children have available to them . . . a free appropriate public education which emphasizes special education and related services designed to meet unique needs." It links compliance to the civil rights of those being served: "No qualified handicapped individual 3 through 21 years of age in the United States . . . shall, solely by reason of his handicap, be excluded from participation in, be denied the benefits of, or be subjected to discrimination under any program receiving federal assistance."

PL 94–142 includes three major sections. First, schools are required to provide the *least restrictive educational environment* for each handicapped child. To implement this, schools have *mainstreamed* many special education students by integrating them into regular classrooms. Prior to implementation of this act, many school districts organized special classes for students with handicaps, isolating them in separate schools or special wings of regular schools. Special schools for severely handicapped children are considered the most restrictive environment, special classes for part of a school day less restricted, and full placement in regular classes with support for the teacher (mainstreamed) the least restrictive. Schools were required under PL 94-142 to place each student in the least restrictive educational setting possible.

Second, schools must provide an *Individualized Education Program* (IEP) for each handicapped student. An IEP is an individualized plan and educational program for each handicapped child that is developed by educators in consultation with specialists and parents and approved by parents.

Third, parents and guardians of students with handicaps are guaranteed *due process* rights, including access to student records and proposed plans and changes in IEPs. Conferences, called ARDs (for Admission, Review and Dismissal), include the school principal, counselor, special education teacher, parent, and often the student, who decide on next steps in the student's education and then sign off on the plan—a formal procedure to assure due process.

U.S. Department of Education

In 1980, the Department of Education became the thirteenth cabinet-level department in the federal government. Prior to then, education was part of the huge super agency, the Department of Health, Education, and Welfare (HEW). When the Office of Education was a branch of HEW, the chief administrative officer was the U.S. commissioner of education. Shirley Hufstedler, a federal appellate judge, was named by President Carter as the first secretary of the newly-formed Department of Education. The new department had a budget of nearly fifteen billion dollars and about four thousand employees.

Less than a year later, newly-elected President Ronald Reagan called for the department to be abolished. Terrel H. Bell, a former commissioner of education, was named the second secretary of education. He pledged to provide options for the president and to Congress to consider in reorganizing and restricting educational programs in the federal government. One of his first acts was to appoint a prestigious commission to make recommendations about education. Their report, *A Nation At Risk*, was summarized in Chapter 6 as the forerunner of the numerous commission reports critiquing education and focusing national attention on it.

In the debate concerning the viability of education as a department-level agency, the department's supporters were able to build both a political and a logical case for it to continue as a major unit in the federal government. They noted that under HEW, education was only one of many programs and that it often received little attention when competing with social security, health, and welfare programs. A cabinet-level department permitted the secretary of education to communicate directly with the president and Congress. They suggested that such an organization would reduce the layers of bureaucracy by expediting decisions and eliminating overlapping functions. All federal agencies have educational programs in one form or another; having a Department of Education would provide better coordination among them.

Those arguing against the establishment of a Department of Education expressed concern for the encroachment of the federal government on the rights of the states and local agencies. They were concerned that consolidation of education programs would make more vulnerable the various educational programs in other governmental departments. They believed it would increase the regulatory role of the federal government over schools and colleges.

William J. Bennett, the third secretary of education, is an articulate critic of the educational establishment, with a knack for identifying and speaking out on controversial issues. The department is concerned primarily with three areas. The first, providing national leadership, is accomplished by identifying areas of concern such as the quality of education and the improvement of the teaching profession. The second area, helping ensure equality of opportunity, includes application and enforcement of civil rights legislation in education, federal loan guarantees, and educational opportunities for minorities. The third area, promoting quality and efficiency, includes reliable data on the current status and trends in education. Limited resources are provided states and local agencies for quality improvement activities.

The organization of the U.S. Department of Education provides another way to understand its mission and programs. Exhibit 12.2 diagrams its organization. Each assistant secretary heads an office with an extensive professional staff and is charged with applying the three areas of concern to issues and programs in that office.

Judicial Influence on Schools

During the past three decades, courts have considerably expanded their attention to education. As a teacher, your behavior and decisions will be determined to an increasing extent by court decisions. Louis Fischer points out that

> In the field of education it is difficult to find a policy area not touched by judicial scrutiny in recent years. Courts have ruled on matters related to racial desegregation, financial equality, teachers' qualifications, certification, tenure and promotion, curricular decisions, bilingual education, education of the handicapped, the use of standardized tests, locker and student searches, the use of police dogs in schools, political activities by teachers, policies for "RIFing" (reduction in force), and many others. (Fischer 1982, 62)

The courts' involvement often has been based on two principles. First, the "general welfare" clause of the Constitution (Article 1, Section 8) authorizes Congress to act on behalf of the people, and second, the First and Fourteenth Amendments to the Constitution protect the rights of citizens.

The First Amendment protects freedom of religion, speech, and the press. Of particular interest here is part of the first clause:

> Congress shall make no law respecting an establishment of religion, or prohibiting the free exercise thereof; or abridging the freedom of speech, or of the press; or the right of the people peaceably to assemble, and to petition the Government for a redress of grievances.

EXHIBIT 12.2 U.S. Department of Education

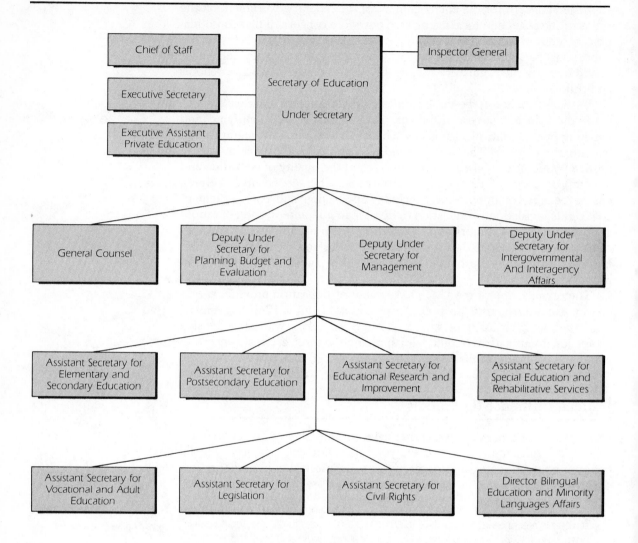

This clause consists of two fundamental concepts. First, the government shall neither establish nor prohibit the free exercise of religion. Two issues raised and in the process of being clarified by the courts include school prayer and Bible reading, and tuition payments and federal aid to private schools. The latter will be considered more fully as one of the issues studied in Chapter 13. The second concept of concern to educators is freedom of speech, which is discussed in greater detail as a student right and a teacher right in the following sections.

The Fourteenth Amendment defines United States citizenship and bars state laws that negatively affect the privileges and immunities of all people. It includes the right to *due process* and *equal protection* of the law. This applies to everyone—students, parents, teachers, and others. The relevant portion of the Fourteenth Amendment reads thusly:

Court decisions at all levels have increasing impact on how schools operate.

No State shall make or enforce any law which shall abridge the privileges or immunities of citizens of the United States; nor shall any State deprive any person of life, liberty, or property without due process of law; nor deny to any person within its jurisdiction the equal protection of the law.

I t can hardly be argued that either students or teachers shed their constitutional rights to freedom of speech or expression at the schoolhouse gate.

Justice Abe Fortas in *Tinker* v. *Des Moines*.

Rights of Students

In working with students, teachers are well advised to study student rights and judicial decisions as a basis for their own actions. Five of these student rights are described in the following paragraphs: freedom of speech, discipline, confidentiality of records, due process, and search and seizure.

Freedom of Speech. The landmark case in student rights to freedom of speech is *Tinker* v. *Des Moines Independent School District* (1969). In December, 1965, after three students let it be known they planned to wear black armbands to protest the Vietnam War, Des Moines, Iowa principals adopted a policy that any student wearing such an armband would be suspended. The three students did and were suspended. The Supreme Court concluded that school officials could not punish students for expressing an opinion when no disorderly conduct ensued. The Supreme Court noted the following in its opinion:

> [T]he wearing of armbands in the circumstances of this case was entirely divorced from actually or potentially disruptive conduct by those participating in it. It was closely akin to "pure speech" which, we have repeatedly held, is entitled to comprehensive protection under the First Amendment. (Tinker, 505–506, 89 S.Ct. 736)

To further clarify the rights considered in *Tinker*, the Supreme Court identified what was *not* involved.

The problem posed by the present case does not relate to regulation of the length of skirts or the type of clothing, to hair style, or deportment. It does not concern aggressive, disruptive action or even group demonstrations. (Tinker, 507–508, 89 S.Ct. 737)

This Court decision placed the burden on school officials, when restricting student activities, to use as the criterion for such action that the activity would "materially and substantially disrupt the work and discipline of the school."

Joseph Cobb summarized several subsequent court decisions related to freedom of speech that were based on *Tinker*.

1. A threat of disruption alone is insufficient reason to abridge student rights (*Westley* v. *Rossi*, 1969).
2. Rules must be relevant to the education function (*Burnside* v. *Byars*, Mississippi, 1966).
3. The school may not discriminate in admission policy (*Burnside* v. *Byars*, Alabama, 1964).
4. Rules must apply equally to female students (*Cash* v. *Hock*, 1970).
5. Denial of a public education may not be arbitrary (*Black* v. *Cothren*, 1970).
6. Regulations must be both preexisting and specific (*Crossen* v. *Fatsi*, 1969).
7. Conduct may not be repressed because of administrative personal disapproval. (Cobb 1981, 107–108)

In *Bethel School District No. 403* v. *Fraser* (1986), the Supreme Court reversed decisions of lower courts to further clarify its decision in *Tinker*. Fraser, a high school senior, made a speech at an assembly that was considered inappropriate and violated the school's disciplinary rules. He had been advised by teachers and an assistant principal prior to the assembly not to deliver it. He did and was suspended for three days. The "Supreme Court held that the school district acted entirely within its permissible authority in imposing sanctions upon Fraser in response to his offensively lewd and indecent speech. The Court stated that there was a marked distinction between the political 'message' of the armband in *Tinker* and the sexual content of Fraser's speech in this case" (Chalk Talk 1987, 122).

School Discipline. Historically, most states and schools have given wide discretion to school administrators in disciplining students. Sametz (1985) summarized the courts' views in the following passage.

In Baker v. Owen (1975) the Court affirmed, without an opinion, a North Carolina ruling sanctioning the teacher's use of corporal punishment over parental objection. The North Carolina court further stipulated that if corporal punishment were to be used certain safeguards apply: Students must be informed as to what behavior led to a spanking; other forms of discipline must be tried prior to the use of corporal punishment; there must be a witness present at the time of the spanking; and, if the *parent(s) request a written reason for the spanking, this must be provided. Thus, the North Carolina court required a limited amount of due process. (29)*

In *Ingraham* v. *Wright* (1976), the Supreme Court decided that schools were not required to give prior notice that corporal punishment would be administered and the opportunity for a student or his/her parents to appeal the decision. The Court found that while corporal punishment was an acceptable method for maintaining school discipline, it should be reasonable. It should not interfere with students' other constitutional rights, and the reasons for the paddling should be well documented. As a teacher, you should be aware, however, that some states, such as New Jersey and Massachusetts, and some school districts prohibit the use of corporal punishment, while others limit the persons and processes empowered to administer such punishment.

Confidentiality of Records.   In 1974, Congress passed the Family Educational Rights and Privacy Act, known as the Buckley Amendment. It grants parents the right to inspect their children's educational records, to challenge any contents they believe inaccurate or misleading, and to restrict access to those records.

The Buckley Amendment was a response to previous abuses of such records. Schools could deny parents access to records while allowing others such as governmental agencies, educational workers, and prospective employers free and unrestricted access. Some records contained sensitive and highly personal information, others outdated or erroneous information. Some were misused, as for example, when a teacher characterized a student as "slow," "lazy," or "troublemaker," thus influencing others' opinion of and actions toward that student. The Buckley Amendment therefore restricted student records to school personnel on a "need-to-know" basis in the absence of parental consent to protect the rights of students.

Due Process.   Students are entitled to due process when they face major disciplinary action such as suspension, expulsion, or other action that might affect them and their future opportunities for education.

The laws of Ohio empowered the principal to suspend a student for misconduct for up to ten days provided the student's parents were notified and given reasons within twenty-four hours and an opportunity existed to appeal the suspension at the next meeting of the board of education. (Fischer 1982, 71–72)

This practice was challenged by parents and students who had been suspended, some for an indefinite period, without notice or hearing. In ruling on the case, *Goss* v. *Lopez* (1975), the Court concluded that, while a brief suspension would not deprive a person of "life," the individual's property and liberty rights might be sufficiently implicated even by a short suspension so as to require some degree of due process.

The total exclusion from the educational process for more than a trivial period, and certainly if the suspension is for ten days, is a serious event in the life of the suspended child. Neither the property interest in educational benefits temporarily denied nor the liberty interest in reputation, which is also implicated, is so insubstantial that suspensions may constitutionally be imposed by any procedure the school chooses, no matter how arbitrary. (Goss 1975, 576)

Two terms are used in this ruling that are important to teachers: *property interests* and *liberty interests*. Since each state provides free public schools, education has become a *right* for every child who is of school age. As a property right, schooling may not be withheld or diminished without due process. Further, students have a liberty interest in their reputations and in their school records, for damages to either may impact their future.

Cobb lists three points on which there is general agreement concerning due process of students.

1. The rules, regulations, and policies of the school should be common knowledge of the student body.
2. A written notice of the hearing should be given to the student. The hearing should take place after the student has had adequate time to prepare a defense and/or an explanation of the charges.
3. The student has the right to confront his accusers at the hearing. (1981, 128)

Search and Seizure.   Students are protected to a certain extent under the Fourth Amendment to the Constitution which reads, "The right of the people to be secure in their persons, houses, papers, and effects, against unreasonable searches and seizures, shall not be violated, . . ." Recent cases involving drugs and other contraband in schools have increased instances of student search and seizure and the involvement of police. Most courts have not subjected public school searches to the same standards as for law enforcement. The constitutional requirement placed on police that there is *probable cause* for a search has been replaced in education by a lesser standard, *reasonable cause*.

Edmund Reutter summarized the factors that courts consider in assessing whether there is sufficient cause for a search:

[T]he source of the information prompting the search, the child's record, the seriousness and prevalence of the problem being addressed by the search and the urgency of making the search without delay. . . . Also of substantial significance in determining whether a search by school authorities is legally permissible is the degree of intrusiveness of the search itself. That which is searched can range from a student's desk or locker, through pockets, purse, or packages, to underclothes or body. Acceptable cause for a search must meet increasingly higher standards as the continuum is traversed, so that for a strip search of a student, 'probable cause' has been held to be necessary. (1985, 693)

A 1985 Supreme Court decision established as the standard for searches of students by educational personnel that of "reasonableness under all the circumstances" (*New Jersey* v. *T.L.O.*, 1985). Reasonableness included two elements: (1) whether circumstances justified the action at its beginning, and (2) whether the scope of the search was reasonable in relation to the situation. The first criterion is met when there is "reasonable grounds for suspecting that the search will turn up evidence that the student has violated or is violating either the law or the rules of the school," while the second criterion considers the intrusiveness of the search in relation to the age and sex of the student and the nature of the infraction.

In *New Jersey* v. *T.L.O.*, an assistant principal searched the purse of a student who denied smoking in the restroom and indicated she did not smoke at all. The assistant principal found not only cigarettes but drug paraphernalia and evidence that the student had sold drugs. The Supreme Court upheld the constitutionality of the search.

For an interesting analysis of what was and was not considered in this case, which also helps us to understand how the Supreme Court thinks about issues, read "New Jersey v. T.L.O.: The Questions the Court Did Not Answer About School Searches" by B. J. Walts in the *Journal of Law & Education*. She points out that the Court "did not define reasonable suspicion with any clarity, identify the necessary elements for conducting a locker search, set the standard by which a search must be conducted if the police are involved, or if the exclusionary rule will allow evidence illegally seized in a school search to be suppressed" (Walts 1985, 437). Further, each state may impose greater restrictions than the Supreme Court; thus school officials also need to review state law.

Student rights are continually being defined more explicitly by the courts of our nation. Some of the current generalizations about them are summarized in Exhibit 12.3.

EXHIBIT 12.3   **Summary of Some Student Rights**

► Students may wear armbands, buttons, or other badges of symbolic expression where they do not intrude on the rights of others or would reasonably lead to disruptions or riots.

► Students can observe their own religion or no religion. They can't be forced to recite a prayer or read Bible verses. They may decline to salute the flag or recite the Pledge of Allegiance.

► Students may assemble in the school or on school grounds, demonstrate and picket peacefully, and collect signatures for dismissal of the principal or others.

► Students can plan public meetings, invite speakers, and distribute literature on the school grounds. School officials can regulate outside visitors who have violated laws and can set rules for students who are distributing literature.

► Students and their parents must have access to student records, but third parties may not have access without the student's or parent's permission.

► Students and their lockers can be searched without warrants if there is reasonable belief that drugs and/or other contraband are present or that they have violated a law or school rule.

► Students cannot be expelled or suspended without the opportunity for a formal hearing, typically before the school board and with representation by an attorney.

► Students cannot be prevented from having an education because of pregnancy and marriage.

► Students' grades should not be affected as a result of punishment, nor diplomas withheld for breaking rules of discipline.

► Schools may administer corporal punishment (unless prohibited by the state or school district), but students are protected by safeguards against unreasonable punishment.

Source: (Abridged from Wiles & Bondi 1985, 91–2) Reprinted with permission.

Rights and Responsibilities of Teachers

Personal and Professional Rights. Teachers have rights both as persons and as teachers. As individuals, teachers enjoy the rights guaranteed by the Constitution to everyone. Under the specific guarantees of the constitu-

*T*eachers and students must always remain free to inquire, to study, and to evaluate to gain new maturity and understanding; otherwise our civilization will stagnate and die.

Chief Justice Earl Warren in *Sweezy* v. *New Hampshire*, 1957.

A reluctance on the part of the teacher to investigate and experiment with new and different ideas is an athema to the entire concept of academic freedom.

Parducci v. *Rutland*, 1970.

tional amendments, teachers are entitled to freedom of religion and expression (First Amendment), freedom from unreasonable search and seizure by governmental authorities (Fourth Amendment), freedom from compelled self-incrimination (Fifth Amendment), and may not be deprived of life, liberty, or property without the due process of law (Fourteenth Amendment).

As teachers, however, their individual freedoms are balanced against the needs of the school with the interests of each limiting, to some extent, the other. Since such rights are relative and shift with each situation, the Supreme Court has considered the specific needs in the context of the teacher-school district relationship.

In *Pickering* v. *Board of Education* (1968), the Supreme Court discussed its position on this balance. After writing a letter critical of the way the school board and superintendent informed, or prevented the informing of, voters relative to proposed new taxes, Marvin Pickering was fired. The letter charged that the board was emphasizing athletics in its budget to the detriment of academics and that the superintendent was attempting to prevent teachers from opposing or criticizing such financial proposals. In ruling against the teacher's dismissal, the Court wrote as follows:

> [F]ree and open debate is vital to informed decision-making by the electorate. Teachers are, as a class, the members of a community most likely to have informed and definite opinions as to how funds allotted to the operation of the schools should be spent. Accordingly, it is essential that they be able to speak out freely on such questions without fear of retaliatory dismissal. (Pickering 1968, 1786)

Teachers may not "constitutionally be compelled to relinquish the First Amendment rights they would otherwise enjoy as citizens to comment on matters of public interest in connection with the operation of the public schools in which they work. . . . The problem in any case is to arrive at a balance between the interests of the teacher, as a citizen, in commenting upon matters of public concern and the interest of the State, as an employer, in promoting the efficiency of the public services it performs through its employees" (*Pickering* 1968, 1734–1735).

In many states, teachers may be awarded tenure after successfully completing a probationary period (typically two or three years). After being tenured, teachers may not be arbitrarily dismissed, demoted, or have their salary reduced without due process and are protected from irresponsible actions by school officials. They are assured continued employment until they resign or retire, subject only to the requirements of improper behavior and financial necessity.

Negligence. Teachers are not immune because they are public employees from liable suits resulting from injuries to students. Cobb clarified the meaning and implications for teachers as follows: "Some injuries are caused by what the law calls a 'pure accident;' that is, it was unforeseeable, unavoidable, and no one was to blame. Other injuries are caused by another person's negligence in allowing or in not preventing the injury. If a teacher's negligence can be proven, he can be held for damages in a tort action brought by the pupil or his parents" (1981, 81).

A *tort* is a civil (as distinguished from a criminal) wrong arising out of a breach of duty that is imposed by law. William Valente points out that "persons are not liable in tort for every accidental injury. Only if a person intentionally or negligently causes injury, will that person be held liable in tort. . . . Most school-related torts involve negligent supervision. The failure to instruct or warn students; to inspect, report, and correct unsafe situations; to arrange student activity in a safe manner; or to aid stricken students all relate to the essential issue of what is proper supervision in particular circumstances" (1980, 349; 357).

Cobb summarized five rights and responsibilities of teachers.

1. As a teacher you enjoy freedom of speech and assembly, but this may be restricted by your position as an example for your students. Any support of unlawful conduct is clearly subject to restriction.
2. Although your mode of dress need not follow student standards, reasonable and nondiscriminatory rules must generally be followed.
3. Your freedom to teach and your selection of subject matter must reasonably relate to the age and maturity level of your students.
4. Employment cannot be conditioned on any political or religious belief or limited by membership in most organizations, nor can a teacher be required to salute the flag.
5. Your responsibility as a teacher carries over into your private life. The commodity you deal in is human minds. The standard to which you are held is high but should not be arbitrary, capricious, or unrelated to sound educational objectives. (1981, 149)

Equal Educational Rights For Minorities

The Fourteenth Amendment has supported considerable legislation aimed at achieving and protecting equal educational opportunities for minority groups. In 1896, *Plessy* v. *Ferguson* enunciated the separate-but-equal doctrine supporting racially segregated schools. Fifty-eight years later, in 1954, *Brown* v. *Board of Education of Topeka* defined a new national policy of racially desegregated public education. Part of the language of *Brown* follows.

> We conclude that in the field of public education the doctrine of "separate but equal" has no place. Separate educational facilities are inherently unequal. Therefore, we hold that the plaintiffs and others similarly situated for whom the actions have been brought are, by reason of the segregation complained of, deprived of the equal protection of the laws guaranteed by the Fourteenth Amendment. This disposition makes unnecessary any discussion whether such segregation also violates the Due Process Clause of the Fourteenth Amendment.

In 1955, the Supreme Court ruled on the meaning of its historic 1954 decision and demanded that "all deliberate speed" be taken to implement its earlier decision (*Brown*, 1955).

Where segregated schools existed, school boards were required to develop plans to eliminate the situation. To desegregate schools, boards of education bused students; modified employment and assignment procedures so that, to the degree possible, the racial proportion of teachers in each school matched that for students in the district; and organized magnet schools that would attract white students to schools with predominantly minority enrollments. These programs have been highly controversial, with rulings from the courts required in thousands of cases at all judicial levels to further interpret the *Brown* principles.

> The federal courts have held that the Brown decisions do not require integration but merely forbid the use of governmental power to enforce segregation (Aaron v. Tucker, 186 F.Supp. 913, 1960); that is, they do not compel the mixing of races nor do they require the reshuffling of the pupils in any school system. Courts have agreed that no child shall be denied admission to a school of his choice on the basis of race or color. (Campbell & Layton 1969, 43)

Since the *Brown* decision in 1954, the federal government has moved from a passive acceptance of dual school systems for whites and blacks toward an active policy of desegregation of such schools to form single systems that serve all children and youth.

Children's rights to equal and free public education were extended in 1982 to illegal, or undocumented, aliens (people who have entered the United States without legal documents). In *Plyler* v. *Doe* (1982), the Supreme Court ruled that even children residing in the United States illegally have rights under the Equal Protection Clause of the Fourteenth Amendment, and that a state may not deny a free public education to them.

The combined Civil Rights Act of 1964 and the Elementary and Secondary Education Act of 1965 linked school desegregation and discrimination to federal aid to education, causing controversy over local

---

The only school de- segregation plan that meets constitutional standards is one that works.

U.S. v. *Jefferson*, 1966

One major impact of governmental influence is expanding educational opportunities.

control of schools and federal intervention into areas considered the domain of the local community and state.

> The federal courts, in recent years, have assumed an increasing role in adjudicating educational problems. One might even say that the schools have become the battle ground where much of our constitutional law is being wrought. These constitutional interpretations become an important part of educational policy. (Campbell & Layton 1969, 45)

The judicial system has influenced educational policy and practice. Educators have charged that the courts have usurped local and state control of schools by expanding their authority. Judges, on the other hand, are ready to apply constitutional principles to school-related controversies and to enforce other laws related to schools. The Supreme Court articulated its position several years ago.

> By and large, public education in our nation is committed to the control of state and local authorities. Courts do not and cannot intervene in the resolution of conflicts which arise in the daily operation of school systems and which do not directly and sharply implicate basic constitutional values. On the other hand, the vigilant protection of constitutional freedoms is nowhere more vital than in the community of American Schools. (Shelton v. Tucker, 1960)

Nationalization and Decentralization

During the past few years, schools across America have become more and more similar; yet, wide variances exist. The curriculum in one state varies somewhat from that in another. States differ widely in the amount of funds provided education, salaries for teachers, and requirements for high-school graduation. Even within a state, a diploma from one school may signify greater achievement than from another. These differences result from the decentralization of authority for schooling.

There are both advantages and disadvantages to this diversity. Central control, as practiced in most countries, leads to the politicizing of education, fosters dogma and singular curricular content, and increases bureaucratic practice.

Decentralization causes problems of articulation. Students transferring from one school to another are often disadvantaged because of differences in content, textbooks, and even the courses required at that level. Teachers' certificates in one state may not be accepted in another because of different requirements. School practices in one community may be idiosyncratic because of local conditions.

The increased mobility of the population of the United States, the need for standardized practice because of court decisions, and the poor quality of some schools have been used as arguments for more similarity in curricula and school organizations. In the coming years, a national policy for education may emerge in this country. Increased federal control, nation-wide standardized tests, and needs for equalizing educational opportunity are three of the arguments used by proponents of such nationalization. Those opposing such a policy point out the rich heritage that America has derived from the diversity of its people.

As a future educational professional, what merits do you perceive in increased or decreased nationalization of schools? Which position—greater nationalization, or greater decentralization—would you support, and why?

States' Responsibility for Public Education

The constitutions of most states specifically refer to public education. For example, Article 11, Section 1 of the New York State Constitution states that "The legislature shall provide for the maintenance and support of a system of free common schools, wherein all the children of this state may be educated."

Within the general guidelines of each state's constitution, the legislature has almost complete power over public schools. The state legislature can prescribe policies that govern any of the school functions in the state. Its actions, however, are tempered by general expressions of the people and subject to review by state and federal courts. Powerful education committees in state legislatures consider legislation and appropriations that consume about *half* the budgets of most states—a strong indication of our social commitment to education.

Five critical educational decisions are made at the state level: creating and modifying school district boundaries (usually with local voter approval); certifying administrative and teaching personnel; determining the curriculum; structuring fiscal support of schools; and setting and maintaining minimum academic standards for public and private schools. Three agencies in each state have responsibilities for schools: the state school board, the state education agency, and the chief state school officer (CSSO).

State School Board

All states but Wisconsin have boards of education that are responsible to the legislature for educational policies and procedures. These boards typically are composed of seven to nine members, but can be larger. For example, the Ohio State Board of Education has twenty-one members—one from each congressional district. In thirty-four states, board members are appointed by the governor. In eight states, they are chosen by popular election. At least four other methods of selection are used in the remaining states. In New York, the legislature elects twelve members of the Board of Regents by congressional districts and four at large. The Texas legislature in 1984 abolished the twenty-three-member elected state board and replaced it with a fifteen-member board appointed by the governor. In 1987, the people voted to return to an elected board with 15 members.

The state board of education typically is responsible for making policies, rules, and regulations for operating schools within the state and has wide discretionary authority in carrying out the law as passed by the legislature.

State Education Agency

The daily responsibility for implementing state policy resides with the state education agency. Departments in different states vary greatly in size and responsibility. Some may have as few as 50 employees, while others have as many as two thousand, with the average being about 350. They supervise a vast number of federal and state programs; review reports from local school districts; maintain financial, attendance, salary, and other records as required by law or the state board of education; and certify teachers.

Chief State School Officer

These state departments of education are administered by a chief state school officer (CSSO), whose title can be state superintendent of education, superintendent of schools, commissioner of education, or superintendent of public instruction. "The chief state school officer is elected by popular vote in nineteen states, appointed by state boards of education in twenty-six states, and appointed by the governor in five states" (Wiles & Bondi 1985, 79).

The CSSO provides the link between lay leaders (state board, legislature, governor) and professional educators in the state. The major responsibility of the CSSO is to provide leadership for educational programs in the state. Other responsibilities include serving as chief budget officer, as hearing officer to whom appeals of educational decisions are directed from local school districts and individual professionals, and as chief executive officer for the board of education.

Intermediate Agencies

Over half of the states have organized intermediate agencies between state and local school districts to provide services that otherwise would not be affordable by individual local school districts. These services include instruction in vocational and special education, inservice training of teachers, media centers, and computer services. In New York these units are called Boards of Cooperative Educational Services (BOCES), while Michigan has County School Districts, and Texas has Regional Service Centers.

Local School Districts

The principle that education is a *state function* and a *local responsibility* was first enunciated in 1647 in the Act of Massachusetts General Court. The act required all towns of a certain size to establish and maintain schools. It placed the responsibility for compliance in the hands of local citizens. During the past half century, schools across the nation have been reorganized and consolidated for two main purposes: first, to overcome the limitations of that early New England model, which consisted of many small, local districts, with its limitations in curriculum offerings, particularly in secondary schools; and second, to promote economy in school operations.

In 1985–86, there were 15,746 school districts in the United States. This represents a dramatic decrease from 127,531 districts in 1931–32 (NEA 1986, 9) and approximately 80,000 in 1950 (Wiles & Bondi 1985, 3). Hawaii is the only state with a single school district for the entire state. Districts are organized by counties in some states (for example, Florida,

Nevada, and Louisiana), while school districts in New England, Indiana, and Pennsylvania are organized on a town or township basis. Some states, such as Illinois, have regional school districts for secondary schools and separate districts for elementary schools.

Local school districts are created by state legislatures and are usually independent of municipal governments, even where their boundaries are the same. Historically, states have passed along discretion for most kinds of policy to local school districts. During the past quarter of a century, states have assumed a larger share of school budgets and greater control of school policies and practices. Despite strong sentiment for local control of education and frustration with bureaucracy, the trend is toward greater state and federal intervention. With an increasingly mobile society, the public seeks general assurance that the variety and quality of education in all communities is strong.

Local school districts parallel state organizations. Each has a school board, a chief executive officer (superintendent), and a staff.

Local Board of Education

School boards are variously called boards of education, boards of trustees, or school committees, depending upon their location. Local school board members are elected by the people in about 85 percent of school districts and appointed, often by the mayor, in the remaining 15 percent.

Legally, school boards act as agents of the state; politically, they represent the local community and its people. They implement the mandates of the state, while acting in the interests of the local school district. They are responsible for making school policies, appointing personnel, approving the annual budget, organizing bond elections when needed, determining tax rates, and overseeing every aspect of the school district's operation.

Superintendent of Schools

Each school board employs a chief executive officer to manage the school district. Except in the smallest districts, this person's title is superintendent of schools.

School systems are governed by boards of education from the local community.

The superintendent of schools is responsible for studying problems, formulating alternative solutions, and presenting proposed actions for the board's approval. A summary of the superintendent's duties follows.

1. Serving as chief executive officer of the board and school system.
2. Helping the board in formulating policies.
3. Providing leadership in planning and carrying out the instructional program.
4. Selecting and recommending personnel for appointment and guiding staff development.
5. Preparing and administering the budget.
6. Determining building needs and administering building programs.
7. Serving as the school leader in the community and as chief spokesman for the educational program (Wiles & Bondi 1985, 104).

In small school districts, the superintendent performs all of these roles; in large ones, a staff assumes most of these duties.

Upon reading this list, a local school superintendent recently told us that his two most important roles were not included—establishing the climate of the school district and working with political forces to improve support for the school.

School District Organization

School districts are organized to promote decision making through line-and-staff organizations that map administrative authority. Exhibit 12.4 illustrates an organizational chart for a mid-size school district.

The organization of public schools is hierarchical. School boards select superintendents who in turn select their staffs, subject to board approval. School principals are supervised by the superintendent and have supervisory responsibility over their faculties.

Line authority is indicated in Exhibit 12.4 by solid lines, staff responsibilities by broken lines. *Line* relationships identify formal chains of responsibilities that flow from the school board through the superintendent to other school employees. *Staff* personnel are specialists who advise and consult with others but have no direct supervisory authority unless it is specifically delegated for special assignments. Titles often indicate whether an individual is line or staff—coordinators, directors, or consultants are usually staff, while principals are line officers. Assistant superintendents may be either, or both; the assistant superintendent for finance, for example, may have supervisory responsibility (line) over a division that maintains fiscal records but staff responsibility to the principals and teachers in the district.

Several activities not readily apparent are conducted or coordinated through central school-district administrative offices. These include organizing and operating school accreditation visits, school lunch programs, district testing program, staff recruitment and selection, personnel benefits and records, plant maintenance activities, student transportation, school health services, purchasing offices, and the development of new instructional resources.

EXHIBIT 12.4   Organization of Medium-sized School District

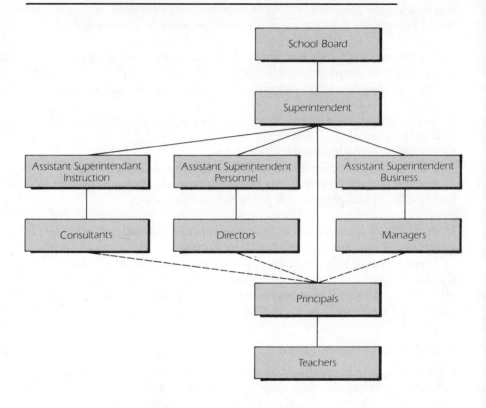

School Levels and Enrollment

Schools are organized into elementary schools, middle schools or junior high schools, and senior high schools. Elementary schools include grades 1–5 or 1–6, often kindergartens (with children attending either half days or full days), and a few prekindergartens or nursery schools. Schools for the preadolescent and early adolescent student include junior high schools (typically grades 7–9) or middle schools (typically grades 6–8). Senior high schools refer both to three-year (grades 10–12) and four-year (grades 9–12) institutions. The organization of district schools often depends on the demography of student populations and the availability of school plants, rather than on educational grounds. Senior high schools typically are larger and more complex than middle schools, junior high schools, or elementary schools, and usually are organized into subject-matter departments.

Table 12.1 details the distribution of the forty million students in American public schools by level for 1982–83 and compares it with that of the forty-five million students in 1970–71. Both the number of schools and the number of students decreased during this period. What other conclusions can you draw from the data in Table 12.1?

*E*ducation is always more essential in our arguments than in our appropriations.

David Cohen, 1984, 12.

TABLE 12.1   Enrollment and Number of Schools by Level

Level	1970–71				1982–83			
	Enrollment in thousands		Schools		Enrollment in thousands		Schools	
	No.	%	No.	%	No.	%	No.	%
Elementary	24,695	54	61,060	67	19,981	50	52,726	62
Junior High or Middle	7,380	16	10,395	11	7,267	18	11,695	14
Secondary, including High School	12,040	27	15,507	17	11,880	30	16,145	19
Combined Elementary/Secondary	844	2	1,330	1	673	2	1,473	2
Not classified	431	1	2,248	2	306	1	2,701	3
Total schools	45,390		90,540		40,107		84,740	

Abstracted from Plisko & Stern, 1985, 28. Source: U.S. Department of Education, National Center for Education Statistics, *Elementary and Secondary General Information Survey, School Universe file, 1970–71* and *1971–72;* and *Common Core of Data, School Universe file, 1982–83,* unpublished tabulations (January 1985).

School Finances

Funding Sources. School funds are derived from federal, state, and local sources. Local districts receive *federal* funds for a variety of categorical purposes—educational programs for children with handicaps, vocational education, school lunch programs, and school desegregation. Some school districts compete for federal grants to support areas such as education for gifted and talented students, curriculum development projects, desegregation plans, and personnel development.

The federal impact on education is far greater than the monies it contributes to schooling. Because its aid is primarily categorical rather than by formula, it targets its funds to priority areas. With funds come regulations that affect other budgets. Most federal grants, for example, require "matching funds"—contributions by the local school in either money or time.

Local school districts, however, depend almost exclusively on real estate (property) taxes for local revenue. Some school-district boundaries include large factories, shopping centers, port facilities, or other property that increase the school's total property value per student far above the state average. Other districts, depending primarily on homes for their tax base, are disadvantaged because few if any students live in factories or businesses, yet the assessed valuation of such property is likely to be higher than for houses. Variations in the tax bases of schools result in differences in services offered to students and salaries paid to teachers.

These differences in educational opportunity caused by the variations in expenditures per student have been the cause of several court cases. In *San Antonio Independent School District* v. *Rodriguez* (1973), for example, the Supreme Court ruled that the basic method of financing education through state and local funds did not violate the equal protection clause of the Constitution. Equity, the Court concluded, must come from state lawmakers and court interpretations. Since then, individual states (for example, California, in *Serrano* v. *Priest,* 1971 and 1976) have formulated varying ways to cope with differences between rich and poor districts.

States allocate funds through formula grants and equalization programs. *Formula* grants are provided to all school districts based on criteria such as the number of students, average daily attendance (ADA) of students, number of teachers, or other uniformly applied measures.

Equalization grants allocate money in *inverse* proportion to local taxpaying ability. Poorer school districts receive more funds per student than richer districts. The purpose of these funds is to equalize educational opportunity across the state, regardless of the wealth of local communities.

In addition to revenue from taxes on property, a few districts have levied sales taxes. Schools also raise money, particularly for building programs, from the sale of bonds. Before being offered for sale, bonds must be approved by the local school board and, in most states, voted on favorably by the local taxpaying public. Bonds, in effect, are ways to borrow money for specific immediate needs to be paid back with future revenue.

Increasing Expenditures. In 1985–86, expenditures for elementary and secondary schools were $134.6 billion, not including $10.7 billion for capital outlay and interest on school debts (NEA 1986, 24–27). The costs of educating students in the United States more than doubled in the decade between 1975–76 and 1985–86, from $1,451 per student in average daily attendance to $3,723. What other trends do you see when examining Table 12.2?

Even when the effects of inflation are considered, the costs of schooling have tended to increase over time. In 1985, the National Center for Education Statistics, a branch of the U.S. Department of Education, calculated the change in expenditures per student in average daily attendance for three years, 1970–71, 1980–81, and 1982–83. Using 1982–83 dollars as a base, they adjusted the costs for the other years to compensate for inflation by using the Consumer Price Index. Because the 1982–83 figures were derived from a different source from those in Table 12.2, they vary slightly ($2,948 rather than $2,949).

TABLE 12.2   **Expenditure Per Student in Average Daily Attendance**

School Year	Amount	Percent Over Previous Year
1975–76	1,451	———
1976–77	1,602	10.4
1977–78	1,781	11.1
1978–79	1,971	10.6
1979–80	2,230	13.1
1980–81	2,489	11.6
1981–82	2,752	10.5
1982–83	2,949	7.1
1983–84	3,172	7.5
1984–85	3,457	9.0
1985–86	3,723	7.7

Source: The National Education Association, *Estimates of School Statistics, 1985–86,* (1986), 25, 1984–85 and 1985–86 figures are updated as revised in NEA, *Rankings of the States, 1986,* 53–54. Used by permission.

When the effects of inflation were eliminated, the average expenditure for schooling per student in average daily attendance in the United States during 1970–71 was $2,252 (when calculated in 1982–83 dollars). Ten years later, in 1980–81, the average expenditure was $2,819, an increase of 25.2 percent. Two years later, in 1982–83, the expenditures were $2,948, an increase of 4.6 percent (Plisko & Stern 1985, 40).

Federal, State, and Local Expenditures for Education.   School revenue is derived from three major sources—federal, state, and local agencies. Examine Table 12.3 to draw any conclusions and determine any trends concerning the source of school revenue.

States are assuming a greater share of the budgets of local schools as they implement policies consistent with equalization legislation and judicial rulings. In 1985–86, states paid for half of local school costs for the first time. With increased expenditures, state legislatures are placing greater controls and demands for accountability and uniform accounting procedures. The percent of school funds from state sources varies from 5 percent for New Hampshire and 27.8 percent for South Dakota to 90.6 percent for Hawaii and 75.6 percent for Washington. Half of the states contribute from 40 to 61 percent, with 50.1 as the average contribution by the state (NEA 1987).

Variation Among States.   States vary widely, both in their capacity to support public schools and in the amount of funding provided to schools. Table 12.4 includes the expenditures by schools per pupil for 1983–84, this amount as a percent of income per capita in each state, and the pupil-teacher ratio. Ranks among the 50 states and the District of Columbia are also provided for comparison. How well does your state support education? Can you think of reasons for this?

TABLE 12.3   **Sources of School Revenue**

School Year	Federal		State		Local And Other Sources	
	Amount*	*% of Total*	*Amount**	*% of Total*	*Amount**	*% of Total*
1975–76	5,949	8.5	30,617	43.7	33,463	47.8
1976–77	6,355	8.4	32,983	43.8	35,965	47.8
1977–78	7,232	8.8	36,369	44.3	38,545	46.9
1978–79	7,769	8.8	41,524	47.3	38,507	43.9
1979–80	9,020	9.2	47,929	49.1	40,686	41.7
1980–81	9,285	8.7	51,376	48.2	45,892	43.1
1981–82	8,409	7.4	54,696	47.9	50,970	44.7
1982–83	8,439	7.0	57,593	47.9	54,292	45.1
1983–84	8,645	6.7	61,877	48.1	58,204	45.2
1984–85	9,269	6.6	69,302	49.6	61,063	43.7
1985–86	9,588	6.4	75,033	50.1	65,067	43.5

* In millions; (e.g., $5,949 = $5 billion, 949 million)

Source: The National Education Association, *Estimates of School Statistics, 1985–86.* (1986). 21. Used by permission.

TABLE 12.4   School Expenditures by State

State	Pupil/Teacher Ratio		Current Expenditures Per Pupil		Expenditures As % of Income Per Capita	
	Ratio	*Rank*	*$*	*Rank*	*%*	*Rank*
Alabama	20.2	44	2,525	50	21.8	43
Alaska	15.8	14	7,843	1	43.1	1
Arizona	19.6	42	2,724	41	21.3	46
Arkansas	17.5	28	2,353	49	22.5	39
California	23.1	50	3,256	27	20.3	50
Colorado	18.4	35	3,697	17	25.0	29
Connecticut	14.0	1	4,738	9	26.2	17
Delaware	16.2	18	4,184	9	29.3	10
Dist. of Col.	14.3	3	4,571	5	25.2	27
Florida	16.6	22	3,238	29	23.6	35
Georgia	18.8	36	2,657	42	21.2	47
Hawaii	22.6	49	3,465	23	25.1	28
Idaho	20.3	45	2,401	45	21.6	45
Illinois	17.8	31	3,538	21	24.0	34
Indiana	18.6	36	3,051	33	24.5	32
Iowa	15.3	11	3,439	24	27.3	14
Kansas	15.4	12	3,560	20	25.8	23
Kentucky	19.2	41	23901	46	21.1	41
Louisiana	18.6	36	2,905	37	25.8	23
Maine	14.5	5	3,024	35	25.4	26
Maryland	17.5	28	4,182	7	25.9	21
Massachusetts	14.9	6	4,026	11	24.6	30
Michigan	20.6	47	3,848	13	28.3	13
Minnesota	17.1	26	3,745	18	26.1	19
Mississippi	18.1	32	2,357	48	25.7	25
Missouri	16.5	20	2,958	36	22.3	40
Montana	15.9	16	3,847	14	35.1	3
Nebraska	15.0	8	3,471	22	26.1	19
Nevada	20.0	43	2,829	40	19.5	51
New Hampshire	15.9	16	3,271	25	21.9	42
New Jersey	15.0	8	4,504	6	26.2	17
New Mexico	18.8	38	3,153	32	28.9	12
New York	15.8	14	5,492	2	34.2	4
N. Carolina	18.8	38	2,625	43	22.6	37
N. Dakota	16.2	18	3,210	30	26.6	16
Ohio	18.3	34	3,257	26	24.6	30
Oklahoma	16.6	22	2,850	39	23.3	36
Oregon	18.2	33	3,889	12	30.8	7
Pennsylvania	16.6	22	4,237	8	31.5	6
Rhode Island	15.1	10	4,285	7	30.8	7
S. Carolina	17.5	28	2,591	44	24.5	32
S. Dakota	14.9	6	2,892	38	25.9	21
Tennessee	20.3	45	23630	47	21.0	49
Texas	17.4	27	3,043	34	22.6	37
Utah	23.6	51	2,220	51	21.2	47
Vermont	14.12	2	3,651	19	30.1	9
Virginia	16.9	25	3,155	31	21.7	44
Washington	20.7	48	3,723	16	26.8	15
West Virginia	15.7	13	3,244	28	31.8	5
Wisconsin	16.5	20	3,816	15	29.0	11
Wyoming	14.4	4	4,799	3	36.3	2
U.S. Average	17.9		3,449		24.9	

Source: Databank, State Education Statistics, *Education Week*, February 18, 1987, 20–21.
   Reprinted with permission.

Decision Making in Schools

If often seems that decisions in schools "come from the top," are made hastily, and are rendered without careful consideration of the consequences. Typically, such is not the case; however, decisions are made on political as well as educational grounds and therefore may not seem rational because the factors considered are unknown to most people viewing the effects of the decision. Perhaps three illustrations will clarify the process and the relative influence of various groups in complex decisions.

Illustration 1: Community Expectations

The Belview School District has two high schools, one (Peters High) in an affluent area and the other (the original and older Belview High) in a working-class neighborhood. This example concerns Peters High, where the parents are especially active in school affairs. The majority of school board members live in the Peters High community, fewer mothers work (and consequently spend time as unpaid helpers in the school), and parents want an outstanding education for their children so that those children will be educationally successful both in college and in life.

For several years, there had been a continuing murmur in the community questioning the quality of education in Peters High School. Finally, parent groups formed and called on board members and the superintendent. In an informal executive session, the board discussed the situation and authorized the superintendent to employ an external review team from nearby universities. The district had employees who had the expertise to conduct the study, but the board wanted an independent audit.

The assistant superintendent was authorized to organize the study. He contacted a professor of education, and after discussing the problem, requested a proposed plan for conducting the study. The professor drew up a proposal, including the names of potential evaluators in each content area taught in the high school, and a budget. This was discussed at length with the superintendent and assistant superintendent, a revised proposal written, and this taken by the superintendent to the board. In a regular session, the school board authorized the study and funds to support it.

As director of the study, the professor first met with the principal of the high school (joined by the assistant superintendent) and then with the consultants who would conduct the study. The study included four facets: (1) observations of classes and analyses of resources; (2) interviews with small groups of students, with parents and, individually, with teachers; (3) analyses of test data and student records; and (4) a survey of graduates from the previous two years. Data were gathered over a six-week period, with each consultant visiting the school for two days, writing a preliminary report, sharing and getting feedback from the study director (and, during a third day, from teachers as to the report's accuracy), then writing a final report.

The final report was positive about the school but nevertheless made a number of recommendations for improving the program. This report was printed and presented orally to the board. Following the study, task forces in the school were formed to assess each recommendation and to plan for implementing needed changes. These task forces included not only teachers and administrators, but also students and parents.

Illustration 2: Pressures from Standardized Testing

In our second illustration, the results of the state-administered basic skills test had just been received by the principal of School B (and are included in this text in Exploration 4 of Chapter 11). The results of the writing test were disastrous: only 39 percent of fifth graders mastered writing, compared with 82 percent who mastered mathematics and 95 percent who passed reading.

During the following summer, the language arts supervisor of the school district worked with a team of teachers from grades 3, 4, 5, and 6 to design a more powerful curriculum in writing. This team studied techniques of writing, ordered and analyzed several programs, engaged a consultant for a few days, and finally completed a set of recommended changes. These recommendations included new elementary-school instructional materials in writing that drew from several commercial sources and from a federally-supported language arts project and a further recommendation that more attention be devoted to writing in the curriculum, particularly in social studies classes. At the fall conference, prior to the first day of school, all teachers were oriented to the new program and told they could call on the language arts supervisor or on any members of the development team if help was needed.

Illustration 3: Substance Abuse

The third example of decision-making began with a drug bust. Just two blocks from the junior high school, a couple were selling marijuana from their apartment. When the police arrested them, they also questioned a number of school-age youngsters who were nearby. One admitted he used drugs, and from follow-up investigations, it was found that a number of students had bought drugs from the couple; furthermore, one student had acted as their agent, even selling marijuana from his locker. Police dogs, trained to sniff out drugs, located three lockers that contained marijuana. The newspaper ran front-page exposés and drugs in schools became the central issue and concern of the community.

Board meetings were crowded; the principal forced to resign (not because of wrongdoing, but for lack of control over school discipline); and classes became disoriented as students and teachers were distracted from their work.

Action came from several sources. In the school, homeroom teachers held class meetings to consider what should be done, and an early group decision was to outlaw any discussion of drugs during classes—homeroom would be the only time in the day for such discussions. The central administration immediately appointed another principal, made public statements about drugs, and initiated a new curriculum on drug education. Individual students, quietly and without publicity, enrolled in drug-treatment programs. Parents joined with the school in a resolve and unity formerly not known.

Within a few months that crisis was over and the school returned to normal. And when drugs were mentioned, everyone—students, teachers, and parents—felt they had faced a crisis and won.

Conclusion

The influence of governmental agencies on the operation of individual schools and on the practices of teachers continues to expand at an ever-increasing rate. At one time in America, schools were primarily a local concern. Parents selected and employed a teacher or teachers for their children. With increased urbanization and greater state concern for education, the organization of state education agencies has become larger and more complex and the regulations affecting schools more prescriptive. Only within the past four decades has the federal government taken responsibility for more than cursory data-collecting activities.

The increased federal role has paralleled its commitment to schools as instruments of social change. The Civil Rights Act and the National Defense Education Act initiated a process that has shaped the American education agenda. Court decisions and federal agency regulations have led, for example, to new approaches to teaching, new curricula, increased concern for compensatory education (minorities, handicapped, women, undereducated, and gifted and talented), desegregation, school busing, and teacher education. Accountability and with it, increased paperwork, have resulted.

Teaching, then, occurs in a context that not only includes the students in your class and the other people in the school, but the organization and support systems of the school district, the state, and the federal government.

Schools are big business today. Expending more than $147.7 billion and employing 2.47 million teachers, principals, supervisors, and other instructional staff, schools comprise a major investment by the public. Three generalizations characterize schools today: (1) they cost more to operate each year, (2) their organization is more complex, and (3) they are controlled more tightly by central governmental regulations and court decisions.

The purpose of this chapter has been to acquaint you with some of the forces that will influence what you do in your classroom. While it is an introduction to the nuances of school organization and judicial actions, this chapter should help you understand the nature of bureaucratic structures and the ways they affect your teaching. As you continue your study of teaching, and as you hear about events in education and proposals for changing structures, programs, and funding priorities, you should now have some basis for understanding them. The information in this chapter also provides an introduction to several of the issues facing educators today that are explored in the next chapter. These perennial issues are manifested in different ways as society attempts to improve education and also to tailor it to the individual needs of students.

Building Reflective Inquiry Skills

Learning About School District Organization, Policies, and Processes

Too few teachers have a working knowledge of the organization of their school districts, actions of the board of education, and ways to influence that organization and those actions. Yet those who do often are able to accomplish more by being able to avail themselves of the district's services and resources.

In this section, we ask you to reflect on the organization and operation of a school district. The following activities outline inquiry procedures in your search. Using this information, draw conclusions about the district's organization, policies, and practices. If possible, compare your findings with those from other districts.

Inquiry 1: Obtain copies of the agenda, supporting materials, and minutes for several meetings of the school board. What items are included? What decisions made?

Inquiry 2: Visit a school-board meeting. Arrive early and talk with people who attend. Why are they there? Who do they represent? What issues are they concerned with? How do they hope to influence board decisions? What were board members doing prior to the meeting? After the meeting? How are they seated? In what ways are visitors recognized? How is the agenda processed?

Inquiry 3: If possible, discuss the responsibilities of the board with one of its members. What are their backgrounds? Why are they on the board? What are their major interests in the school district? What do they perceive as the major challenges facing the dis-

trict? How do they interact with the superintendent?

Inquiry 4: Obtain a copy of the district's policies and procedures manual; select and read one section carefully. What is included? In what detail?

Inquiry 5: Secure an organizational chart of the school district and write names of incumbents in each office. Discuss the organization with an administrator. What are the relations between divisions for finance, personnel, and curriculum? How does the superintendent convey school-board directives and elicit school-district needs? Ask about line and staff officers. How do members of the central office interact with teachers and administrators in schools? What services do they provide, and how do teachers avail themselves of these services? What are the "pet peeves" of the persons you interview?

Inquiry 6: Examine a copy of the budget for the current year. What are the sources of funds? What proportion comes from local, state, federal, and other sources? What is the assessed valuation for the district, the tax rate, and the taxes levied on an average home in the district? How are funds allocated? What proportion is budgeted for each area (for example, personnel, bonded indebtedness, supplies and materials, maintenance of facilities)?

Inquiry 7: Tour the central administration building. What offices are housed there? Use the organizational chart as a guide. Drive by other school-district facilities, such as maintenance shops, bus barns, and storage buildings. What special facilities does the district have and what are their functions?

Explorations

Exploration 1
State Regulations and Teaching
Examine a copy of your state's "School Code" which compiles state laws and regulations. A copy may be found in most university libraries and school-district administrative offices. List the major areas that pertain to responsibilities of classroom teachers.

Exploration 2
Federal Role in Local Education
Organize a debate among members of your class on

the topic, "Resolved: that the federal role in education should be decreased."

Exploration 3
Major Issues in School Governance
Interview a school-board member or legislator to determine what they perceive to be the major issues they face in school governance.

Exploration 4
American and Nationalized Education
Compare your school experiences with those of

classmates who attended schools in other nations. List specific differences in the various educational systems, including their organizations, curricula, and instructional methods.

Exploration 5
School Finance
Secure a copy of the summary of a school-district budget. (The full budget will be so complex as to mask the broader concepts). What are the major ex-penditures? What percent of the total budget is ded-icated to teachers' salaries? To buildings and grounds? To supplies, materials, and textbooks?

Secure the beginning salary schedules for several school districts in the area. Often a county or inter-mediate school agency or the local teacher's associa-tion has these data readily available. The state education agency also has them for the state.

References

Baker v. Owen, 395 F. Supp. 294 (M.D.N.C. 1975), aff'd 423 U.S. 907 (1975).

Bethel School District No. 403 v. Fraser, 106 S.Ct. 3159 (1986).

Black v. Cothren, 316 F.Supp. 468 (Neb. 1970).

Brown v. Board of Education of Topeka, 347 U.S. 483 (1954).

Brown v. Board of Education of Topeka, 349 U.S. 294 (1955).

Burnside v. Byars, 563 F.2d. 744 (Miss. 1966). In *Frontiers of School Law*. Topeka, KS: NOLPE, 1973, *supra* note 25.

Burnside v. Byars, 231 F.Supp. 743 (Ala. 1964). In *Frontiers of School Law*. Topeka, KS: NOLPE, 1973, *supra* note 25.

Campbell, R. F. & Layton, D. H. (1969). *Policy mak-ing for American Education.* Chicago: Midwest Ad-ministration Center, The University of Chicago.

Cash v. Hock, 309 F.Supp. 346 (Wis. 1970). In *Fron-tiers of School Law*. Topeka, KS: NOLPE, 1973, *supra* note 25.

Chalk Talk. (1987). The right of free speech in pub-lic schools: Bethel v. Fraser. *Journal of Law & Education, 16*(1), 119–24.

Cobb, J. J. (1981). *An introduction to educational law.* Springfield, IL: Charles C. Thomas.

Cohen, D. (1984). . . . the condition of teachers' work. . . . *Harvard Educational Review, 54*(1), 12.

Crossen v. Fatsi, 309 F.Supp. 702 (Wis. 1969).

Databank. (1986). State Education Statistics: Student performance, resource inputs, reforms, and pop-ulation characteristics, 1982 and 1986. *Education Week*, February 18, 1987, 20–21.

Fischer, L. (1982). The courts and educational poli-cy. *Policy making in education*, Eighty-first Year-book. Chicago: National Society for the Study of Education.

Goss v. Lopez, 419 U.S. 565, 573 (1975).

Ingraham v. Wright, 430 U.S. 651 (1976).

National Education Association, Professional and Or-ganizational Development/Research Division. (1986). *Estimates of school statistics, 1985–86.* Washington, DC: National Education Association.

National Education Association, Professional and Or-ganizational Development/Research Division. (1987). *Understanding State School Finance Formu-las.* Washington, DC: National Education Association.

New Jersey v. T.L.O., 469 U.S. 325, 105 S.Ct. 68, 83 L.Ed.2d 720 (1985).

Parducci v. Rutland, 316 F.Supp. 352 (N.D. Ala. 1970).

Pickering v. Bd. of Education, 391 U.S. 563, 569 (1968).

Plessy v. Ferguson, 163 U.S. 537, 16 S.Ct. 1138 (1896).

Plisko, V. W. (1983). *The condition of education: 1983 edition.* Washington, DC: U.S. Department of Education, National Center for Education Statistics.

Plisko, V. W. & Stern, J. D. (1985). *The condition of education, 1985 edition.* Washington, DC: U.S. Department of Education, National Center for Education Statistics.

Plyler v. Doe, 457 U.S. 202 (1982).

Reutter, E. E. (1985). *The law of public education,* Third Ed. Mineola, NY: The Foundation Press.

Sametz, L. (1985). Children's constitutional rights. In Sametz, L. & Mcloughlin, C. S. *Educators, Children and the Law.* Springfield, IL: Charles C. Thomas.

San Antonio Independent School District v. Rodriguez, 411 U.S. 1 (1973).

Serrano v. Priest, 5 Cal.3d 584, 96 Cal.Rptr. 601, 487 P.2d 1241 (Cal. 1971).

Serrano v. Priest, 18 Cal.3d 728, 135 Cal.Rptr. 345, 557 P.2d 929 (Cal. 1976).

Sweezy v. New Hampshire, 354 U.S. 234, 77 S.Ct. 1203 (1957).

Sergiovanni, T. J., Burlingame, M., Coombs, F. D. & Thurston, P. W. (1980). *Educational Governance and Administration.* Englewood Cliffs, NJ: Prentice-Hall.

Shelton v. Tucker, 364 U.S. 479, 487 (1960).

Tinker v. Des Moines Independent Community School District, 393 U.S. 503 (1969).

United States v. Jefferson County Bd. of Education, 372 F.2d. 836, 847 (5th Cir. 1966).

Valente, W. D. (1980). *Law in the schools.* Columbus: Charles E. Merrill.

Walts, B. J. (1985). New Jersey v. T.L.O.: The questions the Court did not answer about school searches. *Journal of Law & Education, 14*(3), 421–37.

Westley v. Rossi, 305 F.Supp. 706 (Minn. 1969). In *Frontiers of School Law*, Topeka, KS: NOLPE, 1973, 181.

Wiles, J. & Bondi, J. (1985). *The school board primer: A guide for school board members.* Boston: Allyn and Bacon.

CHAPTER THIRTEEN

Issues Facing Educators Today

OBJECTIVES

By the end of this chapter, you will be able to:

1. Identify some of the important issues that face education in America today.
2. Discuss the major factors impinging on each issue.
3. Articulate your own position and rationale for each position.

KEY WORDS AND CONCEPTS

Basic social institutions—
    family, religious institution, school
Equalized educational opportunities
Evolution and creation science
Excellence in schools
Home schools
Issues
Secular humanism
Societal values
Public and nonpublic schooling
Purpose of schooling
Textbook criteria and censors

*I*n a world of complex and continuing problems, in a world full of frustrations and irritations, America's leadership must be guided by the lights of learning and reason—or else those who confuse rhetoric with reality and the plausible with the possible will gain the popular ascendancy with their seemingly swift and simple solutions in every world problem.

John Kennedy in a speech that was to be delivered in Dallas on the day of his assassination. Reprinted in Jenkins, 1963, 5.

Exploring Educational Issues

In your explorations of teaching, you no doubt have noted two factors: *education is challenging* and *education is challenged*. The first factor reflects the impact teaching has on the teacher. To teach and teach well enough for students to learn is a challenge. It is challenging to keep current on new techniques and research on teaching, current events, content of the curriculum, and needs and interests of students. Every day in a school is different, and every day is challenging.

Education also is being challenged. The future of our nation is so bound up in the education of its citizens that the general public has a major stake in its schools. Few actions go unchallenged; no decisions are final. Those things considered important by one group are not so vital to another. Special interest groups press schools for certain emphases. Waves of change sweep across the nation as each generation grapples with what is important to teach, who is to be taught and to what extent, how taught, by whom, and where.

These are issues in education. They have no definitive answers, and those answers that are given are subject to change. Many of these issues have been considered in previous chapters, but here they are posed as questions that you as a preprofessional can consider and about which you can speculate. Draw upon information from previous chapters, from current events in your community, the nation, and the world, and from your own knowledge and experience.

Think *broadly* in placing these issues in perspective; think *deeply* in considering their implications for the future; think *analytically* in drawing inferences and conclusions from your data base, and think *with others* in your class who have different perspectives, orientations, values, and information so that together a fuller and more complete picture will emerge. Nuances are important. Test your ideas on others and react to theirs.

Things are not always what they may seem. Do you see a vase, or two faces?

Discussing issues in education is both intellectually challenging and interesting. It also can be emotional, as different persons argue their points. Enjoy and learn. Listen to others' words and their meanings. Consider your own rationales for the positions you take. Because there are no correct answers, the process of exploration can be open. Because the issues are important to the future of education, you should begin to understand and to form opinions about them.

Before you read further in this chapter, please turn to Exploration 1 and complete the questionnaire included therein. As you read the chapter, you may revise and extend your responses, and later use the questionnaire as a basis for class discussion.

The Purpose of Schools

Within the context of American society, various institutions have certain expectations they meet and certain roles they perform. Churches, courts, retail businesses, and communication systems each have responsibilities they assume in the fabric of American society. These expectations are implicit and generally known. Within this broad cultural context, what are the expectations for public schools?

ISSUE: What is the major purpose for public schools in America?

This issue is central to the content, organization, and staffing of schools. It is vital for teachers to be able to put the basic purpose of schools into a broader perspective.

Contrasting and Complementary Purposes. Perhaps the only constant element in the world today is change. Particularly in the United States, there is little in education that is static. The major purposes of schools continue to be modified by society. In colonial America, schools trained the clergy and emphasized subjects such as Latin and Greek, History, and Religion. Schools in industrial-age America, according to Toffler (1980), emphasized an invisible, or covert, curriculum (punctuality, obedience, and rote, repetitive work) that prepared students to be workers in America's factories. In today's dynamic social setting, what is the basic purpose of schools?

*O*ne of the major reasons for the calls of crisis in American education is the shifting expectations of the American public.

Harry Passow, 1984, 675.

In one view, the basic purpose of schools is to transmit the culture of the past. Knowledge acquisition is of major importance when this purpose for schools is stressed. This view holds that basic skills such as reading, writing, and arithmetic are vital and stresses cognitive knowledge and information processing. Academic performance is reflected in schools and universities through programs such as the 100 great books program proposed by University of Chicago president, Robert M. Hutchins, and also through achievement tests, poetry memorization, and the traditional content of elementary and secondary curricula.

Some educators believe that the primary responsibility of schools is to teach the three Rs, in order to provide the basic skills needed to learn. In their view, schools should bring about tangible results, such as increased test scores and adequate basic skills by graduates. While other institutions in society (for example, universities, churches, social and cultural groups) are concerned with higher-order cognition and attitude development, only the schools specifically are held accountable for teaching basic skills.

Other educators note that this purpose is much too narrow; that society will not long tolerate such a primary level of achievement. They press for problem solving or transmission of the values that have made America great as the ultimate purpose for schools, citing basic skills simply as a foundation for such higher goals. Basic skills advocates counter with evidence of falling test scores and inadequate skills by graduates who are employed but cannot spell, write coherently, or compute.

Some educators note the rapidly increasing knowledge base and the need to learn how to learn rather than simply the learning of facts and concepts that are soon forgotten or outdated. They focus attention on strategies for learning and motivations to explore, to be inquisitive, and to be open to new ideas. Learning is perceived as a lifelong process and schooling as the beginning.

Schooling may also be perceived as the foundation for work, for a vocation. The content of the curriculum is drawn from needs of the work place. Vocational high schools and magnet schools (such as those described earlier for performing arts, vocational careers, engineering, and science) reflect this stance. So, too, do courses in business, computer science, typing, and homemaking in high school. When asked to identify the primary reasons parents want their children to get an education, respondents to a survey mentioned work and financial reasons most often (Gallup, 1986, 49).

A contrasting purpose for schools—to change society—has been reflected in a number of federal government actions and Supreme Court decisions. Some citizens are discriminated against because of their race, ethnicity, handicaps, sex, or religion. Changes in society to remedy these injustices could occur only if major changes in schools were made. As a result of *Brown* v. *Board of Education* (1954), schools were desegregated. *Lau* v. *Nichols* (1974) required bilingual education for non-English-speaking students. Title IX pressed for actions to eliminate discrimination against females. Public law 94–142 provided for the least restrictive learning environment for students with special learning needs or physical handicaps.

All of these actions hold in common an emphasis on equality of educational opportunity and on changing the ways schools are organized, the substance of the curriculum students study, and the ways in which students are taught. Traditional disciplines are secondary to social action. Through its schools, society would be systematically changed to equalize opportunities of all its citizens.

Balance Needed. Since schools are complex social institutions, none limit themselves to one single purpose. Most schools, however, have a primary purpose and secondary purposes and aims. The major purpose changes over time and with events and problems in a local community or the nation at large. Some events that have shifted school purposes include lowered achievement scores on tests, an international incident that challenged

American ideals, drugs in schools, and expressions of dissatisfaction with the competence of graduates by local businessmen.

The challenge is in achieving balance among various purposes and relevancy related to needs of individual students and society. In your analysis of the purposes of education, you probably concluded that their relative importance was bound to time and place. That is, you would change the order of importance if the community or the times changed. Recognizing the validity of different perspectives and different purposes is important for educators when competing views challenge professionals to make choices.

*O*nly the educated are free.

Epictetus, *Discourse II*, i.

ISSUE: Can Our Educational System Be Both Equal and Excellent?

Equality.   For more than two decades, education marched to the drumbeat of *equality*. The Civil Rights Act of 1964 initiated the search for equality of educational opportunity. Beginning rather slowly, the movement's pace quickened as support for, and successes with, new programs emerged. It became the most comprehensive, most expensive, most visionary movement for human rights in history. The central thrust of the *equality movement* was education. First, the spotlight was on black citizens, then on all racial, ethnic, and religious minorities. The handicapped, then women, then the aged became targets for nationwide attention. The driving force was the federal government, which poured billions of dollars into pro-

Equality of educational opportunity has been a major thrust in the United States for over 20 years.

grams for the poor and the disadvantaged. These programs were undergirded by court actions that legitimized them and federal power that was used to desegregate schools and unlock university doors.

Excellence. By 1983, the tenor of the times had changed. Education in the mid-1980s was galvanized by a series of reports to the public, such as *A Nation At Risk*, by national and regional commissions and task forces. Each report cited the weaknesses in the current system, then made recommendations for solving the problems of schools. Each pressed for *excellence* in education. Only through excellence in its schools could this nation compete economically with other nations. The curriculum became more focused on content and basic skills; testing became more prevalent; minorities scored much lower than whites; and dropouts increased.

The driving force behind education shifted from *equality* to *excellence*. The issue facing educators and the general public today is one of balance. Is one perspective more important, and if so, which? Is it possible to emphasize both, and if so, to what extent should each be emphasized? What are the implications of each position?

Meeting Individual Needs. A related issue is this: to what extent should individual needs be considered in school decisions? Schools tend to group and cluster students for instruction. Based on geographic location, age and educational level, or other criteria, students are assigned to specific schools. Within those schools they are assigned to classes that have specific curriculum objectives. They may attend special classes but seldom are individually taught. Their program of studies is based on state and local requirements; thus the individual needs, desires, and aptitudes of each student may be virtually ignored.

Special Programs. During the past thirty years, a number of actions have occurred to increase individualism within the context of sets of students. Desegregation policy has been designed to improve the educational opportunities of minorities. Bilingual education was instituted for students who do not understand English well enough to participate meaningfully in the educational program. Handicapped students have received special instruction by special teachers on the basis of individual appraisals and instructional programs. Gifted and talented students attend special classes. Magnet schools have been organized for students who are considering the engineering profession, the teaching profession, technologically-oriented careers, theater and music professions, and many others. Each program is an example of the ways in which schools attempt to accommodate individual needs in a group-oriented society.

These special programs tend to be expensive and to benefit a relatively small proportion of the population. Are they effective? Should public schools spend more resources to further enhance their effectiveness? The balance between individual needs and societal expectations is a matter of resources—enough time, enough space and equipment, and enough financial support.

Dropouts. Those who would tailor education to student needs point to the growing student dropout rate as indicative of inadequate school programs. "About 14 percent of high school sophomores leave school before graduating, according to a study by the National Center for Education Statistics. Dropout rates vary sharply by ethnic group and income level. American Indians and Alaska Natives have the highest rate—29 percent. Hispanics and Blacks follow with 18 and 17 percent respectively. The dropout rate for Whites is 12 percent, and it is 3 percent for Asian Americans" (NEA 1984, 85). The study also found that most dropouts later regretted their decision. In cities such as New York, Philadelphia, and Chicago, the high-school dropout rate now exceeds 40 percent (ECS Business Advisory Commission 1985, 10). In concluding a study of dropouts, Ruth Ekstrom and her colleagues identified three special programs that are needed.

> No single program or policy can meet the needs of the diverse dropout population. Three major types of programs are needed: 1) programs to help pregnant teenagers remain in school; 2) programs to help youth with economic needs combine work and education; and 3) programs directed toward students who perform poorly because they are dissatisfied with the school environment. (Ekstrom et al. 1986, 371)

Perhaps this list should be extended to meet the needs of each student, whether they would ultimately drop out of school or whether their education would be enhanced by such an effort.

Dropouts are a result of other conditions, experiences, and attitudes. Should schools attempt to minimize the number of dropouts? This question is related to the issue of equity and excellence; as schools have become more rigorous in their pursuit of excellence, the number of dropouts has increased. Should excellence be diluted to decrease dropouts, or should dropouts receive special instruction? What about social promotion or promotion based on strict adherence to specified standards of achievement? Retaining a child once increases by 40 to 50 percent the risk that he or she will drop out of school later; two retentions increase the risk by 90 percent (Riley 1986, 217).

Summary. The issue of providing both equality and excellence involves the conflict between individual needs, achievements, and aptitudes and societally established minimum standards for success. If one is emphasized, the other suffers. Both are important to an educational program but balance is needed. This applies as much to classes and individual teacher actions as it does to school-wide policies.

Equity based on individual factors such as race, handicaps, home conditions, language, and other needs tends to conflict with excellence based on standards that apply to all. The issue is pervasive to many actions and movements in America over the past four decades.

The schools act as a focal point for societal issues. The old trends are replaced with new directions. The ebb and flow of the values of society are reflected in the schools. These values give direction and purpose to what the students learn and the relationship of that learning to their lives as fully functioning members of society. Much of the school curriculum reflects the basic values of society. Uncertainty and at times conflict may occur when these societal values are in transition.

> *F*ew seem inclined to question the notion that schools are responsible for the many failures of General Motors, or Ford, or Chrysler. It is odd, since schools never were praised for causing earlier successes in that industry.
>
> David Cohen, 1984, 12.

Substance of the School's Curriculum

While the subjects taught in elementary and secondary schools appear to have stabilized, a number of major shifts continue to be made. These occur through changed high-school graduation requirements, new approaches to teaching specific subjects, community concerns, and changes in accreditation requirements (such as those of the New England Association of Colleges and Secondary Schools).

ISSUE: What Content Should Be Emphasized in the Curriculum?

Given the general purposes, aims, and goals for schools, what content should be included in the school's curriculum? Generally accepted, relatively standard content has been identified for each grade level of the school. Elementary schools emphasize reading, arithmetic, and language arts with some instruction in social studies, science, music, art, and physical education. High schools generally require four years of English, two of science, two or three of mathematics, two of physical education, and some electives. While there are variations in different states and in different communities, the curriculum is fairly standard throughout the United States.

Variations do occur and the curriculum does change over time. During the 1960s and 1970s, courses in special subjects proliferated in high schools, but by the mid-1980s state legislatures and local boards of education were increasing the number of required courses in standard disciplines and eliminating many peripheral courses.

Events tend to shape the curriculum. When societal problems become serious, schools are called on to include new programs in their curricula. Thus, tobacco, alcohol, and drug education have become important parts

Who should decide the content of textbooks?

of the program. Driver education followed an increase in traffic deaths, and vocational education was spurred by high unemployment rates. Suicide prevention programs and sex education programs flourish when a rash of teen suicide or teen pregnancy prompt immediate action in the community.

In other instances, special-interest groups have fomented support for certain curricular programs. Veterans' groups challenged the nation; subsequently, patriotism and national pride were included. "Economics with Emphasis on the Free Enterprise System" was required in Texas after business leaders expressed concern about students' lack of knowledge about our economic system. Black Pride Week, Martin Luther King, Jr.'s birthday, and Cinco de Mayo, have become special events because of the efforts of blacks and Hispanics.

Little thought appears to go into whether or not instruction actually will correct a problem. Larry Cuban points out that driver education was offered for decades, with little impact on highway fatality rates. Only when Ralph Nader and others linked car design and highway engineering to road deaths, and the federal government reduced the speed limit to 55 miles per hour did the number of traffic fatalities begin to drop (Cuban 1986, 320).

> *A*ll social movements involve conflicts which are reflected intellectually in controversies. It would not be a sign of health if such an important social interest as education were not also an arena of struggles, practical and theoretical.
>
> John Dewey, 1938, 5.

ISSUE: What responsibility should the school have for teaching socially sensitive areas such as drug education, sex education, and moral values? Should any constraints be placed on such instruction?

The three primary institutions of American society are the *family, religious institutions*, and the *school*. Many of the issues in schools revolve around their responsibility for education in several sensitive areas that could be the domain of one or both of the other primary social institutions.

Teaching moral and ethical values in schools remains highly controversial, with some pressing for the separation of church and state while others are arguing for instruction that is consistent with their concept of Judaic-Christian ideals. During the liberal 1960s and 1970s, schools attempted to remain neutral and open to a wide range of values through an instructional approach called *values clarification*. Using games, dilemmas, and simulations, students clarified their own values, which could have been quite different from those of their teachers or communities. The emphasis in instruction was on process—choosing, prizing, and acting upon values; teachers were to remain neutral rather than expressing their own views. Students wrestled with important issues such as poverty, war and peace, and social relationships.

Prior to this period, schools modeled and taught directly the traditional values of their communities and of American society. The 1980s brought a resurgence of this directional approach to moral education. Parents again called on the schools to teach traditional American values.

Sex education, drug education, and international or peace education are all controversial topics in schools. Is the school the proper place for learning about such topics? Traditionally, when America has faced a serious problem, it has turned to its schools to solve the problem. Even Ann Landers, syndicated columnist, whose advice is read by millions each day, noted that drugs were everywhere and proceeded to list dozens of places and professions in which drugs were of concern. "We must start somewhere to eradicate this all-pervasive problem. The best place is the schools" (Landers 1986).

Are schools the best place to solve problems like drug abuse? Cuban assessed the situation this way: "Schools traffic quite effectively in information and skills, but they tend to be weak when it comes to altering emotionally-based and culturally-conditioned responses. This is especially the case when no consensus exists regarding what should be taught" (1986, 321).

Secular Humanism. While the term has yet to be adequately defined, conservative and fundamentalist Christian groups have used *secular humanism* to describe activities and opinions they believe are at variance with Judaic-Christian beliefs. This is a creed, they maintain, that denies the omnipotence of God by stressing human control over its own destiny; that promotes situational ethics and moral relativism (moral behavior not based on absolutes such as biblical writings, but which vary according to the situation and the person's perception of it); that supports the theory of evolution rather than creation; that promotes nontraditional roles for men and women; that leads to sexual freedom and other forms of hedonism; and that promotes internationalism rather than American patriotism.

During the eighties, conflicting values between secular treatment of content in schools and religious values of parents collided in a series of actions related to secular humanism. Several examples of these clashes during the 1985–86 school year and their dispositions were compiled from press reports and other sources by People for the American Way, a civil-liberties advocacy group.

Parents in San Ramone School District, California, objected to a K–6 drug-abuse prevention program because of "decision-making techniques." The school board appointed a review committee to examine all drug-abuse curricula and recommend an appropriate program.

Parents in Bennett School District, Colorado, objected to a grant to implement a global education program because of a "hidden agenda that de-emphasizes American patriotism," "conflict-resolution" exercises, and "no moral absolutes." The school board withdrew the grant application.

In a Panama City, Florida, junior high school, concerned members of the community objected to two supplementary books because of "language" and "suicide." A review committee recommended keeping the books, but the superintendent ruled that all nontextbooks must be approved. Subsequently, a public hearing was held and all but one of the books were approved.

In Lincoln County, Oregon, parents objected to a reading series because it included such topics as evolution, sex education, and open-ended discussions, and to the adoption of an elementary guidance program because it included values clarification and interference with family values. The reading books remained, but the guidance program was not adopted.

In the Papillion-LaVista School District, Nebraska, a group called Voice for Informed Parents challenged a video series on responsibility and other materials because they "[invade] the privacy of the student and his family" and "[undermine] the traditional values and morals." None of the materials were removed nor altered by the district committee of the school board (summarized from People for the American Way, 1986).

Sex Education.   A controversial and emotional issue, sex education has been taught in schools for more than sixty years. It was initiated as a response to societal concerns about unwed mothers, unwanted pregnancies, and the spread of venereal diseases. The spread of AIDS in the mid-1980s stimulated increased interest in sex education. About 80 percent of public-school students in major U.S. cities now take some kind of sex-education course. In 1986, the Surgeon General of the United States even proposed graphic instruction starting as low as Grade 3.

Americans generally support sex education in schools. Consider the results of Gallup polls conducted in 1981 and 1985 (found in Table 13.1).

In a 1986 poll by Yankelovich, Clancy, and Shulman, 86 percent of respondents agreed that sex education should be taught in school and 83 percent believed that schools should teach children about AIDS, but only 23 percent favored teaching eight-year-olds about AIDS (*Time*, November 24, 1986, 58).

Critics of sex education fear that it encourages experimentation and promiscuity; that discussions of abortion will make it seem like an easy solution; that chastity is not taught as a value; and that homosexuality is depicted as an acceptable alternative life-style. They believe the home is the appropriate place for sex education. "Statistics have demonstrated the ineffectiveness of such courses in reducing sexual activity, unwanted pregnancies, and venereal disease among teenagers" (Cuban 1986, 321).

Proponents of sex education point out that parents cannot be counted on to teach about these sensitive areas to their children. In the 1986 *Time* survey, 69 percent of respondents did not think parents were doing what they should to educate their children about sex, while 39 percent of parents polled indicated that *only a few times* or *not at all* had they had frank and open discussions about sex with their teenagers (*Time* 1986, 58).

Suicide-Prevention Programs.   Suicide is the third most common cause of death (behind accidents and homicide) among persons 15 to 24 years of age, numbering more than 5,000 annually (Strother 1986, 756). Noting that the number of suicides has doubled in the past 30 years, states are implementing suicide-prevention programs for junior and senior high

TABLE 13.1   **Should Sex Education Be Included in Schools?**

	Sex Education			
	In High School		*In Elementary School*	
	1985	*1981*	*1985*	*1981*
Should include	75%	70%	52%	45%
Should not include	19%	22%	43%	48%
Don't know	6%	8%	5%	7%

Source: Gallup, 1985, p. 40. Used by permission.

schools. These programs generally are designed to help students understand depression and suicidal ideas and to teach them strategies for dealing with stress and disappointments. Those who express caution about such instruction point out that cluster suicides (those that occur close together in location and time) may be fueled by such instruction. Others ask if schools are the appropriate institution for such instruction.

Peace Education.   Topics often included in peace education programs include the threat of nuclear war, disarmament, nonviolence, peace, and justice. Many educators believe these topics are of profound importance to the future of our nation and should be fully understood and discussed by young people. Opponents charge that peace education leads to appeasement and the surrender of our national freedom.

Controlled-Substance Abuse.   The use of alcohol and drugs by high school students appears to be increasing. In 1984, a survey of Massachusetts high-school seniors found that 50 percent had started using drugs or alcohol in junior high school and that 29 percent had begun at age 12 or younger. Fifty-four percent of U.S. high-school seniors used marijuana and 92 percent used alcohol in 1985.

Those favoring chemical-abuse education point to the increasing use of drugs and alcohol as a national problem and insist that schools need special programs to help students deal with them. When respondents to a national survey were asked to rate five measures for dealing with the drug problem, 90 percent favored mandatory instruction in the dangers of drugs; 78 percent supported expulsion of students caught using drugs; 69 percent favored using school funds to treat drug users; 67 percent would permit school officials to search lockers; and 49 percent supported urinalysis to detect drug use (Gallup 1986, 46).

Summary.   The extent and depth of the curriculum to be included in the public schools is always in flux. Reading, while a perennial part of the curriculum, includes stories today that have different content, purposes, and vocabulary than did stories used at the beginning of the century. Beyond the more traditional basic skills, what should be included in the curriculum? Does the school have a responsibility to society? Since schools touch most future citizens, do they have a responsibility to society to remedy current problems (for example, the spread of AIDS, the increasing number of teenage mothers, and the use of drugs and controlled substances by youth)? What are the relative responsibilities of schools and of the home and religious institutions?

**ISSUE: Should competing theories be taught in public
schools even though only one is supported by scientific
evidence?**

Theories of Evolution and Creation.   In 1981, the Louisiana Legislature passed the "Balanced Treatment for Creation Science and Evolution Science Act," which required equal treatment of two views of human development. One view is based on Darwin's theory of evolution while the other is based on the biblical story of creation.

Evolution had been widely accepted by scientists as valid and taught as the only theory of how humans came upon the earth. The theory is supported by overwhelming paleontological evidence that humans and many other organisms evolved from simple to more complex forms. Arguing that creation science, like evolutionary science, is not a religious concept but a scientific one, proponents of creationism note that "the abrupt appearance of fossil categories of complex organisms and systematic gaps between different categories of fossil organisms are examples of the scientific evidence supporting their idea of biological creation" (McDonald 1986, 7).

The debate continues from a confrontation 63 years earlier in eastern Tennessee. In 1925, following a highly publicized trial, science teacher John Scopes was convicted of teaching Darwin's theory of evolution that humans and apes share a common ancestry.

For the most part, state and federal courts have rejected such "equal time" provisions for creation science and have ruled that public schools should be allowed to continue to teach evolution. In a similar vein, the Supreme Court declared the Louisiana law invalid, since there is no legitimate secular reason for teaching creationism.

A Public Divided. The public is fairly evenly divided on this issue. A Gallup Poll, conducted in 1982, found that 44 percent of Americans agreed with the statement that "God created man pretty much in his present form at one time within the last 10,000 years," while 38 percent believed humans evolved with God's help over millions of years. Only 9 percent believed that humans evolved by purely natural processes (quoted in *Education Week*, December 10, 1986, p. 7).

Two studies on college campuses found that the majority of students believed in evolution (62 percent at The Ohio State University and 89 percent at Oberlin College). However, these students supported equal time for creation science in the public schools (80 percent at OSU and 58 percent at Oberlin (*Education Week*, December 10, 1986, 7). This makes for an interesting educational dilemma and an issue for educators to consider.

Achieving Its Purpose

A number of issues concerning how schools achieve their purposes and communicate the substance of programs have embroiled educators in debate. Many of these issues involve private schools, home education, the extensiveness of public education, censorship of educational programs and materials, and the rights and responsibilities of individual students. Several of these issues are explored in this section.

ISSUE: To what extent should national, state, and local school officials control public schools? What extinuating factors impact control of schools? In what ways can balance be maintained?

Local control of education is a major issue.

While lip service continues to be paid to local control of public schools, in fact, greater and greater control by state and national bodies is occurring. This perhaps became evident to you as you read Chapter 12. While you may wish to review that chapter in analyzing this issue, one other factor, previously discussed, should be considered.

Two shifts in societal values created the climate favoring greater centralized control of schools. The first was the mounting dissatisfaction with the *quality* of education. Comparisons of U.S. students' achievement with that of students from other nations and lower student scores on national achievement and aptitude tests were sufficient evidence that the quality of schools and schooling in the U.S. was deteriorating rapidly.

The second shift in societal values was the increased demand for justice and *equality*. Beginning in the late 1950s and increasing in scope and intensity through the seventies, the federal government initiated a series of powerful legislative programs that tended to centralize categorical grants for disadvantaged and handicapped children and youth, vocational education, ethnic studies, and bilingual-bicultural education. Each of these programs had its own set of regulations, qualifications, and reporting requirements.

In 1986, a national poll asked respondents to indicate whether, in the future, they wanted more influence or less influence by federal, state, and local agencies in determining the educational program of local public schools. What can you conclude after examining the following table which summarizes their responses?

ISSUE: To what extent should public funds be spent on nonpublic schools?

Early colonial schools in America were private and were supported by tuition paid by parents. Public schools developed as a response to the need

TABLE 13.2   Desired Future Influence on Schools by Federal, State, and
Local Governments

	By Federal Government	By State Government	By Local School Boards
More influence	26%	45%	57%
Less influence	53%	32%	17%
Same as now	12%	16%	17%
Don't know	9%	7%	9%

Source: Gallup, 1986, 49–50. Used by permission.

for an educated populace and to assure separation of church and state. Public schools were supported by public taxes; private and parochial schools by private tuition. Parents who send their children to private schools, then, pay twice. They pay taxes to support public education and they pay tuition to support the private school education of their children. Opponents of aid to private schools counter with the retort, "But they *choose* to do so."

Private and Public Schools.   Studies by the National Center for Education Statistics of the U.S. Department of Education have analyzed the extensiveness of nonpublic schools in America. In 1983, they found that over 5.7 million students attended private schools, over 10 percent of all students in school (Plisko & Stern 1985, 30). In 1980, states with 15 percent or more students in private schools included Delaware, District of Columbia, Hawaii, Illinois, Louisiana, New York, Pennsylvania, Rhode Island, and Wisconsin. When private elementary and secondary schools were analyzed by affiliation, 16 percent of students attended schools that had no religious affiliation; 63.2 percent attended Catholic schools; 4.7 percent, Baptist schools; 4.4 percent, Lutheran schools; 2.3 percent, Christian schools; and 9.4 percent, other religiously-affiliated schools (Plisko 1983, 16–19).

During the past thirty years, the number of private and parochial schools has increased. When asked if this is a good or bad thing for the nation, the public approved of the increase by a 2 to 1 margin (55 percent believing the increase was good and 27 percent bad for the nation). Four years earlier, in 1981, the percent of the public who felt this was a good thing was slightly lower (49 percent), while 30 percent thought it was bad for the nation (Gallup 1985, 45). Should parents have the right to choose where to send their children to school? The rich have always had this choice and often have chosen private schools. Should those parents who are disadvantaged by their financial status also have such a choice? Are private schools divisive along religious, ethnic, or socioeconomic lines, thus posing a threat to national unity?

In *Abington* v. *Schempp*, the Supreme Court ruled against reading the Bible in public schools. In a concurring opinion in that case, Justice William Brennan wrote about the separation of private and public schools.

The public schools are supported entirely, in most communities, by public funds—funds exacted not only from parents, nor alone from those who hold particular religious views, nor indeed from those who subscribe to any creed at all. It is implicit in the history and character of American public education that the public schools serve a uniquely public function: the training of American citizens in an atmosphere free of parochial, divisive, or separatist influences of any sort—an atmosphere in which children may assimilate a heritage common to all American groups and religions (School District of Abington Township v. Schempp, 1963, 241).

Federal legislation and regulations today make available some direct financial support for private schools. Federal grants to public schools and universities often have provisions requiring participation by private schools. Should this practice be extended? Should such assistance be provided only through federal sources, or should states be permitted or required to provide assistance to private and parochial schools? Should such support be equitably distributed according to the number of students served? What impact would such a plan have on public education in America? On private and parochial schools?

Proposals for Funding Nonpublic Schools. With criticisms about the quality of public education and the need of nonpublic schools for increased revenues, several movements have emerged to circumvent the First Amendment restriction on public support of private schools and to increase the amount of tax-based income private schools could receive.

Tuition tax credits would allow individuals paying tuition to deduct from the income taxes they owe to the federal government a specified percentage of the tuition paid. In both 1982 and 1983, tuition tax credit bills were introduced in Congress but not passed. (For a cogent analysis of tuition tax credits, see Thackrey, 1984.)

Vouchers would be issued to parents, who could use them in any school—public, private, or parochial, to pay for the costs of educating their children. The school then would receive funds from the government on the basis of the number of vouchers received.

Privatization would permit school boards to contract with independent corporations for instructional services just as they now often contract for transportation, maintenance, data processing, and other services. A privatization proposal was described by Lieberman (1986) followed by a critical analysis by Mecklenburger (1986).

Proponents of such plans have argued that—

1. Parents should have a choice in the schools their children attend.
2. Public schools would improve through competition.
3. Education of American children and youth would be more effective.
4. Education could be tailored to the specific needs of individual children.

Some of the major arguments against these plans include the following:

1. They are thinly veiled ways to fund private and parochial schools and to avoid Supreme Court decisions that bar direct aid as a violation of the First Amendment.
2. They benefit the rich more than the poor. In proposals to date, tax credits generally are limited to the amount of federal taxes owed.
3. They compromise the principle of equality of educational opportunity and tend to weaken antidiscrimination legislation. Federal courts, however, have ruled that laws permitting vouchers are unconstitutional, because

states may not do indirectly what they may not do directly—support segregated schools.

4. Under voucher and tax credit plans, state standards for teacher preparation, school curriculum, and enrollment limitations probably could not be enforced by them (courts usually give priority to federal statutes over state statutes).

5. A proliferation of nonpublic schools would result, including some with extremist political, religious, and social views.

Summary. The issue of governmental support for private schools revolves around the concept of separation of church and state, rights of citizens to enjoy the privileges afforded by their tax dollars, and the responsibility of government to educate all its children and youth, regardless of their financial ability to pay for their education. Other questions are embedded in this issue, however. What are some of them? What positions have people assumed, and what support do they give for their positions?

ISSUE: Should parents have the freedom to teach their own children at home? What requirements, if any, should society impose to assure quality of such instruction?

One room in a home in Jackson, Mississippi, has tacked to its walls letters of the alphabet with biblical sayings by each. The letter *G* is followed by "God is Love" and *N* by "No man can serve two masters." A biblical time-line poster depicting Christian history winds around three walls of the room. Three children attend school here, in their home.

They are part of an estimated one million children who attend homeschools. Eighteen states require that families receive permission from local school districts to set up home-schools, and in three states (North Dakota, Iowa, and Michigan), home-schooling parents must be certified teachers.

Almost all of the nation's home-schoolers are prompted by the desire to teach religious values to their children. One advocate explained their reasoning this way: "Their religious belief is that the ultimate authority of education for their children is God, not the state. They don't want to be bound by the state." Most parents of home-schoolers are critical of public schools, citing poor results on tests, discipline problems, fear of drugs, and negative peer pressure on their children as reasons for choosing this alternative to public education. In the home-school, instruction occurs primarily through tutoring, with the teacher focusing attention on one or two students. Many parent-teachers rely on religion-oriented publishers for curriculum materials that generally cost from $100 to $200 per child per year.

Opponents of home-schools are concerned that such programs lead children into social isolation and weaken their communication skills and interaction with others. Some note that only one side of an issue is presented, leading to lack of perspective. Others claim that untrained parents cannot teach all the necessary subjects of a school. Other opponents point out that such independent actions weaken the public schools and decrease the cultural balance in the public schools.

ISSUE: At what age should the education of children begin to be supported by public funds?

This issue was clearly articulated in daily newspapers as the nation wrestled with whether or not to institute nursery-school educational programs. Those who favored such programs pointed out that, particularly for at-risk children (those from low-income families with single parents or those with handicaps), nursery-school programs reduced student failure. Those who opposed publicly supported nursery schools pointed to the costs involved and questioned whether the program was designed for all children or only for those with working parents who were seeking cheap child care.

Schools and Working Parent(s). As schooling has become more vital to America, the length of the school day, the school year, and the number of years of schooling have all increased as has the proportion of the population served. During the 1930s and 1940s, elementary-seconary education was extended in most states to twelve grades. During the following three decades, community colleges were expanded to make continuing education more readily available. Each of these expansions has cost money, and thus must be considered in terms of its cost-benefit analysis.

During the 1970s, the number of public kindergartens and nursery schools rapidly increased through the support of federal research and development funds. In 1983, 29 percent of at-risk three- and four-year-olds were enrolled in preschool programs. An issue facing educators today is this: should education be further extended to children of earlier and earlier ages? Should the expense be born by parents, or by all taxpayers?

Respondents to the 1985 Gallup Poll were about evenly divided on these issues. Forty-three percent of the public favored tax-supported child care for preschoolers while 45 percent opposed the proposal, virtually the same results as in the 1981 and 1976 surveys (Gallup 1985, 44). The 1986 Gallup Poll, however, noted a change in perception. Respondents overwhelmingly supported (80 percent) making kindergarten available as a regular part of the school, and 71 percent favored compulsory kindergartens. The public opposed by 64 percent to 29 percent having children start school at age four. In an important exception, 55 percent of nonwhites favored starting public school at age four while 35 percent opposed the idea (Gallup 1986, 55–6).

Single-Parent Homes. This issue is social as well as educational. One child in five lives in a single-parent family. More than half of all black children live with their mothers only (Riley 1986, 215). In 1980, 54 percent of mothers worked, up from 42 percent in 1970 and 36 percent in 1960. In 1983, half of all mothers with children under six had full-time or part-time jobs, compared with only 19 percent in 1960 and 30 percent in 1970 (*Education Week*, Nov. 2, 1983, 18). An estimated 10 percent of public school students are "latch-key children" who lack adult supervision each day before school, after school, or both (Riley 1986, 215).

Advocates of publicly supporting education for children at an earlier age through nursery schools and kindergartens point out that young children need positive role models and stable relationships. When parents are absent, the community—through its schools—must function as an extended family.

Extended Education.   In 1986, the National Governors' Association published *Time for Results: The Governors' 1991 Report on Education*, a comprehensive agenda for educational reform for the five-year period, 1986–1991. Three of its goals relate to extended school experiences. First, the governors recommended that kindergarten be required for all five-year-olds. Second, that high quality developmental programs be provided for at-risk four-year-olds and, where feasible, three-year-olds. Finally, they recommended in-home assistance for first-time, low-income parents of high-risk infants, noting that classes for parents on infant stimulation and early intervention (even prenatal counseling) is particularly helpful when children have multiple handicaps or hearing impairments (Riley 1986, 215–6).

The issue of extended education is bound up in a host of other questions and concerns. Are such extensions educationally sound (some argue that children develop best in a home-like environment through age eight)? Should such programs be restricted to at-risk children or open to all? Should they be publicly supported as part of the community's educational program? What standards should such programs meet (for example, in staff qualifications, teacher to pupil ratios, curriculum guidelines)?

ISSUE: Who should share in decisions concerning textbook selection—publishers, educators, parents, others? How much influence should each group have? What criteria should be used in deciding about the worth of a book or instructional resource?

▶ *A mother in Columbia, South Carolina, demanded that three books be removed from an elementary-school library. She complained that they contained profanity and questionable dialogue about subjects such as menstruation. A review committee denied the request, finding the books included sensitive, realistic treatments of puberty, divorce, and cruelty to obese children.*

▶ *A minister was incensed when a high-school librarian refused his donation of an anti-Mormon book. After weeks of fierce debate, the book was placed on the library's shelves, along with another rebutting its claims.*

▶ *In 1986, fundamentalist parents in Church Hill, Tennessee won a major victory when a federal judge ruled that students could be exempted from attending reading classes in which books were studied that their parents found religiously offensive. Books cited as objectionable included* The Wizard of Oz, *said to include witchcraft, and* The Diary of a Young Girl *by Anne Frank, in which the young Holocaust victim expressed her thoughts on religion.*

▶ *Parents in Campbell County, Wyoming, objected to the* Illustrated Encyclopedia of Family Health *on the grounds that its content was too explicit and lacked morals. After a review, the School District Committee removed the encyclopedia from all libraries.*

▶ *In 1985–86, literary works such as Alice Walker's* The Color Purple, *John Steinbeck's* Of Mice and Men, *and Arthur Miller's* Death of a Salesman *were attacked for "objectionable" language. Shakespeare's* Macbeth *was attacked for dealing with witchcraft and Satanism, and* Romeo and Juliet *for promoting teen suicide and drug abuse. Even dictionaries have been banned in two communities. (Summarized from* People for the American Way, *1986. Reprinted with permission.)*

Self-appointed censorship committees regularly comb through textbooks to identify those with inaccurate content, liberal messages, profanity, and offensive themes and passages they deem improper for children and youth to read. Biology books that include information on evolution are popular targets, as are drug prevention and sex education programs, which opponents claim undermine parental authority and do not teach absolute values. Findings of these groups are reported directly to state textbook committees and local school boards, and when subsequent actions are not acceptable, these groups take legal action.

While parent groups, environmentalists, churches, and patriotic organizations have reviewed textbooks for years, the reasons for censoring books, and censoring itself, has increased in the past decade. One publisher of children's books noted that in the sixties publishers worried about such things as passages in which parents drank beer. Everything changed in the seventies, during which writers championed the "new realism" and explored everything from alcoholism to sex. During the eighties, a conservative trend has led to severe criticisms of books published a decade earlier and a reconsideration of the criteria used as the basis for their adoption.

The American Library Association has tracked censorship incidents for over twenty years. During 1980–1981, the number of such episodes quadrupled to about 1,000 per year and has stablized at this figure. A report by People for the American Way, *Attacks on the Freedom to Learn*, lists 130 censorship attempts that took place in 44 states during the 1985–86 school year. This was an increase of 35 percent over the previous year and over twice as many as for 1982.

These efforts are making an impact. According to *Attacks on the Freedom to Learn*, 39 percent of the incidents in 1985–86 resulted in removal or restricted use of the materials. Further, some textbooks are not adopted when reviewing bodies call attention to certain features, and publishers regularly modify the content and structure of unpublished manuscripts to make them more acceptable to censorship groups.

Those engaged in censorship defend their right to do so in order to protect their children. They believe they have as much right to select textbooks as do librarians, teachers, and other reviewers—and, further, that they are responsibile for the moral development of their children.

Opponents of censorship believe it causes information gaps, not only in libraries but also in school textbooks. A spokesman for the National Council of Teachers of English pointed out that evolution is not even discussed in one-sixth of all biology textbooks and the importance of Christianity to the development of the nation is ignored in most American history texts. Others are concerned that one or two parents may be able to dictate to whole communities. "Banning any book is a violation of the First Amendment," said a sixteen-year-old. "Sure, there's profanity and sex in it, but you hear worse in school halls."

*T*his is a time for courage and a time of challenge. Neither conformity nor complacency will do. Neither the fanatics nor the faint-hearted are needed.

John Kennedy in a speech to have been delivered in Austin the day following his assassination. Reprinted in Jenkins, 1963, 15.

Conclusion

After reading about many of the issues facing our society and subsequently our schools, you may be feeling overwhelmed by the scope of a society in transition. More than any other group, teachers are on the cutting edge of shaping new generations. More than lawyers, accountants, or computer programmers, teachers have the opportunity to shape the future. The words of President John F. Kennedy are as real today as they were when they were spoken in 1961:

> Ask not what your country can do for you. Ask what you can do for your country.

Understanding some of the issues with which our society is grappling, and being able to place school events and decisions in that perspective is part of being a professional reflective inquirer. This chapter and the related study and discussion will introduce you to some issues, sensitize you to the variety of viewpoints to which you will be exposed, and facilitate the development of your own positions and actions. Hopefully, it will be the beginning of a lifelong process of reflecting on issues of great importance to the future of education.

Teaching provides an opportunity to have an impact on the minds of youth who are the future leaders and citizens of our nation. This opportunity is unique to the teaching profession. The foundation of our society in years to come is being built in today's classrooms. You have the opportunity to shape and build this future.

Building Reflective Inquiry Skills

In their book, Models of Teaching, Bruce Joyce and Marsha Weil describe an approach to teaching that has relevance not only as a model for teaching, but also as an approach to exploring the issues raised herein and throughout education. The jurisprudential model was first devised by Donald Oliver and James Shaver to help students analyze and take positions on public issues. They wanted to help students learn to be objective, to act as unbiased judges considering all the evidence.

As you review educational issues, you will note three types of problems: definitional problems, value problems, and factual problems. Definitional problems involve the clarification of words. Often, conflicts in discussions of educational issues revolve around confusing or ambiguous use of words. Until clarity of language is established, the basic issue will continue to be confusing. What is meant by key words in the question within which an issue is posed? Joyce and Weil suggest three ways to clarify communication. "[P]articipants may: (1) appeal to common usage by finding out how most people use a word or by consulting a dictionary; (2) stipulate the meaning of the word for purposes of discussion by listing the agreed criteria; (3) obtain more facts about an example to see if it meets the agreed criteria for a definition" (1986, 266).

When conflicts over values occur, clarification of values, issues, or legal principles is required in order to determine perceptions by those espousing each position of right or wrong, good or bad, or correct or incorrect. Everyone continually makes value judgements—some more important than others. We believe in honesty, "a day's work for a day's pay," the role of government or churches in education, and justice. We also prefer certain clothes, recreational activities, music, and people. Joyce and Weil refer to the latter as "personal preferences" rather than values.

They point out that persons "make decisions on issues involving values because they believe (1) certain consequences will occur; (2) other consequences will be avoided; or (3) important social values will be violated if the decision is not made" (1986, 266). Clarifying the predicted consequences of an issue is one approach to resolving the issue. Another is to compromise a little of each value when two conflict. Oliver and Shaver refer to ideal values—those of absolute value that are either held or not, and to dimensional values—these that have degrees of desirable conditions. Even though various individuals considering an issue may prefer their own specific stances on the issue (ideal position), Oliver and Shaver recommend that some balance be attempted by compromising somewhat on each position. One way to do this is by clarifying the reasons and assumptions undergirding each position. Another is to rely on factual data, and if these data are in dispute, to resolve problems of fact.

Factual problems involve establishing the reality or reliability of conflicting information. Oliver and Shaver suggest two ways to resolve conflicts of fact: "(1) by evoking more specific claims, and (2) by relating it to other general facts accepted as true" (Oliver and Shaver, 1966/1974, 103–104, as guided in Joyce & Weil 1986, 266–267).

Joyce and Weil identified six phases in Oliver and Shaver's jurisprudential inquiry model. The issue is introduced in phase 1, and clarified in phase 2 through synthesizing facts, identifying values and value conflicts, and considering underlying factual and definitional questions. In phase 3, positions are taken on the issue, and in phase 4, the various positions are clarified through establishing points at which different values are violated, clarifying value conflicts with analogies, and setting priorities among values. Phase 5 consists of refining and qualifying various positions, while phase 6 further tests factual assumptions by checking their relevancy and determining predicted consequences of various positions, even under the most extreme conditions (Joyce & Weil 1986, 268–269).

Several phases require confrontation among various positions, which in turn leads to greater understanding of the issue. In discussing issues, it is important that all views are respected and that the focus of the issue be clearly and sharply maintained. The intellectual climate should encourage supporting documentation of varying positions.

Explorations

Exploration 1
Considering the Issues
Prior to reading this chapter, react to the following questions. There are no right or wrong answers. You may alter your responses after reading the chapter or thinking about your answers. Think about what factors you consider in making your choices. You might even want to jot these down for later reference.

1. Which of the following basic purposes for schooling do you consider most important? Rank them from highest (1) to lowest (8).

___ Teach the basic skills of reading, writing, and arithmetic.

___ Teach problem solving.

___ Transmit the basic values of America to its youth.

___ Provide a basis for lifelong learning.

___ Provide the foundation for a vocation.

___ Teach students how to learn.

___ Teach the great ideas of the past.

___ Improve society by equalizing the educational opportunities of all its citizens.

2. Why did you rank these purposes in this order?

_____

_____

3. In 1985, a Gallup poll asked the general public to indicate what subjects should be required of high school students. Using the following list, check those subjects that you believe should be required of all college-bound and all non-college-bound high-school students. Compare your responses with those of your classmates by calculating the percent of members of your class who would require each subject. Then compare your class responses to those found in the Gallup survey provided in Appendix B, Part 2.

Should be Required—

	For Those Who Plan To Attend College.	For Those Who Do Not Plan To Attend College.
Art	_____	_____
Business	_____	_____
Career education	_____	_____
Computer training	_____	_____
English	_____	_____
Foreign language	_____	_____
Health education	_____	_____
History/ U.S. Government	_____	_____
Mathematics	_____	_____
Music	_____	_____
Physical education	_____	_____
Science	_____	_____
Vocational training	_____	_____

4. To what extent should each of the three primary institutions of society (family, school, religious institutions) be responsible for teaching each of the following topics to children and youth?

   a. Primary responsibility for instruction
   b. Some responsibility for instruction
   c. No responsibility for instruction

In the table below, for each topic (for example, sex education), mark a, b, or c to indicate the extent to which a religious institution, then the school, then

the family should be responsible for teaching that topic under ideal conditions. Then, using the same scale, consider the extent of responsibility when taking into account the reality of conditions in society today. Finally, specify the age at which initial instruction should begin.

You might wish to make notes of your reasoning in making these judgements to use in later discussions.

5. In the future, to what extent would you prefer the federal government to influence your local schools? (Check one.)

   _____ a. More influence
   _____ b. Less influence
   _____ c. Same as now
   _____ d. Don't know

Please specify the reasons for your selection.

_____

_____

6. In the future, to what extent would you prefer the state government to influence your local schools? (Check one.)

   _____ a. More influence
   _____ b. Less influence
   _____ c. Same as now
   _____ d. Don't know

Please specify the reasons for your selection.

_____

_____

	Under ideal conditions			Under current conditions			Age
	Religious institution	School	Family	Religious institution	School	Family	
Sex Education	_____	_____	_____	_____	_____	_____	_____
Moral Education	_____	_____	_____	_____	_____	_____	_____
Drug Education	_____	_____	_____	_____	_____	_____	_____
Alcohol Education	_____	_____	_____	_____	_____	_____	_____
Tobacco Education	_____	_____	_____	_____	_____	_____	_____
World Peace Education	_____	_____	_____	_____	_____	_____	_____
Patriotism	_____	_____	_____	_____	_____	_____	_____

7. In the future, to what extent would you prefer the local school board to influence your local schools? (Check one.)

_____ a. More influence
_____ b. Less influence
_____ c. Same as now
_____ d. Don't know

Please specify the reasons for your selection.
_____
_____

8. Should parents of children in your home community have the option of sending their children to public schools or to tax-supported private or parochial schools?

_____ a. Yes
_____ b. No

Why?
_____
_____

9. Should parents in your home community have the option of teaching their children in their own homes?

_____ a. Yes
_____ b. No

Why?
_____
_____

List the requirements you would impose on such instruction if it were permitted.

10. At what age should tax-supported education be begun for all students?

_____ a. Birth
_____ b. Age 1
_____ c. Age 2
_____ d. Age 3
_____ e. Age 4
_____ f. Age 5
_____ g. Age 6

What reasons prompted you to choose this age?
_____
_____

Would you support beginning school earlier for disadvantaged or at-risk students?

_____ a. Yes
_____ b. No

If you answered yes, at what age should school begin for them?

_____ Age

Why?
_____
_____

11. School boards usually decide on the specific textbooks to be used after reviewing the recommendations of professional educators. Textbooks have been analyzed and openly criticized by various groups in America (parent groups, religious groups, patriotic groups). Do you believe such special-interest groups should have any influence on such decisions? To what extent?

_____ a. None at all.
_____ b. Positions of such groups should be made available to decision makers.
_____ c. Such groups should have the opportunity to speak to decision makers about their views and rationales.
_____ d. Decision makers should be required to consider the views of all such groups when considering textbook adoption.

Exploration 2
Debating the Issues

Organize debates on one or more of the issues in this chapter. Each team is composed of two persons, but several teams could work together to build their case.

A debate consists of eight short speeches—four presentations of five minutes each and four rebuttals of two minutes each. The affirmative case is presented in the first five-minute presentation, followed by a five-minute presentation by the opposing team, then the affirmative team's second speaker, and finally, the opposing team's second speaker. Rebuttals are two-minutes each, with one member of the opposing team speaking first.

Following the debate, all four persons discuss the debate and the issue being considered. This provides a process for extending understanding.

Teams taking one side in a debate assume the opposite in the next debate. A class can have several debates transpiring at the same time. There are no winners or losers declared at the end of debates.

Exploration 3
Fish Bowl

Four to six persons are seated in the center of the group (the "fish bowl") to discuss an issue, while the other members of the group observe the discussion. Those outside the fish bowl may observe and listen but may not participate in the discussion.

In one variation, a person on the outside may participate by putting himself or herself in the fish bowl. In another variation, the outside group can ask clarifying questions, but not make statements. Debates described in Exploration 2 can also be conducted in a fish bowl. At the end of the discussion, the entire class may discuss the issue and the major points of each position.

References

Brown v. Board of Education, 347 U.S. 483, 493, 74 S.Ct. 686, 691 (1954).

Cohen, D. K. (1984). . . . the condition of teachers' work . . . *Harvard Educational Review, 54*(1), 11–15.

Cuban, L. (1986). Sex and school reform. *Phi Delta Kappan. 68*(4), 319–21.

Dewey, J. (1938). *Experience & Education* Bloomington, IN: Kappa Delta Pi.

ECS Business Advisory Commission. (1985). *Reconnecting Youth.* Denver: Education Commission of the States.

Ekstrom, R. B., Goertz, M. E., Pollack, J. M. & Rock, D. A. (1986). Who drops out of high school and why? Findings from a national study. *Teachers College Record.* Spring, 356–73.

Education Week. (1986). Nobody home: Social shifts spur early-childhood initiatives. *Education Week.* November 2, 1983, 1; 18.

Gallup, G. (1985). The 17th annual Gallup Poll of the public's attitudes toward the public schools. *Phi Delta Kappan. 67*(1), 35–47.

Gallup, G. (1986). The 18th annual Gallup Poll of the public's attitudes toward the public schools. *Phi Delta Kappan. 68*(1), 43–59.

Jenkins, J. H. (1963). *Neither the fanatics nor the fainthearted.* Austin: Pemberton Press.

Joyce, B. & Weil, M. (1986). *Models of Teaching.* Englewood Cliffs, NJ: Prentice-Hall.

Landers, A. (1986). Ann Landers. *Houston Chronicle,* January 9, 1986, p. 2, sec. 5.

Lau v. Nichols, 414 U.S. 563, 94 S.Ct. 786 (1974).

Lieberman, M. (1986). Privatization and public education. *Phi Delta Kappan. 67*(10), 731–34.

Mecklenburger, J. A. (1986). A diamond in the rough? *Phi Delta Kappan. 67*(10), 735–37.

McDonald, K. (1986). Pervasive belief in 'Creation Science' dismays and perplexes researchers. *Education Week.* December 10, 1986.

National Education Association. (1984). Education 84. *Today's Education.* 80–95.

Oliver, D. & Shaver, J. P. (1966). *Teaching public issues in the high school.* Boston: Houghton Mifflin.

Passow, A. H. (1984). Tackling the reform reports of the 1980s. *Phi Delta Kappan, 65*(10), 674–83.

People for the American Way. (1986). *Attacks on the Freedom to Learn.* Washington, D.C.: People for the American Way.

Plisko, V. W. (1983). *The Condition of Education, 1983 Edition.* Washington, D.C.: U.S. Department of Education, National Center for Educational Statistics.

Plisko, V. W. & Stern, J. D. (1985). *The Condition of Education, 1985 Edition.* Washington, D.C.: U.S. Department of Education, National Center for Educational Statistics.

Riley, R. W. (1986). Can we reduce the risk of failure? *Phi Delta Kappan. 68*(4), 214–9.

School District of Abington Township, Pennsylvania et al. v. Schempp et al., 374 U.S. 203 (1963).

Strother, D. B. (1986). Suicide among the young. *Phi Delta Kappan. 67*(10), 756–59.

Thackrey, R. I. (1984). Some things you may want to know about tuition tax credits. *Phi Delta Kappan. 66(1), 62–65.*

Toffler, A. (1980). *The third wave.* New York: William Morrow.

Don't Trip on the Threshold

OBJECTIVES

By the end of this chapter, you will be able to:

1. Identify the general requirements of the remainder of your preparation program.
2. Discuss professional organizations for teachers and the roles they can play in helping you grow as a professional.
3. Reflect on a personal code of ethics for teaching.
4. Identify means of collecting information for qualifying to teach in various states.

KEY WORDS AND CONCEPTS

Code of ethics
Endorsement
Professional organizations
Teacher supply and demand
Teacher unions
Teaching certificate

In this chapter we explore the paths that will take you from a student of teaching to teacher. First we revisit the decisions you have made at this point about teaching. Now that you have had some experience working in schools and working with teachers, you are ready to make some decisions about the events that will help you become a career teacher. In light of those decisions we discuss the rest of your program and becoming a teacher. The latter part of this chapter focuses on professional development, for as we have implied many times in this text, learning to teach is a process, not a product. Finally, we provide you with means to investigate the possibility of qualifying to teach in various states.

One of the primary purposes in your first course in education is to provide you with information on which to base an informed decision about becoming a teacher. The very personal questions you must address are these:

▶ Do I really want to teach?
▶ Does teaching seem to be a role in which I can grow as a person and benefit the students for whom I will be responsible?
▶ Am I willing to make the necessary commitments to prepare for that role?

Only you can answer those questions, and they take considerable thought. Once you have made that choice in the affirmative, though, and have decided to continue preparing to become a teacher, questions will arise about what will be expected of you in the remainder of your program.

The Rest of Your Program

The purpose of this section is to give you some general ideas about what to anticipate. We have to be cautious, however, because academic programs for teacher preparation vary across the country according to the type of teaching certificate (and perhaps endorsements to that certificate) you want to obtain, individual requirements of the various states, and requirements of the college or university you are attending. Your program may be part of a baccalaureate degree, post-baccalaureate, a five-year program, or a fifth-year program. Patterns vary but the program components are similar. Emphases may differ but the requirements are similar.

How Teacher-Education Programs are Structured

Your preparation to enter the teaching profession will include at least the following elements.

General or Liberal Education. Clearly, teachers must be more than narrow specialists in a particular discipline. To be effective as a teacher at any level and in any specialization, you must know something of cultural heritage, cultural differences and the impact they have on individual development, English, and basic computational skills. You must, in short, be broadly educated. The general education portion of your program will constitute the equivalent of at least two years. If you already hold a baccalaureate degree, you probably completed this as part of that program.

Teaching Specialty.   For middle-school and secondary teachers, one or more content areas form your teaching specialization(s). Elementary teachers usually have a content specialization also, sometimes as a "minor" in your program. This is usually a subject taught in the elementary school, such as mathematics, science, English-language arts, and so on, but may be an interdisciplinary major. The teaching specialty for secondary teachers is usually the major academic field (for example, business education, chemistry, French).

Professional Education.   Research on teaching indicates that not all teaching techniques are equally effective with all ages of students, in all contexts, nor in all subjects. Professional education includes the study of learning theory, cultural foundations, and instructional strategies. Middle-school and secondary teachers are required to study teaching methods in their specific teaching field or fields. Elementary teachers normally are prepared to teach in a broad range of subjects and generally complete coursework and other types of experiences in the teaching of reading, English-language arts, mathematics, science, social studies, art, music, and physical education. Teachers also explore learning theory, cultural foundations, multicultural education, and human growth and development as foundations for teaching. These foundations provide the substantive bases for translating knowledge of the behavioral sciences into teaching. One must know students and be sensitive to the nuances of their actions, their motivations, their needs, their backgrounds, and their dreams. Foundations provide knowledge and skills to better understand these elements.

Clinical Experiences.   During your teacher preparation program you will work with elementary and/or secondary students in schools. Initially, these experiences provide opportunities for general understanding of teaching and for determining whether or not you wish to become a teacher. Several of the activities suggested in this book are designed for these purposes. Quickly, however, school experiences become increasingly task-oriented as you begin to tutor individual students, teach small groups, and perhaps teach full classes under the supervision of a teacher. Near the end of your program, during student teaching or internship, you will be expected to demonstrate your ability to integrate earlier preparation as you teach under supervision.

Types of Certificates

Teaching certificates or *licenses* are issued by each state based on rules and regulations established by the legislature and state education agency of that state. They identify persons who have completed a specified training program and have met all of the stipulated requirements. Employment often is limited to certificate holders.

Endorsements define special expertise for a certificate holder. For example, one teacher may hold an elementary school certificate with kindergarten and bilingual endorsements. This teacher is certified to teach in elementary schools; he or she also may teach kindergarten, bilingual classes at any level of an elementary school, or bilingual kindergartens.

A certificate or license to teach is limited in scope; that is, no single certificate permits a person to teach everything at all levels. Different states have different classes of initial teaching certificates, and the differences are so complex that you are best advised to consult your college or university to find out the different types offered in your state and through your particular institution. Generally, though, several types of certificates are issued.

Early Childhood. This may be a certificate or an endorsement to an elementary certificate. Usually completion of an early childhood program qualifies you to teach preschool through the second or third grade.

Kindergarten. This is usually an endorsement to an elementary certificate which qualifies you to teach in kindergarten classrooms.

Elementary. Elementary certificates in some states qualify holders to teach in grades 1 through 8; in others, grades 1 through 5 or grades 1 through 6.

Middle School/Junior High School. Some states offer specific certificates for middle-school teachers, but not all teacher-education institutions in those states offer such programs. Middle-school certificates generally qualify one to teach grades 5 through 8 or 9 or grades 6 through 8 or 9.

Secondary. Secondary certificates typically qualify holders to teach a specific subject or subjects in secondary schools. Some permit instruction in grades 6 through 12, but most limit secondary certification to grades 9 through 12.

In addition to programs which prepare an individual with the necessary qualifications for an initial license, one may prepare for a number of more specialized areas.

Special Education. Special education teachers are those who work with students who have one or more handicapping conditions. Such conditions include (but are not limited to) speech pathology, deaf or hearing impaired, emotionally disturbed, physically impaired, mentally retarded, or combinations of handicapping conditions. Special education teachers tend to be in high demand in most parts of the country.

Reading Specialists. Reading is one of the most fundamental skills needed for success in school. In most states individuals are in demand who are specialists in helping classroom teachers improve the reading skills of their students, or who work directly with individual students who experience difficulty in reading.

Bilingual Education. Bilingual teachers may help students whose first language is not English by instructing them in their native language. Typically, this is Spanish. The United States is the sixth largest Spanish-speaking nation on earth and experiences continuous immigration from Mexico, Puerto Rico, and other areas where the primary language is Spanish. Expertise in Spanish is normally a prerequisite for admission to bilingual education programs; however, the children with whom bilingual teachers work rarely communicate in the Castilian dialect normally learned in school or college. Dialects can differ greatly depending on the nation of origin and even the social class within that nation.

English as a Second Language. Many languages other than Spanish are spoken in schools. Especially in urban areas, the diversity of primary languages spoken by students is such that individuals are needed to teach them in English, but with special skills in teaching English as a second language (ESL). While bilingual teachers teach students in their native language, ESL teachers teach in English.

The Decision to Specialize

Individuals often enter teacher education and decide to become a high-school mathematics teacher because they have always enjoyed math or to become an elementary teacher because they enjoy working with children.

An additional consideration in choosing a teaching specialty is the likelihood of your being able to find a position after graduation. Finding employment will be greatly affected by the needs of school systems *at the time you complete your program*, not necessarily at the moment when you make your initial choice. As an example, you may be thinking right now that you would like to prepare to teach sociology and psychology in high school. The problem is that very few high schools offer sufficient numbers of such courses to make employing someone with *only* these qualifications practical. Begin now to collect data you will need in order to make teaching specialty decisions later. Here are some suggestions.

1. Interview teachers about their career choices. Do they wish they had prepared for additional, specialized educational positions in their teacher-preparation programs? Have they completed additional work since receiving their initial certificate to qualify them for other educational specializations?
2. Most colleges and universities have placement centers to help their students find appropriate positions. Visit your placement center or placement specialist (specifically in education, if available) and talk with her or him about anticipated needs in the teaching force at the time you expect to complete your program.
3. Become familiar with the requirements for the specific program you are pursuing and also for programs that could qualify you in additional areas. What will it cost you in terms of time, energy, and money to broaden your potential personal marketability as a teacher? To qualify you with endorsements or other certificates? The best sources for such information include the catalog of your college or university and advisors in your school, college, or department of education.

Available Teaching Jobs

More than 2.4 million people teach in public and private schools in America, making teaching the largest professional group in the nation. As Figure 14.1 shows, an increasing number of new teachers are needed. The proportion of college graduates completing teaching-certificate requirements declined by more than half during the 1970s and early eighties. The net effect is an increasing gap between the supply and demand for fully qualified elementary and secondary teachers, at least for the immediate future.

The need for more teachers was felt first in elementary schools (beginning in 1986), while secondary school enrollments—and corresponding needs for secondary teachers—will likely rise after 1988. The greatest needs are in six fields: bilingual education (8.8 new teachers needed per 1,000 current teachers), special education of the speech impaired (6.3 new teachers per 1,000 current teachers), unspecified special education positions (5.0 new per 1,000 current), special education of the seriously emotionally disturbed (3.7 per 1,000), physics (4.5 per 1,000), and computer science (3.7 per 1,000). For comparison, school districts in 1983 reported fewer than 2 shortages (1.6) for every 1,000 current teachers. The

**FIGURE 14.1
Demand for Additional Teachers and Supply of New Teacher Graduates, 1980–1993**

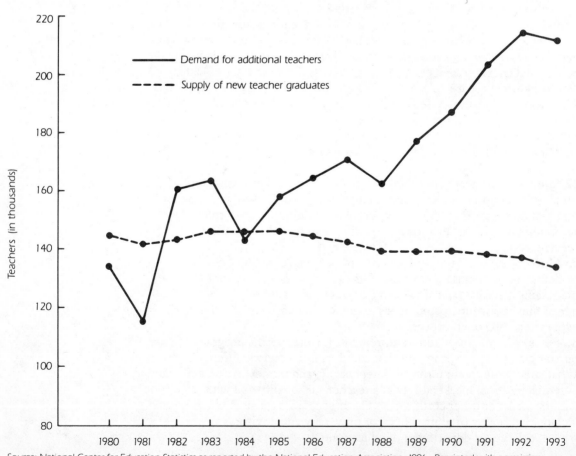

Source: National Center for Education Statistics as reported by the National Education Association, 1986. Reprinted with permission.

greatest shortages, when considering the actual number of teachers, were in special education and elementary education (Plisko & Stern 1985, 146).

Teacher Salaries

College graduates who select careers other than teaching often cite low teacher salaries as a major reason for not entering the teaching field. When beginning salaries for all graduates with a bachelor's degree were compared, teachers' salaries were about 20 percent lower than those offered to engineering, mathematics, and liberal arts majors in 1981. Researchers caution, however, that teacher salaries are for nine or ten months per year, while the other fields are normally quoted on twelve-month contracts (Plisko & Stern 1985, 141–2).

Annual salaries of teachers vary considerably across the nation. In 1986–87, the average teacher's salary rose to $26,704, up 5.9 percent over 1985–86 and up 30 percent in four years. While Alaska paid the most ($43,970), California, Michigan, New York, and Rhode Island paid average teacher salaries of more than $30,000. Table 14.1 includes the average salary for each state, the change from the previous year, and the state's rank.

In short, we agree with Arthur Wise's summary statement in his Foreword to a recent RAND Corporation study: "In absolute terms, teaching has indisputably become a more desirable occupation. Real salaries have increased and working conditions have generally improved (Sedlak & Schlossman 1986, iii)."

There IS Life after Certification!

The end of your first course in preparing to be a teacher is not too early to begin thinking about the career you will have once you are fully certified. The process of becoming a teacher has just begun. A preservice preparation program only provides a background. Once you have completed your preparation program the best that can be said is that you are a safe "beginner." Much of the responsibility for your own professional development beyond the initial certificate and entrance to the profession is yours.

In this concluding section we look at your first year of teaching, at developing a personal code of professional ethics, at the benefits of joining professional organizations for teachers, and at ways of gaining information about teaching in other parts of the country.

Enjoying the first year

If we have been at all successful in our goals as authors of this text, you already know one of the first steps toward enjoying your first year of teaching: learn as much as you can about the community in which your students live before you begin to think about instruction. Conduct a personal community study and use that information to guide your thoughts as you begin to examine the curriculum you will be using.

TABLE 14.1   Average Teacher Salaries, 1986–1987

State	Average Salary *1986–1987*	Change *1985–86 to 1986–87*	Rank
Alabama	$23,500	2.0%	31
Alaska	43,970	6.0	1
Arizona	26,280	6.5	21
Arkansas	19,951	2.1	48
California	31,170	7.0	4
Colorado	27,388	5.8	17
Connecticut	28,902	8.6	8
Delaware	27,467	11.5	15
Florida	23,785	6.9	28
Georgia	24,200	5.0	26
Hawaii	26,815	3.8	18
Idaho	21,469	2.4	44
Illinois	28,430	5.7	10
Indiana	25,684	5.6	23
Iowa	22,603	4.2	38
Kansas	23,550	4.0	30
Kentucky	22,612	7.9	37
Louisiana	21,280	4.0	46
Maine	21,257	8.5	47
Maryland	28,700	7.1	9
Massachusetts	28,410	6.0	11
Michigan	31,500	5.0	3
Minnesota	29,140	6.5	6
Mississippi	19,575	6.0	49
Missouri	23,468	6.9	32
Montana	23,206	3.2	34
Nebraska	22,063	5.4	39
Nevada	26,030	1.6	22
New Hampshire	21,869	7.9	41
New Jersey	28,927	6.5	7
New Mexico	23,977	9.9	27
New York	32,620	7.0	2
North Carolina	23,775	6.4	29
North Dakota	21,848	5.0	42
Ohio	26,317	5.2	20
Oklahoma	22,060	3.0	40
Oregon	26,800	4.4	19
Pennsylvania	27,429	6.1	16
Rhode Island	31,079	5.5	5
South Carolina	23,039	6.8	35
South Dakota	18,781	3.8	50
Tennessee	22,720	6.2	36
Texas	25,308	4.5	25
Utah	23,374	3.4	33
Vermont	21,835	5.0	43
Virginia	25,473	10.3	24
Washington	27,527	5.0	14
West Virginia	21,446	4.0	45
Winsonsin	28,206	7.1	12
Wyoming	27,708	1.8	13
Total/Average	26,704	5.9	

Source: NEA Research. *Estimates of School Statistics, 1986–87.* Used by Permission.

Once you arrive at the school, develop personal relationships with other teachers who share responsibilities similar to yours and begin to plan for your first day and beyond. As we mentioned in Chapter 10, the first day can be a crucial point for first-year teachers because it establishes your ex-

Teachers use their skills
in a variety of settings,
both urban . . .

. . . and rural.

pectations for the students and establishes their expectations of you. Since classroom management is often a concern for first-year teachers (Veenman 1984), beginning the first day in an organized manner may help alleviate this concern (Brooks 1985).

As we discussed in earlier chapters, planning for instruction and evaluating your own instruction is also important. This is another common problem for first year teachers (Johnston & Ryan 1983), but it is not an insurmountable problem. Many of the suggestions offered in this text will help you, but do not hesitate to ask for additional assistance from other teachers and from former instructors. Although new teachers sometimes feel isolated, without opportunity for interaction (Lortie 1980), in most schools this is *not* the case (Little 1982; Rutter 1983), and individual teachers within all schools will be able to respond to your questions and ideas.

If you complete your first year of teaching with the distinct impression that you owe the school system some of your salary back, please do not feel alone. Most strong, reflective, caring teachers do feel that way.

Developing a Personal Code of Ethics

One of the responsibilities incumbent on any professional in any realm of endeavor is the issue of professional ethics. Teaching offers numerous opportunities to be high minded and moral, but it offers challenges as well which twinge the conscience. Here are but three hypothetical situations:

▶ Discussion in the teachers' lounge centers on the incompetence of another faculty member. Do you join in? If the charge of incompetence is accurate, do you do anything about it?
▶ One child reports to you that another child, who happens to be the offspring of a personal friend of yours, is in possession of illegal drugs. Last week you reported an incident concerning another child to your supervisor. What do you do this time? Does it make any difference that friendship is involved here?
▶ A high-school student, in complaining to you about the grade you assigned to him this past term, lets it slip that one of your colleagues gave him a better grade in return for a cash payment. What will you do with this information?

In days past things seemed to be much simpler. Codes of right and wrong were much more straightforward. Now we often find ourselves in situations in which the "right" answer is hardly as clear.

A number of professional organizations for teachers have formulated codes of ethics for their members because professional ethics become increasingly important and complex as society itself becomes more complex. Following is the *Code of Ethics of the Education Profession* published by the National Education Association. We encourage you to read it, study it, reflect on it, and interact with it as you formulate your own personal code of professional ethics. We encourage you to become familiar with other codes as you progress in your process of becoming a teacher. Societal values are no longer as clear-cut on many of the dilemmas teachers face, which may be as traumatic as a troubled teenager confiding to you (because she has to tell *someone*) that she is pregnant and begging you not to tell her parents; or as mundane as struggling with how to grade a paper that you believe was plagiarized though you have no direct evidence of plagiarism.

EXHIBIT 14.1   National Education Association Code of Ethics of the Education Profession

---

Preamble

The educator, believing in the worth and dignity of each human being, recognizes the supreme importance of the pursuit of truth, devotion to excellence, and the nurture of democratic principles. Essential to these goals is the protection of freedom to learn and to teach and the guarantee of equal educational opportunity for all. The educator accepts the responsibility to adhere to the highest ethical standards.

The educator recognizes the magnitude of the responsibility inherent in the teaching process. The desire for the respect and confidence of one's colleagues, of students, of parents, and of the members of the community provides the incentive to attain and maintain the highest possible degree of ethical conduct. The Code of Ethics of the Education Profession indicates the aspiration of all educators and provides standards by which to judge conduct.

The remedies specified by the NEA and/or its affiliates for the violation of any provision of this Code shall be exclusive and no such provision shall be enforceable in any form other than one specifically designated by the NEA or its affiliates.

PRINCIPLE I

Commitment to the Student

The educator strives to help each student realize his or her potential as a worthy and effective member of society. The educator therefore works to stimulate the spirit of inquiry, the acquisition of knowledge and understanding, and the thoughtful formulation of worthy goals.

In fulfillment of the obligation to the student, the educator—

1. Shall not unreasonably restrain the student from independent action in the pursuit of learning.
2. Shall not unreasonably deny the student access to varying points of view.
3. Shall not deliberately suppress or distort subject matter relevant to the student's progress.
4. Shall make reasonable effort to protect the student from conditions harmful to learning or to health and safety.
5. Shall not intentionally expose the student to embarrassment or disparagement.
6. Shall not on the basis of race, color, creed, sex, national origin, marital status, political or religious beliefs, family, social or cultural background, or sexual orientation, unfairly—
   a.   Exclude any student from participation in any program
   b.   Deny benefits to any student
   c.   Grant any advantage to any student.
7. Shall not use professional relationships with students for private advantage.
8. Shall not disclose information about students obtained in the course of professional service, unless disclosure serves a compelling professional purpose or is required by law.

PRINCIPLE II

Commitment to the Profession

The education profession is vested by the public with a trust and responsibility requiring the highest ideals of professional service.

In the belief that the quality of the services of the education profession directly influences the nation and its citizens, the educator shall exert every effort to raise professional standards, to promote a climate that encourages the exercise of professional judgment, to achieve conditions which attract persons worthy of the trust to careers in education, and to assist in preventing the practice of the profession by unqualified persons.

In fulfillment of the obligation to the profession, the educator—

1. Shall not in an application for a professional position deliberately make a false statement or fail to disclose a material fact related to competency and qualifications.

2. Shall not misrepresent his/her professional qualifications.

3. Shall not assist any entry into the profession of a person known to be unqualified in respect to character, education, or other relevant attribute.

4. Shall not knowingly make a false statement concerning the qualifications of a candidate for a professional position.

5. Shall not assist a noneducator in the unauthorized practice of teaching.

6. Shall not disclose information about colleagues obtained in the course of professional service unless disclosure serves a compelling professional purpose or is required by law.

7. Shall not knowingly make false or malicious statements about a colleague.

8. Shall not accept any gratuity, gift, or favor that might impair or appear to influence professional decisions or action.

Teaching is a very human enterprise. It involves daily interaction with young people in the setting of a social institution established to help society's young grow and learn attitudes and skills needed to improve the human condition. Your personal values will be tested in that professional setting and will need to be molded into a system of values that provides you with a sense of integrity as a person and as a professional.

Professional Organizations for Teachers

Because the education industry in the United States is so large, encompassing so many people of varying interests and specializations, a variety of professional organizations for teachers have emerged. These are usually divided into teacher associations, or unions, and subject-matter specialist groups.

The two largest and most powerful teacher associations, or unions, are the National Education Association (NEA) and the American Federation of Teachers (AFT), which is affiliated with the American Federation of Labor/Congress of Industrial Organizations (AFL/CIO). In states allowing collective bargaining for public employees, one of these two is usually the collective bargaining agent for teachers in a given school district. These organizations work for better salaries and working conditions for their members, which is by no means to suggest that they ignore the wellbeing of students. Elements of negotiation between union and school-district representatives often focus on class size, the provision of better services for students, and matters of academic freedom as well as salaries and working conditions. Leaders of both organizations have been active in national educational reform movements discussed earlier in this text. A major thrust of both NEA and AFT is increasing the professional status of teachers and providing teachers with greater autonomy in matters that affect their professional lives and their students.

Membership in NEA (1.7 million) is approximately three times the membership of AFT (600,000), but AFT has gained considerable strength in major urban areas over the past two decades including status as the only bargaining agent for teachers in Chicago, New York City, Washington, D.C., and other major cities. In addition to bargaining for teacher salaries, benefits, and working conditions, both AFT and NEA provide members with a variety of services, including research support, insurance programs, legal support, travel programs, investment opportunities, and many others. At the state and local levels these organizations sponsor opportunities for professional growth of their members through inservice training, provide assistance to teachers whose rights may be endangered, and generally work to improve the status of teachers.

In addition, a number of organizations have arisen that center around teacher commonalities in subject matter and other forms of specialization: the National Council for the Social Studies, the National Council of Teachers of Mathematics, and the National Council of Teachers of English are only three examples. These organizations sponsor publications, conventions, workshops, and communication among their members to improve the teaching of those subjects. Most have state, regional, and local affiliates as well, which work to promote improvement in the teaching of these disciplines. Almost every one of these organizations publishes at least one journal that serves as a primary device for communicating research and new ideas for teaching.

One example may prove helpful. The National Council for the Social Studies (NCSS) is headquartered in Washington, D.C. but has state and local affiliate organizations across the country. Social studies is an important component in the curricula of elementary and secondary schools in every state, and elements of it (citizenship, history, government, and so forth) are taught at literally every grade level.

NCSS's national journal, *Social Education*, devotes much of its space to ideas for teaching social studies concepts, new print and media materials available in the social studies, sample lesson plans and activities, curricular ideas for incorporating African culture (for example) in social studies lessons, and debates about controversial issues in the social studies. NCSS sponsors a national convention each November, which is attended by thousands of teachers interested in the social studies and at which ideas are shared, new materials exhibited, and common interests fostered. In addition, NCSS state affiliates sponsor annual meetings at which members in each state compare ideas and discuss the most recent directions for social studies education in the context of that particular state. State and local organizations may also lobby the state legislature or state board of education on issues affecting social studies education in that particular state.

Other professional organizations for teachers are engaged in similar activities for their members on a continual basis. We believe that active involvement with others of like interests through professional organization activity is a primary mode for continuing your professional development as a teacher. Following is a list of the mailing addresses of the national offices of a number of professional organizations. We encourage you to write to them and ask for information about membership costs and benefits and for information about state, regional, and local affiliates with which you may wish to become involved.

EXHIBIT 14.2   A Partial List of Organizations for Teachers

American Alliance for Health, Physical Education,
Recreation and Dance
1900 Association Drive
Reston, VA 22091

American Federation of Teachers (AFL–CIO)
555 New Jersey Avenue, N.W.
Washington, DC 20001

Association for Educational Communication and
Technology
1126 16th Street, N.W.
Washington, DC 20036

Association for Supervision and Curriculum Development
125 North West Street
Alexandria, VA 22314

Council for Exceptional Children
1920 Association Drive
Reston, VA 22091

International Reading Association
800 Barksdale
P.O. Box 8139
Newark, DE 19711

National Association for Bilingual Education
Room 405, 1201 16th Street, N.W.
Washington, DC 20036

National Association for the Education of Young Children
1824 Connecticut Avenue, N.W.
Washington, DC 20009

National Council of Teachers of English
1111 Kenyon Road
Urbana, IL 61801

National Council for the Social Studies
3501 Newark Street, N.W.
Washington, DC 20016

National Council of Teachers of Mathematics
1906 Association Drive
Reston, VA 22091

National Education Association
1201 16th Street, N.W.
Washington, DC 20036

National Science Teachers Association
1742 Connecticut Avenue, N.W.
Washington, DC 20009

By the way, virtually all of these professional organizations have special student-membership fees which are much reduced and offer a number of benefits beyond their minimal cost. Those benefits are supported out of the dues of the full professional members, which subsidize student-membership benefits.

Teaching in the Various States

Once you have completed your preparation program and are fully certified, the time comes for you to seek a position in which to use the professional skills you have learned. In Chapter 5 we discussed the physical mobility of Americans. Movement from location to location is more common than not. As a result, you are unlikely to teach in one place for the entirety of your career. Since each state controls its own requirements for the certification of teachers, how can you find out about the requirements in other states?

We want to offer you some assistance here. Appendix D is a list of teacher certification offices in the various states from which you can solicit information about what would be required to convert a teaching certificate earned in the state in which you complete your studies, to a certificate honored by another state.

One important element related to teaching in various states is the increasing use of standardized examinations by each state for admission to teacher-education programs and the use of exit examinations as an independent audit after program completion to qualify for a teaching certificate. Exhibit 14.3 shows those states which require examinations for admission to teacher education and/or initial certification. You may find that a state in which you wish to teach requires passage of such examinations before a certificate will be issued.

The Teacher as Learner

As we have intimated throughout this book, effective teachers do not stop learning. Research on effective teaching expands daily. New findings indicate better ways of helping different types of children gain knowledge, skills, and attitudes that are important to their development.

Certified teachers gain new knowledge and skill through staff development programs offered through their schools, by staying abreast of current literature on teaching and in their individual specializations, by involvement with others of like interests through professional organizations, and often through advanced academic coursework and graduate degrees. Effective teachers realize that they must personally take responsibility for their own continued development as professionals.

EXHIBIT 14.3   **State Examination Requirements**

States which mandate or plan entry or exit tests from education programs or for certification

State	Entrance	Exit/Certification
Alabama	*	*
Alaska		
Arizona	*	*
Arkansas		*
California	*	*
Colorado	*	*
Connecticut	*	
Delaware	*	*
District of Columbia		
Florida	*	*
Georgia		*
Hawaii		*
Idaho		
Illinois		*
Indiana		*
Iowa		*
Kansas		*
Kentucky	*	*
Louisiana	*	
Maine		*
Maryland		*
Massachusetts		*
Michigan		

EXHIBIT 14.3 **State Examination Requirements** (Continued)

States which mandate or plan entry or exit tests from education programs or for certification

State	Entrance	Exit/Certification
Minnesota	*	*
Mississippi	*	*
Missouri		*
Montana		*
Nebraska	*	
Nevada	*	
New Hampshire		*
New Jersey		*
New Mexico		*
New York		*
North Carolina		*
North Dakota		*
Ohio		
Oklahoma	*	*
Oregon	*	
Pennsylvania		*
Rhode Island		*
South Carolina	*	*
South Dakota	*	*
Tennessee	*	*
Texas	*	*
Utah		
Vermont		
Virginia		
Washington	*	
West Virginia	*	*
Wisconsin	*	*
Wyoming	*	

Source: American Association of Colleges for Teacher Education. Copyright 1986. Reprinted with permission.

Conclusion

In this book we have attempted to convey an idea of the high sense of mission, the feelings of frustration, the exhilaration and exhaustion, the celebration and hard work that is teaching. Teaching is a profession like no other. In few other professions are the clients *required* to be present. In few other professions can one person impact so many, for better or worse, over the lifetime of a career. In few other realms of endeavor can one stay so closely attuned to youthful ideas and ideals, to challenges and risks, to the cutting edge of the future.

In closing we want to restate what we have said before. We are teachers. We like teaching. We have devoted our careers to improving the quality of learning.

Touch the Future . . .
Teach!

The choice is now yours. You must decide whether to make the strong commitment necessary to become a fully qualified member of the teaching force. We have attempted here to give you a picture of the elements of teaching that are not so apparent to one in the role of student and of the growing body of knowledge about research on teaching, which we feel holds tremendous promise for improving the lives of millions.

In short, we hope you will choose to—**Touch the future: TEACH!**

Building Reflective Inquiry Skills

The Decision to Teach

The most important task before you at the conclusion of this book is to decide whether or not you really wish to continue preparation for teaching. In a spirit of self-assessment we offer the following questions for your rumination.

1. At this point, do I still want to teach?

    Yes   Not Sure   No

2. Do I still want to teach the age or type of students I thought I did at the beginning of this course?

    Yes   Not Sure   No

3. Do I have the patience to work with young, elementary-age children?

    Yes   Not Sure   No

4. Do I need more consistent positive reinforcement from my students than I will likely get as a high-school teacher?

    Yes   Not Sure   No

5. Do I really enjoy helping young people learn?

    Yes   Not Sure   No

6. Am I willing to work positively with parents and other teachers to help young people develop?

    Yes   Not Sure   No

7. Are the subjects in which I am interested in demand in elementary and secondary schools?

    Yes   Not Sure   No

8. Am I willing to commit the time and dedication necessary to become an effective teacher?

    Yes   Not Sure   No

9. Do I have the skills to become an effective teacher?

    Yes   Not Sure   No

10. Does teaching seem to be a career in which I can grow as a person?

    Yes   Not Sure   No

11. Do I have a sense of personal mission that can be addressed by teaching, to make a difference in society?

    Yes   Not Sure   No

References

American Association of Colleges for Teacher Education (1986). *Teacher education policy in the states.* Washington, DC: AACTE.

Brooks, D. M. (1985). Beginning the year in junior high: The first day of school. *Educational Leadership, 42*(8), 76–78.

Johnston, J. & Ryan, K. (1983). Research on the beginning teacher. In K. Howey and W. Gardner (Eds.), *The education of teachers: A look ahead.* New York: Longman.

Little, J. W. (1982). Norms of collegiality and experimentation: Workplace conditions of school success. *American Educational Research Journal, 19,* 325–340.

Lortie, D. (1975). *Schoolteacher.* Chicago: University of Chicago Press.

Plisko, V. W. & Stern, J. D. (1985). *The condition of education.* Washington, DC: U.S. Government Printing Office.

Rutter, M. (1983). School effects on pupil progress: Research findings and policy implications. In L. S. Shulman and G. Sykes (Eds.), *Handbook of teaching and policy.* New York: Longman.

Sedlak, M. & Schlossman, S. (1986, November). *Who will teach? Historical perspectives on the changing appeal of teaching as a profession.* Santa Monica, CA: Center for the Study of the Teaching Profession, RAND Corporation.

Veenman, S. (1984). Perceived problems of beginning teachers. *Review of Educational Research, 54*(2), 143–178.

EXPLORING ELEMENTARY, MIDDLE, AND HIGH SCHOOLS

Facilities: More Than Brick and Mortar

Changes in school construction have evolved from two sources: from educators who design buildings to facilitate educational plans rather than mold educational needs to fit stereotypical building types; and from architects who use new construction techniques and materials to design free-flowing, aesthetic buildings. Gone are the days when a school could be identified because of its shape (a three-story, rectangular box). While the finger-wing, single- or two-story pattern has replaced the school designs of pre–1950, *diverse* is the best descriptor for school plants today. Free-flowing roofs of sprayed and reinforced concrete have drastically changed the contour of the school. They exhibit some of the finest examples of good contemporary architecture in America today.

Classrooms may have only three walls, or none at all, be equipped with movable or temporary partitions which, combined with the space of other classrooms, can be used to make areas for individual student study or instruction for two hundred, or some combination of the two. In elementary schools, there is likely a resource room for special-education students and another resource room (sometimes called a library), which includes books and materials for all students. The secondary school typically includes gymnasiums, shops, an auditorium, special-purpose classrooms, and space for a wide range of activities.

However different individual schools are from one another, certain trends are evident. Modern schools tend to:

- ► Feature flexibility in use of facilities.
- ► Include free and open architectural styles.
- ► Be built on larger sites with areas for off-street parking and recreation.
- ► Feature larger and more flexible teaching areas.
- ► Provide multi-use space (cafetoriums, etc.).
- ► Eliminate basements.
- ► Be acoustically designed for noise control.
- ► Use cheerful colors.

▶ Include more effective fire-resistant, safe, and healthful materials.

▶ Be climate-controlled for maximum year-around comfort (including air conditioning in many schools, particularly in the southern United States).

The word *functional* best describes the revolution in school plant and furniture design of the past twenty years. Building space is designed for maximum use. Functional furniture is designed for flexibility of use. Schools are for use and schools are for education.

Into An Elementary School

The first school we will tour is an elementary school. Valley View, with about eight hundred students, is one of twenty elementary schools in a suburban school district.

Originally, the school population consisted almost exclusively of students from middle-income, single-dwelling families with a few from wealthier families. In recent years the construction of huge apartment complexes and the influx of new immigrants and minorities has changed the student composition. Minority students make up 67 percent of the current Valley View school population, represented primarily by Blacks, Hispanics, and Vietnamese.

Older suburban areas undergoing such changes have been referred to as "interactive areas" as contrasted with "intercity areas" that are experiencing similiar changes. The income level of Valley View is low, with over one-third of students qualifying for free lunches under a federal program. Many families are highly mobile, with several students enrolling and departing each week. Many classes experience a 40 percent turnover by December and nearly 100 percent by the end of the year.

Faculty

The school staff is composed of a principal, an assistant principal (who is responsible for routine administrative matters, handles most discipline problems, and supervises the custodial staff), and thirty-three regular classroom teachers. There are seven half-day kindergartens (three and one-half teachers), eight sections of first grade, seven of second grade, six of third grade, and four each of fourth and fifth grades. Additional instructional personnel include one and one-half librarians, a reading specialist, two special reading teachers and one special mathematics teacher (whose salaries are paid through federal grants to schools with a high proportion of minority students), a counselor, two special education teachers, two physical education teachers (with two aides), two music teachers, a speech therapist, a bilingual aide and an ESL aide, a half-time ESL teacher, a part-time diagnostician, and a registered nurse.

The large Hispanic population necessitates two bilingual classes in the first and second grades and one each in the third and fourth grades. Valley View is a large elementary school with more specialized personnel than most schools; however, many school districts have these same kinds of services available part-time to serve the diverse needs of students.

Building and Grounds

Our first stop is the school office. The administration wing serves several purposes: reception, record-keeping, clerical, conference, counseling, and information. Adjacent to the office is a space for special service personnel. A teachers' lounge, where teachers gather before school and during planning periods, typically includes some professional journals, an overcrowded bulletin board, and a ready coffee pot. (Most teachers' lounges have a "lived in" atmosphere and cookies brought by one of the faculty to munch on.)

In most schools, the instructional resources center is either a separate room (as in Valley View) or an open space in the building and includes books, magazines, listening centers, a television corner, kits, models, and other materials that can be used by children. The American Library Association has made specific recommendations about the quantity of instructional materials in the elementary school library. Check with the school librarian about the adequacy of the collection. Examine the procedures for cataloging, shelving, and use of resources, as well as becoming acquainted with the range and variety of the instructional resources.

A cafeteria, with a separate kitchen and full-time staff, doubles as an auditorium for student assemblies and, with tables folded and moved to the side, for recreational and physical education activities. Fully utilized, it can be occupied from early morning until late in the evening. It is not unusual for a student (in this school and others like it) to take a violin lesson, participate in physical fitness activities, eat lunch, and listen to the high school band in this room—all in a single day.

Being able to move large numbers of students throughout the school day is essential. Adequate corridor space is vital for safety reasons. Outside passageways are becoming common and are found in Valley View as well. Also becoming more common is the use of the hub-designed school, with several classrooms opening onto a central patio or instructional resources center. In many elementary schools, a lavatory is shared by two adjacent rooms, while some have common or gang lavatories.

Normally, classrooms have four walls with at least one wall containing an outside exposure. Classroom wings at Valley View are one room wide, each with a door that opens onto the corridor on the south side and a window wall on the north side. A few experimental schools in the country are windowless, underground, or designed in pie-shaped proportions. In most cases, careful planning provides for the entry of natural light through glass blocks, tinted glass, roof bubbles, or standard windows. Either northern exposure or wide roof overhang eliminates direct glare on student work surfaces.

Light pastel shades have replaced the brindle browns and buff colors of yesteryear. Chalkboards and bulletin boards are now tinted and finished in colors other than black.

Classrooms typically include storage space for children's coats and supplies—often lockers, but sometimes open divided shelves. Individual tables and chairs for pupils are clustered into groups of four or eight. A rug on the carpeted floor signals a location where the teacher brings small groups of pupils or the entire class for group activities or discussions. By having students sit on the floor, each child can be closer to the teacher. Classrooms often contain interest or special work centers.

Curriculum

The guidelines governing curriculum and the number of minutes each subject will be taught are mandated by the local school board following guidelines from the state education agency. The school day for pupils in Valley View begins at 8:00 A.M. and ends at 3:30 P.M. except for half-day kindergarteners.

The time allotted to language arts instruction decreases slightly with each grade: first grade—two hours, 45 minutes; second grade—two hours, 30 minutes; third grade—two hours, 15 minutes; and in the fourth and fifth grades—two hours. This includes reading, composition, spelling, and handwriting.

Mathematics instruction time is one hour, 15 minutes for each grade. Kindergarten pupils receive 20 minutes of physical education and 30 minutes of music instruction daily. For all pupils, the remainder of the time—excluding a 30–minute lunch period—is devoted to social studies, science, art, and health.

Special instructional personnel are involved with special groups of children, and a counselor works with all students. The developmental-counselor concept, adopted by the district, recognizes the importance of a student's self-concept as part of learning. The counselor, who does no disciplining in the school nor any regular classroom instruction, can work with students and their parents in a nonthreatening environment. This work includes individual and group counseling, with referrals by teachers, parents, and self-referrals by students; classroom guidance; and parent and teacher conferences.

Three teachers work with students who need additional instruction in speech, reading, and arithmetic. Their salaries are paid through Chapter I, a federal/state program funded according to the number of students who receive free lunches. They assist students who have academic deficiencies but do not qualify for special education instruction.

A reading specialist provides additional instruction, primarily to students who are above average in academic achievement but who would benefit from enrichment activities. She or he also prescreens students to determine which ones qualify for more extensive testing by the diagnostician.

The language specialists work with students who have English-language deficiencies. The Hispanic bilingual aide assists the six bilingual teachers and works with bilingual pupils in the fifth grade who have no special class. The half-time ESL teacher and ESL aide work primarily with Vietnamese students from all grades.

The primary role and responsibility of the classroom teacher or specialist is instruction. Formerly, classroom teachers supervised their students during lunch periods, but a new state law mandated duty-free lunch and a 45–minute planning period daily for all classroom teachers. Specialists now supervise lunch periods, providing time for teachers to relax.

Discipline is primarily the responsibility of the classroom teacher. An explicit three-step procedure must be followed, involving documentation and parent contact, before a student is referred to the assistant principal for behavior problems.

Teachers are expected to follow a specific instructional model adopted by the district and are observed regularly to assure that they practice correct procedures. This is a new trend in education. Prior to the wave of national criticism in the mid–1980s, most districts permitted teachers to use their professional judgement about which teaching practices to use, but with testing results being made public and compared across schools and districts, school administrators more and more are requiring strict adherence to district instructional policies.

Extra duties for all teaching personnel at Valley View involve occasional bus or passenger-car supervision before and after school. Paper work involves the usual paper grading, report cards, referral forms for after-school tutoring, reading and/or mathematics plans for Chapter I teachers, plus such nonacademic tasks as collecting and recording money for class/school pictures, candy sales, and special-event tickets.

The music teachers plan and direct a yearly PTA musical program. Physical education teachers coordinate an end-of-year Field Day, in which all children participate. In addition, teachers may be asked to serve on an in-building council representing an academic area, such as reading or art, or on a district-wide advisory council. The PTA sponsors a Halloween carnival and a chili supper each year to raise money for school projects.

Middle Schools: Transitions in Education

Middle-school years are a transition period for students. Students during this time are growing rapidly physically, attempting to establish their independence from their parents, and testing their own personhood. The organization of the school also provides students with a transition from elementary school to high school. Teaching styles and the subjects studied often reflect both elementary and high school approaches to education. Faculty may be certified to teach in elementary schools (grades 1–8) or in high schools (6–12), and most schools have some teachers with each type of certificate.

The grades included in middle schools may be sixth, seventh, and eighth or just seventh and eighth. Sometimes they are referred to as junior high schools and include grades 7–8 or 7–9. Unfortunately, the assignment of grade levels to middle schools too often is a reflection of the number and age of students and the configuration of buildings (an administrative decision) rather than an educational decision based primarily on curriculum needs.

Building and Grounds

The Jefferson Middle School we are visiting is located in a small town and is on the same campus as the high school. The grounds are relatively bare;

while some grass grows on the school grounds, it is watered only on the front side of the building, so the playground areas in back are primarily brown. A few untrimmed scrubs dot the front of the school grounds, and several older trees can be seen on the perimeter. Teachers and parents park on a gravel lot adjacent to the side entrance of the school.

The 45-year-old building was originally built as the high school but was converted to a middle school ten years ago when the new high school was built. It is not particularly attractive; grime shows from years of wear without adequate maintenance. The boiler, used for heating, does not always function properly and needs to be replaced.

The two-story building houses classroom facilities for about 450 students. It also has an auditorium (with stage and velvet curtain), cafeteria, resource room/library, principal's office, shop, homemaking suite, and gymnasium.

Curriculum

The school day extends from 8:10 A.M. to 3:15 P.M. and is composed of seven periods. Five of the periods are 50 minutes in length; the first period is 60 minutes to permit announcements and homeroom activities without infringing on class time; the fourth period is 90 minutes long to accommodate lunch. Actual time allocated to instruction is 350 minutes each day (7 periods of 50 minutes each).

The 134 students in the sixth grade take six required courses, including reading, mathematics, science, social studies, English/language arts, and physical education. They may select one elective—band or an exploring elective. The exploring elective is composed of Spanish, art, choir, and oral communication, each studied for nine weeks on a rotating basis. This year, 23 percent of the students chose band and 77 percent chose the exploring elective. Students are randomly assigned to all classes except reading, English/language arts, and mathematics; in the latter classes, they are grouped into sections by level of instruction (with about 14 percent in the above-level group, 74 percent in the regular group, and 12 percent in the below-level group).

Seventh graders (169 in all) continue basically the same required course of study as sixth graders. Students may substitute participation in competitive athletics for the usual physical education requirement, and 36 percent have done so. For their one elective, they may choose art, band, choir, Spanish, or oral communication; or, they can choose to work in the office or library. This year, 35 percent chose art as their elective; 16 percent, band; 14 percent, choral music; 10 percent, oral communication; 12 percent, Spanish; and 13 percent, work experience.

The 152 eighth graders study basically the same subjects as seventh graders—mathematics, reading, English/language arts (all classes grouped by level of achievement, with about the same proportion in each as in the sixth and seventh grades), social studies, and science (heterogeneously grouped). Students can choose either physical education (as did 71 percent of boys and 84 percent of girls) or athletics (29 percent of boys and 16 percent of girls). Electives available to eighth graders and the percent selecting each are art (14 percent), band (14 percent), choral music (7 percent), general shop (22 percent), homemaking (30 percent), Spanish (5 percent), and work experience (8 percent). More than half of the eighth graders selected either general shop or homemaking—two areas not previously available to them.

For several years, the school policy on examinations has read, "Students who have no more than three absences from a class during a semester shall be exempt from the second nine-weeks examination of that semester, provided that student had an academic grade of A, B, or C, for the semester's work." Parents and the school board have recently questioned this policy on the following grounds: first, that final examinations tend to prepare students for high school and college (where such examinations are required); second, that a student could complete eight years of schooling without ever having to prepare either psychologically or educationally for such an experience; and third, that final exams tend to press students to synthesize the content of a semester's work, and thus become a learning experience in themselves. The policy is under review, with the recommendation that such examinations could be taken without the jeopardy of lowered overall grades even if the student did poorly.

Faculty

Of the 34 certified persons on the faculty, five are in their first year of teaching and nine in their second year; thus, about 40 percent of the faculty have less than two years teaching experience. About one-fourth of the faculty, from nine to 32 years of experience. About three-quarters have only a bachelor's degree and one-fourth a master's degree (a lower proportion of master's degrees than the national average but perhaps accounted for by the youth of the faculty and the lack of a nearby university).

The faculty is composed of the principal, counselor, librarian, 4 reading teachers, 4 English/language arts teachers, 1 combination reading/language arts teacher, 5 mathematics teachers, 4 social studies teachers, 4 science teachers, 1 combination homemaking/science teacher, 1 art teacher, 1 band teacher, 1 combination choral music/social studies teacher, 1 combination Spanish/oral communication teacher, 3 physical education teachers/coaches, and 1 shop teacher/coach. Most teachers have at least three preparations; a few have four.

Students

More than three-fourths of Jefferson students come to school by bus. Most live on nearby farms, and the remainder in the small community. The student body is very stable. Forty percent of students were born in this community, 57 percent have attended school only in this district, and 80 percent have lived here at least two years.

Racially, the student body is 88 percent white, 7 percent black, 4 percent Hispanic, and 1 percent Asian or Native American.

Eighth grade students did well on the state test of basic skills. For mathematics, 81 percent met state-specified passing scores; for reading, 88 percent passed; for writing, 87 percent. When asked how many were planning to go to college, 91 percent responded affirmatively; however, school statistics have consistently shown that only 60 percent of this school's graduates ever enter college, and only 25 percent eventually graduate.

High Schools—Comprehensive and Specialized

A high school building is much larger, includes more diverse instructional spaces, and is designed for different instructional objectives than is an elementary or middle school. James Madison High School was built ten years ago and replaced a larger, older building that had been encroached on by the commercial buildings of an expanding downtown district. The school serves as a *magnet school,* one with programs attractive enough to draw students from all across the district. Madison is geared primarily to vocationally-oriented students.

Building and Grounds

The school is an attractive, modern two-story building. The office wing is to the left of the main entrance and has a reception area divided by a counter—with a couch, two chairs, and teacher's boxes in front, and desks for two secretaries behind. Attached are offices for the senior principal, four grade-level principals, a registrar, and an attendance clerk. Across the hall are offices for four counselors, one for each grade level.

Down the corridor are science classrooms, with equipment and heavy tables, running water, gas outlets, models, and supplies. Biology labs differ from the chemistry and physics lab in layout and equipment. Academic classrooms for English, social studies, and mathematics classes are similiar, and most teachers have their own room in which to teach. A few "floaters" teach in several different classrooms, using a room when the regular teacher is on planning period.

The gymnasium and athletic fields of Madison High are similiar to those of most high schools—three tennis courts, a baseball field, and a track surrounding a football field. Separate dressing rooms for boys and girls are off the gym but used for all physical education programs.

What sets Madison apart from most high schools are its vocational facilities. While the commercial art, home economics, and business education rooms are the same height as regular classrooms, they tend to be larger, often composed of suites of rooms, and packed with modern equipment. Shops, however, are two stories high, designed to emulate commercial facilities, with double-garage doors, stacks of materials, and student lockers and washbasins. The wood shop, auto mechanics shop, welding and machine shop, and print shop are set apart from other parts of the building to shield academic areas from the noise of shopwork.

The music wing is also housed separately from academic areas in order to control noise. The bands, choirs, and single small orchestra each have their own special rooms. Individual practice rooms open off of these classrooms and also off of corridors. A cafeteria in the center of the building doubles as an auditorium when the occasion demands.

Students

The enrollment, which has declined by a third in the past decade, is slightly more than 1,000 students, equally divided among the four grades in the school. Ethnically, 5 percent are white, 71 percent black, 23 percent Hispanic, and 1 percent Asian American.

About 70 percent of students work after school, primarily in fast food restaurants or grocery stores; however, many in the twelfth grade have skilled jobs in their chosen vocations. Few will attend college, so their preparation is one for life—or, more accurately, for the present. Their concerns are for money, now! Their needs are for cars and clothes. They're looking for vocations that they can enter directly upon graduation.

Parents of most Madison students have not completed high school. Most work in blue-collar jobs; some are on welfare, particularly since an economic recession that occurred three years ago. Most expect their children to enter vocations similiar to theirs, to be good, solid Americans, and to do well in school.

Curriculum

To graduate, students must complete 4 units of English (one unit equals one hour per day for a year), 3 units of mathematics, 2 units of science, world history or world geography, American history, American government, .5 unit of economics, 2 units of physical education, .5 unit of health, and 7 units of electives, for a total of 22 units. Students in college preparatory programs have only 3 units of electives and take, in addition, 2 units of a foreign language, an extra unit of science, and a unit of humanities or fine arts. Students in cooperative training programs (in which they attend school in the mornings and work in the afternoons) are not required to take physical education.

A new state law requires that all students pass a basic skills competency test in mathematics, reading, and writing in order to graduate. Those who are unable to pass the test (given twice in their junior year and twice in their senior year) are given a certificate of attendance rather than a diploma.

The vocational programs at Madison reflect the needs in the local community (for example, appliance repair, auto body repair, business education, commercial art, commercial foods, distributive education, drafting, home economics, machine shop, printing trades, vocational electronics, and welding).

In addition to athletic teams, band, orchestra, and choir, students may join any one of two dozen clubs. Clubs are related to vocational interests, the school newspaper, and scholastic achievement. The Student Council organizes (with the principal's approval) pep rallies, assemblies, and special days such as Different-Colored-Sock Day, Western Day, Valentine dance, and Faculty Follies. Such activities have been restricted during the past year because of pressure from the Board of Education to spend "as much time on task" as possible. More than 25 students work one period each day in school offices or as a lab assistant and receive an elective credit for the experience.

The school day for students is from 7:50 A.M. to 2:50 P.M. with a 15–minute homeroom the first period and six 55–minute instructional periods. Students are scheduled for one of two 45–minute lunch periods. Teachers are expected to be on duty from 7:40 A.M. to 3:30 P.M. and to be available to tutor students after school.

Faculty

The average age of the eighty-nine faculty members is forty-two, somewhat older than in the nation as a whole. About one-third of the faculty teach academic subjects, while two-thirds teach vocational subjects. Thirty-five percent have a master's degree; vocational teachers have industrial experience, and several have no college degree.

Academic-subject teachers tend to teach in traditional ways. They give short homework assignments because they know that most students work and cannot complete long assignments. Vocational teachers tend to use the apprentice method of teaching—their students learn by actually *doing* things rather than *studying about things;* that is, auto mechanics students learn about cars by repairing them, and commercial art students prepare ads that local stores actually use.

Part 1

THE PUBLIC'S RESPONSES TO GALLUP POLLS FOUND IN CHAPTER 2

In what ways did the Gallup Poll results differ from your responses? Describe the differences between the 1985 results and the earlier poll results for each of the questions. What conclusions could you draw about the difference between the intervening years? Did the survey results provide you with any surprises? How did the members of your class respond to the poll?

School Survey Results

1. Students are often given the grades A, B, C, D, and FAIL to denote the quality of their work. Suppose the public schools themselves, in this community, were graded in the same way. What grade would you give the public schools here? a) A b) B c) C d) D e) FAIL f) don't know

Answer:
Rating of local public schools

	1976	1985
A	13%	9%
B	29%	34%
C	28%	30%
D	10%	10%
FAIL	6%	4%
Don't Know	14%	13%

2. How about the public schools in the nation as a whole? What grade would you give the public schools nationally? a) A b) B c) C d) D e) FAIL f) don't know

Answer:
Rating of national public schools

	1981	1985
A	2%	3%
B	18%	24%
C	43%	43%
D	15%	12%
FAIL	6%	3%
Don't Know	16%	15%

3. Now, what grade would you give the teachers in the public schools in this community? a) A b) B c) C d) D e) FAIL f) don't know

Answer:
Rating of teachers

	1981	1985
A	11%	12%
B	28%	37%
C	31%	26%
D	9%	7%
FAIL	6%	3%
Don't Know	15%	15%

4. Do you think salaries in this community for teachers are: a) too high b) too low c) just about right d) no opinion?

Answer:
Teachers' salaries

	1969	1985
Too High	2%	6%
Too Low	33%	33%
Just Right	43%	43%
No Opinion	22%	18%

5. How do you, yourself, feel about the idea of merit pay for teachers? In general, do you: a) favor it b) oppose it c) have no opinion?

Answer:
Merit pay for teachers

	1984	1985
Favor	65%	60%
Oppose	22%	24%
No Opinion	13%	16%

6. Before they are hired by a school district, do you feel all teachers: a) should or b) should not be required to pass a basic competency test to measure such things as their general knowledge and ability to think? (Or c) do you not know?)

Answer:
Teacher Competency Test Requirement

	1985
Should be required	89%
Should not be required	6%
Don't Know	5%

7. What do you think are the biggest problems with which the public schools in this community must deal? _____

Answer:
Major problems facing schools

	1985	1976
Discipline	25%	22%
Drugs	18%	11%
Poor curriculum/ standards	11%	14%
Lack of good teachers	10%	11%
Lack of financial support	9%	14%
Integration/busing	4%	15%

8. Lack of discipline is often cited as a problem confronting the public schools. Please look over this list and rank order from 1 to 10 which of these possible solutions you think would be most helpful in improving school discipline.

_____ Classes for teachers on how to deal with problem children

_____ Discussion groups with parents of problem children

_____ Required classes for parents of problem children

_____ Suspension of students with extreme behavior problems

_____ Formation of special classes for students who have behavior problems

_____ Creation of a system of work-study programs, with problem children doing useful work half-time and attending school half-time

_____ Classes for administrators to help them create more orderly behavior

_____ Tougher courts, probation systems, and work programs for delinquents

_____ Creation of a curriculum more relevant to the interests and concerns of students

_____ Alternative schools

Answer:
Preferred solutions

Classes for teachers on dealing with problem children	64%
Discussion groups with parents of problem children	62%
Required classes for parents of problem children	50%
Suspension of problem students	46%
Special classes for students with problem behavior	45%

9. How do you feel about the spending of public school funds for special instruction and homework programs for students with learning problems? Do you feel that more public school funds should be spent on students with learning problems than on average students, the same amount, or don't know? _____

Answers:

	1985	1982
More spent	51%	42%
Same amount spent	40%	48%
Less spent	2%	4%
Don't know	7%	6%

10. Should all high school students in the United States be required to pass a standard, nationwide examination in order to get a high school diploma? a) Yes b) No or c) no opinion?

Answers:

	1976	1985
In favor of such a test	63%	50%
Opposed	31%	39%
No opinion	4%	11%

11. Suppose you could choose your child's teachers. Assuming they all had about the same experience and training, what personal qualities would you look for?

_____

_____

_____

Answers:

Qualities named by respondents most often in 1976:

1. The ability to communicate, to understand, to relate
2. The ability to discipline, be firm and fair
3. The ability to inspire, motivate the child
4. High moral character
5. Love of children; concern for them
6. Dedication to teaching profession; enthusiasm
7. Friendly; good personality
8. Good personal appearance, cleanliness

Part 2

THE PUBLIC'S RESPONSES TO GALLUP POLLS FOUND IN CHAPTER 13

Subjects That Should Be Required Of High School Students

	Should be Required—			
	for those who plan to attend college.		for those who do not plan to attend college.	
	Gallup Poll	Your Class	Gallup Poll	Your Class
Art	23%	_____	15%	_____
Business	59%	_____	60%	_____
Career education	57%	_____	57%	_____
Computer training	71%	_____	57%	_____
English	88%	_____	81%	_____
Foreign language	53%	_____	17%	_____
Health education	48%	_____	43%	_____
History/U.S. Government	76%	_____	61%	_____
Mathematics	91%	_____	85%	_____
Music	24%	_____	15%	_____
Physical education	40%	_____	40%	_____
Science	76%	_____	51%	_____
Vocational training	27%	_____	75%	_____

Gallup, 1985, 40. Used by permission.

WORKING IN SCHOOLS

When you first go to a school to observe classes, or to tutor and work with students, or to teach classes, introduce yourself to those with whom you will be working. They will be interested in your background, your interests, and the ways in which you might be able to contribute to the school. The following information, if completed in advance and provided them, has been found to be useful.

Your name:
Address:
Phone numbers where you can be reached:
Experiences with children and youth:
Teaching experience:
Life experiences, hobbies, interests:
College major and minor(s):

Become involved in the life of the school you are visiting. A few suggested activities follow.

a. Help in storing, accounting for, and distributing supplies and materials.
b. Complete records, take daily attendance, and post grades.
c. Collect and account for lunch or book money.
d. Write assignments, lessons, and so forth, on the chalkboard.
e. Assist with hall and lunchroom duties.
f. Assist the principal in the school office.
g. Attend a meeting of school parents.
h. Help with room arrangements, decorations, exhibits.
i. Set up and operate audiovisual equipment.
j. Compile resource materials for a future area of study.
k. Correct and analyze student work.

In all cases, keep in mind that you are a guest in an important social institution and are working under the supervision of professionals who are responsible for the well-being of the school's clients, its students. Each time you arrive at the school, check in at the main office. Your dress and conduct should be professional at all times.

The items listed below are designed to serve as additional suggested activities in which you may engage during your field component. You, together with the teacher or teachers with whom you will work, will decide which activities are the most practical and the most valuable given the specific situation.

1. Help with tutoring.
2. Help with enrichment activities (gifted/talented).
3. Work with the science/history fair. Help set it up; organize.
4. Make a bulletin board with a group of children.
5. Work with small groups on individual problems or skills.
6. Work with students who have special needs (ESL, Basic Classes, etc.)
7. Work with vocabulary development (ESL).
8. Help students with make-up work.
9. Observe teacher duties and participate in hall duty, cafeteria duty, bus duty, etc.
10. Read to the class.
11. Teach a game to the class.
12. Play a learning game with the class.
13. Sit with a reading group.
14. Help with learning centers (both monitoring and developing materials).
15. Monitor seatwork.
16. Teach a remedial lesson to a small group.
17. Operate audiovisual equipment.
18. Take attendance.
19. Grade papers (limited number of papers).
20. Duplicate materials (limited number of materials).
21. Participate in or assist with extracurricular activities.
22. Sit in on a parent conference.
23. Other (describe).

STATE CERTIFICATION OFFICES

Alabama

Teacher Certification
Department of Education
Division of Professional Services
349 State Office Building
Montgomery, AL 36130–3901

Alaska

Certification Analyst
Teacher Education and Certification
Department of Education
Goldbelt Building
P.O. Box F
Juneau, AK 99811

Arizona

Teacher Certification Unit
Department of Education
1535 West Jefferson
Phoenix, AZ 85007

Arkansas

Teacher Education, Certification, Evaluation, and Testing
Department of Education
State Education Bldgs., Rooms 106B/107B
Little Rock, AR 72201

California

Office of Licensing
Commission for Teacher Preparation and Licensing
1020 O Street, Room 222
Sacramento, CA 95814

Colorado

Teacher Education and Certification Unit
Department of Education
105 State Education Building
201 East Colfax Avenue
Denver, CO 80203

Connecticut

Teacher Certification
Bureau of Professional Development
Division of Curriculum and Professional Development
State Department of Education
P.O. Box 2219
Hartford, CT 06115

Delaware

Certification and Personnel Division
State Department of Public Instruction
Townsend Building
P.O. Box 1402
Dover, DE 19903

District of Columbia

Department of Certification and Accreditation
415 12th Street, N.W.
Room 1004
Washington, DC 20004

Florida

Teacher Education and Certification
Department of Education
Collins Building
Tallahassee, FL 32301

Georgia

Division of Teacher Certification
State Department of Education
Twin Towers East
Atlanta, GA 30334

Hawaii

Personnel Certification and Development
Office of Personnel Services
P.O. Box 2360
Honolulu, HI 96804

Idaho

Certification Analyst
Teacher Education and Certification
State Department of Education
Len B. Jordan Office Building
Boise, ID 83720

Illinois

Certification and Placement
State Teacher Certification Board
100 North First Street
Springfield, IL 62777

Indiana

Credentials Specialist
Division of Teacher Education and Certification
State Department of Public Instruction
Room 231, State House
Indianapolis, IN 46204–2798

Iowa

Teacher Education and Certification
Department of Public Instruction
Grimes State Office Building
Des Moines, IA 50319

Kansas

State Department of Education
Certification, Teacher Education and Accreditation
120 East Tenth Street
Topeka, KS 66612

Kentucky

Teacher Education and Certification
State Department of Education
1823 Capital Plaza Tower
Frankfort, KY 40601

Louisiana

Bureau of Higher Education and Teacher Certification
State Department of Education
P.O. Box 94064
Baton Rouge, LA 70804–9064

Maine

Director
Teacher Certification and Placement
Teacher Education and Higher Education
Department of Education and Cultural Services
State House Station 23
Augusta, ME 04333

Maryland

Teacher Education and Certification
State Department of Education
200 W. Baltimore Street
Baltimore, MD 21201

Massachusetts

Bureau of Teacher Preparation/Certification and Placement
Department of Education
1385 Hancock Street
Quincy, MA 02169

Michigan

Teacher Preparation and Certification Services
Department of Education
P.O. Box 30008
Lansing, MI 48909

Minnesota

Personnel Licensing and Placement
State Department of Education
Capitol Square Building
550 Cedar Street
St. Paul, MN 55101

Mississippi

Office of Teacher Certification
Department of Education
P.O. Box 771
Jackson, MS 39205

Missouri

Teacher Education and Certification
Department of Elementary and Secondary Education
P.O. Box 480
Jefferson City, MO 65102

Montana

Teacher Education, Certification and Staff Development
Office of the Superintendent of Public Instruction
Helena, MT 59620

Nebraska

Teacher Education and Certification
Department of Education
301 Centennial Mall South
P.O. Box 94987
Lincoln, NE 68509

Nevada

Teacher Education and Certification
Nevada Department of Education
State Mail Room
215 East Bonanza
Las Vegas, NV 89158

New Hampshire

Office of Teacher Education and Professional Standards
State Department of Education
State Office Park South
101 Pleasant Street
Concord, NH 03301

New Jersey

Bureau of Teacher Preparation and Certification
New Jersey Department of Education
225 West State Street, CN 500
Trenton, NJ 08625

Office of Teacher Certification and Academic Credentials
State Department of Education
3535 Quakerbridge Road, CN 503
Trenton, NJ 08625–0503

New Mexico

Teacher Education and Certification
Education Building
Santa Fe, NM 87503

New York

Teacher Education and Certification
State Department of Education
Cultural Education Center, Room 5A11
Nelson A. Rockefeller Empire State Plaza
Albany, NY 12230

North Carolina

Division of Certification
State Department of Public Instruction
114 West Edenton Street
Raleigh, NC 27611

North Dakota

Teacher Certification
Department of Public Instruction
State Capitol
Bismarck, ND 58505

Ohio

Teacher Education and Certification
Department of Education
65 South Front Street, Room 1012
Columbus, OH 43215

Oklahoma

Teacher Certification Section
State Department of Education
Oliver Hodge Education Building
2500 N. Lincoln Boulevard
Oklahoma City, OK 73105

Oregon

Certification Officer
Teacher Standards and Practices Commission
630 Center St., N.E., Suite 200
Salem, OR 97310–0320

Pennsylvania

Bureau of Teacher Preparation and Certification
State Department of Education
333 Market Street
Harrisburg, PA 17126–0333

Rhode Island

School and Teacher Accreditation
Department of Education
Roger Williams Building
22 Hayes Street
Providence, RI 02908

South Carolina

Teacher Education and Certification
State Department of Education
Room 1004, Rutledge Building
Columbia, SC 29201

South Dakota

Teacher Certification
Division of Education
Department of Education and Cultural Affairs
Kneip Building
700 North Illinois
Pierre, SD 57501–2293

Tennessee

Teacher Education and Certification
State Department of Education
125 Cordell Hull Building
Nashville, TN 37219–5338

Texas

Division of Certification
Texas Education Agency
1701 North Congress Avenue
Austin, TX 78701–1494

Utah

Teacher Certification
Division of Curriculum and Instruction
Utah State Office of Education
250 East Fifth South
Salt Lake City, UT 84111

Vermont

Certification Officer
Educational Resources Unit
State Department of Education
Montpelier, VT 05602

Virginia

Teacher Education, Certification, and Professional Development
Department of Education
P.O. Box 6Q
Richmond, VA 23216–2060

Washington

Professional Certification
Superintendent of Public Instruction
Old Capitol Building, Mail Stop FG–11
Olympia, WA 98504

West Virginia

Certification Unit
Office of General and Professional Education
Department of Education
Capitol Complex
Building #6, Room B–330
Charleston, WV 25305

Wisconsin

Teacher Certification
Bureau for Teacher Education, Certification, and Placement
Department of Public Instruction
125 South Webster Street
P.O. Box 7841
Madison, WI 53707

Wyoming

Certification/Licensing Unit
State Department of Education
Hathaway Building
Cheyenne, WY 82002

Aaron v. *Tucker,* 300
Abington v. *Schempp,* 331
Abortion, 327
Abstract thought, 27, 78, 80
  adults' difficulties in, 81
  Otis-Lennon test and, 262
  rating scales and, 272
Academic awards, 109
Academic learning time, 55-56
Academic objectives (vs.
  managerial), 178
Academic orientation, 57
Academic success, 56-57
  external factors in, 81-93
  home environment and, 105
  self-concept and, 105
Accommodation, 79, 80
Accountability (of schools to
  government), 309, 313
Accountability (of teachers),
  58-59, 177
Accreditation, school, 116, 126,
  305, 324
Action for Excellence 129-130
Active learning, 32, 56, 194, 194
  classroom management and,
  216-217
  grouping and, 207
  in guided discovery, 210
Act of Massachusetts General
  Court, 303
Adams, Henry
Adaptation (in learning), 163
Adler, Mortimer, 63, 131, 174
Administration (of schools),
  68-69
Admission, Review and
  Dismissal (ARD)
  conferences, 290
Adolescents, 82-84
  alienated, 82-83
  suicide by, 83, 325, 326-328
  teachers' reaction to, 132

Adult education, 109. *See also*
  Continuing (life-long)
  education
Advance organizers (in lesson
  design), 181
Affective domain, 162-163
Affective entry characteristics,
  170
Affective objectives, 172,
  177-178
  assessment of, 255, 258-260
Agencies, school, 302-303
Aggressiveness, student, 228
Agriculture, 6
AIDS, education on, 5, 327
Aims of Education, The
  (Whitehead), 32
Alcohol abuse, 324, 328
Alienated adolescents, 82-83
Alienated teachers, 68
Alternative high schools, 5
*America's Competitive
  Challenge: The Need for a
  National Response,* 129-130
American Dream, the, 108
American Federation of
  Labor/Congress of
  Industrial Organizations
  (AFL/CIO), 354
American Federation of
  Teachers (AFT), 354, 355
Americanizing (immigrants),
  103, 144
American Library Association,
  336, 363
American Revolution, 101, 144
Analogies (in tests), 262
Analysis
  by students, 131, 162
  by teachers, 250, 251
Anecdotal records, 266
Anger (by teacher), 230, 236
Anomie, 101

Anthropology, 109-110
Application (intellectual
  process of), 162
Apprentices (during Middle
  Ages), 192
Appropriations committees (in
  Congress), 288
Aptitude tests, 33, 253, 262
  designed for special
  purposes, 262
Aquinas, St. Thomas, 63
Architecture, school, 30, 42,
  361-362
  See also School facilities
Aristotle, 24, 25, 63
Armbands (worn in school),
  293-294
Art education, 42, 78, 90, 257
Art as Experience (Dewey), 32
Articulation (of curriculum),
  148
Asians, 103, 104
Assemblies, school, 121, 369
Assembly, freedom of, 297, 299
Assimilation, 79, 80
Assistant principal, 362, 365
Association (in learning), 75
Association of Colleges and
  Preparatory Schools in the
  Middle States and
  Maryland, 126
Association of Colleges and
  Preparatory Schools of the
  Southern States, 126
Athens, 25
Athletics, school, 298
*Attacks on the Freedom to
  Learn,* 336
Attaining closure (in lesson
  design), 185
Attention (in learning), 54, 77,
  78, 162, 177

Attention-seeking student behavior, 231
Attitude, student, 258-259
Attitude development, 320
Audiovisual aids, 5, 10, 196, 197
Auditorium, school, 361, 368
Autobiographies (for assessment by teachers), 266
Average daily attendance (ADA), 308, 309

Baby boom, 36
Back-to-basics movement, 39, 157
See also Basic Skills
Baker v. *Owen,* 294-295
Balanced Treatment for Creation Science and Evolution Science Act, 328, 329
Ballinger, Charles, 43
Banks, James, 89, 91
Banners, school, 120
Barnes, Donald, 39
Basic skills, 150, 150, 288, 289, 319-320
competency test for, 367, 369
drill and practice for, 204
and purpose of public schools, 319
trend away from emphasis on, 157
See also Back-to-basics movement
Basic Skills Improvement Program, 289
Beauty (schools' teaching of), 117, 122
Bedroom suburbs, 99
Behavior, masculine/feminine, 146
Behavior modification, 225-226, 229-230
Behavior problems, 204, 218, 231-232.
See also Discipline, school
Behavioral-learning theory, 75
Behavioral objectives, 172, 173-174
assessment of, 255-256
evaluation and, 186, 187
vs. problem-solving objectives, 174
Behavioral psychology, 173
Bell, Terrel, 128, 290
Bells, school, 30
Benjamin, Harold, 145
Bennett, Wiliam J., 291
Berra, Yogi, 110

Bethel School District No. 403 v. *Fraser,* 294
Bible
and *The New England Primer,* 106
reading in school, 292, 297, 331-332
vs. secular humanism, 326
Bilingual education, 5, 88-89, 206, 286, 320
example of, 10, 362, 364
individualism and, 322
judicial influence on, 291
objection to, 131
public funding for, 289
requirements for teachers of, 346-347
special-interest groups and, 100
See also ESL (English as a second language) teacher
Bill for the More General Diffusion of Knowledge (Jefferson), 28
Binet, Alfred, 254
Black v. *Cothren,* 294
Black Pride Week, 325
Black students, 33, 90, 103, 334
Block, J. H., 119
Bloom, Benjamin, 55, 119, 162, 170, 201
Boarding schools, 43
Board of Regents examination, 158
Board of trustee, 304
Boards of education, 5, 98, 108, 148, 149, 369
curriculum and, 177
desegregation and, 299-300
responsibilities of, 304
year-round schools and, 43
Bonds (for school funding), 304, 305, 308
Boredom (in students), 198, 201, 203
Bossert, Steven, 59
Boston Latin School, 29
Bower, T. G. R., 78
Boyer, Ernest L., 133
Breakfast, school (free), 5
Brennan, William, 331-332
Briggs, 182
Brimelow, Peter, 39
Bronfenbrenner, Urie, 82, 83
Broudy, Harry S., 98, 99
Brougham, Lord, 7
Brown v. *Board of Education of Topeka,* 299, 300, 320
Bruner, Jerome, 37, 79
Buckley Amendment, 295

Budget, school, 126, 304-305, 309
Building programs, school, 305
Bulletin boards, school, 121, 363
Bureaucracy, school, 133
Burnside v. *Byars,* 294
Business-Higher Education Forum, 129
Business education, 42, 320
Business (and schools), 120-121, 129
Busing, 5, 125, 286, 299, 313

Cafeteria, school, 363, 368
Calmness (of teacher), 223
Career ladders (for teachers), 129
Career schools, 42, 45
Caring (by teacher), 235
Carnegie Foundation for the Advancement of Teaching, 133
Carnegie unit, 151, 153
Carroll, John, 55, 119
Carter, Jimmy, 290
Case studies (for assessment by teachers), 266
Cash v. *Hock,* 294
Castiglione, Baldassare, 26
Categorical legislation, 288-290
Catholic Church (and education during Middle Ages), 25
Causality (in research on effective schools), 122
Censorship of textbooks and reading-list books, 336
Centralization (nationalization), 330
Ceremonies (in schools), 120
Certificate of attendance (instead of diploma), 369
Certification, teacher, 129, 291, 344, 345-347
decentralization of schools and, 301
offices for, 356, 377-384
state responsibility for, 302
state-to-state differences in, 356-358
Chalk-talk lecture, 196
Chalkboards, 196, 197, 200, 363
Charlemagne, 26
Charles, C. M., 230
Chastity, 327
Checking for understanding, 200
Cheerfulness (of teacher), 224

Chief state school officer (CSSO), 302, 303
Child-focusers, 67, 68
Child care
  before and after school, 83, 106, 335
  courses on, 106
  federal funding for, 334
Child development, 80, 81
  Rousseau's theory of, 26, 27-28
Children's Defense Fund, 82
China, ancient, 29
Choral drill, 203
Christianity (neglected in history books), 336
Christians, fundamentalist/conservative, 45, 326, 333, 335. *See also* Religion and education
Cicero (Montaigne), 26
Cinco de Mayo, 325
Civil Rights Act, 38, 300
Civil Rights legislation (and schools), 124-125, 291, 313
Clark, David L., 86
Clarke, John, 29
Classics (in literature), 63, 123
Classification tasks, 256
Class meeting, 9, 10
Classroom learning, 77-78
Classroom management, 58, 194, 201, 216-240
  British study on, 238
  consistency in, 226-228
  definition of, 216-217
  historical perspective of, 223-225
  importance of, 216
  mistakes in, 224-225
  psychological perspectives of, 225-226
Classroom size, 69. *See also* Group learning/grouping
Classroom teaching vs. other duties, 53
Class size, 354
Clubs, school, 120
Cluster suicides, 327
Cobb, Joseph, 294, 298, 299
Cocurricular activities, 109
Code of ethics (teachers' personal), 352-354
Code of Ethics of the Education Profession, 352, 353-354
Cognitive domain, 162, 163
Cognitive entry skills, 170
Cognitive knowledge, 319

Cognitive processes, 75, 77, 78, 79-80
Cognitive psychologists, 74, 75
Cognitive-developmental theory, 75
Cohen, David, 306, 323
Cohen, Elizabeth, 91
Cohesion (in schools), 120
Collective bargaining (for teachers), 354
Collective inquiry, skills for, 123
College Board Scholastic Aptitude Tests (SATs). *See Scholastic Aptitude Tests (SATs)*
College-bound students, 116, 129, 134
College admissions standards, 129, 130
College Entrance Examination Board, 133, 134
Colonial American education, 28-29, 303, 319, 330
Color Purple, The (Walker), 335
Comenius, John Amos, 26
Coming of Age in America (Friedenberg), 39
Coming of Age in Samoa (Mead), 110
Commission on Educational Issues of the National Association of Independent Schools, 133
Commission reports and recommendations (for schools), 127-132, 287, 290, 322
Committee for Economic Development, 122
Committee of Fifteen, 31
Committee on Secondary School Studies, 31
Common schools, 30
Communication (by student), 258
Communication (by teacher), 232-236
Communicative ability, 78
Community
  role of in after-school child care, 83-84
  schools and, 98-111, 311-312, 324
  teachers and, 51, 66, 109-110, 111
Community school, 98-99
Compact-Disk-Interactive (CD-I), 44, 45

Compact disk (CD), 44-45
Comparison questions, 200
Compensatory education, 313
Competency-based education, 119
Competition, student, 60-61, 87
Competitive learning, 60-61
Completion questions, 267, 269
Complex overt response (in learning), 163
Comprehension (intellectual process of), 162
Comprehensive schools, 41, 152-153, 368-370
Computer-intensive schools, 43
Computers
  courses in, 129, 130, 131, 134, 320
  for elite schools, 42
  home schools and, 43
  impact on community, 103
  in schools, 9, 43-44, 36, 103
  software programs for, 43, 44
Conclusion (in lesson design), 185
Conference period, 51, 53
Conferences (for assessment by teacher), 266, 364
Confidentiality of records, 295
Conflict-resolution exercises, 326
Congress (and schools), 288-291
Consistency: The Key to Classroom Management, 226
Constitution (U.S), 28, 86, 98
  general welfare clause of, 291
  schools and, 287, 301
  teachers' rights under, 297-299
Constitutions, state, 302
Construction assignment, 257
Content, subject, 58, 193, 211
  complex vs. simple, 195
  decentralization of schools and, 301
  decisions on, 324-325
  emphasis on, 322
  teaching method and, 194
Contented-conformists, 68
Contests (between schools), 120
Continuing (life-long or adult) education, 109, 320, 334
Continuity (of curriculum), 148
Contracts, teachers', 129
Control Theory in the Classroom (Glasser), 231

Conway, Dorothy, 193-194, 196
Cooking courses, 106
Cooperative action, skills for, 123
Cooperative learning, 60, 61, 91, 206, 207
  group assignments in, 255-256
  peer teachers and, 187
Cooperative training programs, 369
Copyright law, 29
Core curriculum, 31, 63
  proposed reforms for, 131, 134
Corporal punishment, 27, 226, 228
  Baker case on, 294-295
  states prohibiting, 295
Correction (of students), 57
Counselor, school, 5, 364
Counts, George, 124
Course evaluations, 250
Courts (and education), 291-302
Coutier (Castiglione), 26
Covert curriculum, 145, 146, 319
Crane, Stephen, 160
Creation, theory of (creationism), 108, 326, 328-329
Creativity (encouraged in students), 58
Creativity (in education), 39
Cremin, Lawrence, 33
Crisis in the Classroom (Silberman), 39
Criterion-referenced tests, 5, 263, 264-265
Critical judgment, 126-127, 132
Criticism (literary), 64
Crossen v. *Fatsi*, 294
Crowder, Norman, 36
Cruickshank, Donald, 61
Cuban, Larry, 196, 325, 326
Culture (and schools), 5, 6, 100-105, 319
  differences among students, 89-91, 93
  regional differences in, 135
Cultural identification, 91
Cultural pluralism, 89, 104. *See also* Multicultural approach
Culture Wars (Shor), 39
Curricular trends, 154-158, 324-325, 328
  in early 1900s, 31, 32-33
Curriculum, 5, 45, 208-209
  additions to, 145

analyzing the, 169
as criterion of effective school, 126
changes in after Sputnik, 288
concept of, 144-164
contemporary, 149-154
decentralization of schools and, 301
differences from state to state, 301
elementary school example of, 364-365
foreign countries' influence on U.S., 288
factors determining, 194
formal vs. informal (hidden), 145, 146
hidden, 146
high school example of, 369-370
vs. instruction, 159
judicial influence on, 291
middle school example of, 366-367
national defense and, 37
proposed reforms for, 129, 130, 131, 134
school-wide, 172
social messages in, 90
societal changes and, 144-146
state responsibility for, 302
students' previous learning and, 170-172
teacher-proof, 39
terminology for, 147-148
test norms and, 261
traditional, 123, 319
usefulness of, 145
Curriculum development, 144
  funding for, 307
  importance of, 164
  by teachers, 131
Curriculum goals, 160-164, 168
Curriculum guide, 169, 170
Curwin, Rick, 233

Dade Court, 69
Dare the School Build a New Social Order (Counts), 124
Dark Ages, 25
Darwin's theory of evolution. *See* Evolution, Darwin's theory of
Data collection (for teachers' decision making), 250
Day-care, 155
Death at an Early Age (Kozel), 39
Death of a Salesman (Miller), 335

Debriefing (in lesson design), 185, 258
Decentralization, 131, 301-302
Decision making (in schools), 157, 311-313
  by students, 206
  by teachers, 194-195, 223, 250
Delinquency (adolescent), 83
Democracy, education and, 40
Democratic living
  behavior modification and, 230
  classroom management style compatible with, 232
  schools' teaching of, 40, 117, 123
Democratic teachers, 231, 232
Demography of student population, 5, 15-16, 36, 102, 306
  examples of, 362, 367, 369
Demonstration lecture, 196
Departmentalizing, 157
Department of Health, Education and Welfare, 287, 290
Depression (students'), 5, 124, 327
Deschooling Society (Illich), 126
Description (skill of), 110
Desegregation, school, 5, 37, 38, 287, 291, 300
  Brown case on, 299, 320
  funding for, 307
  individualism and, 322
  and public aid to private schools, 333
Detention after school, 226, 228
Developing Attitude Toward Learning (Mager), 144, 250
Developmental-counselor concept, 364
Developmental psychology, 11, 78-79, 87
Dewey, John, 8, 31, 32, 33, 65
  and criteria for quality schools, 123, 132
  progressive movement of, 33, 34
  quote on problems, 208
  quote on social movements, 325
Diagnosticians, 5
Diary of a Young Girl, The (Frank), 335
Didactic instruction, 132
Differential Aptitude Tests, 262

Differentiated diplomas or transcripts, 158
Diplomas, 158, 297, 369
Direct instruction, 57-58
Disabled students, 5. *See also* Handicapped students; Learning-disabled children
Disadvantaged students, 38, 117, 124-125, 288
　intelligence tests and, 254
Disarmament, education on, 327
Discipline, school, 37, 125, 216, 218-219
　in elementary school, 364-365
　example of effective, 222-223, 237-238
　example of ineffective, 221-222, 237-238
　Ginott's theory on, 230-231
　Neill's views on, 238
　rights of students regarding, 293, 294-295
　Roger's theory on, 230
　See also Behavior problems
Discourse II (Epictetus), 321
Discovery learning, 58, 208-211
　in mathematics, 194, 195, 208-211
Discrimination, 300, 320
Discussion (as teaching method), 200, 201
　in guided discovery, 210
　in perennialism, 64, 65
Disruptions, classroom, 217-218
Distractors (in multiple-choice question), 269
District testing programs, 305
Domains of learning, 161-164
Doyle, Walter, 218
Drama education, 42, 78, 151, 257
Dreeben, Robert, 61
Dreikurs, Rudolf, 231, 232
Drills, 159, 194, 195, 202-203
Driver education, 106, 325
Dropouts, school, 90, 322-323
Drug abuse
　treatment programs in schools, 312-313, 326, 328
　school's responsibility·for, 5, 325, 326, 328
　schools and, 5, 83, 312-313, 324
　statistics on students', 328
　school search and seizure and, 296, 297
Du Contract Social (Rousseau), 27

Due process rights, 34, 290, 292-293, 295-296
　applied to teachers, 298
　See also Fourteenth Amendment
Durkheim, Emile, 101

Eastern civilization (and education), 22
Economic Opportunity Act, 38
Economic Policy Institute, 40, 41
Economics education, 150, 158
Economy (and schools), 5, 40, 102-103, 124, 158
Edmonds, Ron, 117
Educating All Our Children (Wilkerson), 116
Educating Americans for the 21st Century, 130
Education, Arts, and Humanities Subcommittee
Education, 5-8, 37-40
　during 1950s, 39, 208
　during 1960s and early 1970s, 37, 39, 209, 325
　during 1980s, 39, 40, 336, 336
　in ancient Greece, 192, 196
　by behavioral objectives, 119
　in Colonial America, 28-29, 303, 319, 330
　crisis in American, 319
　current issues in, 318-337
　during Middle Ages, 192
　economics of, 39, 40
　efficiency in, 291
　　See also Schools, effective
　in eighteenth century, 106, 126, 208
　foreign countries and, 286-288
　inclusive vs. exclusive, 30-31
　during Industrial Age, 319
　national systems of, 286-287
　in nineteenth century, 29-31, 106
　during prehistoric times, 23-24, 145, 192
　as a property right, 296
　in seventeenth century, 144
　student-centered, 28
　trends in, 33-45
　in twentieth century, 31-33
　during World War I, 34, 35
　after World War I, 36
　during World War II, 38, 286
　See also Schools
Educational content, 27
Education and Labor Committee, 288

Education and the Human Quest (Thelen), 58
Education Commission of the States, 129
Education Consolidation and Improvement Act (ECIA), 289
Education Equality Project, 134
Education for All Handicapped Children Act, 92
Education of a Christian Prince, The (Erasmus), 26
Education of Henry Adams, The (Adams), 16
Education of Youth in Pensilvania (Franklin), 29
Egypt, ancient, 29
Eighth Mental Measurements Yearbook, 261
Eight Year Study, 33
Eisenhower, Dwight, 101
Eisner, Elliot, 174, 176
Electives, student, 131, 132, 152, 366-367
Elementary and Secondary Education Act (ESEA), 38, 288, 300
Elementary schools, 10, 80, 150-151, 306
　beginning of, 30
　classroom rules in, 227
　compact disks for, 45
　example of curriculum in, 364-365
　example of faculty in, 362
　example of teaching day of, 9-10, 50, 51
　facilities of, 363-364
　importance of teacher as role model in, 228
　interpersonal interchanges by teachers in, 54
　masculine vs. feminine behavior in, 146
　math and science teachers in, 39
　number of students in classes of, 50, 54
　requirements for teachers of, 346
　teaching shortage in, 349
　Thomas Jefferson and, 28
Eliot, Charles W., 31
Elite schools, 42, 45
Elkind, David, 87, 88
Emile (Rousseau), 26, 27
Emmer, Edmund, 216, 223
Empathy (of teacher), 235
Employment (of teachers), 299, 300

Employment (of students), 82, 84-86, 369

Encoding (memory), 77

Endorsements (teaching), 345-346

Energy (of teacher), 224

Engaged time, 56

Engineering career, 42

England, secondary schools in, 118, 238-239

English, Standard, 88-89

English as a second language (ESL), 52, 100, 206, 347, 364

English courses, 129, 130, 134

Enrollment, school, 42, 306, 333

Environment
 animals and their, 78-79
 classroom, 91, 232, 236-239
 in effective schools, 121
 learning, 57-58, 69
 perceptions of by children, 78
 role of in learning, 75, 76, 77

Epictetus, 321

Episode (Hodgins), 110

Equalization grants, 308, 330

Equal opportunity for education, 287, 291, 320, 321, 330
 as argument for nationalization of schools, 301
 college entrance, 134
 vs. excellence, 323
 and public aid to private schools, 332
 reasons for concern over, 287
 for students of all cultures, 91
 varying tax bases and, 307

Equal protection of the law, 292-293, 300

Equipment, school, 124, 126, 180

Equity (in education), 39

Erasmus, Desiderius, 26

ESL (English as a second language), 52, 100, 206, 347, 364

Essay Concerning Human Understanding, An (Locke), 27, 29

Essay questions, 267-269

Essays in Experimental Logic (Dewey), 32

Essential elements (in curriculum), 149

Essentialism, 63, 64-65, 122, 123

Essential schools, 133

Eternal truths (schools' teaching of), 117, 122-123

Ethics, courses on, 106

Ethics, personal code of for teachers, 352-354

Ethnic identity, 103-105

Europe, education in during Middle Ages, 25

Evaluation
 formative, 186
 intellectual process of, 162
 vs. measurement, 251-252
 summative, 186
 by teachers, 55, 180, 186-187, 250-251, 351
 of teachers, 37, 58.
  See also Teachers, competency/qualifications of

Evaluation and measurement, 250-276

Evaluation assignment, 258

Evaluation questions, 200

Evertson, Carolyn, 206, 223

Evolution, Darwin's theory of, 79, 108
 vs. creationism, 326, 328-329
 neglected in biology books, 336

Examination, final, 250, 367

Excellence (in education), 39, 61, 70, 322
 and economy, 40
 vs. equity, 323

Excellence (in thinking), 64

Excellence fund (for teachers), 134

Exclusionary rule, 297

Existentialism, 63, 66-67

Expectations (students' of teachers), 232-235

Expectations (teachers' of students), 119-120, 146, 194
 British study on, 238
 classroom management and, 226, 232, 233
 classroom rules and, 237
 student awareness of, 233

Expectations (effective schools and), 119-120

Expenses, school, 133, 308-309

Experience (in learning), 27

Experience and Nature (Dewey), 32

Experiential learning, 28

Experimentalism (Dewey's theory of), 32

Experimental studies (on effective schools), 122

Experimentation (in education), 39-40

Experiments in school laboratories, 124

Expert teacher, 192-194

Exploration (in learning), 117, 124, 209, 320

Expressive objectives, 172, 176-177, 178
 assessment of, 255, 256-258
 evaluation and, 186

Expulsion (from school), 295, 297, 328

Extended-day programs, 83

Extended education, 335

Extended family, 105

Extended school year, 130

Externalizing knowledge, 77

Extracurricular activies, 50, 53, 87, 88

Eye contact (student-teacher), 177, 178, 235, 236

Factories (and schools), 30

Faculty, 362, 365, 367, 370
 See also Staff/personnel, school

Fairness (of teacher), 224, 228, 234

Family, nature of American, 105

Family Educational Rights and Privacy Act, 295

Farming community schools, 29-30, 99.
 See also Rural schools

Father of Common Schools, 30

Federal funding for education, 37, 125, 291, 300, 307, 309
 grants for remedial instruction, 362, 264
 private schools and, 292, 331, 332-333
 state-to-state differences, 301

Federal role in education, 38-39, 128, 287-291
 grouping and, 206
 increasing over time, 37, 286, 313
 vs. local and state government, 98, 301, 304
 vs. local government, 330
 proposals for, 130-131

Feedback (to principals), 119

Feedback (to students), 57, 78, 131, 258
 Bloom's theory regarding, 171
 British study on, 238
 computer-provided, 44

effective schools and, 119
on homework, 11
lesson design and, 184
monitoring and, 185, 186
on writing, 204
Feedback (to teachers), 69, 119, 260
Field trips, 10, 177
Fifteen Thousand Hours (Rutter et al), 238
Fifth Amendment (applied to teachers), 298
Films (in schools), 5, 10, 43, 197
Final examinations, 250, 367
Finances, school, 30, 128, 307-310, 313
curriculum and, 150
state responsibility for, 301
Fine arts education, 64, 131, 132, 150
Fine motor skills, 163-164
Firmness (of teacher), 223
First Amendment, 291-292
applied to teachers, 298
censorship of textbooks and, 336
and public aid to private schools, 332
Fischer, Louis, 291
Flash cards, 185, 203
Flavell, John, 79
Foreign language education, 129, 130, 288
Formative evaluation, 186, 250, 251
Formula grants, 308
Fortas, Abe, 293
Founding Fathers Public School, 29
Fourteenth Amendment, 86, 291, 292-293
applied to teachers, 298
minorities and, 299
See also Due process
Fourth Amendment, 296, 298
Frank, Anne, 335
Frankel, Steven, 44, 45
Franklin, Benjamin, 29, 131
Freedom Not License! (Neill), 238
Freedom of assembly, 297, 299
Freedom of choice (in education), 39
Freedom of religion, 291-292, 298, 299
Freedom of speech/expression, 291, 293-294, 298, 299
Freedom to Learn (Rogers), 230

Freedom to teach (academic freedom), 298, 299
Friedenberg, Edgar, 39
Frowning (by teachers), 236
Fuhrmann, Barbara, 233
Fundamentalist Christians, 45, 326, 333, 335. *See also* Religion and education
Future (preparing students for), 158
Future (schools' impact on), 337
Future Farmers of America, 99
Future schools, 6, 40-45, 111, 318-337

Gallup Poll school survey, 371-373
Garfield, James, 31
Gender (differences according to), 146, 205
General welfare clause, 291
Geography education, 150
Gifted students, 100, 125, 128, 307, 313
individualism and, 322
reinforcement for, 229
Ginott, Haim, 230, 231
Glasser, William, 231
Global education, 326. *See also* International (peace) education
Global schools, 41, 42, 45
Goal-oriented instructional systems, 119
Goals, educational, 8, 50, 57, 99
assessment and, 260
curriculum and, 184
in effective schools, 119, 134
expectations and, 232
importance of, 119
mistaken, 231-232
vs. objectives, 160-164
students' individual, 88
Good High School, The (Lightfoot), 132
Goodlad, John, 39, 99, 131
Goodness (schools' teaching of), 117, 122
Goss v. *Lopez,* 295-296
Gould, Stephen Jay, 254
Government influence on schools, 286-313. *See also* Federal role in education; Local government; State government
Government funding of schools, 334-335.

See also Federal funding for education; Local government; State government
Grades, 84, 89, 260
vs. actual learning, 146
mixed messages sent by, 186-187
proposed reforms regarding, 129
students' rights regarding, 297
Grading papers, 51, 52, 53
Graduate work, 15
Graduation requirements, 45, 153-154
example of, 369
proposed reforms for, 129, 133
state-to-state differences in, 273-274, 301
tests for, 273-274, 288
trends in, 158, 324
Grammar, 10
Grammar schools, 28, 29
Grammatical Institute of the English Language, A (Webster), 29
Grants, federal/state, 307, 308
Great Books of the Western World, 64, 123, 319
Great Didactic, The (Comenius), 26
Great Society, 38
Greece, ancient, 24-25, 26, 29
Greene, Maxine, 88
Group learning/grouping, 60, 61, 120, 205-208, 366
advantages/limitations of, 207-208
after lectures, 200
in guided discovery, 210
vs. one-to-one, 192, 195, 205-208
Guidance (by teacher for student), 184
Guided discovery, 206, 208-211. *See also* Discovery learning
Guided note-taking lecture, 196
Guided practice, 203
Guided response (in learning), 163
Gutenberg, Johan, 26
Gymnasium, school, 361, 368

Hall, G. Stanley, 31
Halo effect, 272
Hamilton, Edith, 24, 25
Hand-eye coordination, 163-164

Handicapped students, 92, 100, 130, 205, 288
  Governors' report, 335
  courts and, 291, 313
  intelligence tests and, 254
  funding for, 307
  Public Law 94-142 for, 289, 320
  individualism and, 322
  nursery schools and, 334
  teachers for, 346
  See also Disabled students; Learning-disabled children
Handwriting, 266
Harris-Lanier, 120
Harvard College, 29
Harvard Law School, 29
Harvard University, 31
Hawaii (school system of), 98
Head Start, 38
Health education, 150
Health services, school, 38, 305
Herbert, George, 11
Heterogenous groups (students), 125, 205
Hidden/covert curriculum, 145, 146, 319
High School: A Report on Secondary Education in America (Boyer), 123
High schools, 5, 31, 306
  Boyer's recommendations on, 133-134
  example of curriculum in, 369-370
  example of faculty in, 370
  example of teaching day of, 10-11, 50, 51-52
High-technology schools, 43
Higher-level questions, 201
Higher-level thinking, 194, 200, 201, 208-209
Higher-order skills, 131, 320
Highland Park, Illinois, project, 209
Highlighting key points, 202
Hinge, 38-39
Hispanic students, 90, 103, 104
History education, 90, 150
Hodgins, Eric, 110
Holt, John, 39
Home center, 9
Homemaking courses, 320, 367
Homer, 160
Home schools, 43, 45, 329, 333
Homework, 59, 170, 238
Homicide rates, 40, 41
Homo erectus, 23
Homogenous groups (students), 125, 135, 205
Homosexuality, 327

Hopkins, Mark, 31
Horace's Compromise (Sizer), 120, 133
Hostility (in adolescents), 82-83
House of Representatives, 288
Housing (effect on schools), 15-16, 40, 41
How Children Fail (Holt), 39
Howe, Harold, 83
Hub-designed school, 363
Hufstedler, Shirley, 290
Human Resources Committee, 288
Hunt, James B., Jr., 129
Hunter, Madeline, 119, 182, 184
Hurried Child, The (Elking), 87
Hutchins, Robert, 123, 319
Hypotheses (in learning), 7, 8-9, 80

I.Q. tests, 33, 262
Iliad, The (Homer), 160
Illegal aliens, 300
Illich, Ivan, 126
Illiteracy, functional, 127
Illustrated Encyclopedia of Family Health, 335
Immigrants (to U.S.), 103-105, 130, 144
Inadequacy, student feeling of, 231
Incentives (for students or teachers), 133, 134
Incidental-intentional learning, 119
Income levels (and students), 40, 41
Independence, student, 229
Independent audit (of school), 311
Independent audit (of teachers), 357
Independent thought (in students), 208
India, ancient, 29
Indirect learning, 207, 210
Individuality (of students), 58, 65, 66-67, 322
Individualization (individualized instruction), 27-28
Individualized Education Program (IEP), 290
Individualized Instruction Plan (IIP), 92
Industrial arts, 266
Industrial revolution, 5-6, 29-30
Industry (of teacher), 224

Infant development, 26, 78, 79, 335
Infant mortality, 40, 41
Inflation (and school expenses), 41, 308-309
Information-processing theory, 74-77
Information technology, 102-103
Ingraham v. *Wright,* 295
In Grammar-Schools (Clarke), 29
Inner-city schools, 99, 228-229
In Praise of Diversity (Gold et al), 104
Inquiry, 7, 8, 50, 320
  in progressivism, 65
  instruments, 271-273
  teaching, 58, 159
Instruction, 11
  vs. curriculum, 159
  importance of, 164
  oral and written, 179
  planning for, 178-180
  purposes of, 182-184
Instructional activities, 184-185
Instructional design, 58, 168, 188
  effective teacher's mastery of, 193
  model for classroom design, 178-180
Instructional packages, 43
Instructional resources center, 363
Integration (of curriculum), 148
Intelligence, measurement of, 253-254
Intelligence tests, 253, 254
Interaction (in school), 12, 14, 54, 201.
  See also Relationships
Interactive areas (in demographics), 362
Interactive lecture, 196
Intercity areas, 362
Interdisciplinary approach, 134
International (peace) education, 325, 326, 327
International marketplace. *See* World marketplace and education
Interstate Highway System, 101
Interviews, 266, 271, 272
Introduction (in lesson design), 181
Inventories (for assessment by teachers), 266

Investing in Our Children: Business and the Public Schools, 122
Investments (in U.S.), 41
Israel, ancient, 29

Jackson, Philip, 54, 68
Jacula Prudentum (Herbert), 11
Japan, 40, 41
Jefferson, Thomas, 28-29
Job classifications, 6
Job Corps, 45
Johnson, Lyndon B., 38, 39, 288
Judaic-Christian ideals, 325, 326
Judicial influence on schools, 291-302
Junior high schools, 5, 306, 346
See also Middle schools
Juvenile delinquency, 83

Kennedy, John F., 38, 318, 336, 337
Kennedy, Robert, 44
Keyboarding courses, 103
Kids Don't Learn From People They Don't Like (Aspy), 235
Kindercare, 45
Kindergarten, 334, 335, 346
Knowledge (in ancient civilizations), 29
Knowledge (intellectual process of), 162
Knowledge, externalizing of, 77
Knowledge acquisition, 58, 74, 75
importance of, 319
Piaget's theory about, 79
Kounin, Jacob, 218, 223
Kozel, Jonathan, 39

Laboratories, 126, 255
Landers, Ann, 325
Language (students'), 88-89, 93, 103, 206
Language barriers, 88-89
Language courses, 123, 129, 130, 288
Latch-key children, 82, 105, 334
in middle school, 366-367
Latin grammar schools, 29
Lau v. *Nichols,* 320
Law-enforcement profession, 42
Laws affecting schools, 124-125, 291-302. *See also* Federal role in education
Lawsuits (and education), 106-108, 298-299

Learning, 58, 74-81, 131
enjoyment of, 124
as function of development, 78-79
as function of prior learning, 74-75, 78, 181
manipulation and, 126, 184
theories of, 11, 74-75, 181
Learning centers, 9, 10
Learning-disabled children, 34-35
Learning to learn, 117, 124, 134-135, 320
Least restrictive environment (LRE), 92
Lectures, 64, 132, 194
advantages/limitations of, 196-199
in mathematics, 194
questioning after, 200
Legislature, state, 5
Leinhardt, Gaea, 193
Lesson cycle, 182
Lesson plans, 9, 168, 178, 180-186
Liberal arts career, 42
Liberty interests, 296
Libraries, school, 124, 126, 127, 335-336
books protested, 335-336
in elementary schools, 361
Life-long learning (continuing/adult education), 109, 320, 334
Life expectancy, 40, 41
Lightfoot, Sara Lawrence, 132
Line-and-staff organizations, 305
Lingua franca, 88
Listening center, 9
Literature (schools' teaching of), 90
Literature distribution by students, 297
Local board of education, 148, 149, 304. *See also* Boards of education
Local government and schools, 128, 206, 286, 291
vs. federal government, 301, 304, 330
funding, 307, 309
responsibilities, 303-309
vs. state government, 303, 330
Locke, John, 26, 27, 29
Locker searches, 291, 297, 312, 328
Logic, the Theory of Inquiry (Dewey), 32

Long-term memory, 77, 78, 202
Lortie, Dan, 69
Low-income students, 289
Lunch, school (free), 5, 286, 305, 307
federal grants and, 364
Lunch period, school, 364, 366
Lyceum, 25
Lynd, R. S., 110

Macbeth (Shakespeare), 336
Madeline Hunter method of teaching, 119, 182, 184
Madonna (singer), 87
Magazines, 66
Mager, Robert, 144, 160, 163, 173
quote on intangible results, 250
view on assessing student attitudes, 259
Magnet schools, 42, 125, 320
desegregation and, 300
example of, 368
individualism and, 322
Mainstreaming, 289, 290
Maintaining Sanity in the Classroom (Dreikurs), 231
Management, career in, 6, 42
Management of a City School, The (Perry), 223
Management, classroom. *See* Classroom management
Management by objectives (MBO), 119
Managerial objectives (vs. academic), 178
Manipulation (in memory), 77
Mann, Horace, 30
Manual arts, 63
Manual dexterity, 266
Manufacturing industries, 6
Marriage, student, 297
Martin Luther King, Jr.'s birthday, 325
Mary Kay Cosmetics, 121
Massachusetts Bay Colony, 144
Massachusetts Historical Society, 29
Massachusetts law, 28, 29
Massachusetts State Board of Education, 30
Master craftsman, 192
Master teachers, 131
Mastery learning, 55
Mastery Learning (Block), 119
Matching funds, 307
Matching questions, 271

Mathematics education, 11, 194, 204, 209
  achievement scores and, 128
  career (or magnet) schools for, 42
  changes in teaching of, 37, 41
  debriefing process in, 258
  effective teaching of, 59
  elite schools for, 42
  flash cards for, 185
  in intermediate grades, 151
  proposed reforms in, 129, 130
  after Sputnik, 288
  in U.S. vs. other countries, 41
Mathematics teachers, 39
McGuffey's Reader, 106, 108
Mead, Margaret, 110
Measurement (in education), 252-254
  and evaluation, 250-276
  vs. evaluation, 251-252
  of student progress, 260-273
Mechanism (in learning), 163
Media, effect on schoolchildren, 5, 66, 87, 155
Medical care (in U.S. vs. other countries), 40, 41
Medical schools, women in, 34
Megatrends: Ten New Directions Transforming Our Lives (Naisbitt), 100
"Melting pot," 104
Memorization, 194, 202, 319
Memory, 76-77, 202, 262
Mental discipline, 64
Mental maturity tests, 253
Microcomputers, 5, 44
Microprocessors, 102
Middle Ages, 25
Middle schools, 5, 52-53, 157, 306
  contemporary trend toward, 151
  curriculum in, 366-367
  facilities of, 365-366
  requirements for teachers of, 346
  See also Junior high schools; Suburban schools
Middletown (Lynd), 110
Migration, societal, 102
Miller, Arthur, 335
Mini-lecture, 196
Minorities (and education), 124-125, 299-301, 313
  growth of percentage of, 90
  U.S. Department of Education and, 291
Misbehavior, 204, 218, 231-232

Mismeasure of Man, The (Gould), 254
Mission (goals) of school, 119, 134
Mobility, physical, 101, 287
  as argument for nationalization of schools, 301
  teaching profession and, 357
Mobility, social, 108
Modeling (in learning), 75
Monasteries, 25, 26
Monitoring (of students), 179-180, 185, 186
  for seatwork, 204
  by students, 187
Montaigne, Michel de, 26
Montessori, Maria, 34-35, 124
Montessori schools, 125
Morale of teachers, 58
Moral relativism, 326
Morals (schools' teaching of), 106, 157, 325. *See also* Values
Mormon religion, book against, 335
Motor skills, 163-164
Mount Holyoke College, 194
Mouse (computer), 44
Movie projectors (in schools), 43-44
Multicultural approach, 90-91. *See also* Cultural pluralism
Multilingual teachers, 89
Multiple-choice questions, 185, 267, 269-271
Multiple-response questions, 270
Multiple instructions, 10
Multi-purpose rooms (in schools), 361, 363, 368
Music education, 42, 90, 109, 365, 369

Nader, Ralph, 325
Naisbitt, John, 6, 100, 102
National Association of Secondary School Principals, 133
National Center for Education Statistics, 308, 323, 331
National Commission on Excellence in Education, 127, 128
National Council for Social Studies, 355
National Council for Teachers of English, 336, 355
National Council for Teachers

of Mathematics, 355
National Council of Year-Round Education, 43
National defense (and education), 35-36, 37. *See also* National needs
National Defense Education Act, 37, 124, 288, 313
National Education Association (NEA), 31, 37, 44, 352, 354, 355
National education system, 41-42, 45, 98, 301-302
National Governors' Association, 335
National needs (and education), 117, 124, 291. *See also* National defense (and education)
National schools, 41-42, 45. *See also* Nationalization (of schools)
National Science Board, 130
Nationalization (of schools), 301-302, 330. *See also* National schools
Nation at Risk, A (U.S. Department of Education), 5, 117, 127, 128-129, 290, 322
Neatness (of classroom), 224, 233
NEA Today, 43
Negligence (by teachers), 298-299
Neill, A. S., 238
New Basics, 129
New biology, 37
New England Association of Colleges and Secondary Schools, 126, 324
  See also Colonial American education
New England Primer, The, 106, 108
New Jersey v. *T.L.O.,* 296-297
Newman, 6
New math, 37
New physics, 37
"New realism," 336
Newspapers, 66
New students, 10
"Ninety-day wonders," 35
Nobel Prize professors, 42
Nonverbal communication (by teachers), 235-236
Norm-referenced tests, 263, 265
Normal school, 30
North Central Association of Schools and Colleges, 126

Northwest Association of Secondary and Higher Schools, 126
Nuclear family, 105
Nuclear war, education on, 327
Number cube, 185
Nursery school, 306, 334
Nurses, school, 5

Obedience, 319
Objectives (educational), 36, 160-164
  academic vs. managerial, 178
  assessment and, 255-260
  in classroom instructional plan, 172-178, 186-187, 255-260
  in lesson plans, 9
  in lesson plans vs. unit, 188
  tests and, 276
Objective tests (vs. essay tests), 268
Observation (by teacher of students), 58, 201, 266
Observation (skill of), 110
Observation record, 257, 266
Odyssey of the Mind, 174
Of Mice and Men (Steinbeck), 335
Ohio State University, 61
Olympics of the Mind, 256
One-room school, 41
Operant conditioning, 36
Operationalizing a term, 177
Operational level (in cognitive development), 81
Opinion questions, 200
Oral communication (in classroom), 201
Oral presentations (by students), 255
Orderliness (in classroom), 224, 234
Organization (in learning), 163
See also Classroom management
Organization, school, 128, 150, 303, 313
  different types of, 5
  levels of schools, 306
  from students' viewpoint, 4
  today vs. yesterday, 5, 6
Otis-Lennon School Ability Test, 262
"Ould deluder, Satan," law, 29
Outcome-based learning, 35-36
Outcome-driven conceptualization, 159
Over-choice, 108

Overhead projectors (in school), 5, 10, 43, 197

Paideia Proposal, The (Adler), 63, 131-132
Paper-and-pencil tests, 255
Paperwork (school), 313, 365
Parducci v. *Rutland*, 298
Parental involvement, 83, 228, 364
Parent conferences, 266, 364
Parent groups, 311
Parents
  of adolescents, 83
  single, 5, 105, 106, 334
  working. *See* Working parents
Parochial schools. *See* Private parochial schools
Participant-observer, 110, 111, 146
Passow, Harry, 319
Patriotism, 325, 326
Patterson, C. H., 26
Pauper School Act, 29
Peace Corps, 45
Peace education, 325, 327
Pedagogy, 58, 65, 70
Peddiwell, J. Abner, 145
Peer-matching network (for students), 127
Peer pressure, 83
Peer tutoring, 187, 206
People for the American Way, 326, 336
Pep rallies, 120, 369
Perception (in learning), 27, 78, 79-80, 163
Perception (selective nature of), 111
Perennialism, 63-64, 122, 123
Performance (of teachers), 58, 59, 129
Permissive education, 39, 231
Perry, Arthur C., 223, 225
Personality tests, 254
Personnel/staff, school, 5, 117, 304, 305, 307
Phi Delta Kappa, 59
Philosophers, 24, 25, 27
Philosophy of teaching, 50, 62-68
  and lesson design, 183
  personal, 62-63, 67, 70, 183, 229, 240
Physical education, 28, 63, 266
  in essentialism, 64
  example of, 365, 368
  in intermediate grades, 151
  in primary grades, 150

separation by gender for, 205
Physical performance exercises, 255
Physical proximity (of teachers to students), 236
Piaget, Jean, 78-79, 80-81
Pickering, Marvin, 298
Pickering v. *Board of Education*, 298
Picketing by students, 297
Place Called School, A (Goodlad), 39, 131
Plagiarism, 352
Planning (for teaching), 168-188
  consistency in, 188
  for evaluation, 186-187
  instructional objectives in, 172-178
  normative model for, 178-180
Plant maintenance, 305
Plato, 24, 25, 63
Pledge of Allegiance, 297
Plessy v. *Ferguson*, 299
Plyler v. *Doe*, 300
Poetry memorization, 319
Police dogs in school, 291, 312
Policies/practices, school, 66, 287, 301, 304-305, 365, 367
Political beliefs of teachers, 299
Political influence on schools, 305
Political scientists, 100
Poor Richard's Almanack (Franklin), 29, 131
"Poppa, Don't Preach," 87
"Popular" education, 30-31
Population, school-age children proportion of, 15-16
Post-industrial era, 6
Postdoctoral studies, 37
Poverty (and schools), 43, 288
  students living in, 84, 124, 125, 130
Power tests, 267
Practical vs. theoretical education, 28
Practice (by students), 57, 64, 204
Pragmatism, 32, 67
Praise (of students), 228-229, 235
  British study on, 237, 238
Prayer in schools, 108, 286, 292, 297
Pregnancy, student, 297, 325, 327, 352
Prehistoric times, 23-24
Prekindergartens, 306

Prenatal counseling, 335
Preprofessionals, 9
Preschools, 37, 38, 45
  federal funding for, 334
  increasing use of, 155
  masculine vs. feminine
    behavior in, 146
Primary grades, 150
Principal (school), 118, 119,
  129, 286
Printing press, 26, 30
Private parochial schools, 108,
  125, 205
  federal aid to, 292, 332-333
  tuition payments for, 292, 331
Private schools, 125, 329,
  331-333
Privatization, 332
Probable cause, 296
Problem solving, 123, 124, 320
  grouping for, 206, 207
  in guided discovery, 210
  in progressivism, 65
  in secondary schools, 194
  proposed reforms regarding,
    131
Problem-solving objectives,
  172, 174-176, 178
  assessment of, 255, 256-258
  evaluation and, 186, 187
Process-product research, 116
Process of Education, The
  (Bruner), 37
Productivity (economic
  indicator), , 41
Profanity (in textbooks), 326,
  336
Professional careers, 6
Professional teachers, 11, 67-68
Programmed instruction, 35-36
Programmed textbooks, 36
Progressive education
  (progressivism), 32, 34, 63,
  65, 123, 208
Promiscuity, student, 327
Promotion, 291, 274, 323
Property taxes/interests, 296,
  307
Psychological climate of
  classroom, 11
Psychologists (school), 5
Psychologists/psychology
  (applied to education),
  225-226
Psychomotor domain, 161,
  163-164
PTA, 365
Public address (PA) system
  (loudspeaker), 55, 121
Public control of schools, 30

Public education, 30, 111, 125
  beginning of, 34, 286,
    330-331
  purpose of, 319-323
Punctuality, 319
Punishment/consequences (in
  school), 121, 225, 226, 228,
  232, 237
  British study on, 237-239
  effective schools and, 119
  unreasonable, 295, 297
  See also Corporal
    punishment
Purchasing offices, school, 305
Pure lecture, 196
Purposefulness (in classroom),
  234

Quality Data, 44
Quality of life, 40-41
Quality of schools, 122-126,
  291, 301, 330. *See also*
  Schools, effective
Quest for Certainty, The
  (Dewey), 32
Questioning (as teaching
  method), 195, 199-200
Questionnaires, 271
Questions, test, 267-273

Racial balance in schools, 125,
  286, 103-105
Racial identity, 103-105
Ramps, school, 286
Rating scales, 271, 272
Ratio, student-teacher, 126, 206
Rational thought, 63, 67
Ravitch, Diane, 132
Reading, 59, 200, 235
  effective teaching of, 59
  grouping for, 206
  psychomotor skills in
    learning, 163-164
  right-to-read program, 289
Reading lists, 326, 335-336
Reading specialists, 346, 364
Reagan, Ronald, 130, 290
*Real World of the Public
  Schools, The* (Broudy), 98
Reasonable cause, 296-297
Recall (intellectual process of),
  111, 162, 201
Receiving (in learning), 162
Recitation, 64, 159, 185
Reconstructionists, 124
Records, school, 295, 297
Red Badge of Courage, The
  (Crane), 160

Reference services (for
  teachers), 127
Reflection/reflective practice,
  62, 70
  by students, 186, 267
  by teachers, 195
  on teaching/learning
    process, 55, 61-62
Reflective inquiry, 6, 7-13,
  16-17, 250
  analyzing school experience
    as part of, 14, 16
  and conceptions of quality
    schools, 122
Reforms in schools, 5, 37, 135,
  354
  experimentation and, 39
  as result of research, 116,
    124, 128-134
Rehearsal strategies, 202
Reinforcement, 225, 228-232
Relationships, student-student,
  60, 70, 146, 236
Relationships, teacher-student,
  70, 146, 235-236, 354
  for novice teachers, 61
  in cooperative vs.
    competitive environment,
    59-60
  enjoyment in, 69
  in establishing rules, 227
  existentialism and, 67
  See also Interaction (in
    school)
Relationships, teacher-teacher,
  61-62, 69, 352
Relevance (in education), 39,
  184
Relevance (in learning), 77, 78
Reliability (of test), 254-255,
  272
Religion and education, 144,
  291-292, 326, 331-333
  in ancient Greece, 25
  in Colonial America, 28, 29, 30
  home schools, 43
  during Middle Ages, 25
  students rights regarding, 297
Remedial instruction, 51, 128,
  134, 274
  federal grants for, 362, 364
Renaissance period, 26-28
Repetition, 202
Repetitive work, 319
Research on teaching, 50, 116,
  117-122
  regarding grouping for
    learning, 206
  professional organizations
    and, 355

reflective practice and, 62
Research and development (in U.S.), 41
Reserved powers clause, 98
Reserve Officers Training Corps (ROTC), 153
Resident academies, 43
Resource centers, 363
Resource materials, 52, 53, 69 117, 305
  as criterion for effective schools, 126
  curriculum and, 150
  lesson design and, 180, 183
  principal and, 118
  teaching students to use, 124, 127
Respect (for students/teachers), 234
Responding (in learning), 162, 177
Responsibility of teachers, 54-62, 69-79, 297-299
  for instilling values, 108
Responsibility of schools, 5, 40, 105-109
  drug abuse and, 5, 106, 144
  vs. family or church, 144
  vs. personal responsibility, 127, 133
  sexual relationships and, 144
  as surrogate parent, 105-106
  in teaching values, 108, 163
Restlessness of students, 10
Restrooms/lavatories, school, 9, 10, 286, 363
Retaining students (from promotion), 323
Retrieval (of memory), 77, 78
Reutter, Edmund, 296
Revenge, student desire for, 231
Reward-and-ignore system, 229-230
Rewards (in school), 225, 226, 228-229, 237
  British study on, 237, 238
RIF (reduction in force), 291
Right-to-read program, 289
Rights of students, 5, 287, 292, 293-297
Rights of teachers, 297-299
Ripple effect, 218
Robotics, 103
Rock music (effect on schoolchildren), 87
Rogerian philosophy, 225, 230, 232
Rogers, Carl R., 225, 230

Role playing, 258, 266
Roles, male/female, 326
Roman Empire (destruction of), 25
Rome, ancient, 25-26, 29
Romeo and Juliet (Shakespeare), 336
Rosenshine, Barak, 57, 58, 68, 182, 200
Rote learning, 108, 157, 319
Rousseau, Jean Jacques, 26, 27, 28, 31, 208
Rowe, Mary Bude, 201
Rules, classroom, 226-228, 231, 232
  at beginning of school year, 236-237, 238
  controversy about, 239
Rural schools, 41-42, 51, 99
  in nineteenth century, 29-30
Rush, Benjamin, 29
Rust Belt, 102
Ryan, Kevin, 61

Saber-Tooth Curriculum, The (Benjamin), 145
Safety (in classroom), 234-235
Salaries of teachers, 58, 129, 134, 301, 349, 350
  collective bargaining for, 354, 355
Sales taxes (as funding for schools), 308
Salutatorian, 104
Saluting the flag, 299
San Antonio Independent School District v. *Rodriguez,* 307
Santayana, George, 24
Sarcasm/ridicule (by teacher/students), 224, 234
Satellite technology for schools, 41-42
Schaefer, Robert, 33
Schedule, school, 151-152
Scholastic Aptitude Tests (SATs), 39, 128
Schon, Donald, 62
School and Society, The (Dewey), 8, 32
School closings, 106
School committee, 304
School District of Abington Township v. *Schempp,* 332
School districts, 169, 276, 305
  boundaries, 302, 303-304
  poor vs. rich, 307, 308
  tests and, 276
School facilities, 361-362

  for elementary schools, 363-364
  for high schools, 361, 368-369
  for middle schools, 365-366
School office, 363, 369
School policies/practices, 66, 287, 301, 304-305, 365, 367
School year, 42-43
School settings, 12, 59, 61
  impact on teachers, 69
  studies on effective, 5
Schooling in Capitalist America (Bowles et al), 108
Schools
  analyzing, 13-14
  choice of, 125-126, 135
  as communal acculturation agency, 108
  community and, 98-111
  dynamic atmosphere of, 4-6
  history of, 22-33
  quality of, 116-135
  reputations of, 116
  response to changes in community, 100-105
  responsibility of. See Responsibility of schools
  social change and, 38, 105-109
  students' perception of, 59
  See also Education
Schools, effective, 116-122
  faculty in, 120-121
  high expectations and, 119-120
  principals and, 118, 119
Science education, 42, 59, 124
  achievement scores and, 128
  changes in, 37, 41
  debriefing process in, 258
  in intermediate grades, 151
  in primary grades, 150
  proposed reforms in, 129, 130
  after Sputnik, 288
Science teachers, 39
Scientific investigation, 64
Scientific method, 33, 37
Scolding (by teacher), 224
Scopes, John, 329
Search and seizure, 291, 296-297, 298
Seatwork, 56, 57, 204
Secondary schools, 50, 54
  classroom rules in, 227
  facilities in, 361, 368-369
  grouping and, 208
  during nineteenth century, 31

teachers in, 80-81, 194, 346

Secular humanism, 326-327

Segregation, school, 38, 299

Selection questions, 267

Self-checks/evaluation for students, 185, 187

Self-concept/self-esteem (of students), 68, 88, 89, 230

Self-contained teaching kits, 5

Senior high schools, 306

Sensitive periods (in child development), 34

Sensory channels, 76, 77

Separate-but-equal doctrine, 299

Separation of church and state, 28, 125

Sequence (of curriculum), 148

Sequence (in tests), 262

Serial polygamy, 105

Serrano v. *Priest,* 307

"Sesame Street, " 155

Set (in learning), 163

Sewing courses, 106

Sex (in textbooks), 336

Sex discrimination, 320. *See also* Women

Sex education, 106, 325, 327

Sex segregation, 205

Sexual activity, teenage, 83, 326, 327

Shakespeare, William, 63, 336

Shelton v. *Tucker,* 301

Shops (work), school, 361, 367, 368

Shor, Ira, 38

Shorehan, New York, project, 209

Short-answer questions, 267, 268-269

Short-term memory, 76-77, 202

Silberman, Charles, 39

Silence (by teacher), 236

Simon, Martin, 194, 209

Simulation, 258

Single-parent families, 5, 105, 106, 334

Situational ethics, 326

Sizer, Theodore, 133, 120

Skill exchanges (for students), 127

Skinner, B. F., 36, 225, 226

Skinnerian philosophy, 225, 226, 232

Slavery, 103

Slide projector, 197

Small-town schools, 99

Smiling (by teacher), 235, 236

Smoking, cigarette (and schools), 297, 324

Social-learning theory, 75

Social class, 108

Social conduct/knowledge (in schools), 65

Social needs (of students), 207

Social reconstructionism, 63, 65-66

Social sensitivity (schools' teaching of), 123

Social skills, 88, 206

Social studies education, 42, 124, 129, 258

in intermediate grades, 150-151

in primary grades, 150

Social traditions, knowledge of, 65

Social values, 5, 6, 323

in essentialism, 65

impact on schools, 38, 144, 105-109

purpose of schools and, 319

schools' role in transmitting, 106-108, 124-125, 320

social reconstructionism and, 66

See also Society and schools

Social welfare professions, 42

Social workers (school), 5

Societal trends, 100-105

Society and schools, 17, 22-23, 40, 124-125, 320, 337. *See also* Social values

Socioeconomic status (SES), 86-87, 117, 118, 218-219

Sociograms, 266

Sociologists/sociology (applied to education), 54, 59, 69, 109-110

Sociometric devices, 271

Socrates, 24, 25

Socratic dialogue, 64

Software programs, 43, 44

Some Thoughts on Education (Locke), 26

Space race and education, 36-37, 39, 208

Sparta, 25

Special education, 286, 289-290

in elementary schools, 361

requirements for teachers of, 346

resource teachers for, 5, 51

teaching shortage in, 349

Special-interest groups, 100, 116, 318

Special-purpose classrooms, 361

Specialization, subject, 156-157

Special programs, 322

Speed tests, 267

Spelling, 10

Sports, school, 109, 369

Sputnik, 36-37, 41, 124, 128, 288

SRA Achievement Series, 263

Staff/personnel, school, 5, 117, 304, 305, 307

in effective schools, 120-121

in elementary school, 362, 365, 367

Stances (teaching), 67-68, 70

Standard English dialect, 88-89

Standard error of measurement, 255, 262

Standards, school, 302, 333

Stanford Binet, 262

Stanford University, 68

State-approved textbooks, 169

State-wide achievement tests, 286

State-wide curriculum, 149

State-wide school district, 303

State education agency, 302-303

State examinations for certification, 356-358

State government (and schools) 128, 206, 286

budget for education, 302

curriculum and, 148, 149

educational resources provided by, 291

vs. federal government, 301, 304

funding for schools, 307, 309, 310

vs. local government, 303, 330

responsibility for, 302-303, 313

State school board, 302

State universities, 30

Steinbeck, John, 335

Stem (of question), 269

Stevens, Robert, 57, 68, 182, 200

Stevenson, R. L., 105

System (Stevenson), 105

Stickers, school, 120

Stimuli (in learning), 75, 76, 211

Storage (of memory), 77, 78, 181

Strategies, learning, 77, 320

Strategies, teaching, 8, 58, 193, 195

evaluation and, 251

See also Teaching methods

Street Corner Society (Whyte), 110

Stress (students'), 328
Strip search, 296
Student, experience as, 4, 12-13
Student-centered education, 28
Student choices (in schools), 63, 65, 117, 135
    in establishing classroom rules, 226, 231
Student-focused strategies, 195, 196, 205-211
Student rights, 5, 287, 292, 293-297
Student-teacher ratio, 126, 206
Student teachers, 227
Students, 12, 50, 74
    authority figures and, 146
    competition with peers, 146
    life outside the classroom for, 81-93
    perception of teachers and schools, 59
    pressure to achieve on, 87-88
    searches of, 291
    self-concepts of, 68
    self-discipline by, 218, 219, 220, 230
    self-expression by, 78
    social interactions among, 12, 91
    socioeconomic status (SES) of, 86-87
    in U.S. vs. other countries, 41
Substitute teachers, 55
Suburban schools, 38, 99. *See also* Middle schools
Suicide (by students), 83, 326
Suicide-prevention programs in schools, 325, 327-328
Summarizing (by students), 200
Summary (in lesson design), 185-186
Summating review (in lesson design), 185
Summative evaluations, 186, 250, 251
SummerMath for Teachers, 209
Summer school, 15, 134
Summer workshops, 91
Sunbelt states, 102, 287
Superintendent of schools, 276, 304-305
Super schools, 43
Supervisory responsibility, 53, 305, 364
Supply questions, 267
Supreme Court rulings, 5, 287, 301, 320
    against Bible reading in schools, 331-332
    on creationism, 329

on corporal punishment, 294-295
on school funding, 307
on searches of students, 296-297
on segregation/desegregation, 299-301
on students' freedom of speech, 293-294
Suspension (from school), 226, 295, 297
Sweden, 40, 41
Symbols, school, 120, 146
Sympathy (of teacher), 224
Synergistic process, 13
Synthesis (intellectual process of), 58, 162
Synthesis questions, 200
Systematic education, 160, 162, 164, 211
Systemized teacher evaluation, 5
Systems of education (in U.S.), 98

Table of specifications, 266
Tabula rasa, 26, 27
Talking during class (behavior problem of), 217, 218
Tanner, Daniel, 160
Tardiness, student, 218
Task-focusers, 67, 68
Task Force on Education for Economic Growth, 129
Task forces, 311-312, 322
Tax rates, school, local government and, 304, 305
Taxes for support of schools, 28, 308, 331
Taxonomies, 161, 163, 201
Teacher, transition from student to, 12-13
Teacher and Child (Ginott), 230
Teacher Corps Legislation, 38
Teacher-education programs, 344-345, 357
Teacher-focused strategies, 195-204
Teacher preparation, 344-347, 349-352
    British study on, 238
    field work for, 375-376
    and public aid to private schools, 333
    See also Training (for teachers)
Teacher Professional Development Term, 134
Teacher-proof curriculum, 39
Teacher shortage, 37-38, 129,

348-349
Teachers, 12-13, 77-78
    ambivalence in, 68
    in ancient civilizations, 29
    administrative burden on, 129
    autocratic, 231
    changes in role of, 50
    compact disks' effect on, 44, 45
    competency/qualifications of, 5, 37, 58, 288, 291
    current issues facing, 318-337
    with doctorates/graduate degrees, 43, 367
    demand and supply of, 15-16, 348-349
    elementary school, 80
    liberal education for, 132
    as mentors and role models, 51
    minority, 38
    personal code of ethics of, 352-354
    political activities by, 291
    principals and, 119
    as professionals, 11
    proposed reforms for, 129, 130, 131, 134
    as role models, 226, 228, 230, 238
    secondary school, 80-81, 194, 346
    students' perception of, 59
    substandard credentials of, 37
    as theorists, 8-9
    top researchers as, 42
Teachers, beginning, 61, 68, 238, 252
    recommendations for, 349-354
Teachers, effective, 116, 120-121, 129, 160, 192-194
    British study on, 238-239
    classroom rules and, 237
    continued self-development by, 357
    proposed rewards/incentives for, 133, 134
    time management by, 220-223
    traits and management skills of, 223-225
    See also Teaching, effective
Teachers' colleges, 30
Teachers' lounge, 363
Teaching, 9, 12-13, 24, 50
    origins of, 22-30, 145, 192
    reasons for enjoyment of, 68-69

Teaching, effective
elements of, 194-196
importance of first day, 350-351
varying instruction for, 192-211
Teaching certificate, 15
Teaching day, 50-54
Teaching jobs available, 348-349
Teaching/learning process, 55, 61-62, 211
during Middle Ages, 192
Teaching methods, 193, 194
content-specific and general, 195
new, 4, 5
studies on effective, 5, 57
See also Strategies, teaching
Teaching profession
career decision on, 344
characteristics of, 16
code of ethics for, 352, 353-354
deciding on career in, 108
how it differs from others, 358-359
in various states, 356-357
journals for, 355
magnet school for, 42
organizations for, 352, 354-356
paperwork required in, 51-52
reasons to enter, 14-16
working hours of, 51, 52, 53
working year of, 51
workweek of, 15
Teaching responsibilities, 54-62, 69-70
See also Supervisory responsibilities
Teaching specialties, 345, 346, 347-348
Team building, 120-121
Technical jobs, 6
Technology
courses in, 130
effect on schools, 5, 102-103, 145, 209
in schools, 36, 43-44
Television
effect on children, 5, 66, 155
in schools, 5, 36, 43
Tenth Amendment, 287
Tenure (for teachers), 291, 298
Test norms, 261
Test of Cognitive Skills, 262
Test-taking skills, 261
Testing and research department, 276

Tests
analysis of by teachers, 250
designing, 266-273
educational, 252
for evaluation by teachers, 55
national movement for, 273-275, 276
as proof of teacher effectiveness, 116
patterns of, 274
psychological, 252, 254
scores for year-round students on, 43
teacher-prepared, 266
uniform, 45
U.S. scores vs. foreign students', 330
Tests, achievement, 33, 116, 250, 263
effective schools and, 117, 118, 122
criterion-referenced, 263, 264-265
international comparisons, 127-128
norm-referenced, 263, 265
purpose of schools and, 319
reliability of, 255
state-wide, 286
subtests on, 263
validity of, 254
See also Tests, standardized
Tests, aptitude, 33, 253, 262
Tests, commercial, 260-265
Tests, educational, 33
Tests, standardized, 58, 59, 250, 260-265, 301
criticism of, 87
curriculum and, 261
declining scores in, 320, 330
for admission to teacher-education programs, 357
for teaching certificate, 357
judicial influence on use of, 291
proper and improper use in instruction, 261
proposed reforms regarding, 129
reforms precipitated by, 312
reliability of, 255
trend toward increased use of, 158
validity of, 254
See also Tests, achievement
Texas Educational Assessment of Minimum Skills, 264-265
Textbooks, 64, 65, 335-336
censorship committees for, 336

classroom instructional design and, 169
decentralization of schools and, 301
proposed reforms regarding, 132
social messages in, 90
in social reconstructionism, 66
Thomas Jefferson's views on, 28-29
The Greek Way (Hamilton), 25
The Schools We Deserve: Reflections on the Educational Crisis of Our Time (Ravitch), 132
Thelen, Herbert, 58
Theoretical constructs, 9
Theoretical vs. practical education, 28
Third Wave, 6
Thoughts upon the Mode of Education (Rush), 29
Threatening (by teacher), 224
Time-on-task research, 11
Time allocation/management, 55-57, 121, 131, 150, 194, 220-223
lesson design and, 183, 184
in analyzing the curriculum, 169-170
in elementary school, 151
in guided discovery, 210
in high schools, 152-153
in middle schools/junior high schools, 151-152
Time for Results: The Governors' 1991 Report of Education, 335
Time servers, 68
Tinker v. *Des Moines Independent School District,* 293-294
Toffler, Alvin, 6
Torts (school-related), 299
Town schools, 41. *See also* City schools vs. country schools
Trade in U.S. and education, 40, 41
Traditional knowledge (in school curricula), 123
Training programs (for teachers), 59, 194, 288. *See also* Teacher preparation
Transcripts, differentiated, 158
Transportation, student, 305. *See also* Busing
Travel fund (for teachers), 134
Trends, societal, 100-105
Trends in education, 208-209, 291

True-false questions, 267, 270-271
Truths, eternal (schools' teaching of), 117, 122-123
Tucson Education Association, 216
Tuition tax credits (for private schools), 332, 333
Tuskegee Institute, 33
Tutoring, 52, 53, 370, 375
  in ancient Greece, 192
  of students by students, 59
  See also Remedial instruction
Twentieth Century Fund's Task Force on Federal Elementary and Secondary Education Policy, 130
Tyler, Ralph, 32
Typing courses, 103, 164, 320

U.S. v. *Jefferson,* 300
U.S. Department of Education, 5, 58, 116, 117, 287
  beginnings of, 290-291
  organization of, 291
U.S. Office of Education, 287, 290
Understanding, checking for, 200
Undocumented aliens, 300
Unemployment, 5, 6, 40, 41
  effect of on community's perception of schools, 99
  effect on school population, 16
Unit plan, 168, 187-188
Urbanization, 101-102, 104, 313
Urban (city) schools, 38, 89
  example of teaching day of, 51-52
  external factors in academic success in, 81-93
  in nineteenth century, 29-30
Urinalysis (for drug abuse detection), 328
Using Behavioral Objectives in the Classroom (Tanner), 260

Valedictorian, 104
Valente, William, 299
Validity (of test), 254-255, 272
Value complex, 163
Value systems, personal, 110, 111

Values (schools' teaching of), 108, 127, 133, 144, 163
  change in, and schools, 323
  characterization by, 163
  controversy about, 163
  internalized, 163
  See also Morals
Values clarification, 325
Valuing (in learning), 163
Variability (in teaching methods), 193, 194, 195, 211
  grouping and, 207
Variance (in tests), 255
VCR cassettes, 5
Veneral disease (teenage), 327
Verbal achievement scores, 128
Verbal fluency, 88-89
Verbal reasoning (testing of), 262
Verbal skills, grouping and, 206
Veterans' groups, 325
Video display terminal (VDT), 44
Videotapes, 66
Vietnamese students, 103, 104
Vietnam War, 37, 39, 293-294
Vigilance (of teacher), 224
Violence (in schools), 219, 235
Virtue (Locke's theory of), 27
Vocational education, 27, 100, 153
  example of, 368, 369
  funding for, 307
  proposed reforms for, 129, 131
  qualifications of teachers in, 370
  salary of teachers in, 286
  unemployment rates as spur for, 325
Vocational high schools, 320
Voice for Informed Parents, 326
Voice synthesizers, 44
Voluntary actions by students, 177-178, 259-260
Voucher system, 125, 332, 333

Walker, Alice, 335
Waller, Willard, 54
Walt Disney World, 120
Walts, B. J., 297
Warner, W. Lloyd, 110
War of Poverty, 38, 45, 299
Warren, Earl, 298

Washington, Booker T., 33, 34
Webster, Noah, 29
Western civilization (and education), 22
Western College Association, 126
West German, 40, 41
Westley v. *Rossi,* 294
What Works: Research about Teaching and Learning (U.S. Department of Education), 58, 83
Whitehead, Alfred North, 32
Whyte, William F., 110
Wilkerson, Doxey, 116
William Penn Charter School, 29
Williams College, 31
Wilson, Woodrow, 30, 31
Wise, Arthur, 349
Wizard of Oz, The, 335
Women, 124, 288, 313
  education during Renaissance and, 27
  in medical school, 34
  See also Sex discrimination; Sex segregation
Wood, Robert, 130
Work ethic, 11
Working memory, 76-77
Working parents, 5, 82, 83, 105
  and federal funding for child care, 334
  nursery schools and, 334
  and school as child-care agency, 106
World marketplace and education, 40, 45, 124, 130, 209, 322
World War II, 34, 35, 38, 120
Writing, 255, 257
  by elementary students, 10
  effective teaching of, 59
  non-graded, 78
  practice and feedback for, 204
  proposed reforms regarding, 131, 134
  psychomotor skills in learning, 163-164

Year, school, 130
Year-round schools, 42-43, 45